PageMaker 4
by Example

Macintosh Version

*Pica -
6th of an inch*

*Marta Hayoso
786 - 6958*

PageMaker 4
by Example

Macintosh Version

David Webster
Tony Webster

Adapted to PageMaker 4 by
Paul Webster
Caroline Webster

M&T Books
A Division of M&T Publishing, Inc.
501 Galveston Drive
Redwood City, CA 94063

© 1990 by M&T Publishing, Inc.

Printed in the United States of America
First Edition published 1990

Library of Congress Cataloging in Publication Data

ISBN 1-55851-121-0   (book/disk) $34.95
ISBN 1-55851-105-9   (book) $24.95
ISBN 1-55851-122-9   (disk) $20.00

93 92 91   4 3 2

Preface

This book was written to make PageMaker 4 as easy to understand and use as possible.

Its contents and approach are based on over 1,000 hours of classroom training with a variety of desktop publishing packages. It can be used as a self-paced training book for individual teaching or as the workbook for classroom training.

The book is broken up into modules, where each progressive module covers more detailed operation of PageMaker. Each module includes an information section as well as a detailed exercise (except for Module 1).

Self-Paced Operation

For those PageMaker users who purchase this book to help them learn the many new concepts of version 4, the approach outlined in the following paragraphs is suggested.

As indicated above, each module contains an information section which is designed to introduce and outline the associated concepts. This part of each module should be read first. This information section complements the PageMaker manuals by providing many examples of how different concepts are utilized. Extensive use of screen illustrations helps to reinforce the learning process.

Following on from the information section is an exercise for each module (except the first). These exercises are summarized on one page at the front, so that people of all levels of experience with PageMaker can use them to gain maximum benefit. Those people, for example, who are feeling confident, can attempt the exercises without further assistance. For those who need further prompting, the detailed steps for each exercise are also included. Again, extensive screen illustrations are included with each exercise solution, making them as simple as possible to understand.

These exercises use sample files that are included with the PageMaker system. Depending upon your geographical location, publications or templates that you open with PageMaker may be designed for A4 or Letter pages. In some cases, your sample files may differ slightly from those contained in our exercises. This should not make any difference to the thrust of these exercises, however.

Classroom Operation

In classroom use, the attendees work through each module in conjunction with the course instructor. Instead of the user reading the information section of each module, the instructor would explain the concepts in front of the class. The attendees are strongly recommended to keep this information on hand for future reference.

The exercise sections are then attempted by the attendees on their own as part of the classroom tuition. As for the self-paced approach, these exercises may be attempted without assistance, or worked through by following the detailed steps that are included.

There are eighteen modules contained within this book. Each one covers a separate section of PageMaker and can be considered individually. Later modules, however, require knowledge which is explained in earlier sections.

Good luck in learning PageMaker. We hope this book contibutes to your success with this package.

Acknowledgments

We would like to acknowledge the assistance of the following organizations and people who helped in the production of this book:

- Aldus Corporation, including Freda Stephen and Craig Danuloff
- Brenda MaLaughlin of M&T Publishing
- Paul Webster and Caroline Webster who adapted this book to PageMaker 4

Limits of Liability and Disclaimer of Warranty

The Authors and Publisher of this book have used their best efforts in preparing the book and the examples contained in it. These efforts include the development, research, and testing of the theories and programs to determine their effectiveness.

The Authors and Publisher make no warranty of any kind, expressed or implied, with regard to these programs or the documentation contained in this book. The Authors and Publisher shall not be liable in any event for incidental or consequential damages in connection with, or arising out of, the furnishing, performance, or use of these examples.

Contents

Module 1

Learning the Basics

Learning the Basics

In this first module we are going to look at PageMaker basics, including the screen, menus, palettes, and other tools, and see how these are used together to create, modify, close, and open your publications.

This training material is not designed to teach you how to use a Macintosh. It is assumed throughout that you know how to work with the system and how to do all the necessary things such as operating the mouse, opening and closing documents, and working with pull-down menus.

We will start from the position as shown in Figure 1 — a view of the Macintosh desktop with PageMaker 4 already installed in its own folder.

Figure 1. Here we have PageMaker 4 installed and sitting in its own PageMaker folder.

To start PageMaker, click on the PageMaker icon to highlight it and choose *Open* from the **File** menu. Alternatively, quickly double-clicking in the PageMaker 4 icon will open the program.

After performing the operation as listed above, your screen will appear as shown in Figure 2. This is the PageMaker desktop; at this stage we have not yet created a new publication or opened a current one. This requires additional steps.

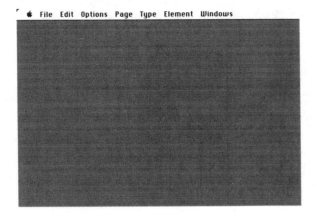

Figure 2. *Upon opening PageMaker, after the Aldus PageMaker 4 screen has briefly come and gone, you will be greeted with a screen similar to this.*

Menus

For the moment, let's look at PageMaker's menus (Figure 3).

The menu names include: **File, Edit, Options, Page, Type, Element,** and **Windows**. Each one of these menus contains several commands that are used to help put a publication together.

To see the contents of these pull-down menus, move the mouse over any of the menu names and hold down the mouse button. What will drop is the list of commands relevant to that menu (Figure 4). To get rid of the menu invoked, move the mouse away from that menu, and release the mouse button. The menu will then disappear.

 File   Edit   Options   Page   Type   Element   Windows

Figure 3. *The menu bar.*

In any particular menu, there are a varying number of commands listed. Some of these commands appear in black, while others are listed in gray. If a command is listed in gray, it cannot be selected at the current time. Some other function must be performed before the command can be selected.

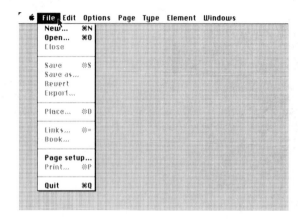

Figure 4. *A menu is activated by moving the mouse so that the cursor is on top of one of the seven menu names, and then clicking and holding down the mouse button.*

Commands listed in black are selected by running the mouse down the column after a menu has been invoked, until a command in the menu is highlighted in reverse video (Figure 5). Release the mouse button, and the highlighted command will be selected.

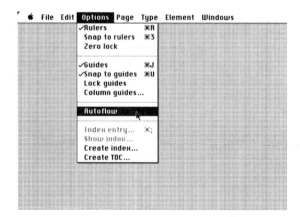

Figure 5. *A command is activated by holding the mouse button down, running it down the menu, highlighting commands as you go. Release the mouse button on the command you would like to use.*

An alternative to selecting a command in this fashion is to select a command using the shortcut key method. Note that to the right of many menu commands there are several keys listed (Figure 6). These are the shortcut keys for invoking that special command.

For example, holding down the Command key while typing R will activate the rulers. There is no need to invoke the menu (in this case the **Options** menu) if you use the shortcut keys to select a command.

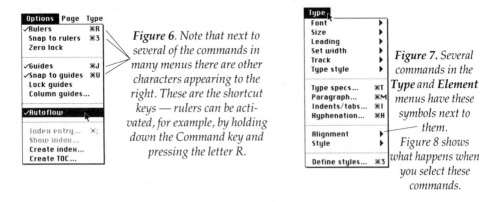

Figure 6. Note that next to several of the commands in many menus there are other characters appearing to the right. These are the shortcut keys — rulers can be activated, for example, by holding down the Command key and pressing the letter R.

Figure 7. Several commands in the **Type** and **Element** menus have these symbols next to them. Figure 8 shows what happens when you select these commands.

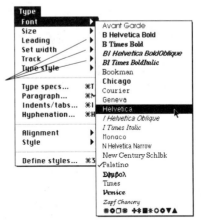

Figure 8. To activate a command that uses this symbol, you must not release the mouse button immediately. To select your choice, run the mouse down the secondary menu that automatically appears.

If a menu command is followed by the ▶ symbol (see Figures 7 and 8), this means that that command must be selected in a slightly different way. You will find that when the mouse is held down on one of these commands, a secondary menu is immediately invoked either to the left or to the right of that command. To select a choice from this menu, you must keep the mouse button held down, and move it down the new list of choices. Release the mouse button on the choice you would like to select from those offered. These types of menu commands are found exclusively in the **Type** and **Element** menus.

Other commands within different menus have ellipsis marks following them (for example, the *New, Open, Save as, Export, Place, Links, Book, Page setup,* and *Print* commands from the **File** menu, as shown in Figure 9). All of these commands (and they occur in a number of different menus) open a dialog box.

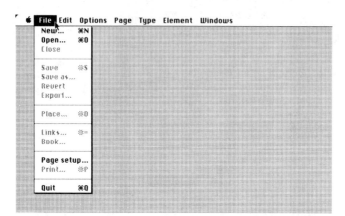

*Figure 9. The different commands within the **File** menu that include the ellipsis are clearly seen.*

A dialog box (Figures 10 and 11) is basically a number of choices presented to invoke the selected command. A dialog box appears as a rectangular outlined window sitting within the page, containing several choices. Many commands use dialog boxes, and most dialog boxes are vastly different from each other.

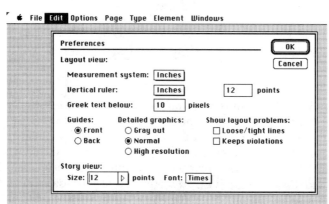

*Figure 10. Dialog boxes appear after invoking many of the commands in the PageMaker menus. A dialog box simply gives you extra choices over the execution of the command you have chosen. This dialog box represents the Preferences command from the **Edit** menu.*

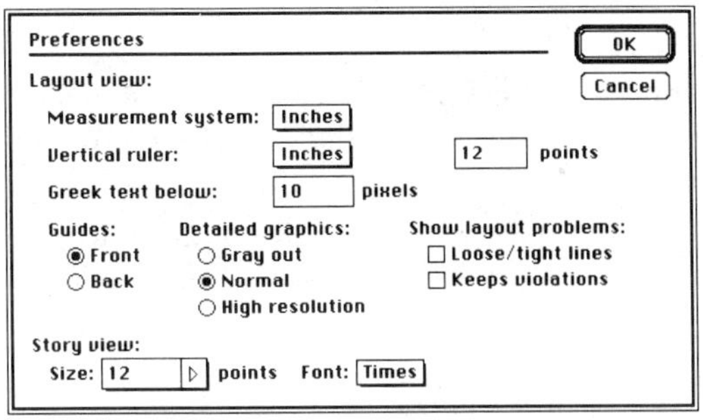

Figure 11. Choices can be made from the dialog box by clicking the mouse button in the circles, boxes, or text areas.

Although circles and boxes within a dialog box represent options to be selected, a group of circles usually means that only one option can be selected at any one time. Small squares usually represent several options which can be invoked together. A filled circle or a checked box is a selected option.

Text squares, the larger rectangles, require you to click in the squares with the mouse, and use the backspace or delete key to erase the current words or numbers (if there are any), then use the keyboard to insert the new values. Alternatively, if you double-click in a rectangle, it then assumes a reverse video appearance, allowing you to type in directly without deleting anything that may have already been in there.

For example, see Figure 13. Under Page size, only one selection can be made (in this case, Letter). Under Options are the small squares, and in this case we have checked both. The Orientation may be Tall or Wide, but not both. The larger text squares include the different Margin dimensions. We have typed our own values into these. After selecting all the choices you like within a dialog box, either select OK by clicking on it, or press the Return key.

If you invoke a dialog box by accident, or you select options within a dialog box you do not wish to use, click on the Cancel button.

Three things may happen after selecting a command in a menu. First, it may appear as though absolutely nothing has happened. In this case, you may simply have activated a command that does not become apparent until a certain task is performed. Second, you may be confronted with a dialog box. Third, a visible change may take place on the screen.

Creating a new document

A PageMaker document is referred to as a *publication*. By opening a publication we bring it into the computer's memory and onto the screen.

As you open PageMaker you are not immediately thrust into a new publication as we indicated above. It is up to you to decide whether you want to open up a new or an existing publication.

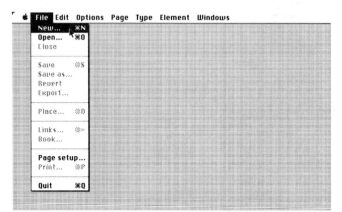

*Figure 12. A new PageMaker publication is opened by selecting the New command from the **File** menu. Alternatively, you could have chosen an existing publication by selecting Open.*

To open up a new publication you must select the *New* command from the **File** menu (Figure 12). Upon doing so, you will be presented with the dialog box of Figure 13. This is the dialog box you will be confronted with every time you wish to create a new publication.

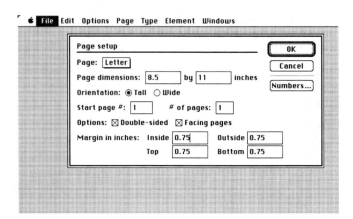

Figure 13. Every time the New command is opened, this dialog box appears. Basically, it is asking what kind of page (and how many) do you want to use for this new document.

Your first choice is what page size to use (Figure 14). All the traditional sizes are included, but if they are not appropriate, you can create your own special page. Every time a page size is selected, its actual size is listed in the two boxes next to the words Page Dimensions. If you want to create a special page, select Custom by highlighting it, and insert whatever page size you like in the two boxes to the right.

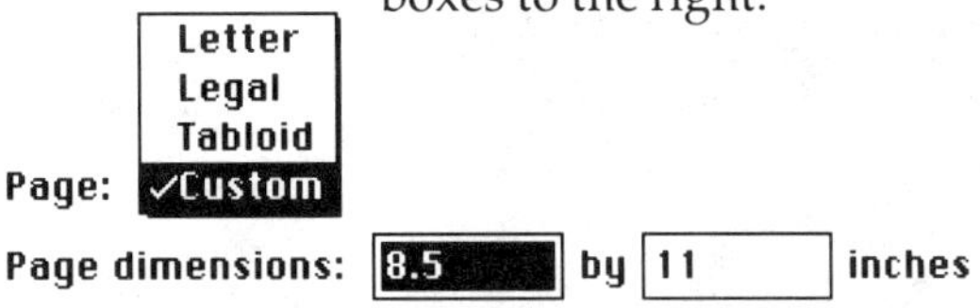

Letter
Legal
Tabloid

Page: ✓**Custom**

Page dimensions: **8.5** by 11 inches

OK

Cancel

Figure 14. The Page size options.

Your next choice is whether to use a portrait (vertical or tall) or a landscape (horizontal or wide) page (Figure 15). These two types of pages cannot be mixed in the same publication.

Orientation: ⊙ **Tall** ○ **Wide**

Figure 15. The page orientation options.

*Tall aka portrait
Wide '' landscape
view*

The next line asks you what page number you would like to start on, and how many pages you would like to use in this publication (Figure 16). Keep in mind that any of the choices made in this dialog box can be altered after the publication has been opened, except for the number of pages. (This is changed differently as we will see later.)

Start page #: 1   # of pages: 1

Figure 16..The Start page and number of pages options.

Your further options are whether to use Double-sided pages, and whether or not to use facing pages (Figure 17). You will find that it becomes much easier if both of these commands are selected (they are selected if a cross appears in the little box next to each command). When these two choices are selected, it is possible to view and work with two pages at one time.

Obviously, you would not choose Double-sided if you are working with a publication that only prints on one side of the page.

Options: ☒ **Double-sided** ☒ **Facing pages**

Figure 17. The Double-sided and Facing pages options.

Your final choice is the margins for your particular page (Figure 18). These creates guides on the page — guides that will not print, but will display to make sure text and graphics are contained in the right position on the page.

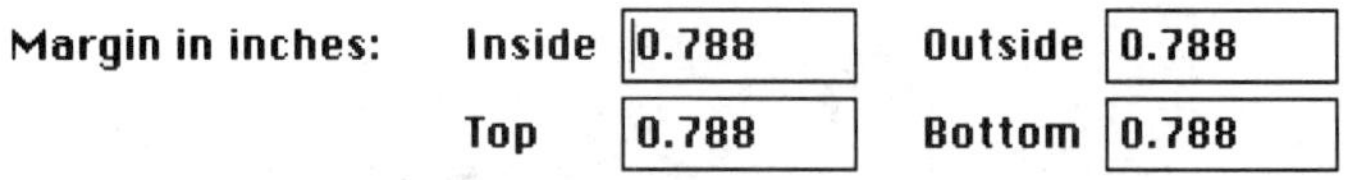

Margin in inches:	Inside	0.788	Outside	0.788
	Top	0.788	Bottom	0.788

Figure 18. The page Margin options.

After choosing the correct page setup details as shown in Figures 13 to 18, click on OK (or press the Return key) to bring you into the initial publication window. This is shown in Figure 19.

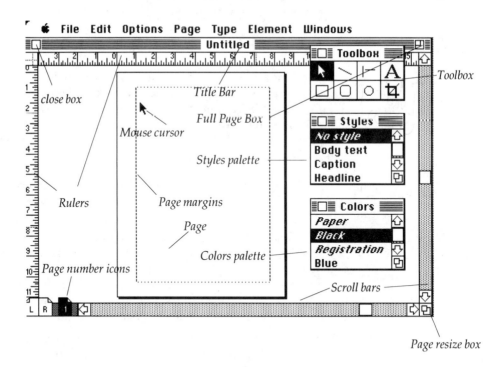

Figure 19. *The initial publication window. Not everything in this window will appear on your screen at first, so there is no need to panic.*

Before we look at the page itself, note that the *Page setup* command in the **File** menu, once invoked, uses a dialog box similar to that of *New* (Figure 13). The majority of the options selected when you choose *New* can be altered using this *Page setup* command while inside the publication.

The Title bar

The title bar is the lined strip just below the menu names. At this stage, the name in the middle of this bar of Figure 19 reads "Untitled." This means that a new publication has just been opened, and has not yet been saved. After a publication has been saved, its name replaces the word Untitled.

This title bar also has three other properties. First, if the mouse button is held down anywhere in the title bar , moving the mouse will move the entire PageMaker window. As the mouse button is released, the window will reformat in its new position (see Figure 20).

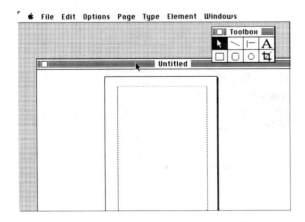

Figure 20. Holding the mouse button down on the title bar while moving the mouse will drag the entire PageMaker window.

Second, the title bar contains the "close box," a small open box in the top left-hand corner of the title bar. This is the box that, when clicked, will close the current publication. If you have not saved the publication before you click this box, you will be prompted to save your changes before the window is closed.

In the top right-hand corner of the title bar is the full page box. When clicked, the PageMaker publication expands to its maximum size on the screen. When a publication is opened, it will always open to maximum size, so the full page box only needs to be used if the publication has been resized in some other way.

The Toolbox

The Toolbox (Figure 21) is a PageMaker feature that is used quite often. It is, literally, the box from which we select a tool to achieve a certain task. To select a certain tool, simply click the mouse on that tool.

Before we actually look at each of the available tools in more detail, note that the Toolbox has its own title bar, one with similar properties to the publication title bar. The Toolbox can be closed or moved in the same way as described above. If you accidentally remove the Toolbox from the screen by clicking on its close box, select the *Toolbox* command from the **Windows** menu. The Toolbox will then appear on screen.

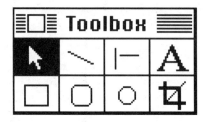

Figure 21. A blown-up picture of the Toolbox — usually situated near the top right-hand corner of the screen — although it can be moved around at will. Currently the pointer tool is selected.

Figure 22. The pointer tool.

The painter tool is used most of the time, as it is the one that must be used to select most elements on the page. Its use will become much more apparent as you use PageMaker more and more.

Figure 23. The diagonal-line drawing tool.

The line drawing tool allows only straight lines in any direction to be created. Freehand drawings cannot be created within Page-Maker. Holding down the shift key allows this tool to become identical to the perpendicular line drawing tool (below).

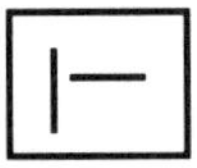

Figure 24. The perpendicular-line drawing tool.

The perpendicular-line drawing tool allows only straight lines in 45-degree increments to be created. This is especially useful for creating forms, intercolumnn rules, and for any lines that must be either horizontal or vertical.

Figure 25. The text tool.

Select the text tool to edit text in PageMaker, to create text, or to change the properties of existing text.

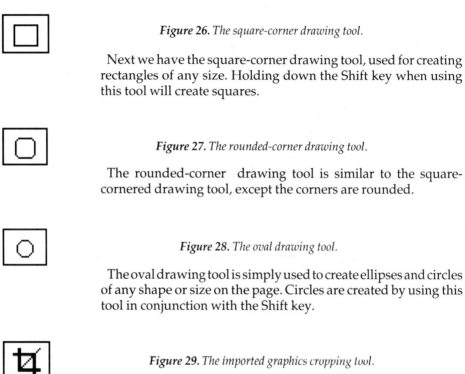

Figure 26. The square-corner drawing tool.

Next we have the square-corner drawing tool, used for creating rectangles of any size. Holding down the Shift key when using this tool will create squares.

Figure 27. The rounded-corner drawing tool.

The rounded-corner drawing tool is similar to the square-cornered drawing tool, except the corners are rounded.

Figure 28. The oval drawing tool.

The oval drawing tool is simply used to create ellipses and circles of any shape or size on the page. Circles are created by using this tool in conjunction with the Shift key.

Figure 29. The imported graphics cropping tool.

Finally on the Toolbox is the graphics cropping tool. This tool is used to remove portions of imported graphics — much like a knife.

Style and Color palettes

Figures 30 and 31 indicate the *Style* and *Color* palettes offered with PageMaker.

The *Style palette* allows you to select text and change its style according to a preset style type. For example, you may decide that your normal text within a publication is to be set at 10 point Palatino with 12 point line spacing, 2 point spacing after each paragraph, justified, a first line indent, and two tabs set at particular intervals. This can all be preset and named as a style type. Any text brought into the publication can be selected and applied this style type.

Figure 30. Style palette.

Figure 31. Color palette.

Similarly, subheadings can be, say, 12 point Bold Palatino with certain spacing above and below, with or without indenting. This also can be preset, given a name and applied to all relevant sub-headings. This approach to document assembly leads to increased productivity and a more consistent publication layout. A style's specifications may be revised at any time. PageMaker will then apply those new specifications to any paragraphs that have been applied that style.

PageMaker comes with five default styles: Body text, Caption, Headline, Subhead 1, and Subhead 2.

The *Color palette* allows color to be added to selected text or graphics. Again, any number of color types can be named, specified, and added to the Figure 31 palette. If you have a color monitor, the results will be immediately apparent. The color approach still works with black and white monitors — the resulting printout on a color printer will then indicate the results.

Preset colors defined for PageMaker 4 include: Paper, Black, Registration, Blue, Green, and Red.

Don't try to use too many of these tools or palettes yet — all are covered in great detail in following modules. If you are still unsure as to the functions of these tools, don't worry — they will be discussed later in the book.

Page number icons

Down in the bottom left-hand corner of the page are the page number icons. Depending on how your document is set up, you may see a few or many icons in this area. At the very least, you will see an *L*, an *R*, and a *1*. The 1 tells you this is page 1 of the current document. As we start creating larger documents, the 1 icon will be accompanied by a 2, a 3, a 4, and so on up to 999. The icon currently highlighted in reverse video is the page currently shown on the screen. In this way, you can move to a specific page in your document simply by clicking on its page number icon.

The L and the R represent the master pages. The use of these master pages is covered in detail in a later module.

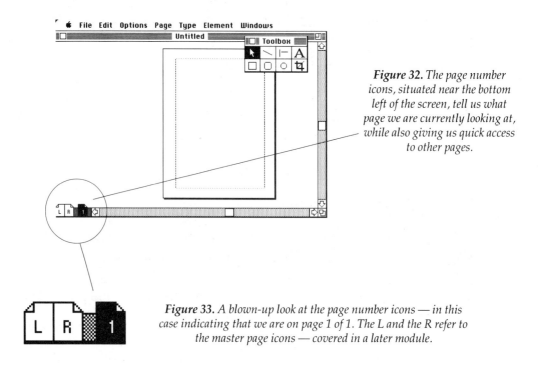

Figure 32. The page number icons, situated near the bottom left of the screen, tell us what page we are currently looking at, while also giving us quick access to other pages.

Figure 33. A blown-up look at the page number icons — in this case indicating that we are on page 1 of 1. The L and the R refer to the master page icons — covered in a later module.

Any single PageMaker document can hold up 999 pages. It is not possible to show this many page icons at the bottom of the screen. Depending on your screen size, no more than about 30 will be present. To accommodate the extra pages, left and right arrows, at the beginning and end of the page icons, will appear (Figure 34). The right arrow lets you scroll through the page numbers in ascending order. The left arrow is for scrolling back to find previous pages.

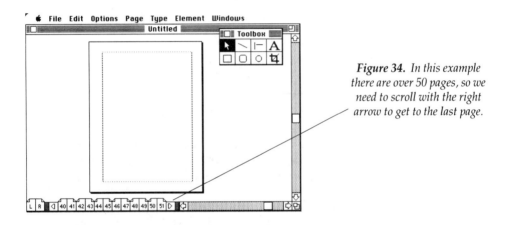

Figure 34. In this example there are over 50 pages, so we need to scroll with the right arrow to get to the last page.

Although 999 pages is the maximum size of a publication, it is possible to number pages up to four digits in length. The maximum (automatic) page number allowed in PageMaker 4 is therefore 9999, subject to the overall publication being no larger than 999 pages.

The page

The first thing you will probably notice in opening a new publication, is the representation of the page on the screen. This representation is based on the choices you selected upon opening up a new document. The outline of the page itself should be visible, as should the dotted margins defined for that page (Figure 35). If we had columns defined for this page, column guides would also be visible.

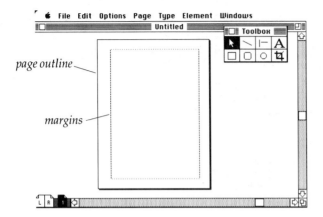

page outline

margins

*Figure 35. The outline of the page itself is very easy to spot. The dotted lines on the inside of the page indicate the page margins as described in the Page setup dialog box of Figure 13 (the dialog box that appears after selecting New from the **File** menu).*

The pasteboard

The pasteboard is the area around the page that can be used to store any imported or created text or graphics. If we look at the page as an actual page, then the pasteboard should be viewed as the desk around the page. We can place all possible articles and pictures in this pasteboard area and choose between them. This pasteboard area remains constant no matter what page you are looking at in the publication. Nothing in the pasteboard area will print, and the pasteboard is always saved with the publication.

The rulers

Through the *Rulers* command in the **Options** menu, it is possible to choose to display, or not display, horizontal and vertical rulers on the screen. Figures 19 and 36 show the rulers displayed. These rulers can be of considerable assistance in placing text and graphics on the page, and can be used in conjunction with special horizontal and vertical ruler guides.

Figure 36 shows the top left-hand corner of the page. Normally, for a single page viewed on screen, the ruler's zero position will begin at this point. For Facing pages view, this is not necessarily true. In either case, it is possible to change the zero position both horizontally and vertically.

The use and flexibility of rulers are explained in more detail in a later module.

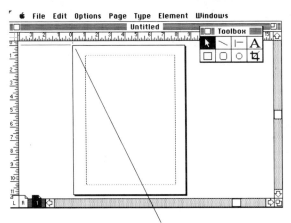

Figure 36. The ruler zero point can be seen at the top left-hand corner of the page.

Notice the 0,0 horizontal and vertical ruler positions are aligned with the top left-hand corner of the page.

The scroll bars

Along the bottom and the right-hand side of the page are the scroll bars. These are the bars that allow you to move around the page to view different sections of the page in certain views.

On large high-resolution screens, scroll bars are used very little. When the whole page can be viewed and read at the same time, there is no real need to use the scroll bars. However, on the normal Macintosh screen, there is no way you can view a whole page of text and be able to read it at the same time — the screen is just too small. To read the text, you will find that you will only be able to see about one third of the page at a time. Consequently, the scroll bars must be used to move yourself around the page. They can be manipulated in a variety of ways as described below.

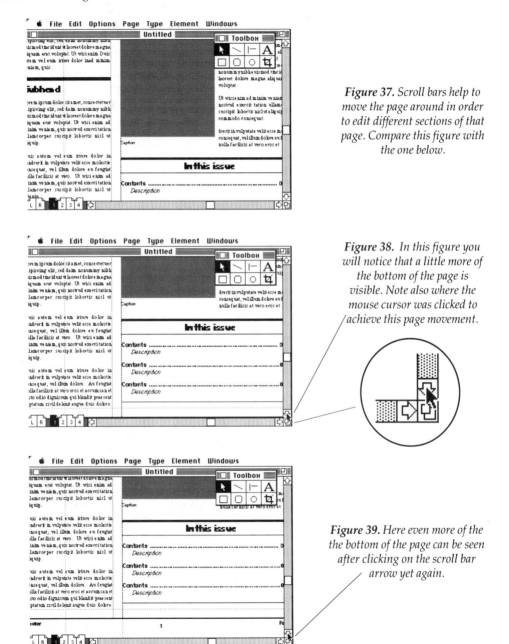

Figure 37. Scroll bars help to move the page around in order to edit different sections of that page. Compare this figure with the one below.

Figure 38. In this figure you will notice that a little more of the bottom of the page is visible. Note also where the mouse cursor was clicked to achieve this page movement.

Figure 39. Here even more of the the bottom of the page can be seen after clicking on the scroll bar arrow yet again.

Both sets of scroll bars have an arrow in each corner (top, bottom, left, and right). Clicking on any arrow will move you in that direction in relation to the page. Many people get a little confused here — they tend to think that clicking on a certain arrow is going to take them in one direction, when in fact, it takes them in the other. Experiment to see which way clicking on a certain arrow is going to take you.

Without having text on the screen, it can be a little tricky following exactly which way the scroll bars are moving.

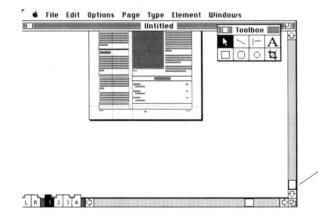

Figure 40. Even in reduced (Fit in window) view (described in the next section) the screen can be scrolled. When we are looking at the bottom of the page, note where the white square is situated in the vertical scroll bar — also at the bottom.

Clicking on these arrows is the slow way to move around the page. If you click on the gray areas in the scroll bars you will move around much more quickly — on the smaller screens about a screen at a time. Before you try this however, note one thing about the scroll bars: they both have a little white square in them. This white square represents what part of the page you are looking at in relation to the total screen area. For example, if this white square is situated near the bottom of the right-hand side scroll bar, this means that you are looking at or near the bottom of the page. If the square is near the top of the scroll bar, you are looking at somewhere near the top of the page. When you click in the gray area of the scroll bar to move around, whatever side of the white square you click on is the direction you are going to move. As you scroll, watch the white squares change position in the scroll bars.

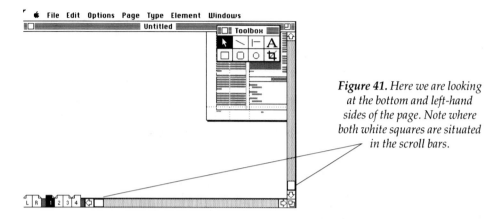

Figure 41. Here we are looking at the bottom and left-hand sides of the page. Note where both white squares are situated in the scroll bars.

Another way to scroll around the screen, and perhaps the easiest way, is to hold the mouse button down on one of the white squares, and move it up or down (or left or right). Release it when it appears that the white square is going to be situated where you want the page to be. For example, if you are looking at the top of a page and would like to look at the bottom, hold the mouse button down on the right-hand side white square, move the mouse down the page until the white square is situated near the bottom of the scroll bar, and release the mouse button. The whole PageMaker screen will reformat so that you are looking at the bottom of your page.

The final way to move around the PageMaker screen is to use the grabber hand. By holding down the Option key and the mouse button, the pointer turns into a hand. The screen then moves in the direction that the mouse is moved. Holding down the Shift key restrains the movement, horizontally or vertically.

The Page resize box

The page resize box is located in the bottom right-hand corner of the PageMaker window (Figure 42). Holding the mouse button down on this little box allows you to resize the publication window at any time. This may be done when working with the multitasking Finder, or perhaps using some of the Macintosh utilities (calculator, clock, etc.). Anytime you wish to return the publication window back to its full size, simply click on the full page box at the right-hand side of the title bar to do so.

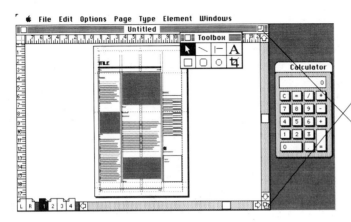

Figure 42. The page resize box can be used to resize the PageMaker window — to make room for something like the Macintosh calculator, for example. Clicking on the full page box returns the PageMaker window to its full size.

Page views

Before we go any further we must look at the different ways we can view the PageMaker publication currently open. In Figure 43 we are viewing the full page of a document. This is generally the default way to view the page and is called the *Fit in window* view.

To view the general layout of your page, *Fit in window* is generally the best choice. When *Fit in window* is selected (**Page** menu), the page appears as big as is possible given the current screen size. However, many screens are of a size that makes it impossible to do any editing when a page is at *Fit in window* size. There are other choices, however.

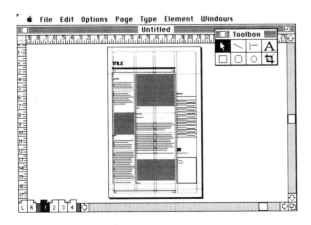

Figure 43. Here we see a publication opened in reduced, or Fit in window view.

Listed in the **Page** menu are all the possible page sizes that can be selected to view the page. Experiment yourself by selecting different page views to see how a certain page size can be used for editing, another for viewing layout, another for precisely aligning graphics, and so on. PageMaker has a great variety of ways to view the currently open publication.

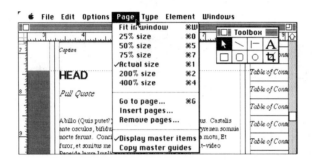

Figure 44. The Page menu gives you a wide range of ways to view your PageMaker publications.

One additional page view is achieved by holding down the Shift key while selecting *Fit in window* from the **Page** menu. What you get in this case is shown in Figure 45 — the whole pasteboard area as well as the page or pages. This is useful when you wish to view the whole pasteboard area. Figures 46 through 51 show 6 different views of the same publication.

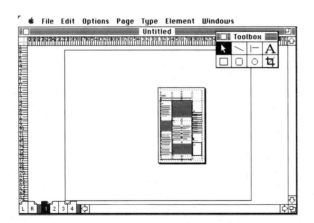

Figure 45. This view shows you the total pasteboard area around the page or pages, and is achieved by using the Shift key while selecting Fit in window view.

[handwritten note: ⌘-opt-click switch back and forth]

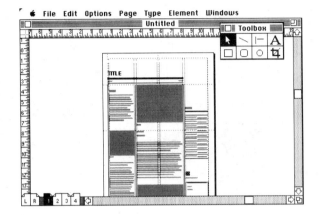

Figure 46. *Here we see the same page as Figure 43, at 25% ...*

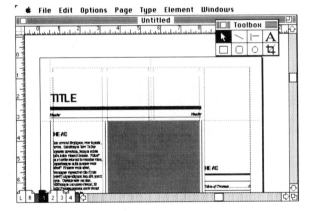

Figure 47. *... and again at 50% ...*

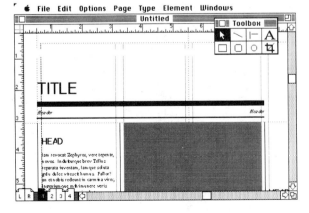

Figure 48. *... and again at 75%....*

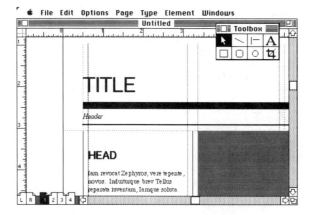

Figure 49. ... *and again at actual size*.....

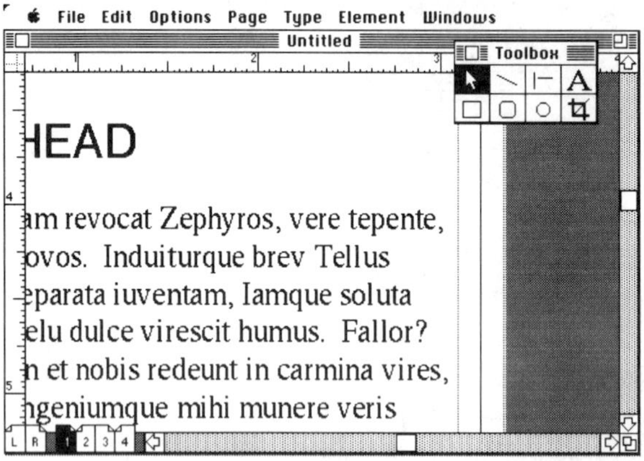

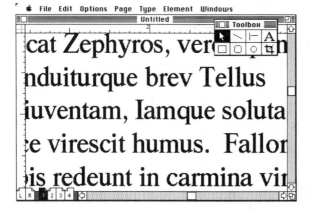

Figure 50. ... *and now at 200%*...

Figure 51. ... *and finally at 400%*.

The Preferences command

It's a good idea to look at the *Preferences* command before we go any further, as it helps you customize PageMaker to your own liking. Invoke the *Preferences* command in the **Edit** menu.

From this command there is a major choice to be made — which measurement units should be used. There are several units to choose from, so choose wisely — measurement units turn up everywhere in PageMaker. Whichever measurement unit is chosen is the one that appears in all future dialog boxes. This may be overridden at any time, as we will see later. It is also possible to set different measurements for the horizontal and vertical rulers in the dialog box of Figure 52. Again, this will be discussed in a future module.

Other choices within the *Preferences* dialog box will be discussed in later modules.

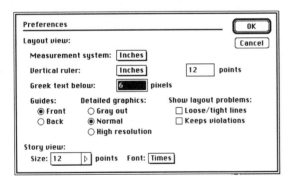

*Figure 52. The choices in the Preferences dialog box, accessed through the Preferences command in the **Edit** menu, help to customize PageMaker to your special preferences.*

The Undo command

Located at the top of the **Edit** menu is the *Undo* command. This is a safety factor that allows you to undo virtually all PageMaker functions — including moves, deletes, copies, pastes, and so on. Always remember this command is here — however, remember it cannot undo everything, and it will only undo the very last step you have taken.

41

The Close command

The *Close* command in the **File** menu (Figure 53) is used to close the currently open publication. Choosing *Close* prompts you to save the changes you have made to this publication (unless you had just saved those changes). You can choose *OK*, *No*, or *Cancel* (Figure 54). *No* closes the publication, saving no changes — everything you changed since you last saved has been lost. *Cancel* takes you back to the PageMaker page. *OK* will save all changes to the publication. The saving process is discussed in more detail later.

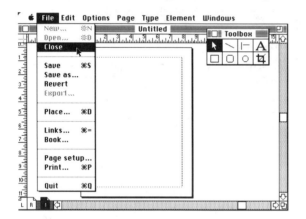

Figure 53. The Close command will remove the currently open publication from the screen — regardless of whether it was a new publication or an existing one.

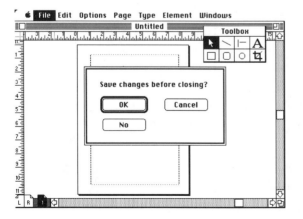

Figure 54. This warning will appear if you have not saved your work before quitting. For now, clock on Cancel if confronted with this woaring. We will discuss saving in a later module.

The Quit command

The *Quit* command from the **File** menu (Figure 55) works in exactly the same way as the *Close* command, although it returns you not to the PageMaker opening desktop, but to the Macintosh desktop.

At the conclusion of every information section and exercise (where applicable) in this book, you should close the current publication and not save the changes.

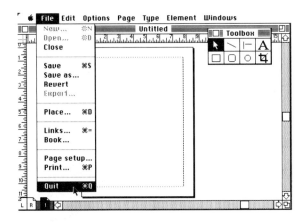

*Figure 55. The Quit command, located at the bottom of the **File** menu, will return you to the Macintosh desktop.*

Opening an existing publication

In this module, we have looked at ways to start up PageMaker as a new publication, including major options. For loading and opening previously saved publications, please refer to Module 2.

Module 2

Loading Files

Loading Files

PageMaker allows us to manipulate and put together files that are usually created using other computer applications. Although we can create many publications using PageMaker alone, its real strength lies in the fact that it can accept formatted files from virtually all other major Macintosh applications. Text files are best created in dedicated word processor packages, like Microsoft Word (Figure 1), while more effective and professional graphics can be created in packages such as Freehand, MacPaint (Figure 2), Illustrator (Figure 3), and CA Draw. Files created in these, and other applications, can be placed directly into PageMaker.

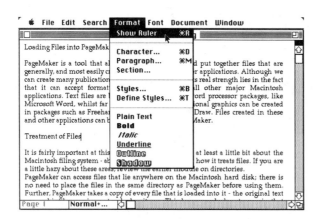

Figure 1. Microsoft Word was used to create the text for this book.

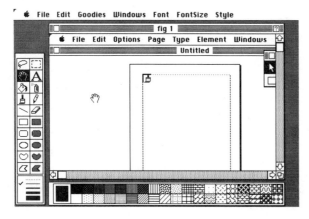

Figure 2. All the screen shots used in this book are in MacPaint format, and could have been edited in this program before importation into PageMaker.

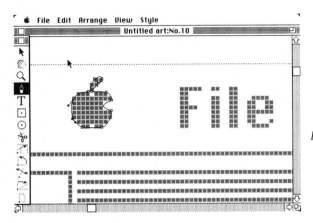

Figure 3. *Adobe Illustrator could have been used to dress up our Figure 2 MacPaint image if necessary.*

Treatment of files

It is fairly important at this stage that you understand at least a little bit about the Macintosh filing system — how it uses folders and how it treats files.

PageMaker can access files that lie anywhere on the Macintosh hard disk; there is no need to place the files in the same folder as PageMaker before using them. Furthermore, PageMaker takes a copy of every file that's loaded into it — the original text or graphic file remains untouched as it was. This has several advantages: the original file can now be used in other applications as well, and the PageMaker publication is treated as one file rather than a mixture of several. Files imported to PageMaker from graphics or word processing programs can now also be linked to your PageMaker file, so that any changes made in either PageMaker or the outside program will reflect in both programs. (See Module 15 on **Linking Files**.)

Most of the time, outside files can be accessed in their original form. Occasionally, you may have to do something a little different to a file to allow it to be used in PageMaker. For example, PageMaker cannot accept CA Draw files in the CA Draw format — the default format for such files. PageMaker can, however, accept CA Draw files in their EPSF or PICT formats. Other packages have similar options for saving their graphics in a compatible format.

Loading files

All types of files, whether text or graphics, are accessed through the *Place* command (Figure 4) in the **File** menu. After selecting this command, you will be presented with the dialog box of Figure 5. To help you understand the concepts of this module, you may find it useful to work with PageMaker as you read our comments.

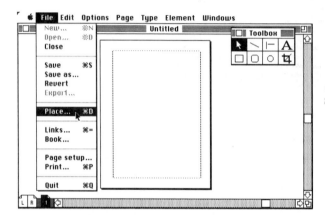

Figure 4. *The Place command is used to gain access to the files on the hard disk, and/or floppy disks.*

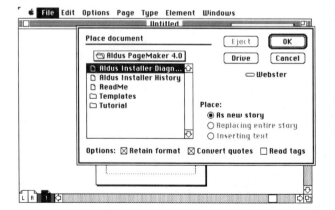

Figure 5. *This is an example of the dialog box that appears on selecting the Place command. Yours may look a little different.*

This is where the idea of folders becomes so important. In order for you to change folders to access different files, it is vital to understand what you are doing.

In Figure 5, we are viewing files and folders from the folder in which the PageMaker program is resident. This is named Aldus PageMaker 4 and this name is shown in the rectangular box above the list of files and folders.

Compatible files are denoted by the small page to the left of the file name. Incompatible files will not be listed at all. Other folders are included in the list and are denoted by the small folder to the left of their name. See Figure 6 for a description of the *Place* command dialog box.

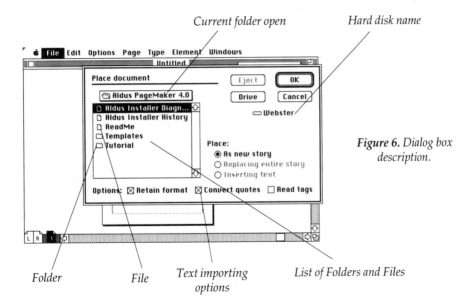

Current folder open

Hard disk name

Figure 6. *Dialog box description.*

Folder   *File*   *Text importing options*   *List of Folders and Files*

Most of the time you will find that the file you are after is not resident in this current folder at all, so we must change folders. There are two possibilities here, depending on whether the new folder is contained within or outside of the current folder.

To move to a folder within the current folder, move the mouse over the name of that folder, and click the mouse button twice in succession. You will then be viewing the files and folders from within the new folder (Figures 7 and 8). Alternatively, you can click on the new folder once, to select it, and then click on the OK button.

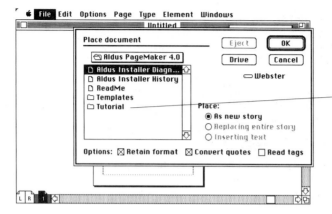

Figure 7. To gain access to the files and folders in the Tutorial folder, which is within the PageMaker folder, you must double-click on that folder name. Alternatively, you may select that folder by clicking on it once, and then clicking on the OK button.

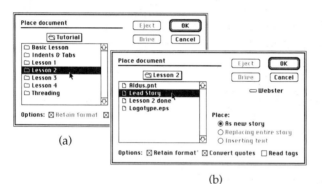

(a)

(b)

Figure 8. The file we want to place later in this module is called Lead Story, inside the folder Lesson 2, which is inside the Tutorial folder. Once we have located it as shown, we can select it using the methods described in the paragraphs below.

To change to other folders not contained within the PageMaker 4 folder, which is often the most common first move, a different technique must be used. You must move the mouse over the name of the current folder open — that is, the name in the small rectangular box above the list of files and folders. In Figures 5, 6, and 7, this is named Aldus PageMaker 4. Hold the mouse button down on this name (Figure 9).

What you will then see is a kind of menu drop — a menu that lists several different names. At the bottom of this menu (it will be a different length depending on where the PageMaker 4 folder was located on your hard disk) will be the name of your hard disk, with a little hard disk icon to the left of it. If you release the mouse button while the hard disk is selected, you will move to the Macintosh desktop. Do this now.

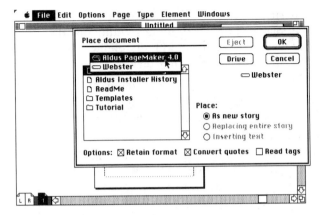

Figure 9. This is the same dialog box as Figure 7. Instead of moving within the Page-Maker folder, move up towards the Macintosh desktop. To do this, hold down the mouse button on the folder name (Aldus PageMaker 4 in this figure) and all higher folders will be listed. Move the mouse to the hard disk icon and release the button. In our case we did not have any higher level folders — just our hard disk.

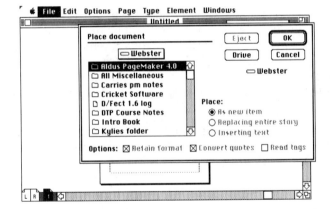

Figure 10. If we move the mouse cursor down the list in Figure 9 to select Webster, we will be presented with the view from the hard disk. Nearly every name in the list is a folder.

Once you are looking at the Macintosh desktop of Figure 10, you should see mainly a list of folders rather than files. From here, you can select the folder to move down to using the technique described below. You may need to scroll down this list of folders if it contains any more than eight names.

When you find the name of the folder you would like to move into, click on it twice. From within this folder, you may either select the file you are after, or move down another folder level. Finding folders or files within different levels of folders is called "hierarchical filing." It is the standard method within the Macintosh environment. If you are familiar with the Macintosh, then you will be familiar with this filing structure. If you are not however, do not worry that it is confusing. Try to imagine it is a filing cabinet where you may place a number of folders within one file. It is a very effective way to build up your library of information rather than having it all resident at the same level.

If you are sure the file exists in this folder, but is not listed in this window, it may exist in a format incompatible with PageMaker. Return to the program in which it was created to change its format.

In our case we are going to select and load the Lead Story file located by following the steps outlined in Figures 7 and 8. To load this file, you can choose one of the same two methods discussed above for moving into folders. Click on Lead Story and then click OK or just double-click on the file. Additional options required in selecting your file are described at the end of this module.

After a few seconds (the time depends upon the format and the size of the file being loaded), you will be returned to the Page-Maker page, with very little apparent difference. However, the mouse cursor will have changed its appearance, once again depending on the type of file that is being loaded. If you have just loaded PageMaker and not changed any default settings, it will look like figure 11.

Text files loaded in will cause the mouse cursor to change its appearance to any one of the three options shown in Figures 11, 12, and 13. Graphics files, however, will cause the mouse cursor to take on a variety of different forms, depending on their format. These are shown in Figures 14 through 17. The different text and graphics possibilities are briefly discussed below. The detailed operations of these different place methods are described in future modules.

Figure 11. *When text has been selected to load into PageMaker using the Place command, the mouse cursor may change appearance to look like this. This is called manual text flow and is the PageMaker default mode.*

Figure 12. *This is the semi-automatic text flow cursor appearance.*

Figure 13. The automatic text flow mode.

Figure 14. The EPS or PostScript mouse cursor.

EPS graphic files will cause the mouse cursor to look like Figure 14. Files from programs such as Adobe Illustrator, CA Draw, and Aldus Freehand can be imported in this format.

Figure 15. The draw-type cursor.

Draw (or PICT) type files will cause the mouse cursor to take on this appearance. Files from MacDraw, MacDraft, CA Draw, and other similar applications will cause the mouse cursor to look like a pencil.

Figure 16. The TIFF, or scanned image cursor

TIFF files, which are usually scanned files, or files transported from an MS-DOS PC, will cause the mouse cursor to take on the appearance of a checkerboard.

Figure 17. The paint-type mouse cursor.

Paint files, such as those from MacPaint, SuperPaint, and Full-Paint, cause the mouse cursor to take on the appearance of a paintbrush.

Once you have changed the mouse cursor, through the *Place* command, to indicate a file has been loaded, you must get the file from memory to the page. In Figure 18, we are about to load the file Lead Story, through the process described earlier in this module.

Before you click the mouse button, you must locate the mouse cursor where you would like the text or graphic to start flowing. If it is a text file you are loading (as in our case), make sure that the mouse cursor is flush with the left margin of the page. It should snap to this margin (see Figure 18). If you click the mouse cursor now, the text will flow from where the mouse is located, across and down the page (Figure 19). This text file is now loaded. Such an operation may take a few seconds.

Before clicking the mouse, ensure that the mouse cursor looks the same as Figure 18 (which is the manual text flow mode as illustrated in Figure 11). If not, go to the **Options** menu and choose the *Autoflow* command. (The reasons for doing this are explained in the next module.)

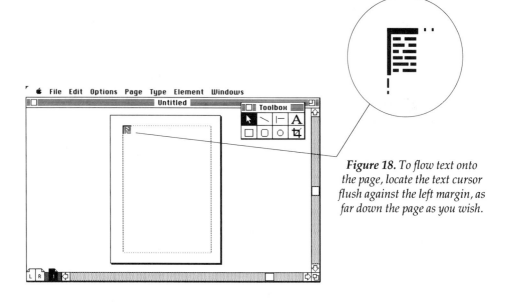

Figure 18. To flow text onto the page, locate the text cursor flush against the left margin, as far down the page as you wish.

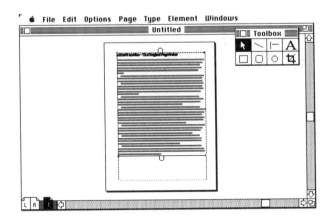

Figure 19. Here we located the text cursor in the top left-hand corner of the margin before we clicked the mouse button. The text flows within the bounds of the left, right, top, and bottom margins.

There is a second method that can be used to flow text and/or graphics onto the page (this is the method that should always be used with graphics). Position the mouse where you would like the top left-hand corner of the file to be, and hold down the mouse button. Now move the mouse down and to the right of the page, keeping the mouse button held down. A box will be drawn indicating the area in which the text or graphics is going to flow. Once the mouse button is released, the text or graphics will flow into the area bounded by the box. See the example shown in Figures 20 and 21.

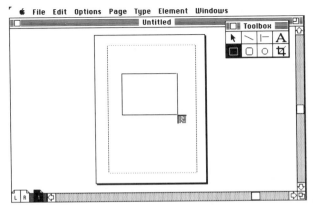

Figure 20. This is an alternative method to Figures 18 and 19 of loading the text onto the page. After you have chosen Lead Story, through the Place command, and you are returned to your page with the text cursor of Figure 11, hold down the mouse button and drag the mouse diagonally to the right and down the page. Now see Figure 21.

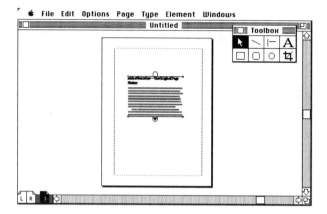

Figure 21. Release the mouse button when the box is the desired size. The text now flows to fill this box.

If you have already flowed your text, go back to earlier in this module and repeat the steps to load Lead Story. If the file you just loaded fills the page, perform these steps in the pasteboard area at the side of the page.

Figures 22, 23, and 24, show loading the Anchor.TIF file from within the Lesson 4 folder using the *Place* command. This is being loaded using the method described in Figures 20 and 21 —that is, loading a file into a designated box area. Note that it is possible with this approach to upset the correct proportions of a graphic. Don't worry, this is easily fixed and is described in Module 7.

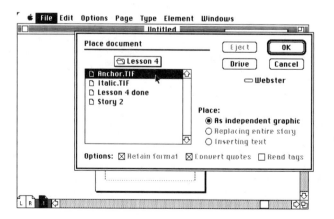

Figure 22. Here we have selected the file Anchor.TIF to load onto the PageMaker page.

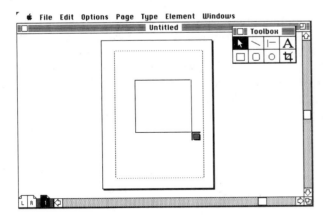

Figure 23. *We hold the mouse button down and once again draw a box the size that we would like our picture to be. If your page is filled with text from the previous examples, use the area on either side of the page.*

Figure 24. *When we release the mouse button, the image fills the box we created for it.*

Saving Files

The *Save* command in the **File** menu (Figure 25) will save all changes that you recently made to the publication, document, or template you are currently working on. The *Save* command can be used at any time without your having to leave the work you are doing. The saving of both text and/or graphics forms a Page-Maker publication. The first time you execute the *Save* command, the *Save publication as* dialog box (Figure 26) will appear. This lets you give your publication a name, and lets you choose where you want to save this publication. The *Save as* command can also be used at any time during your working on a publication. If your publication has already been named, the *Save as* command lets you re name it and/or change the disk or folder it is on. The *Save as* command will also reduce the size of your publication, after editing, which means less disk space is used.

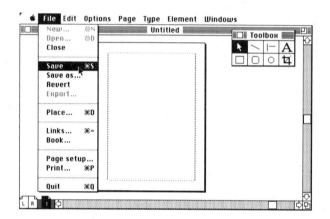

Figure 25. The Save command in the File menu will save all changes you have made to the current publication. It is a good idea to use this command often to prevent the loss of valuable work.

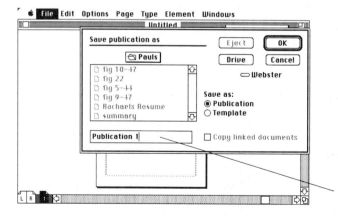

Figure 26. The Save publication as *dialog box appears either by selecting the* Save *command in a publication for the first time, or selecting the* Save as *command in the* **File** *menu. After moving the folders and files to the place you would like your file to be saved, type in the name you would like to call the publication, as we have done here.*

Opening an existing publication

So far we have discussed opening PageMaker for a new publication. Opening previously saved publications can be done in one of two ways. One way is to open the saved publication from within PageMaker 4 using the *Open* command. Start up Page-Maker as normal, and instead of choosing *New* from the **File** menu, choose *Open* (Figure 27). The *Open* publication dialog box will now appear. This gives you the opportunity to move around the files and folders on your Macintosh to where you saved your PageMaker 4 publication. Once you find it, simply double-click on it, or highlight it with your mouse and click on OK. Figures 27 and 28 show how this is done.

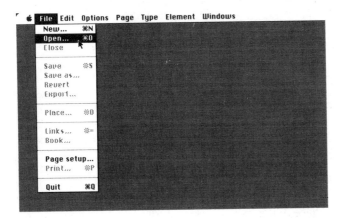

Figure 27. After starting up PageMaker from the desktop, select the Open command instead of the New command to open a previously saved PageMaker publication.

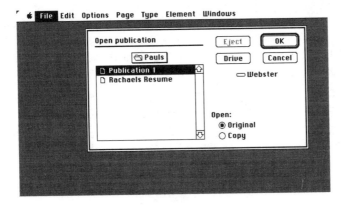

Figure 28. Once your PageMaker publication has been located, double-click on it, or select it and click on OK, to open the publication.

The second way to open a previously saved PageMaker publication is to open it directly from the Macintosh desktop. You do not have to open PageMaker 4 itself to do it this way. After locating your file on the desktop, double-click on the icon or file name and it will open (Figure 29).

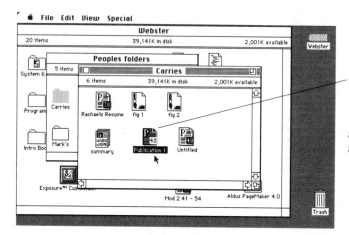

Figure 29. *The file is located in its folder, and double-clicked on to open. A PageMaker 4 document icon is recognized by a P in the top left, and a 4.0 in the bottom right, of the icon.*

Options for importing text

You may have noticed several choices that can be made when importing text files — the choices that appear along the bottom of the Place dialog box. These include *Retain format*, *Convert quotes*, and *Read tags* (Figure 30).

Retain format will, if selected, make sure that any formatting applied to text at the word processor level still applies in PageMaker. If it is not selected, the text come through with none of the formatting applied in the word processor.

Convert quotes will convert the " and ' quotes often used by word processors to the more professional ", ", ', and '.

Read tags (discussed in more detail in Module 11, **PageMaker Style Sheets**), will read formatting codes imbedded in the text at the word processor level.

The other options, located to the right of the window, include *As new story, Replacing entire story,* and *Inserting text.* These are discussed in Module 10, **PageMaker Templates.**

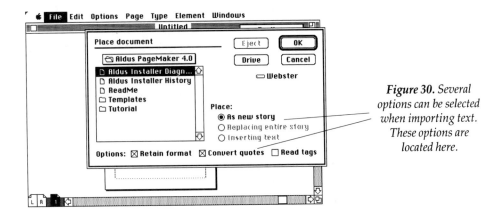

Figure 30. Several options can be selected when importing text. These options are located here.

Module 2 Exercise

Loading Files

Module 2 Exercise — Loading Files

In this exercise we are going to load files into PageMaker, both graphics and text. We will also go through the process of locating these files on the hard disk from the PageMaker *Place* command dialog box.

This training material is structured so that people of all levels of expertise with PageMaker can use it to gain maximum benefit. In order to do this, we have structured this material so that the bare exercise is listed below this paragraph on just one page, with no hints. The following pages contain the steps needed to complete this exercise for those that need additional prompting. This module should be referenced if you need further help or explanations.

Module 2 exercise steps

1. *Start PageMaker.*

2. *Create a new PageMaker document, using these parameters:*

     Letter page

     0.75 inch margins all around the page

     Double-sided, Facing pages

     Four pages long

     Orientation tall (portrait)

3. *Set the measurement preferences to use inches.*

4. *Load in a text file called Lead Story from the Lesson 2 folder, which is located in the Tutorial folder. Flow this text onto the first page using the manual flow method.*

5. *Load in the graphic Logotype.eps from the Lesson 2 folder, and place it at the bottom of the page.*

6. *Change the page view to Actual size and scroll to the top right-hand corner of the page.*

The detailed steps to complete this exercise are located on the following pages.

The steps in detail

1. Start PageMaker.

   This first step is achieved by locating the PageMaker 4 folder (this is where the PageMaker program is most likely to be) and finding the program PageMaker 4. It has a very distinctive icon. Double-click on this icon (Figures 1 and 2).

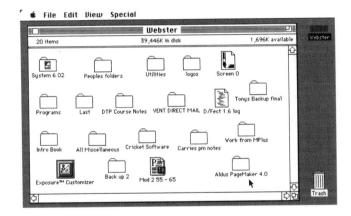

Figure 1. Although there is very little chance that your desktop will look anything like this one, there should at least be a folder named PageMaker 4. This folder needs to be opened by double-clicking with the mouse to find the Page-Maker program.

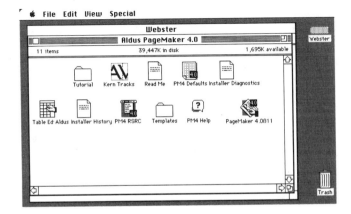

Figure 2. Within the PageMaker 4 folder should be files similar to these — although not necessarily the same. Locate the file named PageMaker 4 and double-click on it to open it.

2. *Create a new PageMaker document, using these parameters:*

Letter page

0.75 inch margins all around the page

Double-sided, Facing pages

Four pages long

Orientation tall (portrait)

After starting PageMaker, a new document is created by selecting the *New* command (Figure 3) from the **File** menu. From this command comes the dialog box of Figure 4.

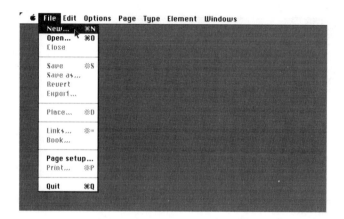

*Figure 3. The New command from the **File** menu must be used to create a new PageMaker publication.*

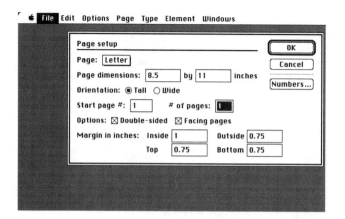

Figure 4. The New dialog box contains all the options we need to create the page described in step 2 of this exercise. This figure shows current default values. Figure 5 shows the new values required for this exercise.

In this dialog box, the default parameters of Letter size, Double-sided, Facing-pages, and Orientation (Tall) do not have to be changed. Just change the number of pages to 4 and the Inside margin to 0.75.

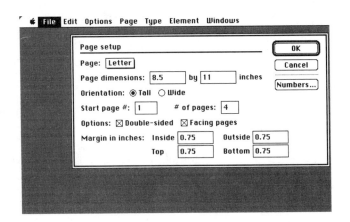

Figure 5. Your dialog box should be set up exactly like this one.

3. *Set the measurement preferences to inches.*

These preferences are set using the *Preferences* command in the **Edit** menu. Invoke this command (Figure 6), and set up the dialog box as shown in Figure 7.

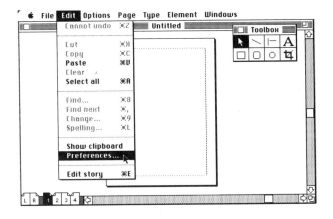

Figure 6. Use the Preferences command to set measurement units.

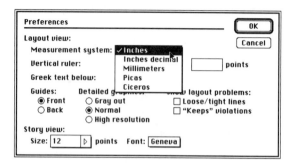

Figure 7. Select the correct measurement unit and click on OK.

As this is only an example of using the *Preferences* command, you may, in fact, prefer to set the measurement units to something else more suitable to you — perhaps millimeters. Remember, this unit of measure can always be overridden by inserting m for millimeters, p for picas, and i for inches in any dialog box.

4. Load in a text file called Lead Story from the Lesson 2 folder, which is located in the Tutorial folder. Flow this text onto the first page using the manual flow method.

The first step here is to use the *Place* command from the **File** menu (Figure 8). From there you will be presented with the dialog box of Figure 9.

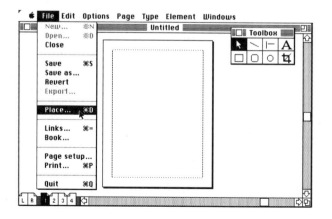

Figure 8. The Place command is used to import all files into PageMaker.

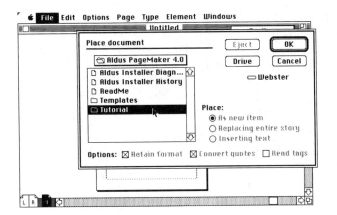

Figure 9. If you opened PageMaker from the Page-Maker 4 folder, you will be presented with a list that contains the Tutorial folder, which includes the lesson folders.

If you opened up PageMaker from the PageMaker 4 folder, you will see something similar Figure 9 — the folder Tutorial should be listed. If it is, double-click on Tutorial. If it's not, hold the mouse button down on the currently open folder name, run the mouse down to the name of the hard disk, and release the mouse button. Now search for the PageMaker 4 folder (or something similar), and then the Tutorial folder within this.

Once you have entered the Tutorial folder you should have no trouble locating the Lesson 2 folder. Double-click on this and then on Lead Story (Figure 10) and wait a few seconds to be returned to the PageMaker page. Your Tutorial or Lesson 2 folder may have slightly different files than ours. This doesn't matter — just find and select Lead Story.

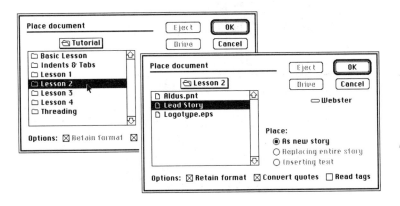

*Figure 10.
Double-click on the Tutorial folder and on Lesson 2, and double-click again on the file Lead Story.*

Your mouse cursor will, of course, change shape after the file loads. It should be the same as shown in Figure 11 — the manual flow mode. If it is not, go to the **Options** menu and choose the *Autoflow* command. To load this file onto the page, move the mouse cursor to the top left-hand corner of the page margins (Figure 11), and click the mouse once. The text will then flow onto the page (Figure 12).

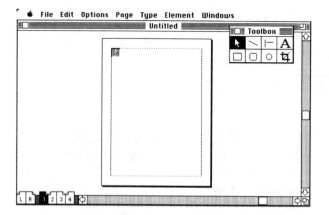

Figure 11. Note the shape of the mouse cursor, denoting a file is waiting to be loaded in manual mode. Position the mouse cursor where you want the text to flow from (normally the top of the page).

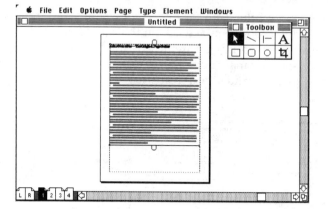

Figure 12. The text will flow across and down the page until it runs out.

5. *Load in the graphic Logotype.eps from the Lesson 2 folder, and place it at the bottom of your page.*

The *Place* command once again is used to load in a file, no matter what format it exists in. This time however, you will see the contents of the Lesson 2 folder, as this is where we retrieved our last file.

Locate the file Logotype.eps, and double-click on the filename (Figure 13).

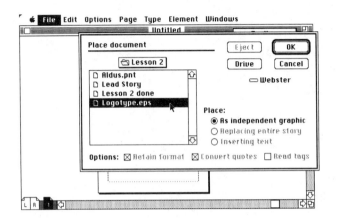

Figure 13. *Select the file Logotype.eps after selecting the Place command again. You will be taken to the same folder as you retrieved the last file from — in this case the Lesson 2 folder.*

To place this file at the bottom of your page, move the mouse from the page to the area you want it placed (see Figure 14). You can deposit the graphic using one of two techniques — either the one-click method we used above for the text flow, or the box-draw method. To use the latter method, hold down the mouse button, move the mouse down and across to the right of the page, and release it when the box is the desired size (Figure 15).

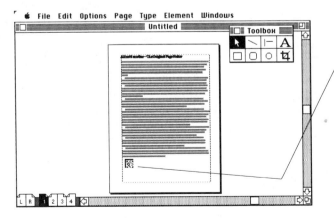

Figure 14. *Note the different shape of the mouse cursor. Move it to the bottom of your page and drag the mouse down and across the screen, to the bottom right-hand margin, and release it. The image file will appear on the screen (see figure 15).*

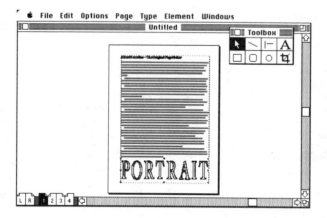

Figure 15. The graphic at the bottom of the page.

6. *Change the page view to Actual size and scroll to the top right-hand corner of the page.*

The page view is changed via the **Page** menu. Select the command *Actual size* from this menu (Figure 16).

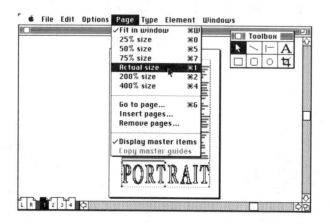

Figure 16. Changing to Actual size view can be done in a variety of ways, but this way is the most straightforward.

Initially, you will see the top right-hand corner of the page — in fact, it could be anywhere on the page. The scroll bars must be used to move the page around.

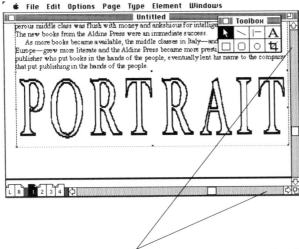

Figure 17. *Initially changing to Actual size could put you anywhere on the page.*

These two areas move you to the top right of the page. Two mouse clicks in each of these areas will get you to the desired area. You could, of course, use the top right and lower right arrows (circled in Figure 18), but this would be slower.

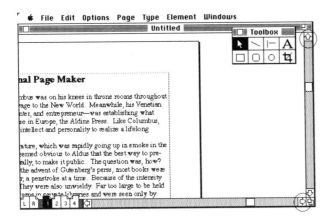

Figure 18. *We clicked twice in the areas indicated in Figure 17 to get this result — a look at the top right-hand corner of the page.*

After completing this exercise you should be familiar with the basic techniques involved in the use of PageMaker: how menus work, how dialog boxes work, how to load files, and how to move around the screen. This is a good start for moving to the next module.

Module 3

Working with Text Blocks

Working with Text Blocks

As already discussed, we can import text from other applications onto the PageMaker page. It is possible, however, to have greater control over the text and manipulate text blocks in various ways.

To follow with the discussion in this module, load any text onto the page. The Lead Story file as loaded in Module 2 would be suitable. Use the load method discussed in Figures 20 and 21 in Module 2 to get your text onto the page similar to that shown in Figure 1.

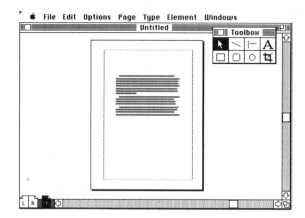

Figure 1. To follow with the discussion in this module, first set up a page similar to this one.

Before we begin, make sure that you have the selector (pointer) tool activated in the Toolbox. This will allow you to select and manipulate text (Figure 1).

We are not going to look at sentences, letters, and words in this module, but rather the manipulation of the whole block of text (or "text block") as one unit.

If it is not selected, click once on the text block. Once selected, you several things will appear around the edge of this text block (Figure 2). These include a line above and below the text, a "windowshade handle" above and below the text, and a dot (or small square) in each corner of the text block. These indicate that the text block is selected, and each one of these selection indicators can be used in a different way to manipulate that text block.

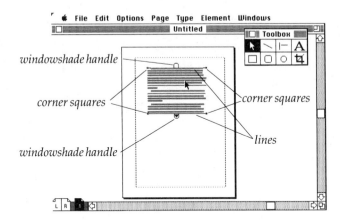

windowshade handle

corner squares

corner squares

lines

windowshade handle

Figure 2. *Note the features of the selected text. A line above and below, a windowshade handle above and below, and a dot or small square in every corner.*

Moving text

Any text block can be easily moved to anywhere else on the page without changing its shape in any way. There are, in fact, two ways to do this. First, hold down the mouse button on the block of text, somewhere near the middle of the text. Hold the mouse button down and don't move the mouse for a few seconds. The arrow cursor changes to a four-arrow type, the handles and corner squares disappear, and the text is bounded by dotted lines. Now move the mouse anywhere on the desk, with the mouse button still held down, and the text will move wherever you want. This method is illustrated in Figure 3.

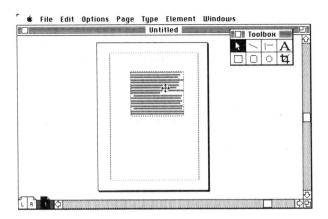

Figure 3. *Here we have held down the mouse button on the text block, waited several seconds, and then moved the mouse. The entire text block moves with the mouse in the manner shown.*

Alternatively, you can hold the mouse button down on the text and move the mouse immediately. What this does is move the selected text block, but only in a boxed outline form. Once the mouse button is released, the text will reformat in its new position. This is illustrated in Figure 4.

Clicking anywhere outside the text block will deselect that block.

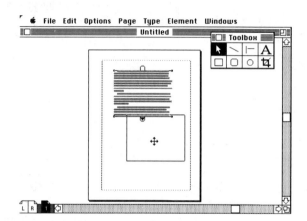

Figure 4. Here we have held down the mouse button on the text block and moved the mouse immediately. Only a boxed outline of the text follows the mouse in this case — often a quicker, yet less exact way to move text.

Resizing text blocks

Text blocks can be resized as simply as they can be moved. Once again, there are several ways in which a text block can be resized. We will look at each one in turn.

People often think they must define their column width, number of columns, page breaks, and so on from the word processor they used to create the text. However, this kind of work is done from within PageMaker and can be altered at will, regardless of how the text was created in the word processor. The word processor is used basically as a text input medium — very little formatting work need be done at this early stage.

Resizing vertically

When resizing a text block vertically, the width of the text block is not altered at all. Before we do this, however, let's get one thing straight — using these methods, there is no way that you will lose any text. It may look as though text has disappeared, but rest assured, it will come back.

With reference to Figure 5, note the handles above and below the selected block of text. The top handle should be empty, while the bottom handle has a small down arrow (▼) in it. This indicates that this text block contains more text than is currently visible. If the handle has no symbol, this would indicate the end of a particular text block.

Let's say we want to alter the length of this text block vertically. The way this is done is as follows. Hold the mouse button down on the bottom handle (with the down arrow sign). You must be fairly exact when doing this, and you must make sure that you do not simply click once — you must hold the mouse button down. You can now move the mouse up and down as much as you like. Wherever you release the mouse button is where the new length of the text block will end (see Figures 5 and 6). If you move the mouse up, text will have disappeared from the page. However, if you move the mouse button down, more text will appear on the page. (Unless, of course, the text file runs out of text; in which case the bottom handle will be empty.)

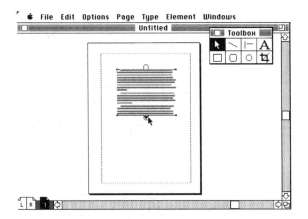

Figure 5. *To resize the text block vertically, hold down the mouse button directly on top of the bottom handle (which contains a ▼symbol, indicating more text is contained in the text block than is visible).*

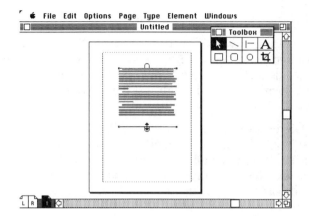

Figure 6. Hold the mouse button down on this symbol and move the mouse down or up. After releasing the mouse button, the text will reformat at its new size.

Alternatively, the text block could have been resized using the same method on the top handle. Holding the mouse button down on this handle will allow you to resize the text in the exact same way (Figure 7). However, if you shorten the text block from the top, the text will disappear from the bottom of the block. You cannot hide text from the top of a block using this method.

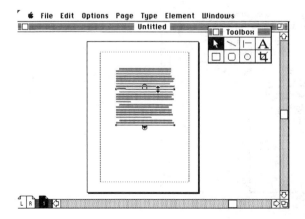

Figure 7. Text blocks can also be vertically resized by "grabbing" (holding down the mouse button on) the top handle and moving the mouse down.

Resizing horizontally

If you would like to horizontally increase or decrease the width of a text block, hold down the mouse button on any dot in any corner of the text block. You must be fairly exact when doing this, and you may at first miss the dot altogether. If you do, reselect the text block, and try again till you get it. When you have selected it correctly moving the mouse button causes the effect shown in Figure 8.

This method of grabbing a corner dot with the mouse allows you to resize text both horizontally and vertically.

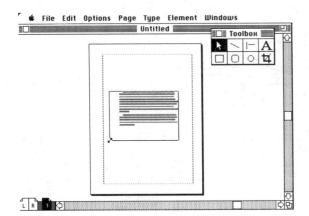

Figure 8. *To resize text blocks horizontally, hold down the mouse button on any corner of a selected text block. In every corner of this block there should be a dot — this is what you grab. As you move the mouse, a rectangle is created on screen indicating the new size of the text block. Text blocks can also be resized vertically in this fashion.*

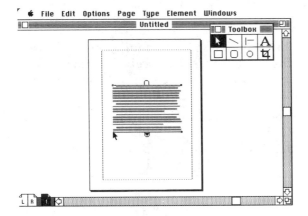

Figure 9. *After we release the mouse button, the text block formats to the exact size of the rectangle of Figure 8.*

The box that appears on screen is indicative of the new dimensions of the text block when you release the mouse button. The text block can be adjusted both horizontally and vertically at the same time, and the text will reflow immediately.

Column guides

There are several guides that exist in PageMaker for exercising control over text blocks. Perhaps the most common guides that you will use are the column guides.

To adjust the number of columns on the page, select the *Column guides* command from the **Options** menu (Figure 10). You will see the dialog box in Figure 11.

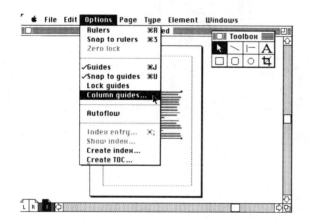

Figure 10. The Column guides command in the **Options** menu is used to select the number of columns for the page.

Within this dialog box, input the number of columns you want, and then the amount of desired space between the columns. Upon clicking on OK, you will notice some column guides have now been added to the page (Figure 12).

Text will not immediately flow into these columns — it is up to us to flow the text into these columns. These column guides initially appear in the background. Text currently on the page stays at its previously defined width.

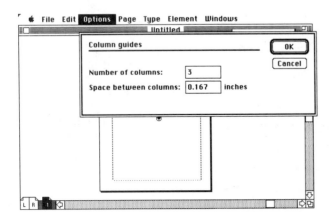

Figure 11. The Column guides command dialog box. Here we have defined three columns with .167 inches between each one.

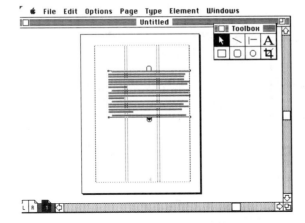

Figure 12. Although existing text on the page will not flow into the three columns automatically, the guides will appear on the page, and any text now added to the page will flow into these new columns.

To continue following our operations, select your text as shown in Figure 12, and press the Delete (or Backspace) key. This text is then deleted. Choose the Lead Story example file with the *Place* command and flow it down column 1 of the page as shown in Figures 13 and 14. To find this file, double-click on Tutorial in the PageMaker 4 file, and then again on Lesson 2.

Whenever a new text file is flowed, it will obey the bounds of a column guide. See Figures 13 and 14, which illustrate this point.

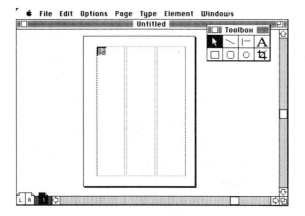

Figure 13. On a page defined with three columns, we are about to flow the Lead Story text file down column 1.

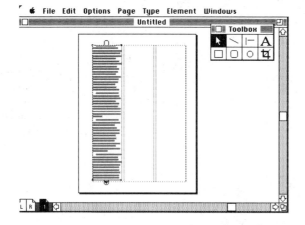

Figure 14. Note how the text flows down the first column, rather than across the whole page, as it would if no columns were defined.

The *Column guides* dialog box only selects equal size columns. Irregular columns may be achieved by manually moving the column guides themselves. To do this, hold down the mouse button directly on a column guide, away from text if possible, and move the mouse button to the left or the right. The column guide will move with the mouse. You cannot just pull one column guide. The set of column guides moves together, as shown in Figure 15.

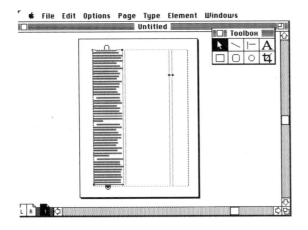

Figure 15. Irregular columns can be created by holding the mouse button down on a set of column guides and "dragging" it to the left or right.

Margin guides

We have already discussed margin guides in Modules 1 and 2; the guides we can see around the inside edges of the page. These are defined when we start a particular publication; however, they can be altered manually if we wish. To do this, hold down the mouse button on either the left or the right margin, and move the mouse to the left or the right. A dotted margin guide will follow the mouse, and where it is released will be the new text margin (Figure 16). Any text now flowed onto this page will obey these new margins.

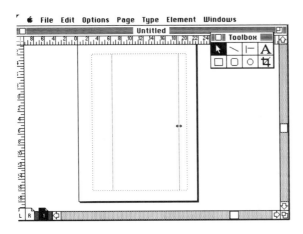

Figure 16. The left and/or right margin guides for the page can be altered from within a publication by holding down the mouse button on the left or right margin, and dragging them where necessary. To better illustrate this we have temporarily changed from 3 columns to 1 column through the Figure 11 dialog box.

All guides on the page, whether margin, column, or ruler (which we'll look at a little later on), are affected by several commands in the **Options** menu. Bear in mind these guides never appear on the printed output. They are simply there to help control the layout of your document. The first command which modifies guides is the *Guides* command. This hides or shows all guides (Figures 17 and 18).

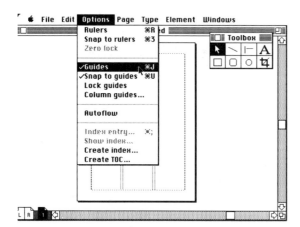

Figure 17. Selecting the Guides command will alternately hide and show column guides on the screen. Note that with all such commands, a check to the left indicates that the command is on.

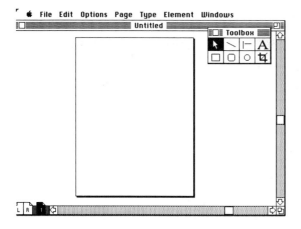

Figure 18. Here the guides are hidden from the page — it gives a better indication of what the page will look like when printed.

The *Snap to guides command* (Figure 19) allows all text and graphics on the PageMaker page to "magnetically snap" to the various page guides, whenever they are in close proximity. This feature is usually best left on, for it makes sure that all text and graphics blocks are flush with margins, which is generally the requirement. It is often turned off when working close to a particular guide that you do not want to to be flush with.

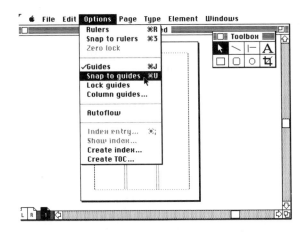

Figure 19. Selecting the Snap to guides *command, which is on by default, allows text and graphics to snap flush to guides, if they are close to these guides.*

Lock guides is, as the name suggests, a lock for all guides on the page (Figure 20). With this command activated, no guides can be moved at all until this command is reselected. It makes sure you don't accidentally move guides that were accurately positioned.

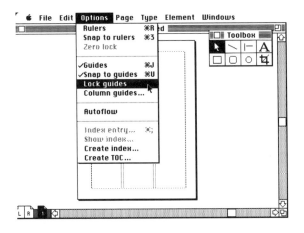

Figure 20. All guides can be locked into position using this command to prevent accidental movement of precisely placed guides.

Warning about guides

All guides can occupy a position above or below any text or graphic objects on the page. What this means is, if you try to select text or graphics exactly where a guide is, the guide or the object may be selected first.

This can be controlled through the *Preferences* command in the **Edit** menu (Figure 21). The associated dialog box (Figure 22) provides you with a choice of setting the guides at the front or the back. Alternatively, even if the guides are set to the front, it is possible to choose the *Guides* command in the **Options** menu to temporarily hide the guides from the screen. The particular object can then be selected. You can also select an object behind a guide by holding down the Command key while selecting the object.

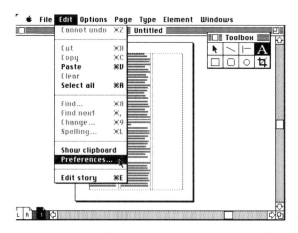

Figure 21. To control whether guides should be behind or in front of other objects on the screen, first choose the Preferences command from the **Edit** menu ...

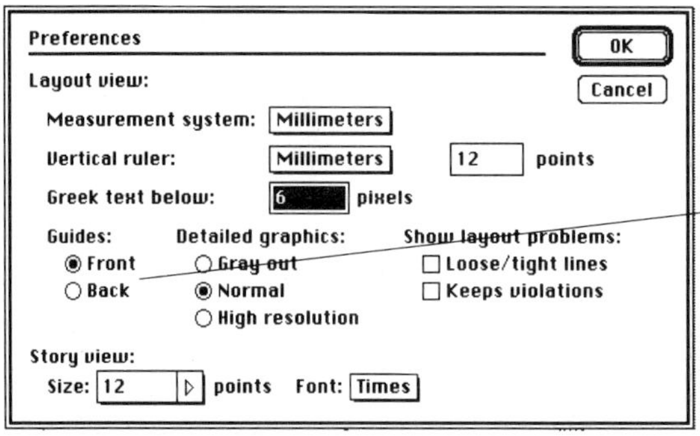

Figure 22. ... then, from the dialog box that appears, make your choice. We have chosen to have the guides appear at the front.

Reflowing text

By now, several questions about the movement of text may have entered your mind. How do we get to see all of a text file? How do we flow the same file down several columns? How do we continue a text file from one page to the next? Right now we will look at exactly how to do these things.

The first thing we will look at is how to continue text from one text block to another. This has to be done if you want to flow text down several columns on the same page, or even if you want to flow text from one page to another. As you might have guessed, there are again several ways to do this.

Figures 23 to 31 on the following pages show how to flow text manually into three columns across the page. If you wish to follow this approach, define three columns and select the example file Lead Story through the *Place* command in the **File** menu. After a few seconds, your screen should look like Figure 23. Now, flow the text down one column as shown in Figure 24. Any text or graphics currently on the page can be erased by clicking on it to select it, and pressing the Delete or Backspace key.

The easiest way to continue text from an existing block to a new one is as follows. With the pointer tool, select the text block that contains the hidden text (such as column 1 of Figure 24) that you wish to flow onto a new text block. Click once on the bottom handle that contains a down arrow symbol (Figure 25). After doing this, you will have a new text paragraph mouse cursor, the same one that appears immediately when loading a new file (Figure 26). You can now flow text anywhere or anyhow you like, with the knowledge that this new text block you are about to create continues exactly where the text block you just selected leaves off.

Follow Figures 27 through 31 to flow a full text file across multiple blocks. To summarize this operation, study carefully the captions of Figures 23 through 31.

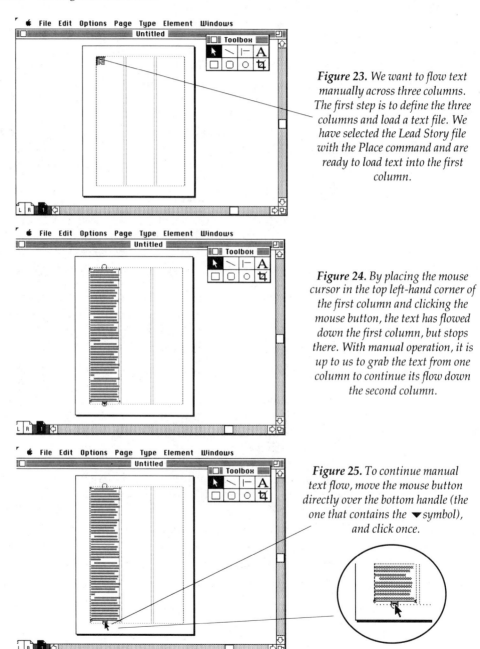

Figure 23. *We want to flow text manually across three columns. The first step is to define the three columns and load a text file. We have selected the Lead Story file with the Place command and are ready to load text into the first column.*

Figure 24. *By placing the mouse cursor in the top left-hand corner of the first column and clicking the mouse button, the text has flowed down the first column, but stops there. With manual operation, it is up to us to grab the text from one column to continue its flow down the second column.*

Figure 25. *To continue manual text flow, move the mouse button directly over the bottom handle (the one that contains the ▼symbol), and click once.*

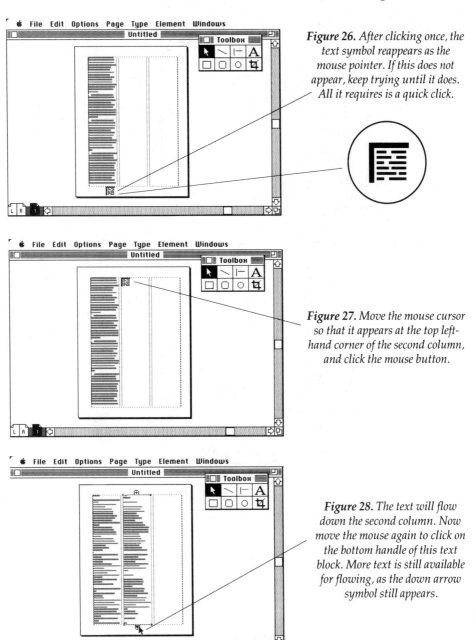

Figure 26. After clicking once, the text symbol reappears as the mouse pointer. If this does not appear, keep trying until it does. All it requires is a quick click.

Figure 27. Move the mouse cursor so that it appears at the top left-hand corner of the second column, and click the mouse button.

Figure 28. The text will flow down the second column. Now move the mouse again to click on the bottom handle of this text block. More text is still available for flowing, as the down arrow symbol still appears.

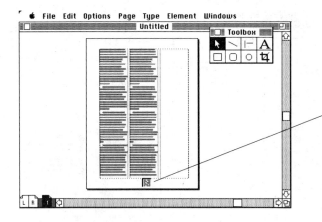

***Figure 29.** Once again the mouse cursor will change shape.*

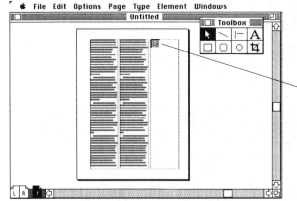

***Figure 30.** Now move the mouse cursor so that it appears at the top left-hand corner of the third column and click the mouse button.*

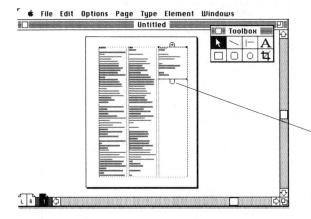

***Figure 31.** In our case the text in the file we are using ran out before it reached the end of the column. Apart from the fact that it does not fill the column, we are also aware of this because the bottom handle of this third text block is empty.*

If a text block contains the ▼ symbol in its bottom handle, this means that it can be clicked on again, and the rest of the following text can be flowed into a new text block. If you click on this handle by accident, and get the paragraph mouse cursor when you don't want it, simply reselect the pointer tool and it will disappear.

In Figure 31, we know we have reached the end of the text file, as the bottom handle of the third column is empty and does not contain a ▼ symbol.

Automatic text flow

Text can be made to run across columns and pages automatically, without operator intervention. To do this, select the command *Autoflow* from the **Options** menu (Figure 32). When this command is selected, the mouse cursor will look like this 🗊 rather than like this 🗊 (Figure 33). When you click the mouse to flow the text, it will flow across columns and pages fairly quickly, creating any pages it needs as it goes (Figure 34). This process, which can take a bit of time with large text files, can be stopped by clicking the mouse button.

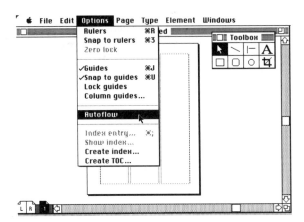

*Figure 32. Selecting the Autoflow command in the **Options** menu, before text is flowed, allows text to run automatically across columns and pages.*

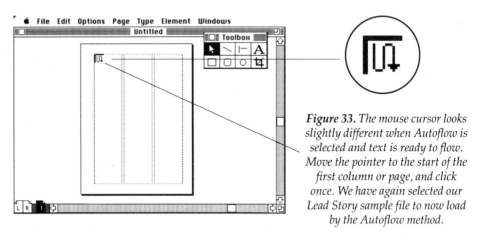

Figure 33. *The mouse cursor looks slightly different when Autoflow is selected and text is ready to flow. Move the pointer to the start of the first column or page, and click once. We have again selected our Lead Story sample file to now load by the Autoflow method.*

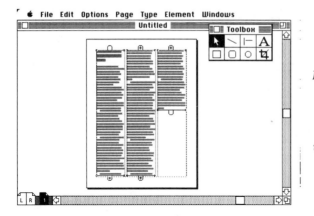

Figure 34. *Text will flow across all three columns without operator intervention at the end of every column. If this text file had been longer than one page, new pages would have been created automatically.*

Semi-automatic text flow

Semi-automatic text flow is just as it sounds — a midway point between manual and automatic text flow. In manual flow, you must click the loaded mouse cursor at the top of every column or page, go to the bottom of that column or page, click on the bottom windowshade handle to reload the cursor, go to the top of the next column or page, and repeat the steps. With automatic text flow, you simply click the loaded mouse cursor on the first column or page, and the rest is done automatically.

By holding down the Shift key as you are about to click the mouse cursor to flow the text for the first time (regardless of whether the *Autoflow* command has been selected), the mouse cursor will change appearance to look like this: ⎮⎡⎯⎤. When it does, the text will flow down the first column or page and stop, and the mouse cursor will be loaded automatically, as the text finishes flowing down that column or page. You are then free to click at the top of the second column or page, without having to first click on the bottom windowshade handle of the first column.

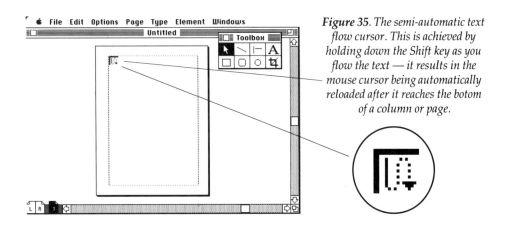

Figure 35. The semi-automatic text flow cursor. This is achieved by holding down the Shift key as you flow the text — it results in the mouse cursor being automatically reloaded after it reaches the botom of a column or page.

Semi-automatic text flow is perhaps best used when you want to flow text more quickly than you can manually, but not regularly across the full length of all columns and pages, as automatic text flow does by default.

Temporarily changing text flow modes

Automatic to semi-automatic

1. Select *Autoflow* on from the **Options** Menu.

2. Hold down the Shift key, position the mouse cursor where text is to reflow, and click on the mouse button.

The mouse icon changes to the semi-automatic icon and returns to automatic when the Shift key is released.

Automatic to manual follows similar steps except that the Command key is used instead of the Shift key.

Manual to semi-automatic

1. Select manual text flow mode (*Autoflow* off in the **Options** menu).

2. Press the Shift key and click the mouse button.

The mouse icon changes to the semi-automatic icon and returns to manual when the shift key is released.

Manual to automatic follows similar steps except that the Command key replaces the Shift key. Text will flow to the end of file, or until you click the mouse button again.

Resizing multiple text blocks

Whenever a text block is split into several text blocks, any of the individual blocks can be resized and moved without ever losing continuity of text between the blocks. When the first block in a series of blocks is resized, for example, by raising the bottom windowshade handle (Figure 36), text is forced back into the following text blocks. No other text blocks change size. The last text block (in our case column 3 of Figure 36) would have a down arrow symbol in the bottom windowshade handle, if we clicked on it with the pointer tool. This indicates there is now more text available to flow into the third column.

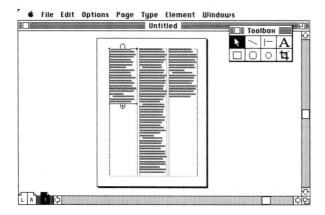

Figure 36. Any text block in the sequence can be resized without drastic consequences or loss of text. Here we have resized the first column of the page in Figure 34. Note the third column has not changed size, but would have more text available for further flowing, if required.

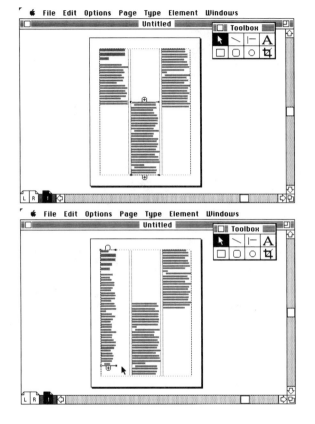

Figure 37. Even the middle block in a series of text blocks can be resized without ever losing text or continuity of text.

Figure 38. Here the first column has been narrowed, still without any loss in the flow and readability of the text. Column 3, in both Figures 37 and 38, has not changed its length, but now has more text available for flowing, to compensate for the reduction in columns 1 and 2.

Removing text blocks

Text blocks can be selected with the pointer tool and then deleted using the *Cut* or *Clear* commands from the **Edit** menu. The Delete key also deletes a text block once selected. When this happens, that text block is removed from the "chain." In other words, the text loses all continuity. Because of this, never use these commands to remove a text block if you want to keep text continuity.

The simple way to remove a text block is related to the way we resized text blocks earlier. However, instead of resizing the text block a little, hold down the mouse button on the bottom handle, and pull the mouse cursor up to the start of the text block (Figures 39 through 42). The entire text block will disappear with only the two handles remaining, as shown in Figure 42.

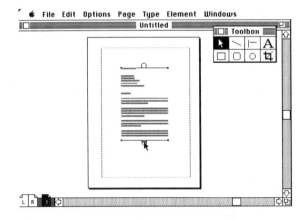

Figure 39. Let's say that we want to get rid of this text block. We initially act as though we are going to resize it.

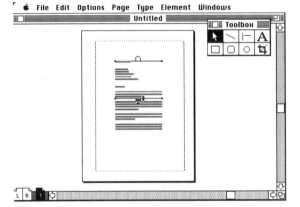

Figure 40. Hold down the mouse button on the bottom handle, and pull the mouse cursor up the page. However, instead of releasing the mouse button half-way up the column...

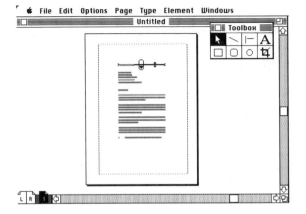

Figure 41. ...take it all the way to the top.

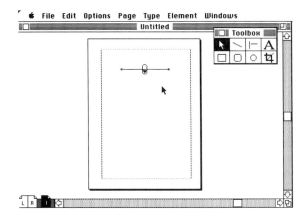

Figure 42. After releasing the mouse button above the text block, the two handles will appear together on the page.

When just these two handles remain, there are two things you can do. First, if you click anywhere else on the page, they will disappear. Second, if you click on the bottom handle once, they will both still disappear, but you now have a loaded mouse cursor with which you can reflow the text elsewhere (Figure 43).

This method could have been used to remove the middle column of text in, say, Figure 34. Text continuity is not lost; all the text in the middle block that is removed using the above method moves into the third column, and is available for flowing into the rest of the column and onto another page if necessary.

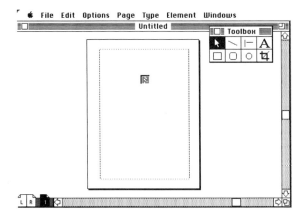

Figure 43. If the mouse button is clicked on the bottom handle of the text block of Figure 42, the text can be completely reflowed. Text will never be lost — neither will continuity, if this method is used.

Separating a text block

When a text block has flowed onto the page, it may not be in the desired layout or format. For example, the page may have three columns, and your text occupies the first column only. Instead, you would like it to be placed in the top half of the page, with sections of text in all three columns. This is achieved by breaking the text block in the first column into two other sections. These two sections can then be placed in the two other columns. To follow through with us in this section, make sure you have a page with three columns and enough text to fill the first column.

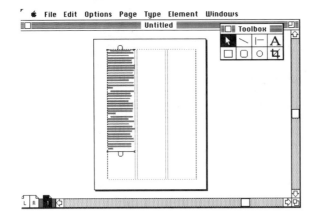

Figure 44. The text on this page occupies the first column only. If this is not how you want your layout to look, you can break a larger text block into smaller text blocks, so they can be moved around individually. The first step in breaking apart a text block is to select it with the pointer tool, and then place your mouse over the bottom window-shade handle.

To break the text block, first select it with the pointer tool (Figure 44). While still pressing the mouse button, move the bottom windowshade handle up to where you would like the text in column one to end. Upon stopping, you'll notice the bottom text handle now has the down arrow symbol inside it. By clicking once on the down arrow, you will get either the manual flow icon or the autoflow icon, depending on whether *Autoflow* from the **Options** menu has been selected or not. For this exercise, *Autoflow* should be switched off. Then flow the text into the second column. Follow the same steps with the text block in column two to create a third text block. Figures 45 through 49 explain these steps in detail.

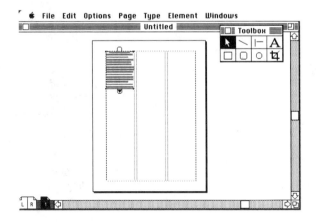

Figure 45. Push the bottom middle handle up as though you are resizing the text block. Once you've released your finger from the mouse at the desired point, the bottom text handle will have the down arrow symbol.

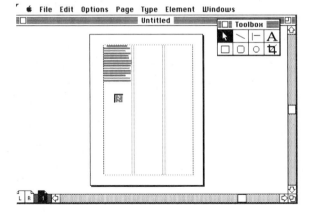

*Figure 46. Upon clicking on the down arrow symbol, the text flow icon will appear. If the Autoflow icon appears, go to the **Options** menu and deselect Autoflow.*

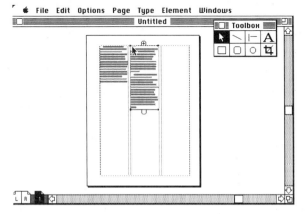

Figure 47. Now flow text into the second column.

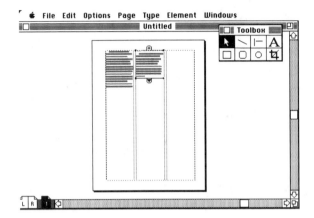

Figure 48. Follow the same steps with this text block as you did with the first one. Push up the bottom handle to the place in the text you wish to break the block. Now click the mouse on the down arrow, and you will get the manual text flow icon again.

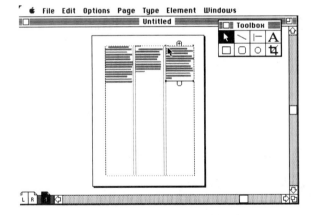

Figure 49. Again reflow the text, but this time into the third column. Now you have three individual text blocks.

These three text blocks can now be moved anywhere around the page without affecting each other. Note that these three text blocks are still threaded together, and form what PageMaker calls a single story. Resizing of any of these text blocks will not lose text continuity, and will have the same operations as discussed earlier in resizing multiple text blocks in Figures 36, 37, and 38.

Combining text blocks

If your current document is made up of numerous text blocks, you may wish to join some or all of them, making it easier to move text around. If there are two text blocks which are part of the same story you would like to join, first select the last one with the pointer tool. Place the mouse over the bottom windowshade handle and pull it all the way up to the top, as you did in Figures 40 and 41 in this module. Figures 50 and 51 also repeat this operation.

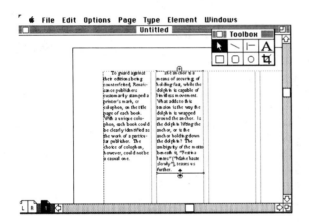

Figure 50. *Hold the mouse down on the bottom handle and start pulling it all the way up to the top handle.*

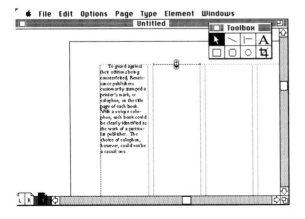

Figure 51. *You should be left with no text from the second block, and just the two handles showing a plus in the top one, and a down arrow symbol in the bottom one.*

Now there should be a plus symbol and a down arrow symbol left in the handles of column 2 (Figure 51). Next, select the first text block. Once selected, the bottom window handle will now have the down arrow symbol. Place your mouse over this handle, and pull it down, to reveal the text you have now recombined with the text of column 1.

Alternatively, you could have just selected the column one text and pulled down on the bottom windowshade handle. The text from column two would have flowed into column one.

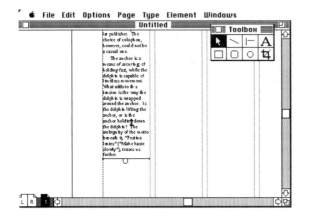

Figure 52. The mouse is held on the down arrow and pulled down to reveal the text we have just recombined from column 2 into column 1.

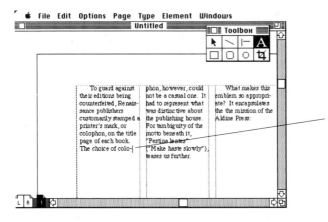

Figure 53. Here we have three text blocks we would like to join, so we have placed the text cursor at the end of the first text block.

If you have more than two text blocks to join of the same threaded story, you could continue doing what we have just described for multiple blocks. Alternatively, use the text tool and place the flashing cursor at the end of the first text block.

The next step is to choose the *Select all* command from the **Edit** menu. All your text should be selected and shown on the screen in reverse video. Again, from the **Edit** menu you next choose *Cut*. All text on your screen should totally disappear, but don't worry. If you now select *Paste* from the **Edit** menu, all text will flow back on to your screen as one block.

Figures 53 through 57 summarize this process.

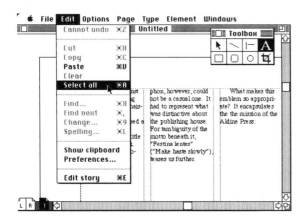

Figure 54. *To follow the steps explained above, you should next choose* Select all.

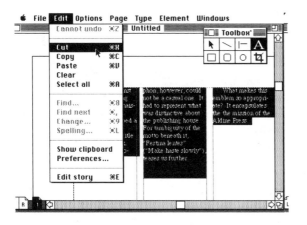

Figure 55. *After all the text is selected, we then execute the* Cut *command. All text on your screen should disappear.*

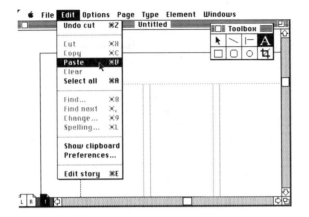

Figure 56. To finalize the joining of multiple text blocks, select the Paste *command from the* **Edit** *menu. Note all text has gone from the page, prior to executing the* Paste *command.*

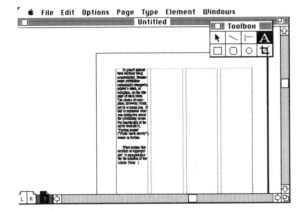

Figure 57. After the Paste *command is used the text reflows as one block. The finished result is obvious when we look at the page in reduced view. The three text blocks have become one larger text block. If your text is longer than one column, you will now have to continue reflowing it, until all text is placed.*

Unthreading and threading text

Unthreading text is when text blocks that belong to the same story are separated so they become individual text blocks. The new text blocks will remain unaffected by changes made to text blocks that were once part of the same story. That is, if you have a text block that is part of a large story, and would like to edit or change its layout without affecting the rest of the text, you can unthread this text block and make necessary changes. This un-threaded text block can always be rethreaded back into the original story. Figures 58 through 62 explain this process in detail.

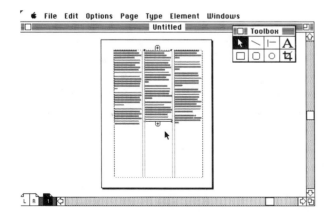

Figure 58. When unthreading text blocks that belong to the same story, first select the text block you wish to separate with the pointer tool.

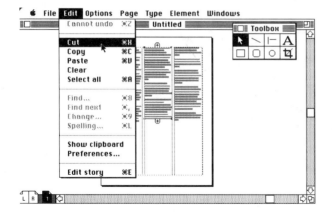

Figure 59. After selecting the appropriate text block, we then move to the Cut *command in the* **Edit** *menu.*

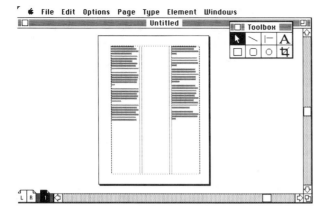

Figure 60. The selected text block has now been cut from the screen.

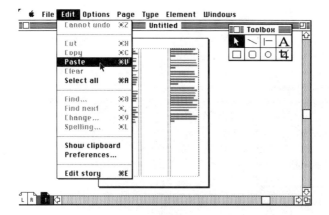

Figure 61. *The next step is to move again to the* **Edit** *menu and select the* Paste *command.*

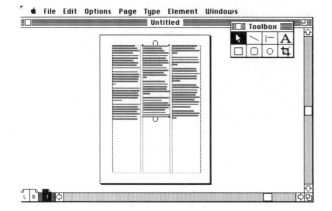

Figure 62. *The text block has now been pasted back onto your page but as a separate and individual text block. You can now edit, manipulate, and change the layout of this text block without affecting the other text blocks on the page.*

Because this text block we unthreaded is no longer part of the larger story, any changes we would like to make to the whole story will not affect the unthreaded text. Therefore, once you have made changes to the unthreaded text, you can rethread it back into the larger story.

To rethread the text block we originally unthreaded, first select it with the pointer tool. Now choose the *Cut* command, and the text block should again disappear from the screen. Next, place the text cursor at the point in which you would like to rethread your text. The text block does not have to be rethreaded into the story at the place it was unthreaded. After selecting the *Paste* command, the text will flow back onto the page as part of the larger story.

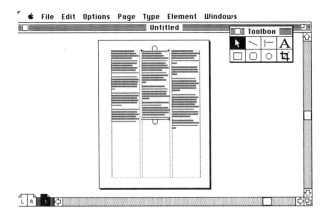

Figure 63. *To rethread the middle text block back into the larger story, we first select it with the pointer tool.*

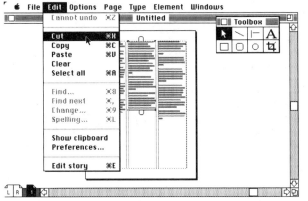

Figure 64. *The Cut command is then executed.*

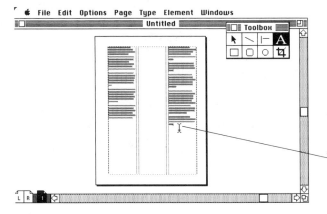

Figure 65. *After cutting the text block from the page, select the text tool, and place the cursor in the story where you would like to rethread the text. In our case we placed the flashing cursor at the end of the text block in the third column.*

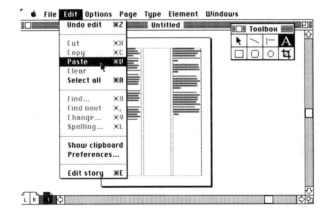

Figure 66. After placing the text cursor at the end of the text in the third column, we then select the Paste command.

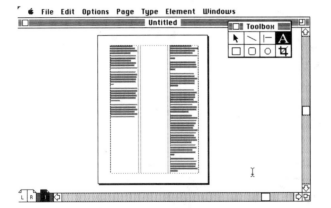

Figure 67. The text flows back onto the page and has been rethreaded back into the original story.

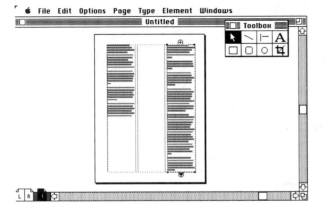

Figure 68. On selecting the now longer text block with the pointer tool, you can see that there is still more text to flow. This larger text block can now be broken down into smaller text blocks, or moved around the page. Now that the text blocks form one story again, any changes made to the story will affect the whole text.

Rotating text blocks

The *Text rotation* command is contained within the **Element** menu. With this command you have the ability to rotate text blocks in 90 degree angles. Text that you want rotated must be selected by the pointer tool, and only one text block can be rotated at a time. If you wish to work with us, type your name anywhere onto an empty PageMaker page, and make the font size 48 point. Then move to *Actual size* so we can see what we are doing. See Figures 69 through 72 for further instructions.

Figure 69. *The first step when rotating text is to make sure there is a text block on the page. So type in your name and make it at least 48 point.*

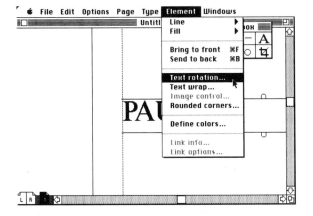

Figure 70. *Making sure your text block has been selected by the pointer tool, then move to the* Text rotation *command in the* **Element** *menu.*

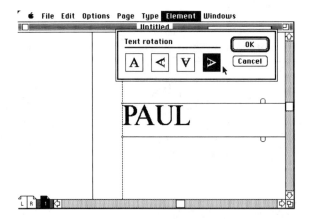

Figure 71. The Text rotation *dialog box will give you four choices, in 90 degree increments, on how you would like your text to be rotated. Select the angle by clicking on the icon showing the direction you would like the text to rotate.*

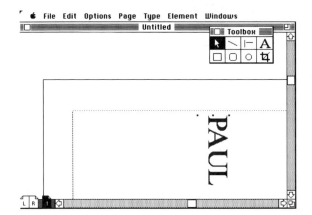

Figure 72. After clicking OK *in the* Text rotation *dialog box, the text block will have been rotated in the direction selected.*

The rotated text will probably not appear back on the page in its original position. If you cannot see the text block, scan the screen using the scroll bars, or move to *Fit in window* mode. Larger text blocks can just as easily be rotated by going over the same procedure (see Figures 73 and 74). All rotated text will immediately wrap around any graphics you have defined with text wrap attributes, if they happen to clash.

Editing rotated text blocks can only be done through the *Edit story* command, which is fully explained in a later module. You can, however, use the pointer tool to change the layout and line breaks of rotated text. When selected with the pointer tool, the

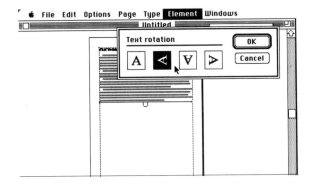

Figure 73. With this larger text block we still follow the same steps. After selecting it with the pointer tool and choosing Text rotation from the **Element** menu, we clicked on the second rotation option. Figure 69 shows the result we achieved after clicking on OK.

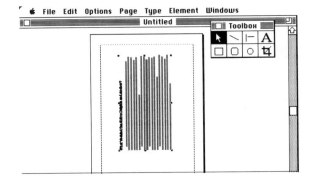

Figure 74. The whole text block has been rotated corresponding to the icon we selected in the previous dialog box.

rotated text block will have eight handles around it, just like a graphic. Changing the layout of the text is done by holding the mouse down on one of these handles, and adjusting it to a new position and/or size (Figure 75).

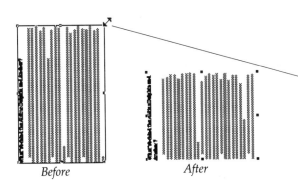

Before   *After*

Figure 75. The layout of this rotated text block has been changed by moving it with the top right handle.

Module 3 Exercise

Working with Text Blocks

Module 3 Exercise
Working with Text Blocks

In this exercise we will flow text into columns and manipulate text files and blocks once we have loaded them in. We will resize the columns, horizontally and vertically, and reflow the text.

This training material is structured so that people of all levels of expertise with PageMaker can use it to gain maximum benefit. In order to do this, we have structured this material so that the bare exercise is listed below this paragraph on just one page, with no hints. The following pages contain the steps needed to complete this exercise for those that need additional prompting. The **Working with Text Blocks** module should be referenced if you need further help or explanations.

Module 3 exercise steps

1. *Create a PageMaker document consisting of four Letter pages, 0.75 inch margins all around, and three columns on each of the four pages.*

2. *Load in the text file Lead Story from the Lesson 2 folder, within the Pagemaker Tutorial folder, and flow this file manually down the first column only of the first page.*

3. *Resize the text block in the first column so that it only flows halfway down that column.*

4. *Continue the text flow from halfway down the first column on the first page, to the top of the first column on the second page.*

5. *Move back to the first page and change the number of column guides to two. Resize the existing text block so that it fills the first column entirely. Continue the flow from the first column to the second.*

The steps to complete this exercise are located on the following pages.

The steps in detail

1. Create a PageMaker document consisting of four Letter pages, 0.75 inch margins all around, and three columns on each of the four pages.

The PageMaker publication itself is created by selecting the *New* command from the **File** menu (Figure 1). If a PageMaker publication or template is already open, you will have to choose the *Close* command from the **File** menu before you may select *New*.

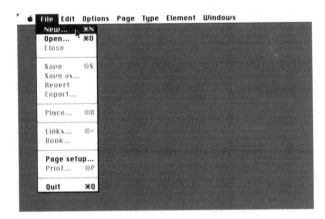

Figure 1. The New command must be used to create a new PageMaker publication.

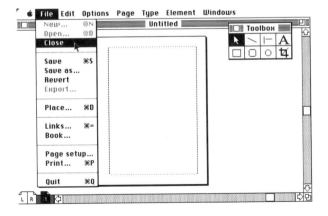

Figure 2. If a publication is currently open, the Close command will have to be chosen before the New command can be accessed. In other words, only one Page-Maker document can be open at a time.

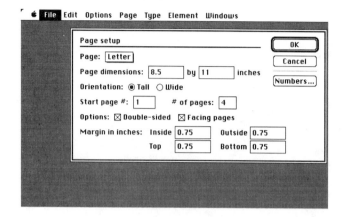

Figure 3. *The New dialog box should be set up like this — a Letter page, four pages long, and 0.75 inch margins all around.*

The Letter page size and the 0.75 inch margins are set from the dialog box that appears upon selecting *New* (Figure 3). You should also set, within this dialog box, 4 for the number of pages.

Once you have set up the box as per Figure 3, click on OK. The first page of the publication will then appear on screen.

To set the three column guides on the page, you must use the *Column guides* command in the **Options** menu (Figure 4). In the dialog box that appears upon selecting this command (Figure 5), insert the number 3 for number of columns. The space between columns can stay at the figure indicated of 0.167 inches.

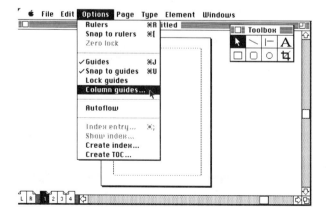

Figure 4. *The Column guides command from the* **Options** *menu must be used to create column guides for the page.*

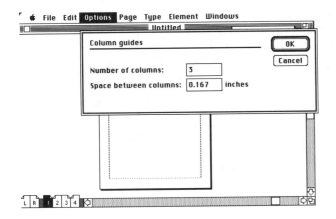

Figure 5. Insert a 3 for the number of columns for the page. The space between the columns, often called the "gutter," does not matter in this case.

2. Load in the text file Lead Story from the Lesson 2 folder, within the PageMaker 4 Tutorial folder, and flow this file manually down the first column only of the first page.

To load in the file Lead Story you must use the *Place* command from the **File** menu (Figure 6). If, after using this command, you are unsure as to how to locate the folder Lesson 2, review the steps in detail for step 4 of the Module 2 Exercise. Figures 7–9, below, briefly summarize these steps.

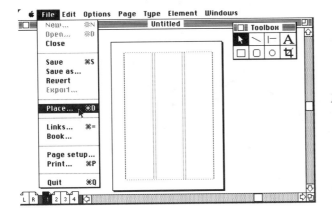

Figure 6. Choose the Place command to load in any files.

Module 3 Exercise - Working with Text Blocks

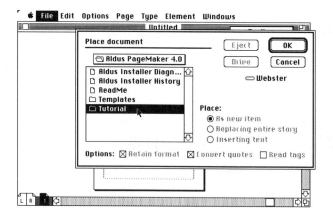

Figure 7. This dialog box will appear after selecting Place. *Double-click on the folder name Tutorial to access the needed file.*

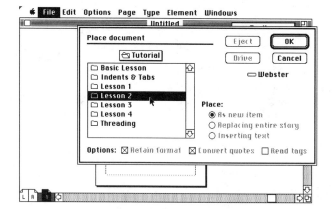

Figure 8. In this list of folders, double-click on Lesson 2.

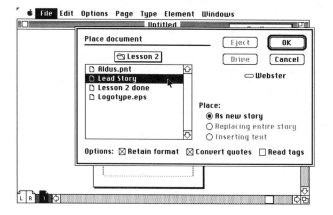

Figure 9. Then from this list of files double click on Lead Story.

Before you flow the text down the first column, make sure that the *Autoflow* command has not been left on. Have a look at the **Options** menu, and if the *Autoflow* command has a check next to it, this means that it is on. Select the command and it will then turn off. If it has no check next to it (as in Figure 10), just exit the menu.

Once the text file is ready to load into memory as in Figure 11, position the mouse cursor so that it appears in the very top left-hand corner of the first column of the page. From here, click the mouse button once. The text will flow down the first column and stop as shown in Figure 12.

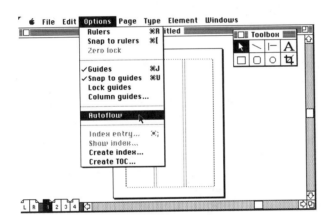

Figure 10. Before you actually flow any text, make sure the Autoflow command in the Options menu has no tick next to it. This will ensure that we are in manual mode and that the text only flows down one column at a time.

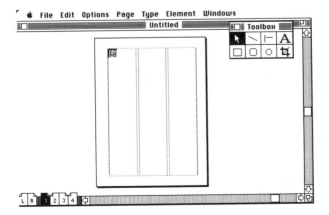

Figure 11. Position the mouse cursor at the very top left-hand corner of the first column, and click the mouse button once.

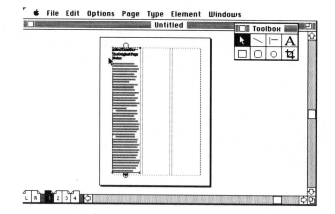

Figure 12. The text will flow down the first column and stop.

3. Resize the text block in the first column so that it only flows halfway down that column.

Before you resize this first text block, make sure that the pointer tool has been selected. This is the tool in the top left-hand corner of the Toolbox.

Click once anywhere inside this text block to select it. Once selected, a handle will appear at the bottom of the text with a small down arrow symbol in it. Move the mouse cursor over this handle and hold the mouse button down. (If all other handles of the text block suddenly disappear, it means that you were not quite on the bottom handle — reselect the text block and try again.) Once

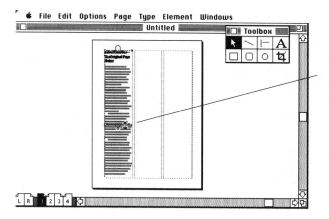

Figure 13. In this figure notice the position of the mouse cursor, which is actually now a two-sided arrow. We are in the process of resizing the column — achieved by holding the mouse button down on the bottom handle, and moving the mouse up the column.

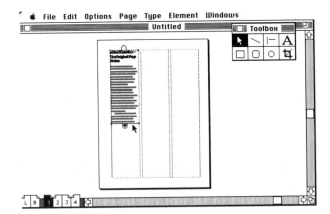

Figure 14. Release the mouse button when you have resized it to your liking.

the mouse button is held down, move the mouse to about halfway up the column (Figure 13), and release the mouse button (Figure 14). The text will now end exactly where you released the mouse.

4. Continue the text flow from halfway down the first column on the first page, to the top of the first column on the second page.

To continue text from one text block to another, regardless of where the second text block is going to flow, you must click once on the bottom handle of the existing text block (make sure this block is selected to make the handle visible). Once this is done, the mouse cursor will change appearance (Figure 15); if it does not, try this again until it does.

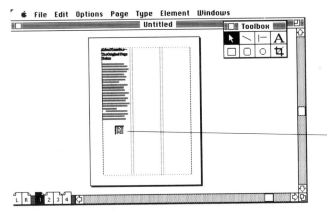

Figure 15. To continue text flow somewhere else, locate the same handle that you held the mouse button down on to resize the column, but this time click on it once so that the paragraph mouse cursor comes back.

After you have obtained the new mouse cursor, click on the Page 2 icon near the bottom left-hand corner of the page. You will move to page 2. Page 3 will also show on the screen (Figure 16).

Initially, page 2 will not have three columns. To give page 2 three columns, use the *Column guides* command from the **Options** menu, as we did for page 1 earlier. You can set the column guides even while you have the special loaded text mouse cursor.

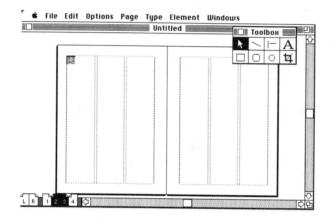

Figure 16. Click on the number 2 page icon in the bottom left-hand corner of the screen. Because we are using the PageMaker Facing pages selection, we see page 3 as well. We have also set three columns for these pages through the Column guides command from the **Options** menu.

Position the mouse cursor exactly as we did for page 1 — at the top left-hand corner of the first column (Figure 16) — and click the mouse button once. Text will flow down the first column of the second page (Figure 17).

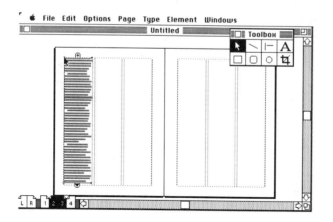

Figure 17. As long as the mouse cursor is positioned correctly at the top of the left-hand column, and you click the mouse button once, text will flow down this column and stop.

5. Move back to the first page and change the number of column guides to two. Resize the existing text block so that it fills the first column entirely. Continue the flow from the first column to the second.

Click on the page 1 icon to return to page 1.

To change the number of column guides, use the *Column guides* command in the **Options** menu. Change the 3 in this dialog box to 2 (Figure 18).

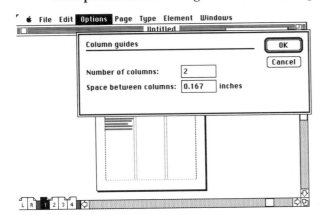

Figure 18. After clicking on the 1 icon in the bottom left-hand corner to return to page 1, use the Column guides command from the Options menu to change the 3 columns to 2.

When you return to the page, the text block will appear not to run into the newly created columns (Figure 19). We must now resize the block so that it does. Since the text block begins in the correct place (the top left-hand corner of the first column) we only need to resize this text block using one of its handles — in this case the bottom right-hand corner handle. These handles will appear after you select this text block with the pointer tool.

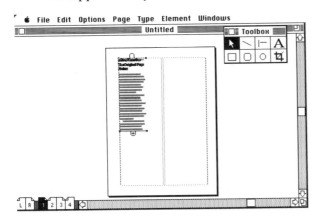

Figure 19. Because this text flowed when three column guides were on the page, it does not appear to fit the new two column format. To resize it so that it does, you must first select the text block by clicking on it once with the pointer tool. Now move to Figure 20.

Make sure the text block is selected with the pointer tool, and locate the bottom right-hand handle (the small dot). Hold the mouse button down on this dot until the mouse cursor changes to a two-sided diagonal arrow, and move the mouse until the box that is created fills the entire column (Figure 20). Release the mouse button, and the text will reflow to fill the column (Figure 21).

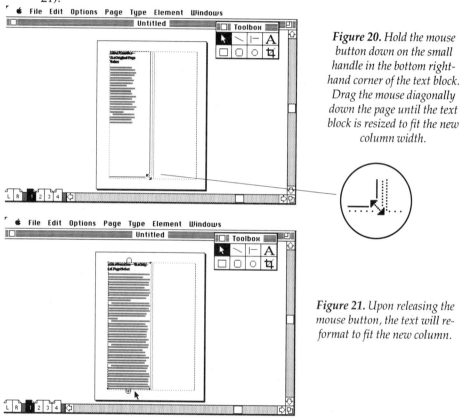

Figure 20. Hold the mouse button down on the small handle in the bottom right-hand corner of the text block. Drag the mouse diagonally down the page until the text block is resized to fit the new column width.

Figure 21. Upon releasing the mouse button, the text will re-format to fit the new column.

To continue the flow from the first column to the second column, make sure that the first column has been selected. Now, click once on the bottom handle of the first column where the plus sign is, so that the mouse cursor changes once again to the manual flow mode (Figure 22). Move the mouse cursor to the top left-hand corner of the second column and click the mouse button (Figure 23). The text will not quite fill the second column as it runs out (Figure 24). The text that was put onto page 2 from step 4 will now have disappeared, as all text has been reflowed onto page 1.

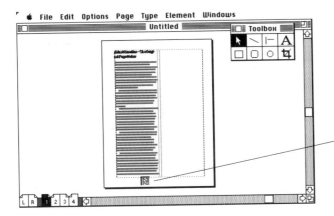

Figure 22. *To continue the text flow from the first column to the second, click on the bottom handle of the first text block. (Note the position of the mouse cursor in Figure 21.) The mouse cursor will then change to the manual flow mode of this figure.*

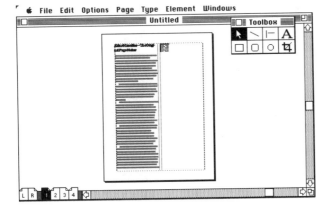

Figure 23. *Position the mouse cursor in the top left-hand corner of the second column and click once.*

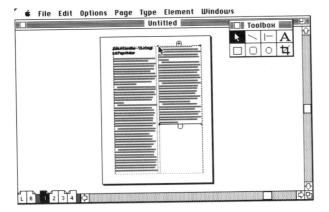

Figure 24. *Text will then flow down the text column until the end. In this case the text file ends before the column does. Any text that we had flowed onto page 2 from step 4 has now moved back to page 1.*

Module 4

Editing Text

Editing Text

Any text file that is imported into PageMaker isn't permanent — it can be deleted, edited, or added to, and also have its text attributes changed. Text can even be entered directly into Page-Maker. In this module we will be looking at Editing PageMaker text in what is called the layout view. With PageMaker 4, it is now possible to edit text and apply a number of useful word processing functions to text using the story editor. The story editor is detailed in Module 5.

Correcting errors

We will look first at how we can correct errors from any text on the PageMaker page or pasteboard area. This includes correcting simple errors, as well as deleting text, and adding a few words or lines to text. If you wish to follow our examples in this module on your PageMaker program, load the file Lead Story onto a three column, Letter page. Change to *Actual size* view and move to the top left-hand corner of the page (Figure 1).

Figures 2 through 6 show how to delete and add text directly on the PageMaker page.

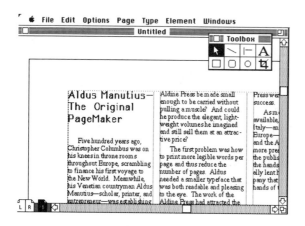

Figure 1. Load the file Lead Story into three columns to follow this information section more clearly.

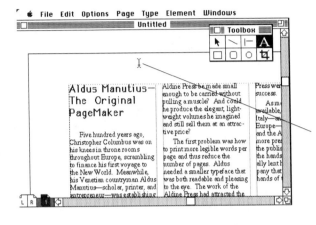

Figure 2. *Select the A tool from the Toolbox to do any text editing. The cursor changes to the text editing I-beam.*

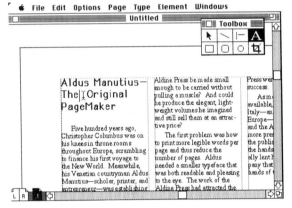

Figure 3. *Move the mouse cursor to the right of the letter to delete, and click the mouse button once. A flashing text cursor will appear under the mouse cursor.*

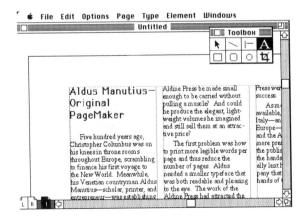

Figure 4. *After the flashing text cursor has been inserted, pressing the Delete key will remove the character to the left of the cursor, in this case we have deleted the word "The."*

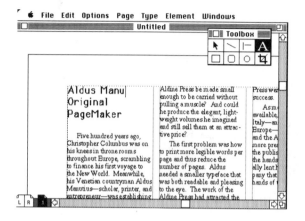

Figure 5. Every time the Delete key is hit, another character to the left is deleted.

Figure 6. The keyboard can also be used to add letters to any imported text. Here we have added some text to the first headline paragraph.

Moving the flashing cursor

The flashing text cursor obviously has to move around from time to time to allow you to correct errors all over the page. This itself can be done two ways. The first method involves the keyboard and is best used when the distance to move the flashing cursor is not far. The directional keys on the keypad are functional with PageMaker, so hitting the right direction key will move the flashing cursor one letter space to the right. The up arrow key will move the mouse cursor one line up, the down arrow key one line down, and so on (see Figures 7 and 8).

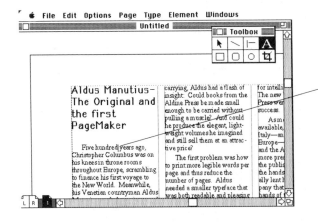

Figure 7. Note the position of the flashing text cursor now. We used the down arrow key on the keyboard, to move the cursor down a line at a time, from where it was in Figure 6.

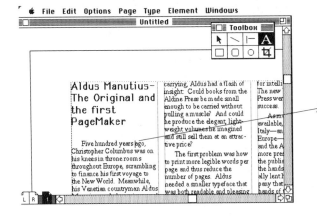

Figure 8. The text cursor has moved again from where it was in Figure 7, this time as a result of the right arrow key on the keyboard being tapped a couple of times.

The second method of cursor movement involves the mouse. It is basically a repeat of how we inserted the text cursor in the text anyway. Regardless of where the flashing text cursor appears in the text now, grab the mouse, and its cursor should reappear on the screen. Now move the mouse cursor where you would like to reinsert the flashing cursor, and click the mouse button. The flashing cursor will become imbedded in this new position. (Figure 9).

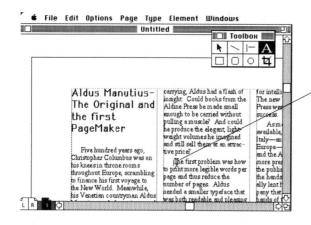

Figure 9. The mouse cursor can be found (it is hidden as text is added and deleted) by moving the mouse. It can be inserted anywhere else in the text in the same way it was inserted initially, as indicated in Figure 3.

Deleting more than one character at a time

Obviously, using the Delete key to erase one character at a time is not a satisfactory way to delete any more than a couple of characters at once. There are other ways that words, paragraphs, and entire documents can be deleted and edited in one swift movement.

Before more than one character can be acted on, it must be selected. There are several selection techniques you can use, depending on exactly how much text you would like to delete. The first technique we will look at must be used when you want to select an irregular amount of text — that is, an amount of text that is not exactly one word, one paragraph, or one file.

Move the mouse cursor to the start of the text you would like to select. Now hold the mouse button down and move the mouse cursor to the end of the text you would like to select. As you move the mouse over the text, it will become highlighted in reverse video — indicating that this text is selected (see Figures 10 through 13).

There are several other methods that make it much quicker to select the text you are after. If, for example, you wanted to select one word, you may select that word by moving the mouse cursor anywhere over the word, and clicking twice. The entire word will become selected automatically (Figure 14).

click-shift cleak
sel p137

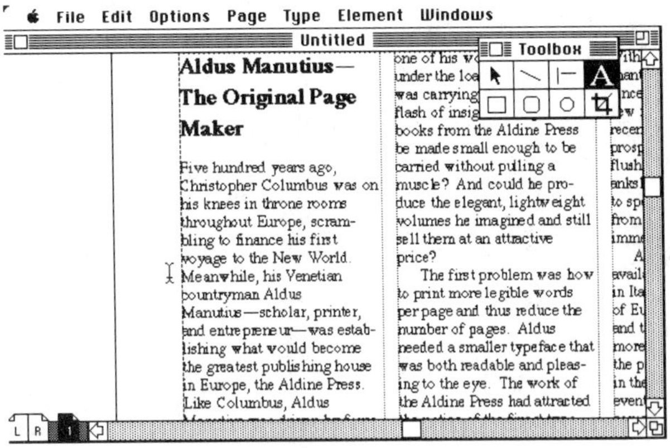

Figure 10. *Here we are going to select the whole line that reads "Meanwhile, his Venetian" (about seven lines down the second paragraph). To do this, we move the mouse cursor so that it is positioned at the very start of the first word we want to select. Hold the mouse button down here.*

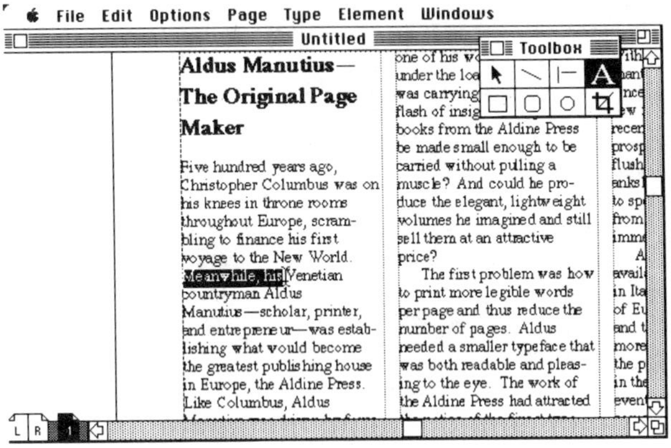

Figure 11. *With the mouse button held down, move the mouse over the text. Everything the mouse passes is highlighted in reverse video. This indicates that the text is selected.*

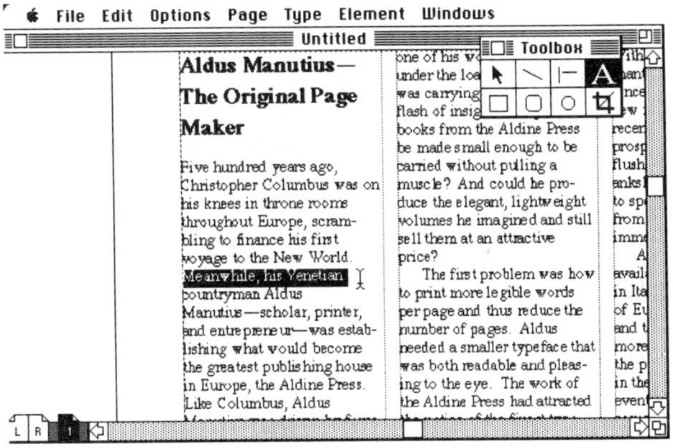

Figure 12. *Release the mouse button when the desired text is selected.*

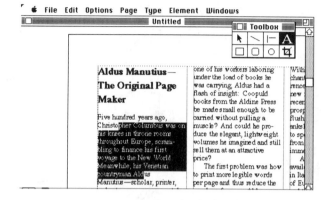

Figure 13. Any amount of text can be selected using the method shown in Figures 10 to 12 — not just full words, paragraphs, or lines.

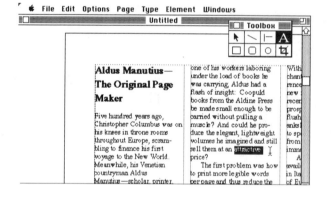

Figure 14. To select a single word, move the mouse cursor over the desired word and double-click the mouse. The entire word will be selected automatically.

An entire paragraph can be selected in a similar method. Move the mouse cursor over the paragraph you would like to select, and triple-click the mouse. The entire paragraph will become selected (Figure 15).

If you select any text with the double or triple-click methods, you can still combine it with the original method of selection we talked about. After you double- or triple-click, keep the mouse button held down and run it over the text. Words and paragraphs will be selected as you go, depending on whether you double or triple-clicked initially.

Any text selected in the above methods will be acted on as a group. If we decide to bold text for example (which we'll look at

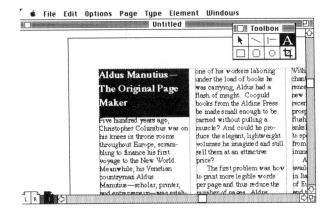

Figure 15. An entire para-graph can be selected in the same way as words — except a triple-click replaces the double-click.

soon), all the selected text will become bold. If we press the Delete key on the keyboard, all the selected text will be deleted.

Another method for selecting irregular amounts of text is to insert the flashing text cursor at the start of the block, move to the end of the block, hold down the Shift key, and insert the text cursor again. The entire block is selected. Finally, it is also possible to select, in one go, the entire text file loaded or being loaded. Simply place the cursor anywhere in the text and choose the *Select all* command from the **Edit** menu (Figure 16).

Once selected, text can then be cut, copied, or pasted elsewhere. All these commands are in the **Edit** menu. The *Cut* command

Figure 16. An entire text file can be selected by inserting the text cursor anywhere in the text, and choosing the Select all command in the Edit menu. This selects an entire file — not just text on the screen, but even text that has yet to be inserted.

deletes text from the screen, *Copy* copies it, and *Paste* will reinsert at the text cursor the very last text block cut or copied.

The *Cut* and *Copy* commands store their text in a place called the *Clipboard*. The Clipboard only stores one block of text at a time. The last *Cut* or *Copy* command is the one that remains in the Clipboard, and it is from here that the *Paste* command will take its text. If you wish to delete text without changing the contents of the clipboard, then use the *Clear* command from the **Edit** menu.

Changing text attributes (Type menu)

In this module we will show how to change text attributes using different commands within the **Type** menu. PageMaker 4 also offers a shortcut method for applying attributes to text using style sheets.

The basic theory discussed in this module, however, is important to understanding the concept behind style sheets, which are discussed in Module 11.

All text in PageMaker can have certain styles applied to it, regardless of whether or not a font and size was applied to the text at the word processor stage. To effect any changes to any text on the screen, the text must be selected using the techniques described above, and options from the **Type** menu applied to it.

Have a look at the **Type** menu (Figure 17). We are going to look at the first six commands in this menu and how they relate to the text itself.

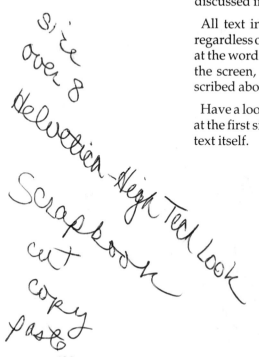

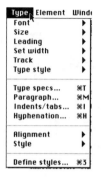

*Figure 17. Several commands in the **Type** menu will change the selected text.*

Type Menu - top six commands

First, make sure that you have some text selected on the page, say the first paragraph, so you can see how the changes we are about to make alter the text. The first six commands require that you keep the mouse button held down on the command you are after, and a sub-menu will appear either to the left or the right of the selected command (Figure 18). Keep the mouse button held, and run the mouse down the new menu. This may require a few honing skills at first to actually use the new sub-menu.

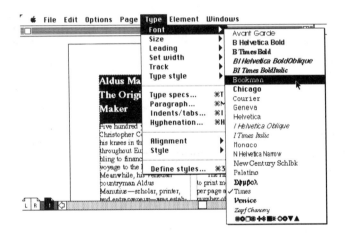

Figure 18. Hold down the mouse button on the Font command, and run the mouse down the sub-menu to select a font.

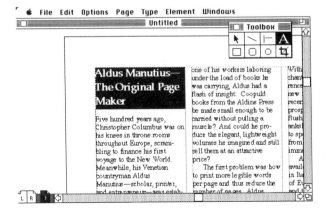

Figure 19. The font Bookman, which we selected above, is reflected on the screen with a different screen font.

Look first at the *Font* command (Figure 18). Listed in the sub-menu that appears in this figure is the selection of fonts available for use. The range of fonts will depend on how many are loaded into your system and the printer you use. Each one of these type-faces will have its own screen representation, which will change when another font is selected.

By choosing the Bookman font from Figure 18, we have changed the first paragraph to Bookman, as seen in Figure 19.

The *Size* command allows you to manipulate the point size of the selected text, from 4 to 650 points in increments as small as 0.1 points. By choosing *Size*, a different sub-menu appears as shown in Figure 20. To access a point size not listed in this sub-menu, choose Other at the top of the sub-menu. Alternatively a command further down the **Type** menu (*Type specs*) must be used. Select the type size that you would like to employ, in our case 10 points in Figure 20. Once again, this will be reflected in the text selected (Figure 21).

Leading (also known as line spacing) is accessed through the *Leading* sub-menu in the *Leading* command. Leading determines exactly how the text is going to look. In the *Leading* sub-menu (Figure 22), you will see numerous values, in half-point incre-ments, that you can set the leading to.

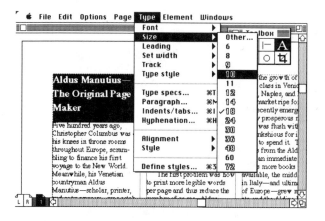

Figure 20. The Size command is used in the same way as the Font command and Font sub-menu — run the mouse down the new Size sub-menu to select a size for the text.

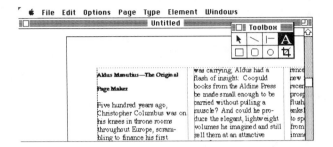

Figure 21. The size of text is then reflected on the screen. In our case 10 point text for the first paragraph.

You will also note a value that reads "Auto." When Auto is selected as the leading value, it is set by default to twenty percent greater than the size of the text. The default value for Auto leading can be adjusted through the Spacing option in the *Paragraph specifications* dialog box (discussed later in this module). Auto leading automatically adjusts to line spacing whenever the point size of the text is altered. This can be important, because if your document uses 10 point type with 11 point leading (commonly called 10 on 11 , or 10/11), and you decide to change the point size to 12 points, the leading will remain at 11 points until you change it. If the leading was automatic it would not necessarily need changing at all.

In the *Leading* sub-menu (Figure 22), you can therefore choose a predetermined size, Auto or Other. Other allows you to choose a leading value from 0 to 1300 points in 0.1 point increments. Leading can also be set in a similar way using the *Type Specs* command further down the **Type** menu.

Below leading is the *Set width* command (Figure 23). This feature controls the width of the characters from 1 to 250% in 0.1% increments. Normal will be set by default in the sub-menu of Figure 23, or it will indicate whatever the selected text may have previously been altered to. To change to a different value, run down the sub-menu to make your selection. Other may be selected to choose a specific value within the available range indicated above.

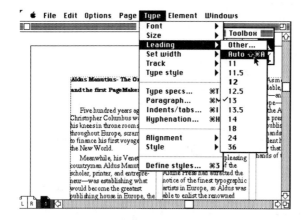

Figure 22. Once again the leading command works as do the commands above it — as it is selected, a sub-menu appears from which you must select a leading value.

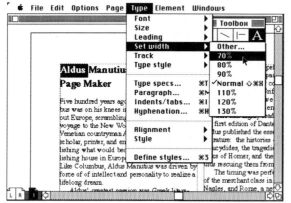

Figure 23. The Set width command alters the width of your text characters. Here we are changing the word "Aldus" to 70% of its original width. Figure 24 shows the result.

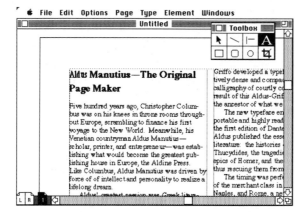

Figure 24. The result of what we did in the previous figure. The width of the text has been reduced.

The next command in the **Type** menu is the *Track* command. This refers to the amount of spacing between characters. The choices you have here, when the mouse is held down, will expand or decrease the space between the text based on the point size of the type. An example of this is shown in Figures 25 and 26.

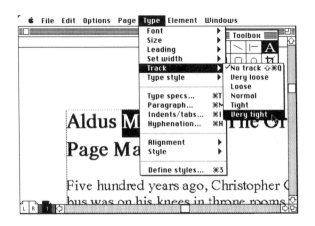

Figure 25. Here we are changing the inter-character spacing of the word "Manutius" using the Track command.

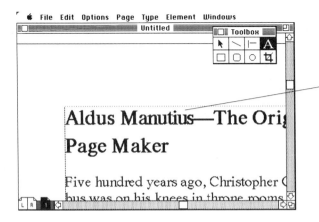

Figure 26. In moving to Actual size view, you will notice that the inter-character spacing of the word we selected is tighter than the other words.

Next, look at the *Type style* command. In this, simple style changes are made to the text, including Bold, Italic, Underline, Strikethru, Outline, Shadow, Reverse, etc. (Figure 27). This will be reflected on the screen, and different styles can be built on top of each other. To get a bold italic effect for example, you must first select Bold, and then reselect the command to choose Italic. This way, multiple type style effects can be applied to any selected text (Figure 28).

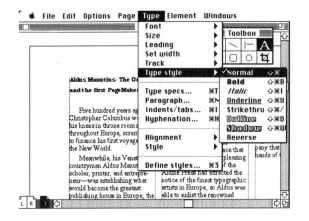

Figure 27. The type styles can only be applied one at a time, but can be applied one on top of the other for multiple effects.

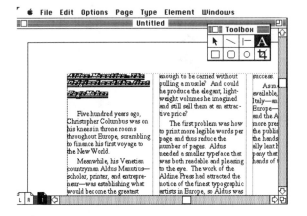

Figure 28. All the Style commands have been applied to this paragraph.

Examples of fonts, sizes, and examples:

Bookman 12 point italic

Times 14 point bold

Avant-Garde 10 point normal

Zapf Chancery 18 point italic

Helvetica 36 point

Type specs command

The commands described above — *Font, Size, Leading, Set width, Track, Type style* — are used as a kind of shortcut to changing text attributes. Although almost all type specifications can be changed using these commands, they can also be changed in one dialog box using the *Type specs* command. This command is located about halfway down the **Type** menu (Figure 29).

Within the dialog box that appears on choosing the *Type specs* command (Figure 30), there are several obvious choices which can be made, others not so obvious.

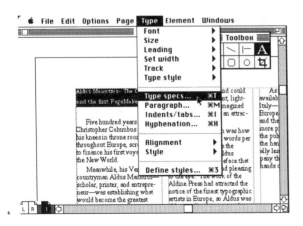

Figure 29. Selecting the Type specs command will allow you to apply all the options found in the six commands above it, plus more — all as a group.

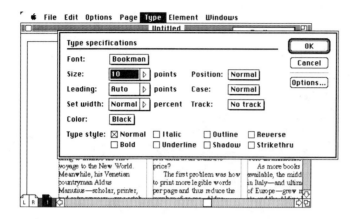

Figure 30. This is the Type specs dialog box — reflecting all the current settings for the selected text.

The line at the top reads "Font: name of font ." Replacing *name of font* will be the actual font the selected text uses. In our case, Figure 30 indicates Bookman. If you would like to change the font the selected text uses, hold down the mouse button on the actual name of the font. The same sub-menu that appears when the actual *Font* command is selected further up the menu also appears here (Figure 31). Run the mouse up or down the sub-menu and release it on the font you would like to use. The *name of font* will be replaced with the new font.

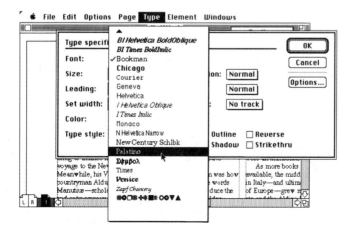

Figure 31. When you hold down the mouse button on the current font name, this sub-menu will appear from which you may select a new font.

footnotes -superscript

Underneath the Font line is the *Size* line. Here, the size of the text can be altered in two different ways. As you select the *Type Specs* command, the actual size of the text will be listed in reverse video next to *Size*. Whenever a line is highlighted like this, the new selection can be typed in without even positioning the mouse button. Therefore, in this case you can simply type in the new size of the text, from 4 to 650 points. In Figure 32 we have typed in 12.

The other way to change the size is to hold down the mouse button on the little arrow symbol just to the right of the point size. The *Size* sub-menu will appear (Figure 33), and you can run the mouse button up or down this sub-menu to select the size you are after. This change will be reflected in the size box.

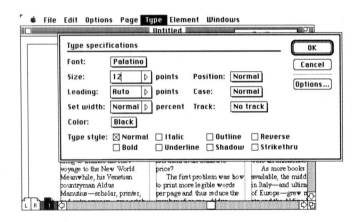

Figure 32. To change the Size of the selected type, you can simply type a new size straight in...

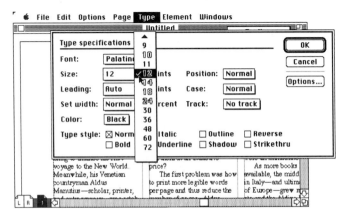

Figure 33. ... or hold down the mouse button on the little arrow to the right of the Size, and select a Size from the sub-menu.

147

The next command in the *Type specs* dialog box is the *Leading* selection. This again will read whatever the selected text is set to at the moment. To change this figure, hold down the mouse button on the little arrow just to the right. The Leading sub-menu will appear (Figure 34), from which you can highlight the Leading figure for the selected text.

It is also possible to key in your own figure over what is contained in the Leading box. Simply double-click in the box and it will change to reverse video. Key in your new figure at this time.

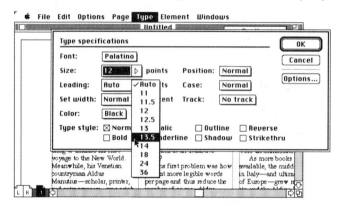

Figure 34. The Leading is altered in much the same way as the actual Size of the text.

Underneath Leading is the *Set width* option. The same procedure is used here to change the setting. The mouse is placed over the arrow and the sub-menu will appear (Figure 35). Or you can double-click in the relevant square and type in your own figure.

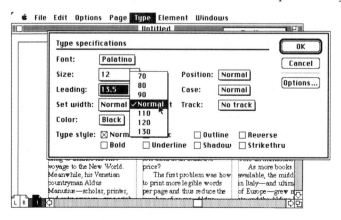

Figure 35. The Set width command has its own sub-menu, or a figure can be typed in the corresponding box.

The *Color* choice will only apply to those using either a color screen or a color printer. It also has a sub-menu that is activated by holding the mouse button down over the color that is currently displayed. Changing the color here will reflect in the selected text. For a more detailed description on color in PageMaker, please see Module 13 in this book.

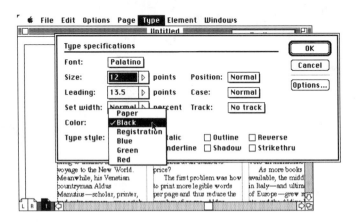

Figure 36. The Color command will affect selected text or text you are about to create.

To the right of this dialog box is the *Position* command. Once again this will probably read Normal, but if you hold down the mouse button on Normal, you may select either Superscript or Subscript text (Figure 37). These choices shift the text slightly higher or slightly lower than the baseline of the text, respectively.

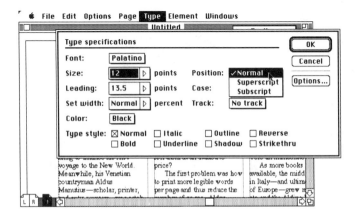

Figure 37. The position of the text, although generally set to Normal, can be superscripted or subscripted for such things as footnotes, formulas, and so on.

Underneath *Position* is *Case*. In most cases it will read Normal, but if you hold down the mouse button on the word Normal, another little sub-menu will appear, one that reads Normal, All caps, and Small caps (Figure 38).

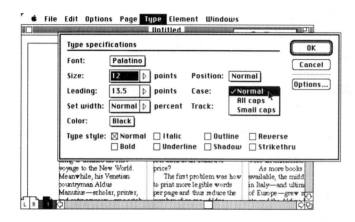

Figure 38. The Case of the text can be adjusted automatically — a quite handy feature for converting lowercase to uppercase or vice versa.

The All caps selection changes all letters to full-size capitals. The Small caps alternative changes lowercase letters to small capitals. The Normal selection reverts all text back to how it was originally placed or entered on the page.

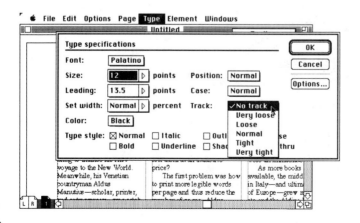

*Figure 39. The Track command controls the inter-character spacing. The choices here are the same as are available directly from the **Type** menu (Figure 25).*

The *Track* command underneath *Case* gives you exactly the same choices as it does in the **Type** menu, and again is activated by holding the mouse button down on the current selection.

At the bottom of the dialog box you are given eight different style changes you can make to text. These are the same as available in the *Type style* command previously indicated in Figure 27. With the approach using the *Type style* selections of Figure 40, you are able to select multiple styles at one go. Simply click the mouse button in every box that you would like applied to your text.

Type style: ☒ **Normal** ☐ **Italic**   ☐ **Outline** ☐ **Reverse**
　　　　　　　☐ **Bold**　 ☐ **Underline** ☐ **Shadow** ☐ **Strikethru**

*Figure 40. The eight choices available at the bottom of the
Type specs dialog box are selected by clicking the mouse
inside the little squares. Multiple styles may be selected.*

On the right side of the *Type specs* dialog box, and under the OK and Cancel choices, is another selection. It is the *Options* command, which reveals the *Type options* dialog box when clicked (Figure 41). This dialog box relates directly to the size of your small caps and superscript and subscript characters. Also, it controls the position of your superscript and subscript characters in relation to your other text. All changes made here are done in percentages.

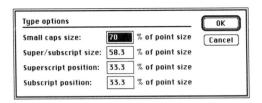

*Figure 41. The Type options
dialog box. The choices here relate
to small caps and superscript and
subscript characters.*

The *Small caps size* option changes the size of your small caps in relation to the current point size. For example, if you wanted the small caps of your selected text to appear larger or smaller, compared to the full size capitals, this can be altered to a specific percentage (Figure 42).

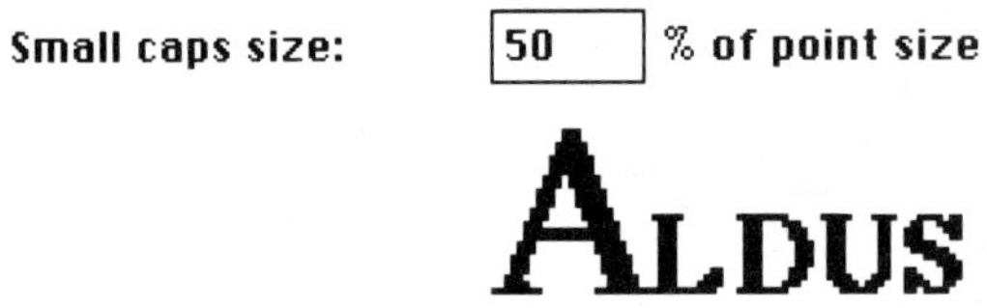

Small caps size: `50` % of point size

ALDUS

Figure 42. Here we have adjusted the small caps of this text to be 50% the size of the larger caps.

The same principle applies with the *Super/subscript size* option. The size of these characters can be set to your liking by double-clicking over the number already set in the box. It will now appear in reverse video, and your own percentage can be typed in (Figures 43 and 44).

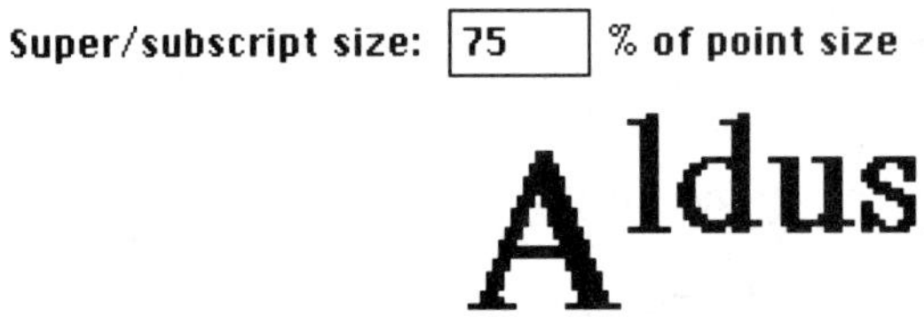

Super/subscript size: `75` % of point size

A ldus

Figure 43. The size of the superscript characters have been changed to 75% of the current point size.

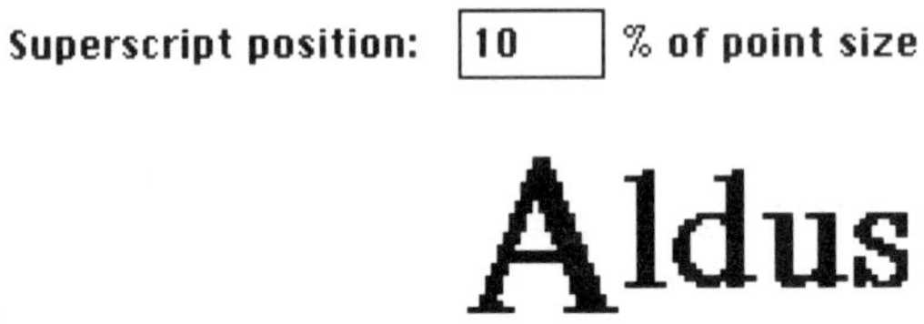

Superscript position: `10` % of point size

A ldus

Figure 44. The position of the superscript characters have been altered to 10%. The same rule applies when changing the position of subscript characters, only they are below the rest of the text.

After changing everything about the text you require in the *Type specs* dialog box, either click the OK button or hit Return on the keypad. All set changes will be applied to selected text. If no text was selected, and the pointer tool is active in the Toolbox, everything you set up will be the new default values for all text entered into this particular PageMaker publication via the keyboard.

Paragraph command

All options in this command apply to entire paragraphs rather than just text. The entire paragraph does not have to be selected, as all paragraphs partially selected, or the paragraph that contains the text cursor inserted in it, will be fully affected by this command.

Keep the first paragraph on the page highlighted and select the *Paragraph* command in the **Type** menu, just below the *Type specs* command (Figure 45). You will then see the dialog box of Figure 46.

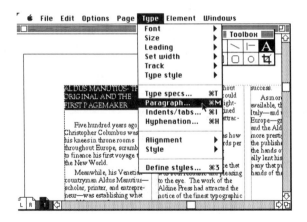

Figure 45. The Paragraph command gives us access to a series of settings that apply to entire paragraphs rather than just selected text.

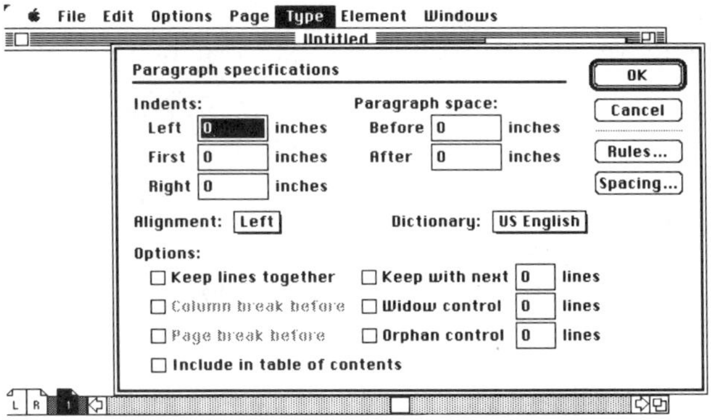

Figure 46. The dialog box that appears with the Paragraph command shows the current settings for the selected text (in our case the first paragraph). If several paragraphs are selected that use different settings, some boxes in this dialog box and others may be empty.

The first part of the *Paragraph specifications* dialog box are the *Indents* selections. Each of the three indents, *Left*, *First*, and *Right*, adjust the text in slightly different ways. The figure in the rectangle next to the Left indent is the figure that the entire paragraph will be indented from the left of the margin. It must be zero or a positive number. White space will run down the left of the paragraph for whatever width is in this dialog box.

The First indent refers to how far the very first line in the paragraph is indented compared to the rest of the paragraph. A positive number here refers to a normal first line indent—a good way to denote the start of the paragraph. A negative number provides a hanging indent, where the first line is not indented, but all subsequent lines are.

The Right indent is the distance that the paragraph is indented from the right margin, similar to the left margin except on the other side. This can only be set to zero or a positive number.

Indenting examples

> This paragraph has been indented three inches from the left. Note the strange word spacing, as this paragraph has the alignment set to Justify, which we'll talk about next.

This paragraph is indented 1 inch from the left, .15 from the right. The word spacing over a large block of text looks better than the paragraph above.

This paragraph has a hanging indent in which the second and subsequent lines are indented from the first line. It also has a 1 inch indent from the right, and a .50 inch indent from the left for the first line.

From the *Paragraph* specifications dialog box, you may also select which way your paragraph(s) should be aligned. Different effects are created by selecting either Left, Right, Center, Justify, or Force justify. Run down the sub-menu of the *Alignment* selection (Figure 47) for the way you would like to align text. Some examples follow:

This paragraph is centered

This paragraph is left justified

This paragraph is right justified

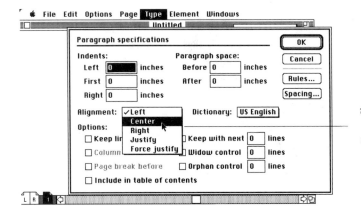

Figure 47. If you want to change the alignment of the text, click the mouse button over the boxed word next to "Alignment" and run the mouse down the list. Choose either Left, Center, Right, Justify, or Force Justify. We have chosen Center.

The *Paragraph space* selection (including *Before* and *After*) on the top right of the dialog box inserts white space above and below the selected paragraph. Body text, for example, may have some space before (or after) every paragraph to make reading easier. Headings may have a quarter of an inch below them to break them from the rest of the text. Whatever the use, each figure above and below will be the amount of white space above and/or below paragraphs. In Figure 48, we have inserted 1.180 inches space below our paragraph. Figure 49 shows the results of the Figure 48 settings.

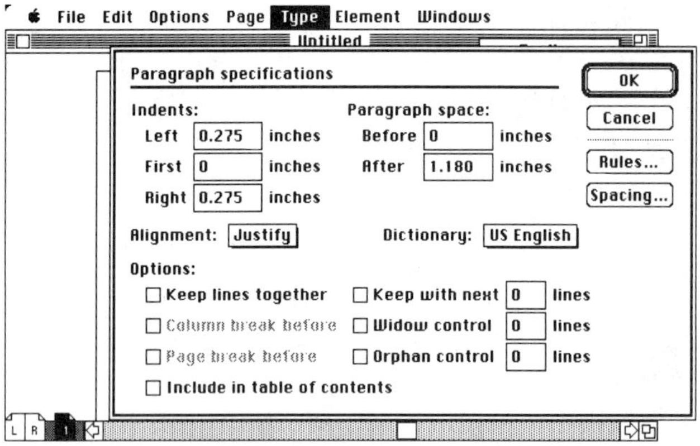

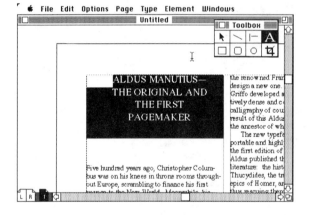

Figure 48. *Here we have centered the paragraph, set indents to the left and to the right, and given a 1.18 inch space after the selected paragraph.*

Figure 49. *The results of our settings of Figure 48 applied to the initial heading. The text is centered, indented from either side, and has 1.180 inches of space after.*

Shortcut paragraph alignment changes may be made using the *Alignment* command at the bottom of the **Type** menu. Holding the mouse button down on *Alignment* produces a sub-menu allowing you to choose between the five types of alignment already discussed and shown in Figure 47. As shown in Figure 50, however, the *Alignment* command can be a faster way of setting this paragraph function.

By holding the mouse down on the currently displayed dictionary, within the *Dictionary* option (Figure 51), all the installed language dictionaries will be displayed. The language dictionary is

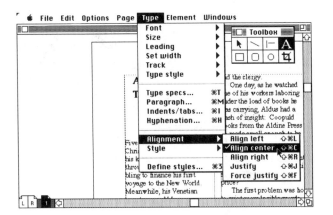

Figure 50. *The Alignment command can be used to quickly set the justification of selected text.*

used for both spelling and hyphenation, which is discussed later. PageMaker can support up to 10 installed hyphenation and spelling dictionaries, but using more than one dictionary in a publication can slow the text composition and spelling checker.

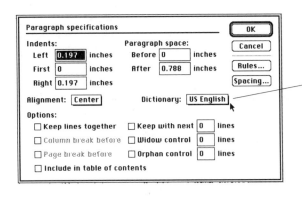

Figure 51. *The Dictionary command in the Paragraph dialog box is currently set to US English. This option is used when checking spelling and hyphenating.*

The seven Options that appear in the bottom half of the *Paragraph* dialog box are activated by simply clicking inside the squares with your mouse. The first available option here is *Keep lines together*. Selecting this will ensure that an intended paragraph will not separate over columns, pages or graphics. Graphics, with text-wrap attributes defined, can sometimes split paragraphs because they are unusually shaped. This can be averted simply by choosing the *Keep lines together* option.

When *Column break before* is checked, the selected paragraph or the next one created will begin a new column. The same applies with the *Page break before* option, only the paragraph will obviously start a new page.

If you have a heading or a paragraph that you want to be part of the table of contents, select the intended text, and click on the *Include in table of contents* option. PageMaker will automatically include this in your contents. Refer to Module 17, **Table of Contents** to find out how to use this feature.

The *Keep with next ☐ lines* option gives you the choice of having a selected paragraph being placed with either 1 to 3 lines of the following paragraph. This option is useful for keeping titles and subtitles with their appropriate text, if they are likely to be separated by a column or page.

Widow control determines how many lines are left at the end of a paragraph at the start of a new column or page. This option is available so that one line does not have to be left on its own at the top of a column. PageMaker gives you a choice of a minimum of 1 to 3 lines to be left alone. The same applies to *Orphan Control*: a minimum number of lines, to be determined by you at the beginning of a paragraph, left alone at the bottom of a column or page. The widow and orphan control should be predetermined when auto-flowing longer documents. With smaller publications, these two functions aren't very useful, because the laying out of text can easily and quickly be changed manually.

Below the Cancel option in the *Paragraph* specifications dialog box is the word *Rules*. By clicking on this, The *Paragraph rules* dialog box (Figure 52) will appear. This dialog box specifies size, color, width, style, and placement of horizontal rules above and / or below a selected paragraph. These lines, once placed, cannot be moved separately with the pointer tool, as they will now be part of the text block. The only way they can be altered is through the *Paragraph rules* dialog box.

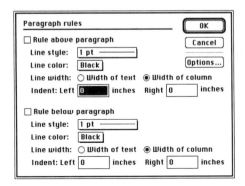

Figure. 52 The Paragraph rules dialog box is activated by clicking on the option "Rules" in the Paragraph specifications dialog box.

By clicking inside the square to the left of the words *"Rule above paragraph"* and *"Rule below paragraph,"* you can place rules above and below your selected text. If you only want one of these rules, this is done simply by just clicking in the corresponding box. Your above and below rules can be set up to have different attributes.

By holding down the mouse over the Line style and Line color rectangles, the attributes of the rule above or below your selected paragraph are determined. The Line style choice is identical to the choices available in the *Line* option under the **Element** menu. By holding your mouse down on the rectangle to the right of the option Line style, a sub-menu of choices will appear (Figure 53).

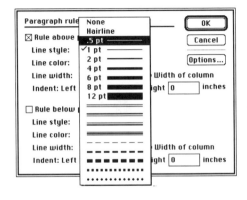

Figure 53. The Line style for Rule above has been set to .5 pt.

Line colors are also selected in the same way (Figure 54). The width of your rule can either be the width of your text or the width of your column. Click inside the circle for the width you want, as we have done in Figure 54.

Figure 54. The color is selected from the color sub-menu and the rule is given a Line width of column wide.

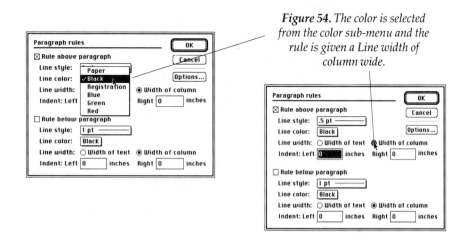

The rules can also be indented on both the right and left sides, so they can actually fall short of the text or column, or somewhere in between. The indents are set up by double-clicking inside the squares to the right of the words *Indent: Left/Right*, and typing in the required measurements (Figure 55). Figure 56 shows the results of our settings for the first paragraph. Figures 57 and 58 show an example of the use of a rule below a paragraph.

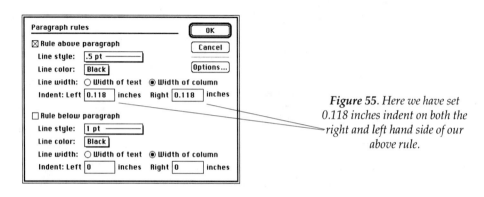

Figure 55. Here we have set 0.118 inches indent on both the right and left hand side of our above rule.

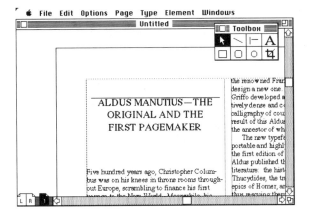

Figure 56. The final result of our settings for the rule above our selected paragraph (from Figures 53 through 55).

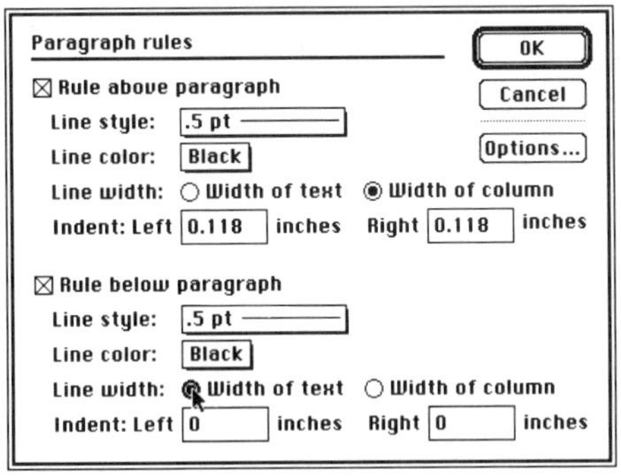

Paragraph rules

☒ **Rule above paragraph**
Line style: .5 pt ————
Line color: Black
Line width: ○ Width of text ● Width of column
Indent: Left 0.118 inches Right 0.118 inches

☒ **Rule below paragraph**
Line style: .5 pt ————
Line color: Black
Line width: ● Width of text ○ Width of column
Indent: Left 0 inches Right 0 inches

OK
Cancel
Options...

Figure 57. The rule below the paragraph is set to almost the same as the above one, but this time we choose Width of text as our line width.

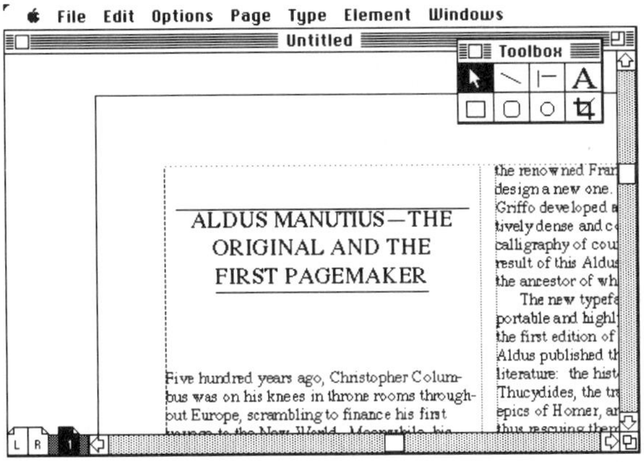

 File Edit Options Page Type Element Windows
Untitled
Toolbox

ALDUS MANUTIUS—THE
ORIGINAL AND THE
FIRST PAGEMAKER

the renowned Fran
design a new one.
Griffo developed a
tively dense and c
calligraphy of cou
result of this Aldus
the ancestor of wh
    The new typefa
portable and highl
the first edition of
Aldus published th
literature: the hist
Thucydides, the tr
epics of Homer, an

Five hundred years ago, Christopher Colum-
bus was on his knees in throne rooms throughout Europe, scrambling to finance his first

Figure 58. The rule below the paragraph has the attributes we have just defined in the previous figure.

161

The *Paragraph rules* dialog box of Figure 52 has an additional Options button on the right hand side. This takes us into the *Paragraph rule options* dialog box of Figure 59. By default it should say "Auto" in the inches above and below baseline boxes, for both the top and the bottom rule. If you double-click in these boxes, you can set your own measurement for spacing above and below the baseline for the rules we created in Figure 58.

See Figures 60 and 61 for what happens when we change these figures.

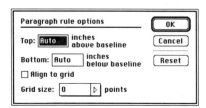

Figure 59. The Paragraph rule options dialog box, which is accessed through the Paragraph rules dialog box of Figure 52.

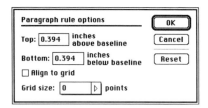

Figure 60. We have selected the relevant paragraph and set the top rule to be 0.394 inches above the baseline and the bottom rule to be 0.394 inches below the baseline.

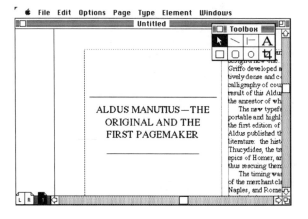

Figure 61. The result of what we did in the previous figure.

The *Align to grid* feature, also in the Paragraph rule options dialog box, is used when you are working with mutiple text columns. When *Align to grid* is checked, the baselines of the body text will align horizontally. The grid size should be set to the same as body text leading. See examples in Figures 62 through 64.

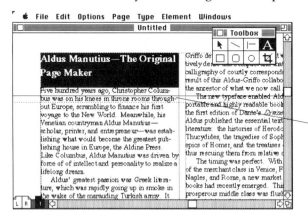

Figure 62. *On placing the file Lead Story again, we can see that the two text blocks, in column 1 and 2, are out of alignment.*

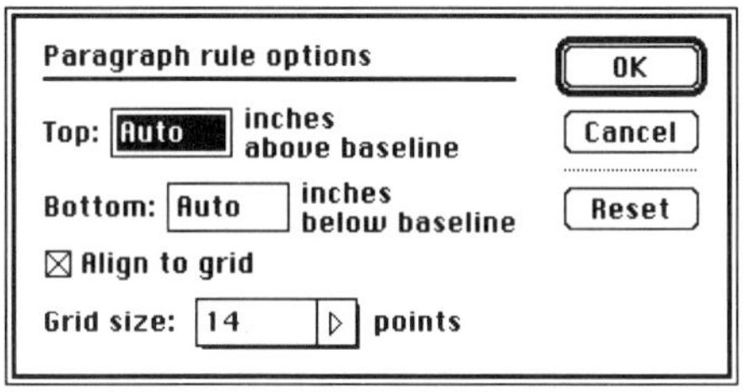

Figure 63. *Now by turning the Align to grid on, and setting the grid size to 14 (the body text's leading), the text blocks will now align.*

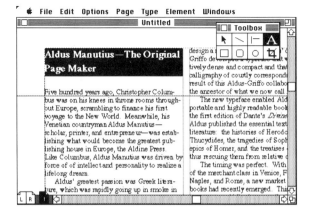

Figure 64. *The two text blocks in corresponding columns are now aligned. Notice that we had the heading paragraph selected to initiate this procedure.*

On returning to the *Paragraph* specifications dialog box (Figure 65), we can see the *Spacing* option under the Rules option. When clicked on, this will take us to the *Spacing attributes* dialog box (Figure 66).

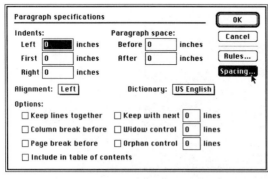

Figure 65. The Spacing attributes box is accessed by clicking on the word "Spacing" in the Paragraph specifications dialog box.

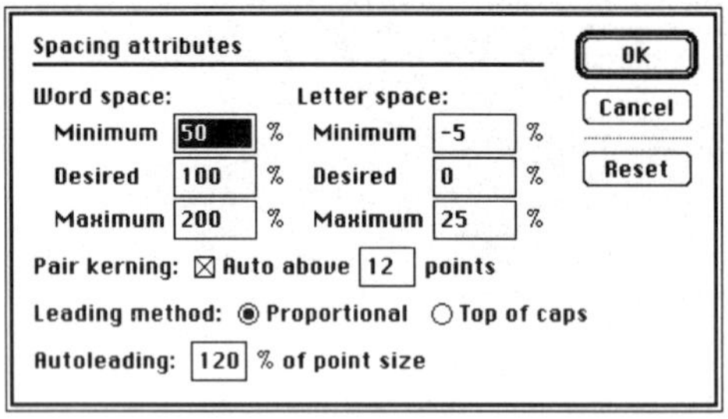

Figure 66. The Spacing attributes dialog box. You may prefer to leave this command alone unless you have very precise requirements for text spacing.

The *Spacing attributes* dialog box gives you control over text spacing. However, the default setting for text spacing is usually sufficient for most uses.

Note: Do not confuse this *Spacing* command, which adjusts the amount of horizontal spacing between letters and words, with the Spacing selection in the *Paragraph* command of Figure 48. This latter selection, as we have discussed previously, simply adjusts the amount of vertical spacing between paragraphs.

The *Spacing attributes* dialog box is associated with adjusting the amount of spacing between words and letters. *Word space*, the first selection, is used to set the space between words on the page. The designer of the font being used has set a value of 100% as the optimum space between words. The *Desired* space between words is, by default, set at 100%. By decreasing this value, as well as the corresponding *Maximum* and *Minimum* values, the text will appear more tightly spaced. Increasing these values will cause the text to be more loosely spaced.

Word space works for both justified and unjustified text. You can change *Desired* to any figure between 0% and 500%. The limits for *Minimum* and *Maximum* are 0% and 500% of *Desired*.

Letter space, the next selection, is the figure that PageMaker is allowed to insert between letters in text when justifying. This selection does not apply to unjustified text. By having zero in all three boxes, PageMaker will not insert extra spaces between letters at all. By putting a figure of 25% in *Maximum*, PageMaker is allowed to insert, at maximum, 25% of word space between letters.

The range limits for *Minimum* and *Maximum* are -200% to +200%. *Desired* must be between *Minimum* and *Maximum*.

See the following examples (Figures 67 through 71) of various word and letter spacing commands on text. These examples illustrate that text spacing can be modified many ways, some of which are unacceptable and some of which are useful for various applications. The look of the text in many instances is up to you.

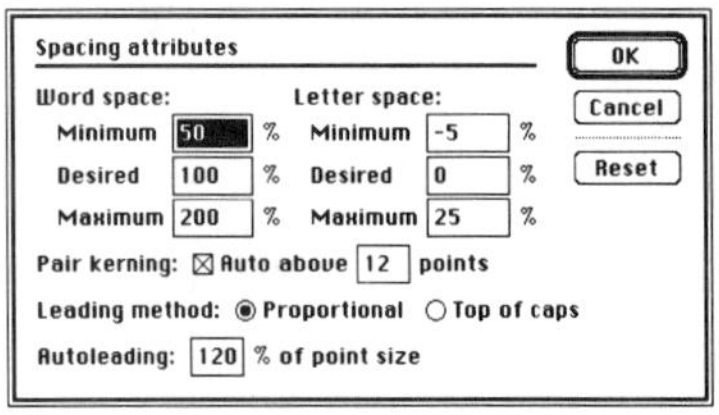

Figure 67. The paragraph on the right shows the results of the PageMaker default settings on the left.

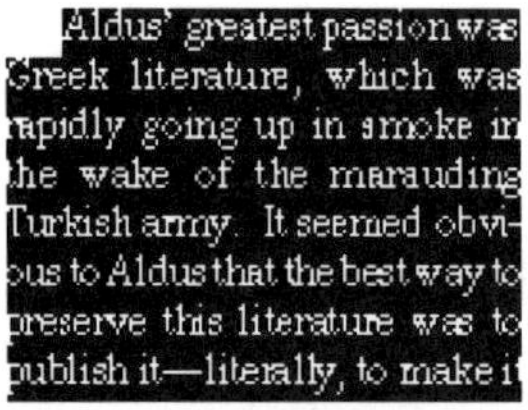

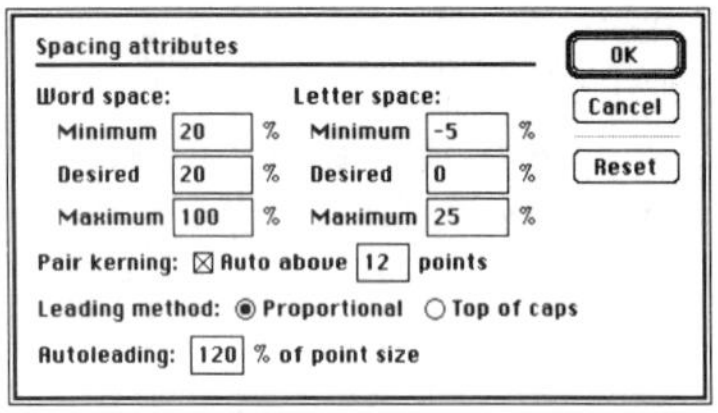

Figure 68. We have tightened up on the word spacing settings on the left to give the results on the right.

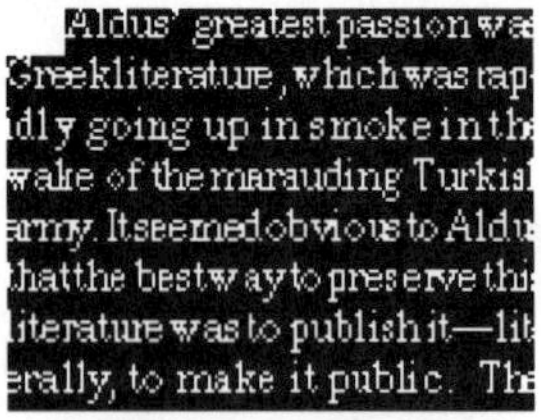

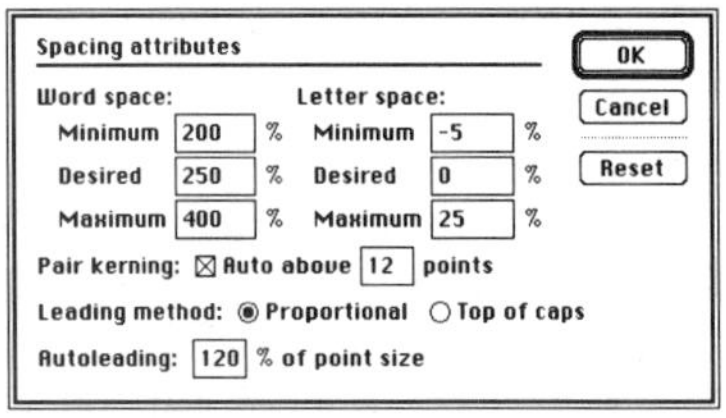

Figure 69. We have now loosened the word spacing to produce the results on the right.

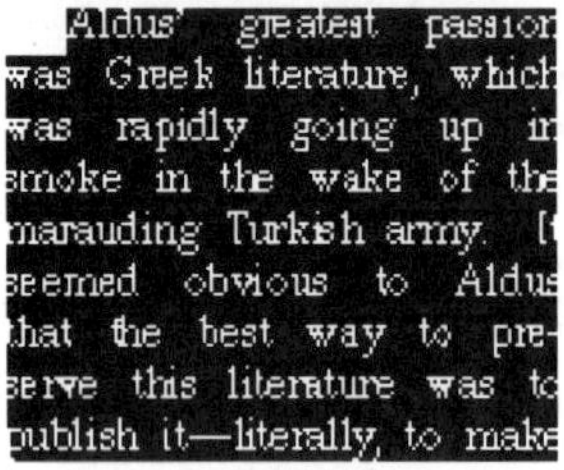

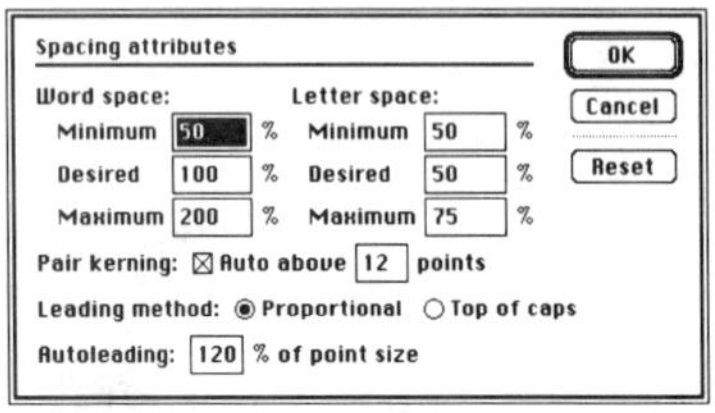

Figure 70. We have now adjusted the letter spacing by allowing more space between letters. The result is on the right. Compare to Figure 67 which uses the same word spacing.

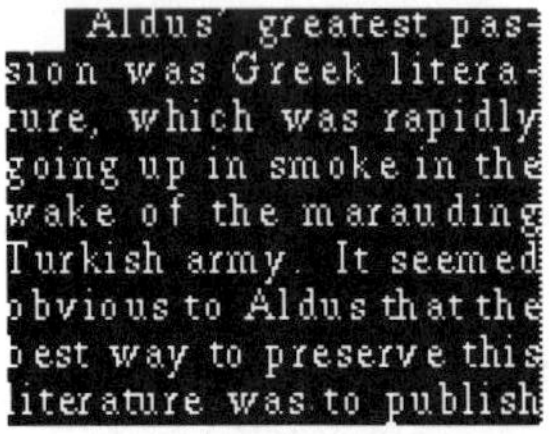

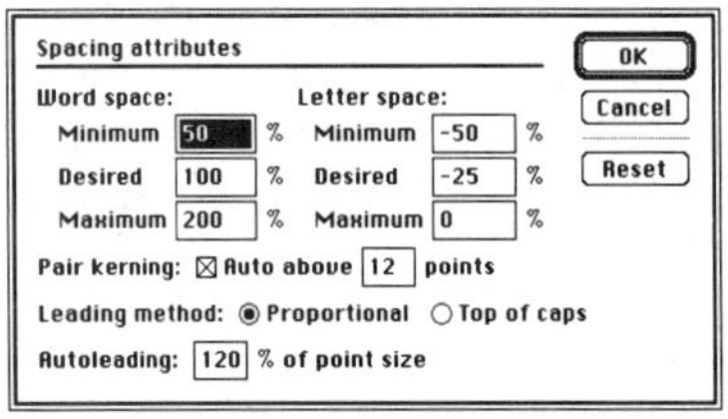

Figure 71. Letter spacing has now been tightened to provide the results as shown.

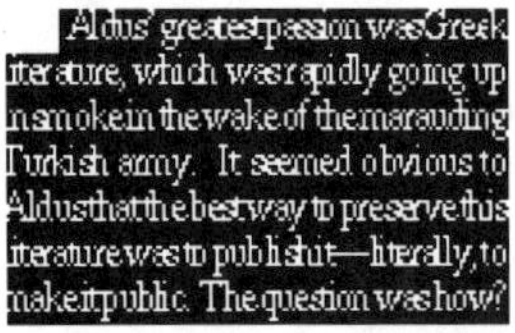

Below word and letter spacing is the *Pair kerning* control. Kerning is the moving together of two letters that might otherwise appear too widely spaced. Generally, it is a good idea to leave kerning on (it is on if the check appears in the *Auto above* box next to Pair kerning in Figure 66). Being able to control the size above which text should be kerned allows you to kern perhaps only your headings, which may be 36 point, and not your body text, which may be 12 point or less.

(These letters are kerned)

(These letters are not kerned)

The value set for *Auto leading* in Figure 66 is the amount Page-Maker uses by default (120%) when Auto leading is selected for text either through the *Leading* or *Type specs* commands. The figure is taken as a proportion of the text size, so to achieve leading at 10 percent of the text size, you would insert the figure of 110% in this rectangle.

A *Leading method* must be selected — either *Proportional* or *Top of caps*. Both use different parameters to judge the leading distance. Proportional is based on the largest character in the line; a line of 10 point text that contains a 14 point character will be leaded based on the 14 point character. It is the preferred method of use.

The Top of caps method is included for compatibility with PageMaker 2.0 and should not be used for new work.

Indents/tabs command

As we discussed above, and as shown in Figure 46, it is possible to select Left, First, and Right indents of paragraphs using the *Paragraph* command in the **Type** menu. It is possible to do this as well, plus more, with the *Indents/tabs* command (Figure 72) also from the **Type** menu. The *Indents/tabs* dialog box, which results from selecting the command, is indicated in Figure 73.

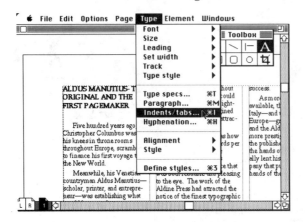

*Figure 72. The Indents/tabs command from the **Type** menu can be used for setting tabs and indents. The latter capability is similar to that available with the Paragraph command.*

Figure 73 shows the default PageMaker tab settings of one every 0.5 of an inch (or .5 cm for international versions). Figure 74 expands upon this dialog box by showing the variety of other user-settable tabs that are available. These include left justified, right justified, centered, and decimal tabs.

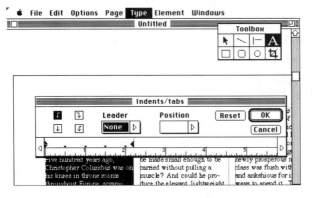

Figure 73. The Indents/tabs dialog box. Note the tabs that are set by default to every 0.5 of an inch.

To change the default settings of Figure 73 for a single publication requires the pointer tool in the Toolbox to be selected. Once the pointer is selected, it is simply a matter of going to the dialog box of Figure 73, and adjusting indents and tabs to your requirements. Wherever you then click on the page to type text, it will automatically assume the new default values. Text already on the page may have its indents and/or tabs changed by selecting it with the text tool, and then changing the settings in the *Indents/tabs* dialog box.

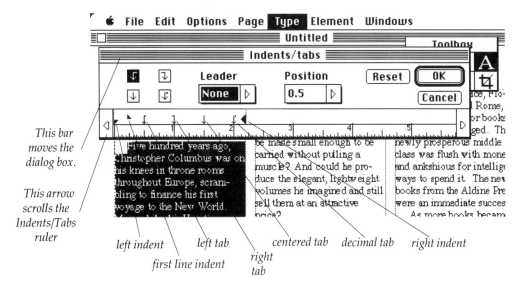

Figure 74. *The various components that make up the Indents/tabs dialog box are indicated. One of the important points to note in this figure is the way we have aligned the zero point of the dialog box's ruler with the left-hand column guide for the left column. This makes it easier to set up indents and tabs for the column widths you may be working with.*

We will now provide some examples to illustrate the indents/tabs concept of PageMaker. Again, if you would like to follow this, you may wish to reload Lead Story into a single, three-column, A4 or Letter page.

In Figure 75, we have selected the first body text paragraph with the text tool, and then chosen the *Indents/tabs* command leading to the dialog box indicated in the figure. From this box we can see that there are no indents at all, and only the default tab settings are showing.

In Figure 76 we have set left, right, and first indents. Note the interrelationship between the *Indents/tabs* and *Paragraph* commands which can be seen by comparing Figures 76 and 77. Figure 77 is the dialog box associated with the *Paragraph* command while the first paragraph of Figure 76 is still selected. The values given for first, left, and right indents correspond with the settings shown in the *Indents/tabs* dialog box of Figure 76.

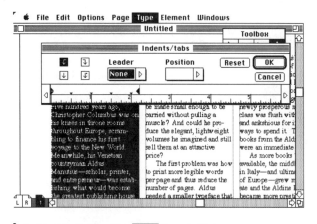

Figure 75. The initial paragraph we have selected has no indents set and only the default tabs. Compare this to Figure 76 after we have made some adjustments.

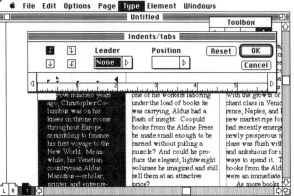

Figure 76. We have now set first, left, and right indents. Note that aligning the zero point of the ruler with the left margin allows us to pictorially view our settings and compare with the actual text. The tab ruler automatically aligns with the left-hand margin if text is selected when the Indents/tabs command is chosen.

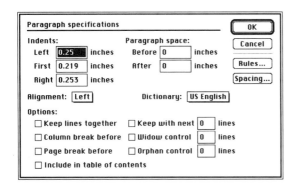

Figure 77. Compare the settings of this Paragraph command dialog box with the same settings in the Indents/ tabs dialog box of Figure 76. You'll see that the two lots of settings are identical showing the interrelationship between the two commands.

In the final two examples below, we have gone to the bottom of the third column on our page to an empty area, clicked on the text tool, and then typed the numbers 1 to 5 with a tab after each one. The result, as shown in Figure 78(a), is simply tabs every 0.5 of an inch which is the default setting. We then selected this text and changed the tab settings. The new tab settings (now spaced every inch) and the result as shown in Figure 78(b).

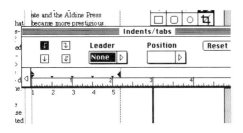

Figure 78(a). By clicking on the text tool, and typing in the above numbers separated by tabs, we are using the default tab values of one every 0.5 of an inch.

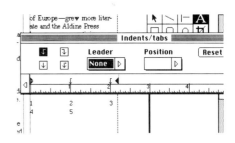

Figure 78(b). Here we have selected the numbers keyed in in Figure 78(a) and have changed the tab settings to one every inch. This results in the changed settings as shown.

The Tab Leader choice from Figure 79, when turned on, places a repetitive line of characters on your page each time you do a tab. Leader is set to None by default, and a leader must be selected before the tabs are set. The choices other than None can be seen when the mouse is held down over the appropriate arrow (Figure 79).

If none of the choices available are what you want, you can select Custom and type your own character in the box that originally said None.

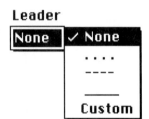

Figure 79. The Leader choices that are available include dots, dashes, and lines. Whereas choosing Custom lets you type in your own choice of character for your leader. Below is an example of using the dots as leaders. We set the tab for 1 inch and applied it to the text on the page.

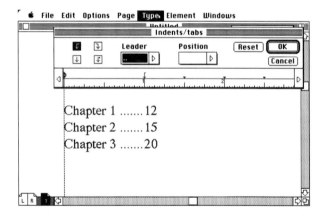

Next to the Leader box is the Position box (Figure 80). This lets you Add, Delete, Move, and Repeat tabs quicker, easier, and with more accuracy. The Add tab choice will place a tab in whatever point you specify in the position box. For example, if you placed a 2 in the position box, and highlighted the Add tab choice from the Position sub-menu, PageMaker will put a tab at the 2 inch point.The Delete tab option simply removes a highlighted marker, or if none is highlighted, it will remove the tab at the point you specify in the Position box.

Move tab will change the point of a highlighted tab to the setting requested in the Position box. For example, if you want your tab at 2 inches to be moved to 2.35 inches, type this setting in the Position box, and PageMaker will quickly and accurately change the position of the highlighted tab.

Repeat tab will speed up the process of multiple tabs at equal distances. You may want tabs set at every half an inch. Instead of placing them there yourself, simply place one tab at the first half inch, and while this tab is still highlighted, select Repeat tab, and tabs will be placed at every half inch point along your ruler.

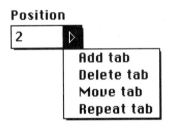

Figure 80. The choices available in the Position sub menu let you accurately Add, Delete, Move, and Repeat tabs. Below we typed 2 in the Position box and chose Add tab. PageMaker puts a tab at the 2 inch point on the ruler. We then applied this setting to the text on our page with the Leader still on dots. As you can see, our second tab is exactly one inch away from our first.

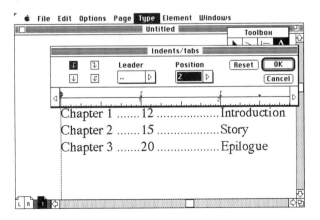

Hyphenation

The *Hyphenation* dialog box is available directly through the **Type** menu (Figures 81 and 82). It is also obtainable through the *Edit style* dialog box, which comes from the *Define styles* dialog box in the **Type** menu. The *Define styles* dialog box is explained in Module 11, **PageMaker Style Sheets.**

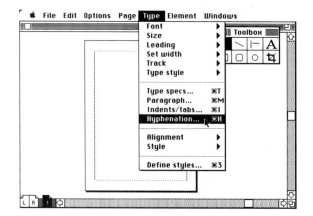

*Figure 81. The Hyphenation dialog box is accessed through the **Type** Menu.*

The *Hyphenation* command has to be turned 'On' in this dialog box (Figure 82) before it can operate. By default it will already be on. How PageMaker hyphenates depends upon your method of choice. Your first preference is *Manual only*. On selecting this choice, PageMaker hyphenates only at the discretionary hyphens you place in the text yourself. A discretionary hyphen is activated by pressing the *Command + hyphen* keys. The discretionary hyphens placed in text are not seen until needed.

The *Manual plus dictionary* choice allows PageMaker to hyphenate words according to the dictionary, while still recognizing discretionary hyphens. The third choice is *Manual plus algorithm*. This has the features of the previous two, as well as having a dictionary algorithm. PageMaker will determine the best places for hyphenating your words in a logical way. The layout of your work is a determining factor in the decision PageMaker makes on where to put hyphens. The *Manual plus algorithm* choice has an advantage over the *Manual plus dictionary* choice, as the latter will only hyphenate words it recognizes. The dictionary algorithm will hyphenate words that aren't recognized by the normal dictionary, as well as ones that are.

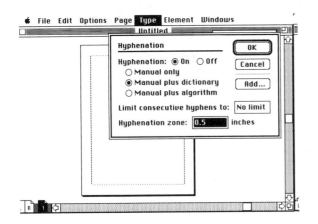

Figure 82. The Hyphenation dialog box gives you three choices on how to hyphenate your text. The Manual plus dictionary choice is selected by default.

The total amount of hyphens appearing in one paragraph can also be determined. By double clicking in the box after *Limit consecutive hyphens to*: you can put in your own figure from 1 to 255. By default it will say "No Limit." With this selected, there will be no limit to the number of hyphens PageMaker will place in your text. Depending on how long your paragraph is, it is recommended that a number no greater than 10 be used, as the paragraph may become too clustered with hyphens.

Adjusting the *Hyphenation zone* command will change the amount of space at the end of a line, for which hyphenation will occur. The larger the hyphenation zone, the less hyphens will occur and the smaller the zone, the more hyphens.

The *Add* word option lets you add an unlisted word to the dictionary. While adding this word to the dictionary you also insert discretionary hyphens. The number of discretionary hyphens you put together indicates your preference on how Page-Maker should hyphenate the word. Figure 83 gives an example of this.

175

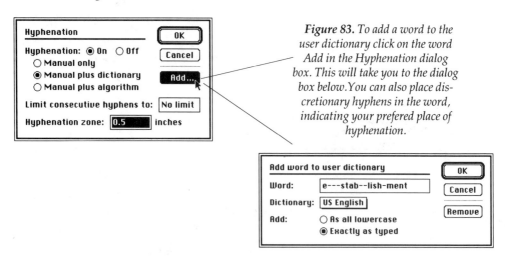

Figure 83. To add a word to the user dictionary click on the word Add in the Hyphenation dialog box. This will take you to the dialog box below. You can also place discretionary hyphens in the word, indicating your prefered place of hyphenation.

When adding discretionary hyphens to the words in this dialog box, one hyphen indicates the most preferable place for hyphenation. Two hyphens is your second choice, and three, the least preferable. If a word you add is already in the dictionary, the new discretionary hyphens you put in will replace the current settings. The *As all lowercase* option saves the word in the dictionary as lowercase characters and not necessarily as you typed it in. Whereas the *Exactly as typed* option will save the word exactly as you input it. Selecting *Remove* takes the displayed word out of the dictionary. If you have a word that you never want hyphenated, put a discretionary hyphen in front of the word in the *Add word to user dictionary* dialog box.

Alignment command

This sub-menu is a shortcut approach to paragraph alignment outlined previously under the *Paragraph* command. See Figures 47 and 50 in this module for details.

Define styles and Style command

These two commands are described in Module 11 — **Page-Maker Style Sheets.**

Creating new text files

Rather then creating your files solely from a word processor, and then loading them into PageMaker, files of quite considerable length can be created totally from within PageMaker itself, in normal layout view. With PageMaker 4, it is also possible to do faster text entry and editing in the new story editor mode. Module 5 provides more details on story editor.

For simple headings and captions, however, it is sometimes easier to just create them in normal layout view. Figures 84 to 87 illustrate this approach.

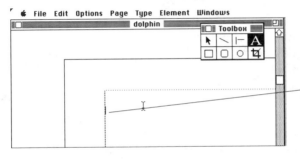

Figure 84. Choose the text tool, move to the area on the page you would like to start typing, and click the mouse button once. A flashing text cursor will appear, in this case at the left margin.

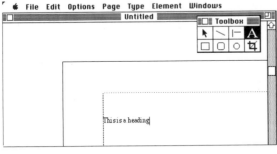

Figure 85. After the flashing text cursor has been inserted, you are free to add text as you see fit.

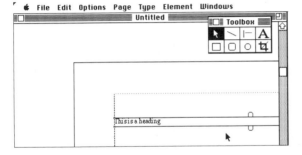

Figure 86. This new text file we have created occupies its own text block, as every new text file does (note the change of tool in the Toolbox).

177

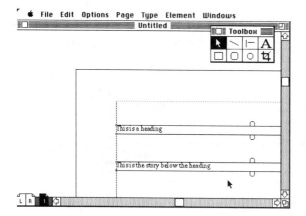

Figure 87. Every time the mouse cursor is clicked in a new position and text is entered, a new text block is created.

When entering text in layout view, the flashing cursor may not always be where you clicked the mouse cursor. Where it does end up depends on how the defaults for text are set. (Defaults are looked at in another module.) For example, if you tried to click the mouse cursor in the center of an empty page, and the default text setting is left justified, the flashing cursor will appear to the left side of the page. If you want the text centered, type it in, select it, and center it. Alternatively, go to the **Type** menu, choose *Alignment*, and then Align center.

For these reasons it is often easier to move off to the side of the page to create smaller text files. Quite often such things as headings, captions, footnotes, etc., are created in this way. After they have been formatted off the side of the page, move them into position on the page. Figures 88 to 91 illustrate this approach.

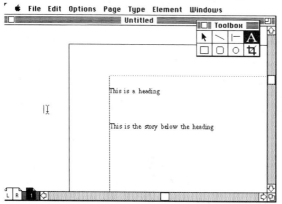

Figure 88. It is often easier to create small text blocks, for such things as headings or captions, off the actual page in the pasteboard area, and move them onto the page later.

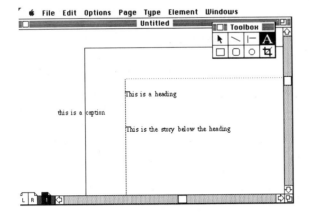

Figure 89. This text we have added on the side of the page will now also occupy its own little text block...

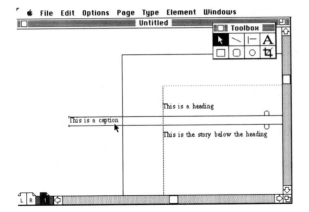

Figure 90.... which can now be moved onto the page from the clipboard area using the pointer tool...

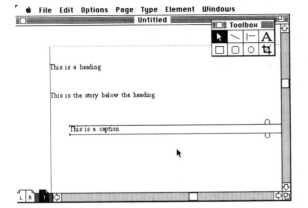

Figure 91.... as we have done here.

Exporting Text

Text from within PageMaker, whether it was imported or created within PageMaker, can be exported in word processor format for use in a word processor or other such application.

The first step is to select the text you would like to export to a file. If you wish to export a whole file, insert your text cursor within the story and choose *Select all* from the **Edit** menu, before you choose *Export*. Otherwise, simply select the text you would like to export (perhaps just a few words or paragraphs as shown in Figure 92).

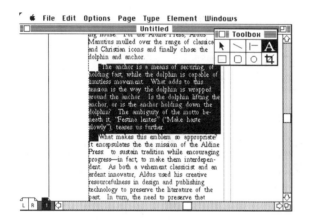

Figure 92. Here we have selected a single paragraph to export to a word processor file.

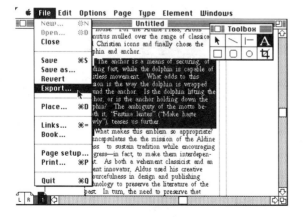

*Figure 93. After selecting the text to export, choose the Export command from the **File** menu.*

After perfoming either of these steps, choose the *Export* command from the **File** menu (Figure 93). The Figure 94 dialog box will appear.

Insert the name of the word processor file you wish to create in the rectangle provided, as well as the format next to this rectangle. The format you choose will depend on exactly what word processor you use, or what you want to use the file for. We have chosen 'Example name' in Microsoft Word 3.0 format (Figure 95).

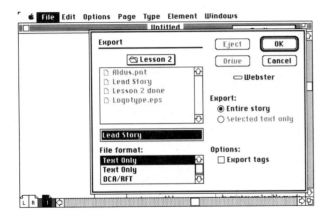

Figure 94. The Export command dialog box.

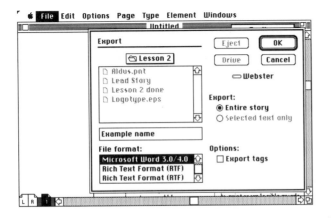

Figure 95. Insert the name of the file-to-be in the rectangle (we inserted the name Example name).

After doing this, click on OK; after a few seconds a word processor file has been created and placed on disk (Figure 96).

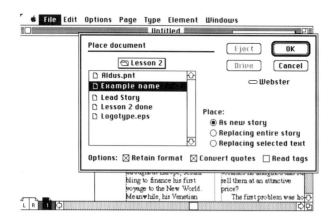

Figure 96. Upon selecting the Place command (after we clicked on OK from Figure 98), we can see the text file Example name now on disk.

Module 4 Exercise

Editing Text

Module 4 Exercise
Editing Text

In this exercise we will edit text — correct simple errors, select text, and apply simple styles and formatting information.

This training material is structured so that people of all levels of expertise with PageMaker can use it to gain maximum benefit. To do this, we have structured this material so that the bare exercise is listed below this paragraph on just one page, with no hints. The following pages contain the steps needed to complete this exercise for those that need additional prompting. The **Editing Text** module should be referenced if you need further help or explanations.

Module 4 exercise steps

1.   *Open up the template* Newsletter 2 from the Templates Folder.*

2.   *At the top of the page is the major heading "Title" and directly below is the word "Headline." We are going to rename these. First, change the word "Title" to "April News " and then the word "Headline" to "What's New?"*

3.   *The two paragraphs below our new heading, "What's New?" have to be bolded. Next, move to the bottom half of the first column. The first two paragraphs under the word Subhead have to be italicized.*

4.   *The subheading "What's New?" must now be centered. Next change the font of the heading "April News " to Palatino, with a point size of 30, and then also center this.*

5.   *Change the leading of the two paragraphs, in the first column that we italicized, to 15 points.*

6.   *Give these same two paragraphs a first line indent of 0.2 of an inch, changing one paragraph at a time.*

*At this point consider a template the same as a PageMaker publication. The special properties of templates are discussed in Module 10.

The steps in detail

1. Open up the template Newsletter 2 from the Templates Folder.
   Opening up an existing publication or template is a little different from starting a new one. The command used to open a publication or template is

the *Open* command from the **File** menu. (Templates are similar to publications. The different properties of templates are discussed in Module 10.)

After choosing this command you are presented with a dialog box similar to when we choose the *Place* command. However, this time only saved publications or templates are there for you to choose, whereas before we we researching for files. Locate the Templates folder (Figure 2), which will be listed in this dialog box, and double-click on it. Within that folder is the Newsletter 2 template (Figure 3). Double-click on its name.

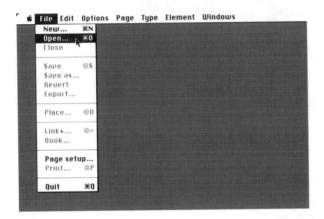

Figure 1. The Open command must be used to access an existing publication or template.

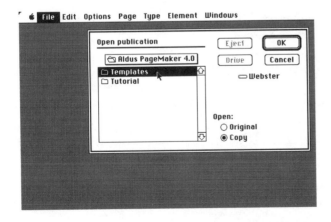

Figure 2. The Newsletter 2 publication is located in the Templates folder.

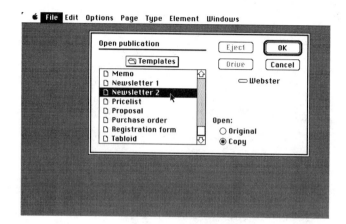

Figure 3. *Locate the publication entitled Newsletter 2 and double-click on it.*

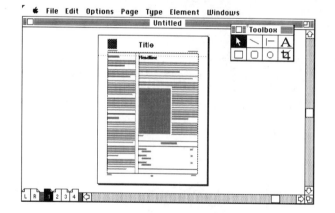

Figure 4. *Newsletter 2 will look like this when set to Fit in window view.*

2. At the top of the page is the major heading "Title" and directly below is the word "Headline." We are going to rename these. First, change the word "Title" to "April News" and then the word headline to "What's New?"

There are several ways that we can delete these two words and replace them. First, however, change to *Actual size* view and use the scroll bars to move the page so that you can actually read this heading (Figures 5 and 6). Alternatively, by holding down the Option and Command keys, and simultaneously clicking the mouse with the cursor located where you wish to go, you can move to *Actual size* view with the page already positioned at the correct point.

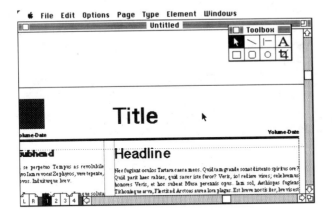

Figure 5. *Change to Actual size view so that the text can be read.*

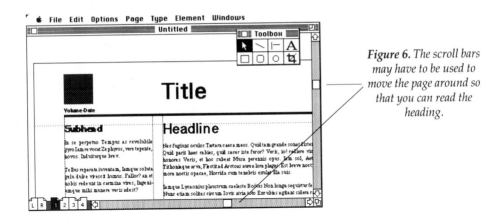

Figure 6. *The scroll bars may have to be used to move the page around so that you can read the heading.*

Make sure the text cursor is selected before you start. When it is, move the mouse cursor over the first word we are going to replace—Title. Now double-click the mouse, and the word will become selected (Figure 7). If it does not, wait a second and double-click the mouse again, until it is highlighted in reverse video.

Once the word Title is highlighted, you can type in the replacement words — April News. There is no need to delete the existing word first — just type the new words. As soon as you touch the first key on the keyboard, the highlighted word disappears — to be replaced by the new characters you are typing (Figure 8). This applies whenever a selection of text is highlighted within PageMaker. Any text keyed in simply replaces the highlighted text.

The method described above is now used to replace the word Headline (just below Title). The steps are highlighted in Figures 10 through 12.

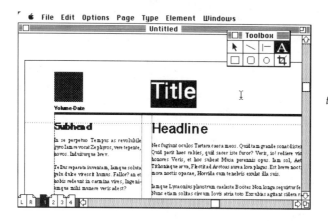

Figure 7. Making sure that the text cursor is selected (note the text tool selected in the Toolbox), move the mouse cursor over the word Title, and click the mouse twice quickly. The word will become selected.

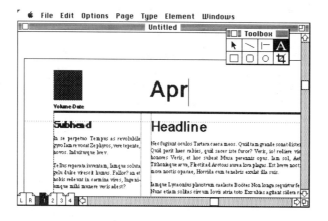

Figure 8. As soon as you start typing the new word in, the old word disappears. Continue typing until the new word or words have been entered.

Figure 9. *The new title completed.*

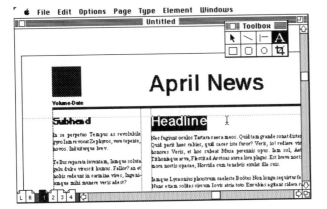

Figure 10. *The same steps can be followed to replace entirely the word Headline. Double-click on this word...*

Figure 11. *...and type in the new words.*

Figure 12. Headline has now been reworded with What's New?

3. The two paragraphs below our new heading "What's New?" have to be bold. Next, move to the bottom half of the first column. The first two paragraphs under the word Subhead have to be italicized.

Move the screen slightly down and across so that you can see the first group of information we are going to edit (the two paragraphs under the subheading "What's New?"). Once again, there are several ways that we can select this text, as this is what we must do before we can bold it.

The most straightforward way to select the text is as follows: Making sure the text cursor is still selected, move the mouse cursor to the start of the text you would like to select. Hold the mouse button down here and keep it down. Now run the mouse cursor over the text, releasing the mouse button only when it appears to the right of the very last letter you would like to select. The entire two paragraphs will be highlighted (Figures 14 and 15).

Figure 13. We are now to select the two paragraphs below the heading "What's New?"

Figure 14. *Run the mouse cursor over the text, keeping the mouse button held down, and all text will become highlighted as you go.*

Figure 15. *Release the mouse button when the mouse cursor is to the right of the very last letter you want to select. All letters in between the start and end point will be selected.*

Two other methods could have been used to select the text. You could have clicked once to insert the text cursor at the start of the text to select, held down the Shift key, and clicked at the end of the text block. You could also have triple-clicked on the first paragraph, held the mouse button down on the third click, and moved the mouse anywhere into the second paragraph. If you are unsure of either of these methods, stick to the first method described.

Once the text is selected, move to the *Type style* command in the **Type** menu (Figure 16). Remember that this command is a little different to some others, in that you must hold the mouse button down on the command and run the mouse button down the resulting sub-menu (Figure 16). Select the style *Bold* from this sub-menu.

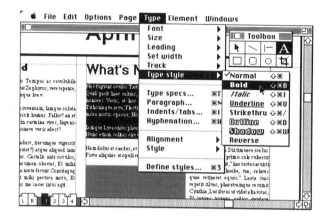

Figure 16. *After selecting the text, choose the Bold style from the Type style command in the* **Type** *menu.*

Figure 17. *The entire two paragraphs that were selected now change to bold on the screen.*

The two paragraphs have now changed to bold style (Figure 17). You could have also bolded these paragraphs in two other ways. The shortcut keyboard method could have used Command + Shift + B. Alternatively, you could have selected the *Type specs* command from the **Type** menu, and chosen Bold from the subsequent dialog box.

After having successfully completed this, move to the bottom left of the page to view the next two paragraphs we are changing (underneath the word Subhead in the bottom half of the first column), and select those as well, using the methods described earlier in this step. This time however, select the style *Italic* from the *Type style* command. See Figures 18 to 20 for the steps involved.

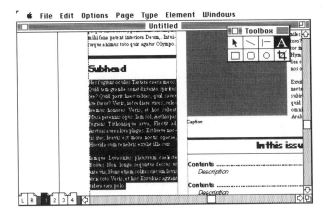

Figure 18. Use the scroll bars to move yourself down to the bottom left of the page, enough to select the appropriate paragraphs under the word Subhead. Use the same method as described earlier to select the text.

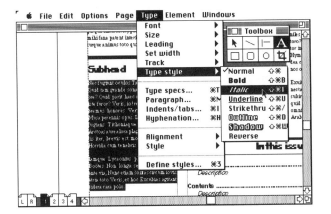

Figure 19. After selecting the text, use the Type style command again to change this text to Italic.

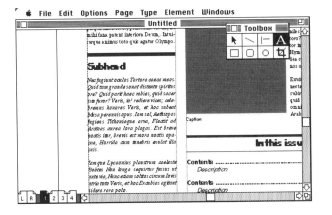

Figure 20. The italicized text. As for bolding, you could have chosen one of the other two alternatives - shortcut keys of Command + Shift + I or used the Type specs dialog box, also from the **Type** menu.

4. The subheading "What's New?" must now be centered. Next change the font of the heading "April News" to Palatino, with a point size of 30, and then also center this.

Move the page back to the heading "What's New?", and select it. After selecting this (Figure 21), select the *Alignment* command in the **Type** menu, and choose *Align center* for alignment (Figure 22). The selected paragraph will instantly be centered (Figure 23).

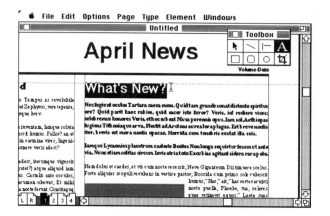

Figure 21. *Our next task is to alter the justification of the heading "What's New?" Locate the heading and select it.*

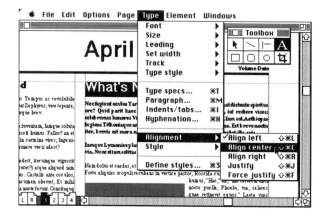

Figure 22. *Use the Alignment command from the Type menu to center the selected text. The shortcut key method (Command + Shift + C) or the Paragraph command from the Type menu could also have been used.*

Figure 23. The result of centering the subheading "What's New?"

Move to the major heading that reads "April News" and select it (Figure 24). To change the size and font of the text, choose the *Type specs* command from the **Type** menu (Figure 25).

Figure 24. Use the scroll bars once again to move the page up a little to read the heading. Select the heading as shown.

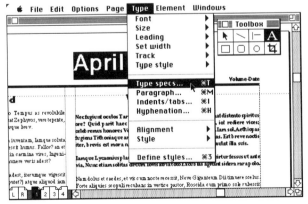

*Figure 25. After selecting the heading, select the Type specs command from the **Type** menu.*

Within the *Type specs* command dialog box (Figure 26), select the Palatino font by clicking and holding down the mouse button on the current Font name. Select Palatino from the sub-menu that appears (Figure 27).

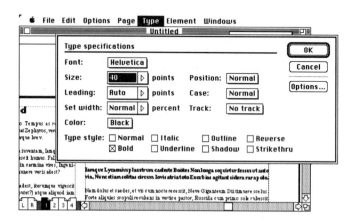

Figure 26. The Type specs dialog box will return the current type face, size, etc., of the selected text.

To change the size of the text, simply type in the new size (Figure 28). The size box will already be highlighted so there is no need to select that box first. Figure 29 shows the results of Figures 27 and 28.

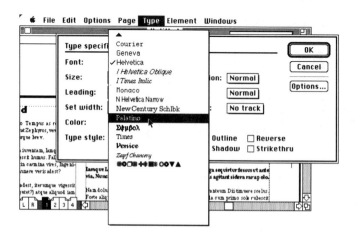

Figure 27. To change the font being used, hold the mouse button down on the current font, and run the mouse down the sub-menu that appears. Then choose Palatino.

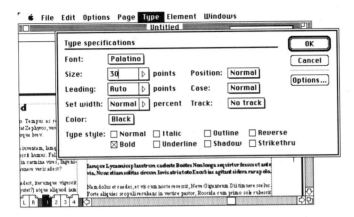

Figure 28. The new size for the text can be typed straight in — no need to position the mouse anywhere.

Figure 29. Here we see the result of the heading after the Type specs command has been adjusted in Figures 27and 28.We next must center this heading.

Changing the size and font of the text could, of course, been achieved using the *Font* and *Size* commands from the **Type** menu. However, when more than one attribute of text has to be changed, it tends to be easier to change it via the *Type specs* command.

To center the heading, make sure it is still selected, choose the *Alignment* command in the **Type** menu and select *Align center* (Figure 30). The result is shown in Figure 31.

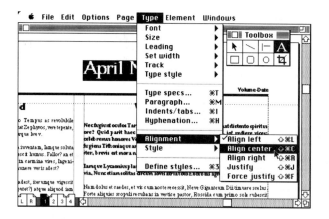

Figure 30. Centering the heading is achieved via the Alignment command in the **Type** menu.

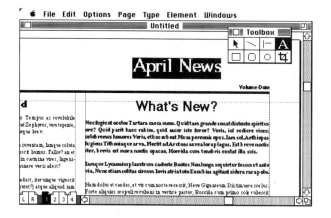

Figure 31. The result.

5. *Change the leading to 15 points in the two paragraph, in the first column that we italicized, to 15 points.*

After scrolling to a position to see these paragraphs, select both paragraphs using the text tool (Figure 32), and then the *Type specs* command (Figure 33). Within this *Type specs* command, select the current Leading figure and change it to 15 points (Figure 34). The space between the lines will change to reflect this new figure after selecting OK (Figure 35).

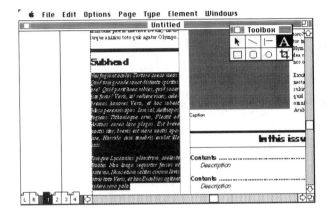

Figure 32. Select the two paragraphs in column one in order to change the interline spacing (leading).

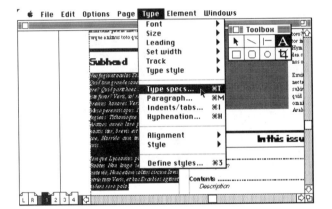

*Figure 33. Select the Type specs command from the **Type** menu.*

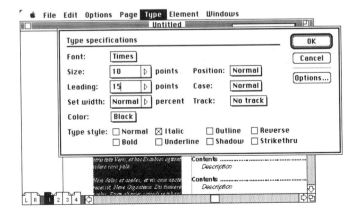

Figure 34. In the Type specs dialog box, change the leading figure to 15 by keying in the number 15 at the Leading box.

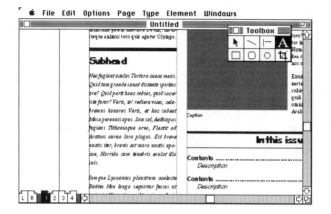

Figure 35. The change of leading in these paragraphs makes them stand out from the rest of the body text.

6. *Give these same two paragraphs a first line indent of 0.2 of an inch, changing one paragraph at a time.*

Select the first paragraph mentioned (Figure 36). After doing this, select the *Paragraph* command from the **Type** menu (Figure 37).

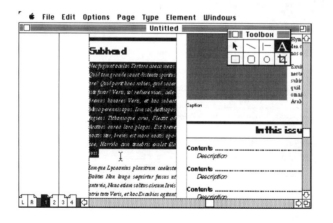

Figure 36. Select the first paragraph under the word Subhead.

Within this command you must alter the number for First, which at the moment should read 0. Change this figure to 0.2 (if in inches) — see Figure 38. If in another unit, insert 0.2i. The first paragraph now reflects the 0.2 inch first line indent (see Figure 39).

Repeat these steps for yourself after selecting the second paragraph underneath.

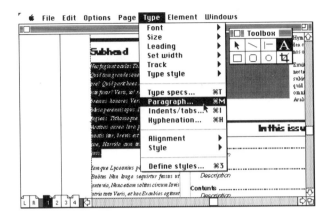

Figure 37. *Now select the Paragraph command in the **Type** menu in order to change the indents of the paragraph.*

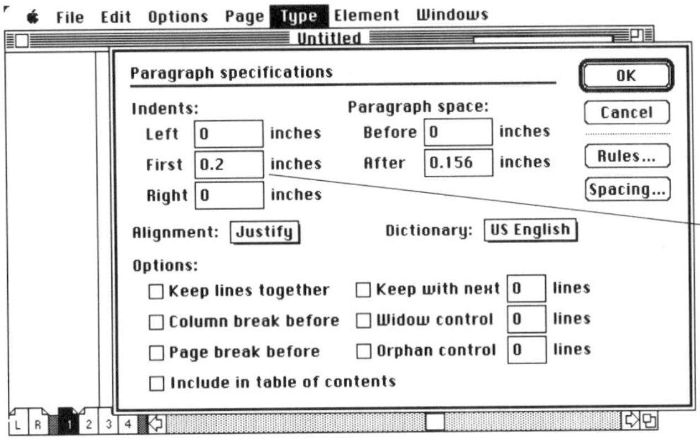

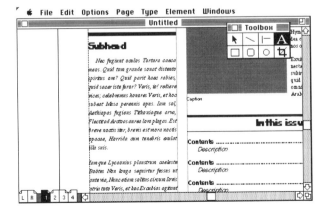

Figure 38. *Change the First rectangle to contain the figure 0.2 (inches). This will cause the first line of the selected paragraph to be indented this amount.*

Figure 39. *The paragraph that was selected now reflects the first line indent we set. Repeat the last few steps yourself (Figures 36 through 38) after selecting the second paragraph underneath. Alternatively, you could try setting this indent using the Indent/tabs command from the **Type** menu.*

Module 5

The Story Editor

Story Editor

The story editor feature in PageMaker gives you many of the important capabilities of a stand-alone word processor. Story editor displays a separate text window on top of the normal publication layout view. It can be used in three ways: (1) to open a text view of a currently placed PageMaker story; (2) to open an empty story window for adding new text; and (3) to import and edit a new word processed file before it is placed into PageMaker.

Each story view opened contains a single PageMaker story file. Multiple stories within a single PageMaker publication can open separate story editor views.

Entering story editor view

By triple-clicking on your text with the pointer tool, the story editor screen appears in a format similar to a word processor. From here you are able to add, delete, or edit text, as well as use the spell checker and the search and replace facilities — just like an external word processor. PageMaker even displays the styles of each paragraph to the left of the text (Figure 1). Notice, in Figure 1, the different menu options available in story view.

As an alternative to triple-clicking on text with the pointer tool, you can click an insertion point with the text tool and choose *Edit story* from the **Edit** menu. Two other methods may also be employed: if a story editor window is already open but behind the normal publication window, click on an exposed part; or choose the story window's name from the **Windows** menu. The **Windows** menu allows you to move at will between story editor and publication layout views.

It is also possible to open up a new, empty, story editor window for adding more text within PageMaker. This is done by choosing *Edit story* from the **Edit** menu without any text selected.

Once a story window is open, you can now edit, delete, or type in text, and use the spell check and search/replace features. To move up or down the text file, use the scroll bar to the right of this

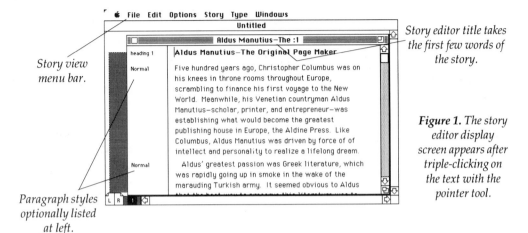

Story view menu bar.

Story editor title takes the first few words of the story.

Paragraph styles optionally listed at left.

Figure 1. *The story editor display screen appears after triple-clicking on the text with the pointer tool.*

screen, in the same way as they are used on the publication layout screen.

You can even use this view to change paragraph styles. (Refer to Module 11, **PageMaker Style Sheets** for more details on style sheets.) Paragraph styles are displayed to the left of the text. A paragraph may be selected in story view by clicking on these style names.

Story view differences

In Figure 1, you can see some of the differences available with the new story view. The menus are slightly different. All text is shown in the font selected in the *Preferences* command from the **Edit** menu. Text styles are shown, but page or line breaks are not displayed. Graphic tools are not available. Story windows are automatically named with the first few words of the actual story.

Color and *Style* palettes may be displayed and utilized. Most changes will only become apparent on return to layout view. The style names listed at left in Figure 1 can be optionally shown or hidden using the *Display style names* in the **Options** menu.

Style sheets and color details are discussed in a later module. Their understanding is not necessary at this point to understand the story editor.

Spell checking

To activate this function select the *Spelling* option in the **Edit** menu (Figure 2). The dialog box of Figure 3 will appear. Spell checking is only possible in story view. Note that in layout view, the *Spelling* command is gray and cannot be selected.

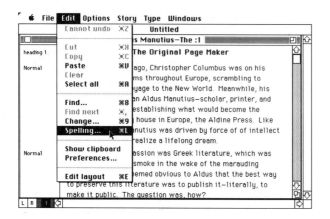

Figure 2. Select the Spelling option in the **Edit** menu. Don't worry what part of the document is displayed on your screen, as PageMaker can check through the entire document regardless.

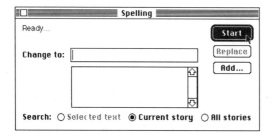

Figure 3. If an insertion point is clicked in the story view, then at the bottom of the dialog box, you can choose Current story or All stories. If a paragraph or portion of text is highlighted, then selected text can also be chosen.

Clicking on the *Start* button of Figure 3 causes spell checking to commence. Once checking is underway, the *Start* button of Figure 3 is replaced with the *Ignore* button of Figure 4.

As each misspelled word is detected, it is displayed at the top of the dialog box, and also in the *Change to:* box (Figure 4). You then have the opportunity to replace the word with the correct spelling, ignore it, or add it to the dictionary. PageMaker will also prompt you, in the large bottom rectangle, with alternative, correctly spelled words for you to choose (Figure 4). The *Add* command, to the right of the Figures 3 and 4 dialog boxes allows you to add words to PageMaker's dictionary (initially 100,000 words for US English, and 80,000 words for International English).

Figure 4. *PageMaker has found an unknown word. We have highlighted one of the suggested alternatives. The next step is to click on the Replace, Ignore or Add commands so that PageMaker can continue its search through the document.*

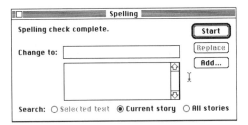

Figure 5. *When the spell checker has reached the end, it will display this in the dialog box.*

To remove the *Spelling* dialog box once you have finished with the spell check, click in the close button in the top left-hand corner.

Search and replace

PageMaker allows you to search for, and optionally replace, text, text attributes, and nonprinting characters. The *Find* command from the **Edit** menu (in story view) produces the dialog box of Figure 6. You enter the text you wish to find, and click the *Find* button. Once PageMaker finds the text, it replaces the *Find* with *Find Next*. You then have the option of continuing on or clicking the close button and exiting. It is possible to search *Selected text*, *Current story* or *All stories* in a publication.

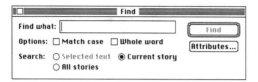

Figure 6. The Find *command dialog box appears on choosing Find from the* **Edit** *menu in story view.*

Clicking on the *Attributes* button of the *Find* command, causes the *Attributes* dialog box to appear (Figure 7). This allows you to search for a range of attributes, not just text. Figure 7, for example, shows the sub-menu for paragraph styles. Any style name in our current style sheet can be selected and searched for.

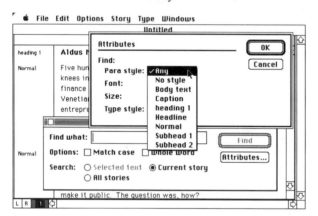

Figure 7. The Find *attributes dialog box. Note we have chosen the Para style: sub-menu and all our style names are available for selection.*

The *Change* command (in the **Edit** menu) searches for a selected item, and changes this item to whatever you have specified. If, for example, you wish to change every occurrence of the word Aldus to Aldose throughout the text, you would do this by setting up the *Change* command dialog box to that shown in Figure 8.

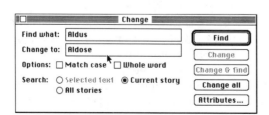

Figure 8. This is what you would enter into the Find what: and Change to: boxes by clicking inside them with the mouse and then typing.

You can choose *Find* (find first occurrence) or *Change all* (change all occurrences). If you choose *Find*, once the first occurrence is found, you then have the choice of choosing *Change, Change & find*, or *Change all*. The *Attributes* button of Figure 8 gives both a *Find* and *Change* attributes dialog box. Its operation is similar to Figure 7, but change attributes are also included.

Importing files to a story window

It is possible to import word processed text, in-line graphics and PageMaker text into story view using the *Import* command from the **Story** menu (Figure 9). This command only operates in story editor mode.

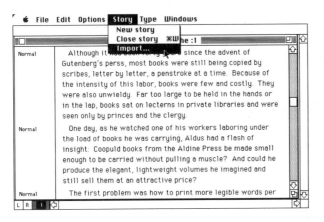

Figure 9. To import text, and in-line graphics while in story view, choose the Import command from the Story menu.

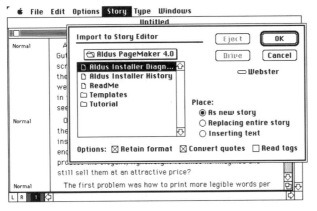

Figure 10. The Import to Story Editor dialog box will appear upon selecting the Import command from the menu in Figure 9.

Using the *Import* command you can load the following:

•*Word processor files*. When selecting *As new story* in the Figure 10 dialog box, the text will be placed into a new story window. When selecting *Inserting text*, it will go into the current active window at the text cursor locations. When selecting *Replacing entire story*, it goes into the currently active window, replacing the original story within.

• *PageMaker 4 files*. A similar set of circumstance applies for word processor text described above. A PageMaker 4 document can, however, include more than one story. You have the option, therefore, through the *Place PageMaker stories* dialog box (Figure 11), to choose one or more stories to import. Multiple stories are imported as a single story with carriage returns between.

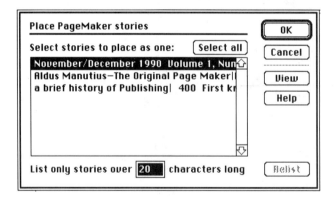

Figure 11. This is the Place PageMaker stories *dialog box from the* Import *command. We have selected to load Lesson 3 done from the Lesson 3 folder in the Tutorial folder. This box tells us there are three different stories we could load. We could choose one, two, or all. The* View *command allows you a small viewing window to view the story contents.*

• *Inline Graphics*. These files will load into the currently open story window with a small graphics marker (▦) showing the insertion point.

Exiting story view

When you have finished with story view, simply click on the box in the top left-hand corner (Figure 12), or choose *Close story* from the **Story** menu. If your story is new, PageMaker will alert you to either Place or Discard the story (Figure 13).

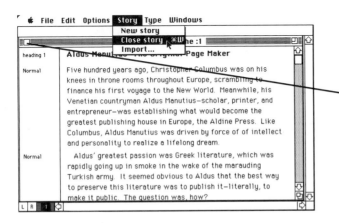

*Figure 12. Click on the close box to return to layout view from story view, or choose Close story from the **Story** menu.*

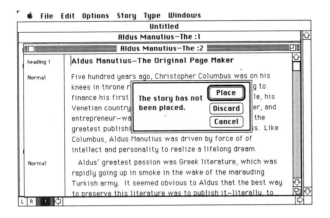

Figure 13. If you have not yet placed a story, PageMaker reminds you as you leave story view.

You may also return to layout view by clicking on an exposed version of the publication, or by choosing *Edit layout* from the **Edit** menu. Any changes made to text in story view will now be automatically included in layout view.

Module 5 Exercise

Story Editor

Module 5 Exercise
The Story Editor

This training material is structured so that people of all levels of expertise with Page-Maker can use it to gain maximum benefit. To do this, we have structured this material so that the bare exercise is listed below this paragraph on just one page, with no hints. The following pages contain the steps needed to complete this exercise for those that need additional prompting. **The Story Editor** module should be referenced if you need further help or explanations.

Module 5 exercise steps.

1. *Place the text file Story 2 into a new PageMaker document.*

2. *Activate the story editor screen.*

3. *Change the heading "What's behind the Aldine Dolphin and Anchor?" to "The Real Story of Aldine Dolphin."*

4. *Activate the Change command, and replace every carriage return with three carriage returns.*

The steps to completing this exercise are on the following pages.

The steps in detail

1. Place the text file Story 2 into a new PageMaker document.

Start a new PageMaker publication, Letter size, of one page in length. If you have trouble with this initial step, please review the first few steps of the Module 3 exercise. Locate the Story 2 file in the Lesson 4 folder inside the Tutorial folder. Go to the *Place* command in the **File** menu, locate Story 2, and load onto your page in one or two columns (your choice).

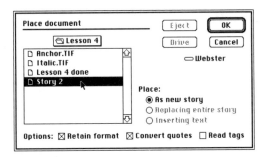

Figure 1. Place the file Story 2 located in the Lesson 4 folder. Load it onto a blank page.

2. Activate the story editor screen.

Triple-click in the text block with the pointer tool to activate the story editor screen.

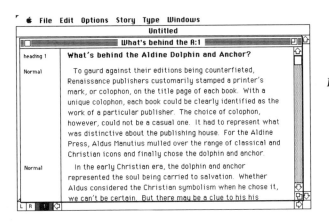

Figure 2. Triple-click in the text block with the mouse. This ensures that the story editor screen opens with the text you clicked on in view.

3. Change the heading "What's behind the Aldine Dolphin and Anchor?" to "The Real Story of Aldine Dolphin."

Select the text tool and highlight the heading (Figure 3). Type in the new heading (Figure 4).

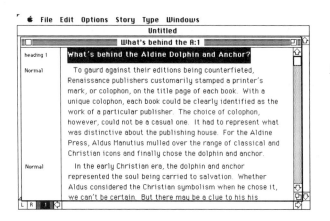

Figure 3. Highlight the heading with the text tool and simply retype the new heading.

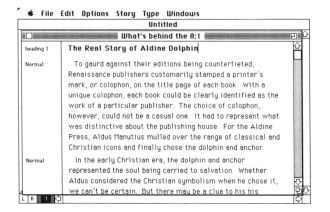

Figure 4. The new heading.

4. Activate the Change command and replace every carriage return with three carriage returns.

Go to the **Edit** menu and select the *Change* command (Figure 5). Read the caption of Figure 6 to perform this operation. The result is shown in Figure 7.

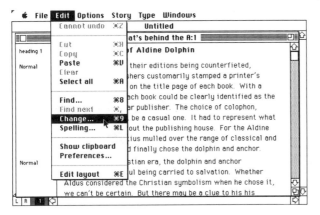

Figure 5. *Select the Change command in the **Edit** Menu.*

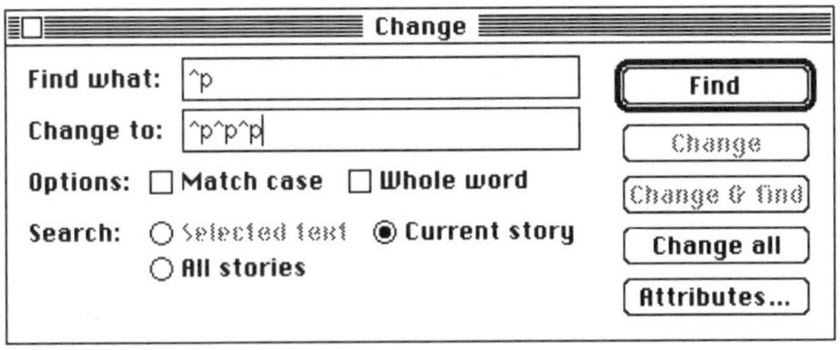

Figure 6. *Enter one carriage return symbol (^p) in the Find what: rectangle, and three in the Change to: rectangle. Then select the option Change all. (Note: the carriage return symbol is option i.)*

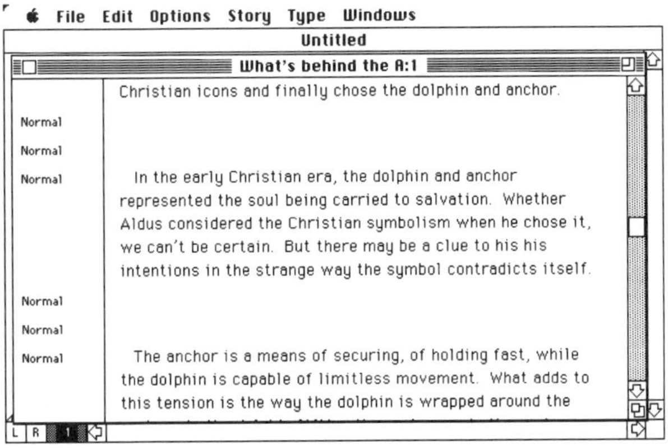

Figure 7. *The result should look something like this. If you choose Display ¶ in the Options menu, you will display three carriage return symbols after each paragraph.*

Module 6

Creating Graphics

Creating Graphics

Most of the time, third-party packages are used to create the complex and professional quality graphics that can be used within PageMaker. There are countless packages available for the Macintosh that make incredible graphics a reality for all types of users — a reality that most of the time cannot be achieved via PageMaker alone.

This is not to say that PageMaker can't create a large array of graphics internally — because it can. When it comes to preparing simple graphics, such as borders, underlines, boxes, circles, simple graphs, and charts, you don't need to look any further than PageMaker itself.

Figure 1 is an example of how graphics can be created within PageMaker in very little time.

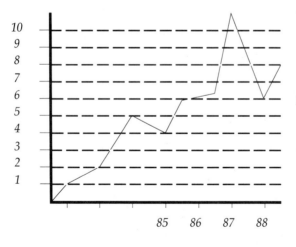

Figure 1. A simple graph created using the PageMaker graphic tools.

All of the PageMaker graphics tools are found in the Toolbox (Figure 2). They include two straight line drawing tools, two rectangular drawing tools, and the oval drawing tool.

Simply select the tool you would like to use from the Toolbox. Let's say we select the square-corner drawing tool first (Figure 3). The mouse cursor changes its appearance to a crosshair.

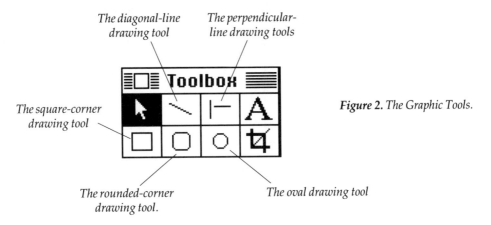

The diagonal-line drawing tool

The perpendicular-line drawing tools

The square-corner drawing tool

The rounded-corner drawing tool.

The oval drawing tool

Figure 2. *The Graphic Tools.*

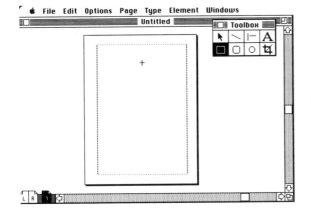

Figure 3. *As soon as any graphic tool is selected, the mouse cursor changes to a crosshair.*

Hold down the mouse cursor where you would like to start drawing the graphic. Dragging the mouse in any direction will cause a box to appear, which will become permanent when the mouse button is released (Figures 4 and 5). All other graphics can be created in exactly this same manner — by selecting it in the Toolbox, and dragging the mouse along the page. Experiment with all the graphic drawing tools to see the results you get, as we have done in Figure 6.

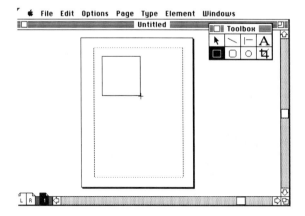

Figure 4. To create a graphic, once you have selected a tool (in this case the square-corner drawing tool), hold the mouse button down and drag the mouse across the page.

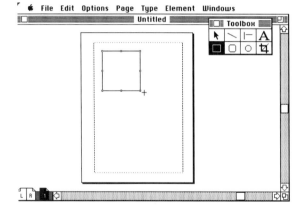

Figure 5. Release the mouse button when the graphic is the correct size. It will then become selected. Note the small square dots (called handles) around the edge of the graphic.

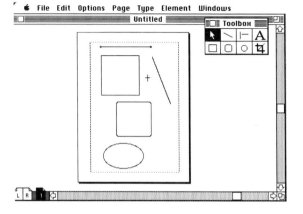

Figure 6. Here is an example of a graphic from each of the graphic drawing tools.

Altering graphics

Once you've drawn a graphic, the graphic is selected — that is to say, it has several small square dots, or handles, around its edge (Figure 5). However, whenever you create another graphic, this new object becomes selected and the previously selected graphic is deselected.

To manipulate a graphic on the page, it must first be selected. This is done by activating the pointer tool in the Toolbox and clicking with the arrow on the border of the graphic. Once selected, a graphic will display the handles around its border (Figure 7). Alternate graphics can be selected simply by clicking anywhere on their border.

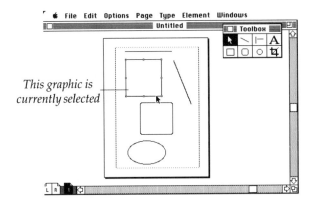

This graphic is currently selected

Figure 7. *To select a graphic, you must first make sure the pointer tool is currently active (note the Toolbox), and click on the border of the graphic you would like to select.*

Changing borders and fills

After selecting a graphic, there are several things that can be done with it. First, we will look at how we can change both the border and/or the fill for that graphic. If you have created a graphic using either of the line drawing tools, you will only be able to adjust the line thickness, because a line has no fill at all.

Make sure a rectangular graphic is selected on screen, similar to Figure 8, and study the *Line* and *Fill* sub-menus under the **Element** menu. Most of the choices in these menus are self-explanatory — line thickness and patterns can be set by selecting the one that appeals to you, as can the shade and pattern to fill a selected graphic. Figures 8 – 14 illustrate some examples.

223

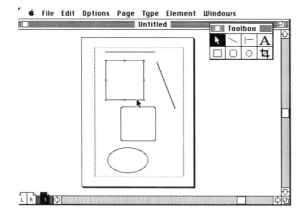

Figure 8. *To change the appearance of a graphic, first select the graphic.*

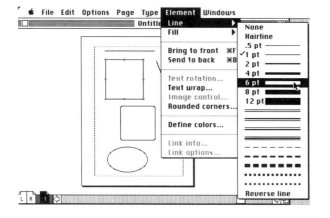

Figure 9. *After selecting the graphic, move to the Line command under the* **Element** *menu, and select the desired line thickness from the relevant sub-menu that appears.*

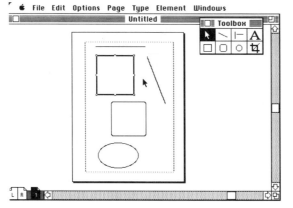

Figure 10. *The graphic will reflect the new line thickness, although it may not be apparent on the screen if the change was slight.*

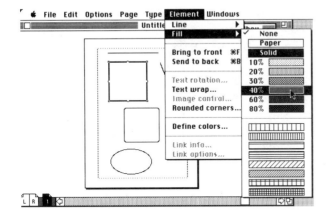

Figure 11. The same idea works when changing the fill pattern of a graphic. Make sure it is selected, then move to the Fill command under the **Element** menu.

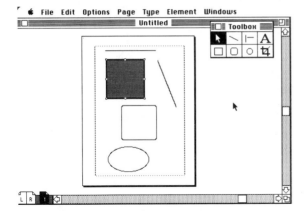

Figure 12. The selected graphic will reflect the new pattern or shade on screen.

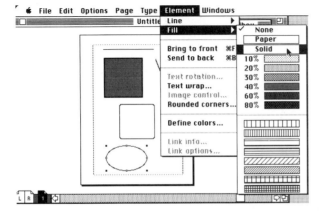

Figure 13. Here we have selected the ellipse near the bottom of the screen, and are in the process of choosing the Solid option, which will be black.

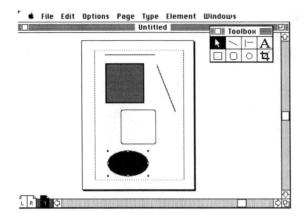

Figure 14. The color black is shown on screen, filling the selected ellipse.

Moving

Graphics can be moved the same way as a text block. Select the pointer tool, hold down the mouse button on the border of the graphic if it is hollow, or anywhere in the graphic if it has a fill pattern, and move the mouse. The graphic will be dragged along with the mouse and will move to where the mouse button is released (Figure 15).

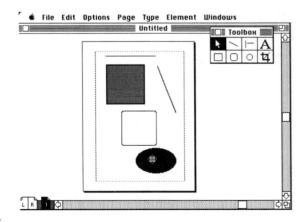

Figure 15. The ellipse has been selected and is in the process of being moved. Note the shape of the mouse cursor indicating this. Wherever the mouse cursor is released will be the new position for the graphic.

Resizing

Any graphic can be resized in any direction, much the same way as a text block can. Only in the case of a graphic, there are more dots around the edge, giving more flexibility in resizing. To resize, first select the graphic using the pointer tool, hold down the mouse button on any handle around the edge of the graphic, and drag it in any direction you like. Release the mouse button when the graphic has been sized correctly.

As you experiment with the resizing of graphics, note that the handle you grab will determine in which direction the graphic can be resized, horizontally, vertically, or diagonally. See Figures 16 to 18, which illustrate this point.

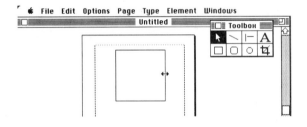

Figure 16. Holding the mouse button down on a side handle means that the graphic can only be resized in that direction (in this case the width of the graphic can be shortened or lengthened, depending on the movement of the mouse).

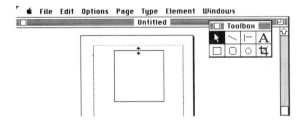

Figure 17. Here we have selected a top handle — allowing us to size the graphic vertically.

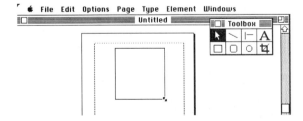

Figure 18. We have now selected a corner handle to size the rectangle diagonally.

227

Editing

Any selected graphic can be deleted, copied, cleared, or pasted to and from the PageMaker screen by using the editing commands in the **Edit** menu. *Cut* will remove the selected graphic from the screen, and keep it in a temporary memory (called the *Clipboard*). The graphic is not yet lost, although it is not visible. *Copy* will put a copy of the selected graphic into the Clipboard and not remove it from the screen.

Paste will transfer the graphic from the Clipboard back to the screen. It will paste the new graphic at a slight offset to its original position. Once the graphic is in the Clipboard, it can be pasted any number of times back onto the page. This has several advantages, one of which is in duplicating a selected graphic any number of times. A graphic can be cleared from the screen without being transferred to the Clipboard by selecting the *Clear* command from the **Edit** menu. The Delete key operates identically to the *Clear* command.

Edit	Options	Page
Cannot undo		⌘Z
Cut		⌘H
Copy		⌘C
Paste		⌘U
Clear		
Select all		⌘A
Find...		⌘8
Find next		⌘,
Change...		⌘9
Spelling...		⌘L
Show clipboard		
Preferences...		
Edit story		⌘E

Figure 19. Cut *removes a selected graphic from the screen and puts it into memory (the Clipboard).* Copy *copies the selected graphic from screen to the Clipboard (the screen graphic is not altered in any way).* Paste *transfers whatever is in the Clipboard back to the middle of the screen, and the* Clear *command removes a graphic from screen and does not put it into the Clipboard.*

Be aware when using the Clipboard that it will only hold one element at a time. Every time you cut or copy something to this temporary memory, the previous element in that memory is lost.

You can view the contents of the Clipboard at any time by choosing the *Show Clipboard* command near the bottom of the **Edit** menu (Figure 19). Figures 20 to 22 provide examples of using the *Copy* command with graphics.

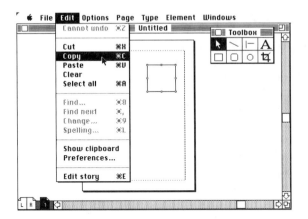

Figure 20. The graphic on this page has been selected. Let's now select the Copy *command. The graphic is then copied to the Clipboard.*

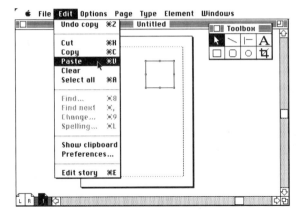

Figure 21. Immediately after choosing Copy *we can choose the* Paste *command. (It does not have to be immediately after, but before something else is cut or copied, or before the Macintosh is turned off.)*

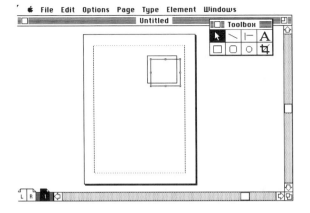

Figure 22. After choosing Paste, *whatever was in the Clipboard is pasted back at a slightly offset position to the original graphic. This process can be repeated to obtain multiple copies of any graphic.*

Changing the printing order of graphics

It's very easy to create graphics that either overlap each other or overlap text on the page. Using two other commands in the **Element** menu, *Send to back* and *Bring to front*, the order of the graphics overlap can be changed. Study Figures 23 to 28 to see examples of this technique.

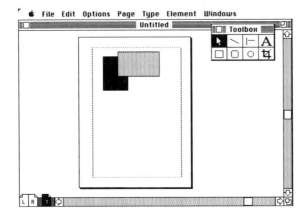

Figure 23. Here we have two graphics that overlap each other. We now want to change the order of the overlap so that the black graphic is on top.

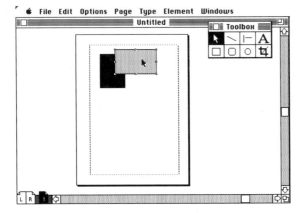

Figure 24. We can select either graphic here, but we will start with the graphic on the top.

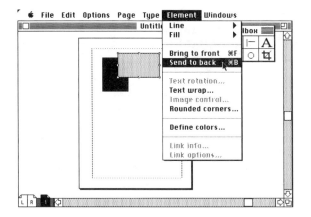

Figure 25. We select the command Send to back *from the* **Element** *menu (because the graphic we have selected is on the top).*

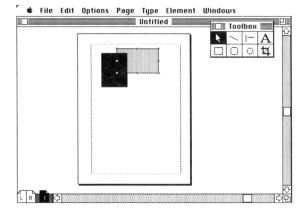

Figure 26. The change can be seen immediately — the black graphic is now on the top.

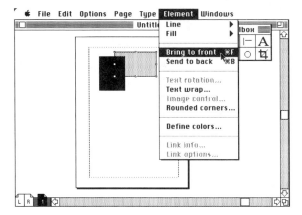

Figure 27. If we now wanted to bring the shaded graphic back to the top, we would need to select the Bring to front *command (because the shaded graphic is still the selected object).*

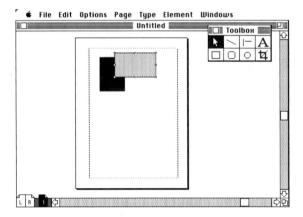

Figure 28. After selecting the command in Figure 27, the shaded graphic now sits on top.

Transparent and solid graphics

Graphics can be filled with transparent and solid selections from the *Fill* sub-menu (Figure 13), as well as a range of shaded options. It is important when using the *None* and *Paper* selections to understand the difference between *None*, which is hollow, and *Paper*, which is usually white. Both look white on the screen.

Note the two overlapping diagrams in Figure 29. In both cases the white rectangle is on the top. In the top example, the white rectangle has a shade selected from the *Fill* sub-menu of *None*, and in the bottom example, the white rectangle has a fill selection of *Paper*.

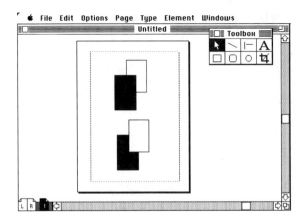

Figure 29. The white rectangle at the top of the page has a fill selection of None. It is hollow and the black rectangle underneath can be totally seen. The bottom rectangle has a fill selection of Paper (which is usually white) and therefore covers the black rectangle underneath it.

Rounded-corner drawing tool

This tool draws rectangles and squares like the square-corner drawing tool, with the obvious difference being it creates rounded corners instead of square corners.

The one step to remember is the *Rounded corners* command is available in the **Element** menu. This command offers a choice of radius for the rounded corners of the rectangle or square. Figure 30 shows an example of the rounded-corner tool and Figure 31 illustrates the dialog box activated with the *Rounded corners* command.

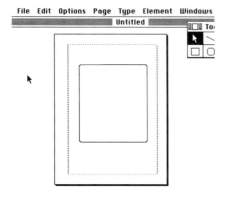

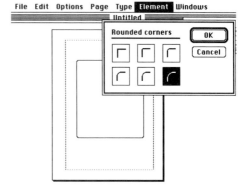

Figure 30. This rectangle was drawn using the rounded-corner drawing tool. The actual radius of the corners can be set using the dialog box of Figure 31.

*Figure 31. This is the Rounded corners dialog box associated with the Rounded corners command from the **Element** menu. You simply choose the radius that suits you.*

Line drawing tools

The diagonal and perpendicular line drawing tools are indicated in the Toolbox diagram of Figure 2. The perpendicular tool draws lines at 45 degree increments, while the diagonal allows straight lines at any angle. The diagonal tool acts like the perpendicular when the Shift key is held down.

The thickness of the lines can be set using the *Line* sub-menu from the **Element** menu (see Figure 9). Some examples are shown in Figure 32.

233

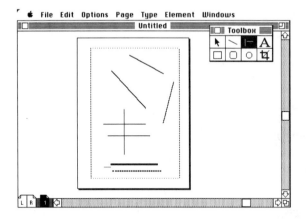

*Figure 32. Examples of the two different line drawing tools are shown. All lines drawn are 1 point in thickness except for the bottom two. The second line from the bottom is 12 points thick, and the bottom line represents one of the pattern selections from the Line command in the **Element** menu.*

Rulers

One element of PageMaker that makes creating and manipulating graphics a lot easier are the PageMaker rulers. These are activated by the *Rulers* command in the **Options** menu (Figure 33).

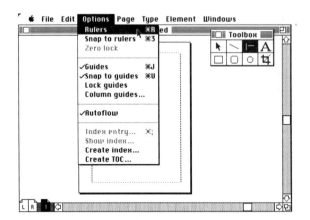

*Figure 33. Selecting the Rulers command from the **Options** menu activates a ruler down the left and across the top of the page (see Figure 34).*

Selecting this command activates a ruler down the left and across the top of the page (Figure 34). These rulers will use units that are controlled by the *Preferences* command in the **Edit** menu. The rulers will always reformat to give accurate measurements on the screen irrespective of the current PageMaker view. The increments in these rulers change depending on the current page view.

234

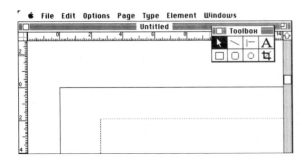

Figure 34. Note that the zero point of the ruler, both vertically and horizontally, is aligned with the top left-hand corner of the page. If the increments in your ruler look a little different, you may have inches or other units set in the Preferences *command in the* Edit *menu. Millimeters are used in this example.*

We can also change where the zero points of both the horizontal and vertical rulers start. By default, the zero point of both these rulers starts at the top left corner of the actual page for single page views. Facing pages view puts the zero point midway between the two pages. Move to *Actual size* through the **Page** menu and look at the top left corner of the page to check this (Figure 34).

To change the zero point of the ruler, move the mouse button to the top left corner where the two rulers intersect (see Figure 35) and hold the mouse button down. Keep this button held down, and slowly move the mouse cursor back onto the page. A crosshair will follow the mouse cursor back down the page (Figure 35). Wherever the mouse button is released is the new zero point of the ruler, both horizontally and vertically. The rulers will reformat to show this as the mouse button is released (Figure 36).

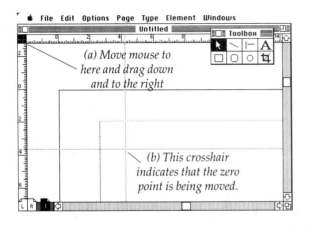

Figure 35. To change the ruler's zero point, hold the mouse button down in the intersecting square of both the rulers and pull the mouse back out onto the page. A crosshair indicating the new zero point of the rulers replaces the mouse cursor. Release the mouse button when the crosshair is positioned correctly.

235

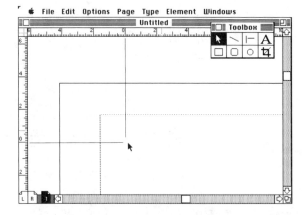

Figure 36. Note the new position of the ruler zero point after Figure 35.

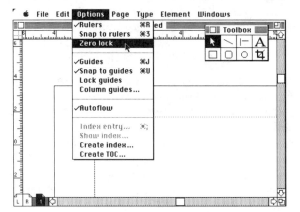

Figure 37. The zero point of the rulers can be locked into position by selecting the Zero lock command from the **Options** menu.

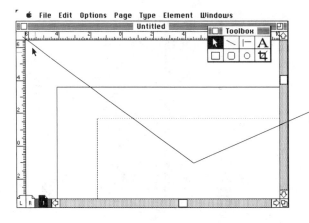

Figure 38. After selecting the command in Figure 37, the intersection of the two rulers now shows a blank square (compare this with Figure 36).

Ruler guides can be "pulled" from the horizontal and vertical rulers, creating a guide that graphics can snap to and align with other graphics.

To use these ruler guides, hold the mouse button down in either ruler, and pull the mouse cursor back down onto the page. As long as the mouse cursor is released on the page, rather than the pasteboard area that surrounds it, a dotted line parallel to the ruler from where this guide originated will be visible on the page (Figure 39).

Multiple guides can be pulled from either ruler (Figures 40 to 42), and it is quite easy to set up a grid with these guides. All guides can be precisely positioned by aligning them with the measurements of the other ruler. More exact alignment is possible at larger page views. Any ruler guide can be moved around on the screen by holding the mouse button down on it and dragging it to a new position (Figure 41). If you want to get rid of one or more ruler guides, simply pull them right off the page (Figure 42), and they will disappear.

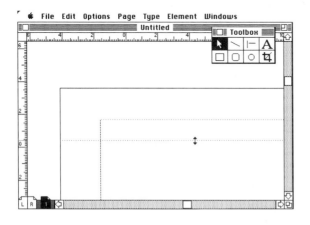

Figure 39. Ruler guides can be pulled from the rulers onto the page by holding the mouse button down in a rule, and dragging it down or right onto the page.

237

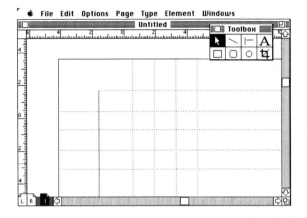

Figure 40. Here we have built up quite a few guides, from both the vertical and horizontal rulers, creating a grid.

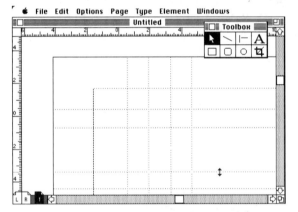

Figure 41. Any guide can be repositioned, by holding the mouse button down on it, and moving to a new position.

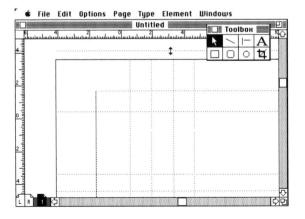

Figure 42. To remove a ruler guide from the page, simply move it so that it is no longer on the page. It will not remain on the pasteboard area when the mouse is released.

Multiple selections

So far we have talked about selecting only one graphic at a time. It is possible, however, to select multiple graphics in a number of different ways. The easiest way to select all graphics on a page is to choose the *Select all* command in the **Edit** menu (Figures 43 and 44). Any operation, whether editing, line, or fill changes, will then affect all selected graphics.

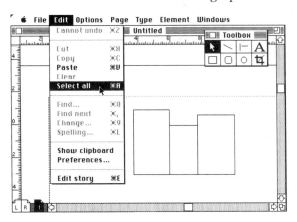

Figure 43. The Select all *command can be used to select all the graphics on a page, but remember that this command will also select any text blocks that may be on the screen.*

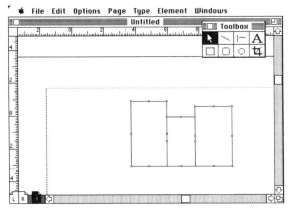

Figure 44. Here are all the graphics selected from Figure 43 using the Select all *command. These graphics can now be deleted, moved, copied, have their line or fill attributes changed, all as a group.*

If a graphics is selected, then selecting another graphic deselects the first graphic. However, if you hold down the Shift key as you select the second and succeeding graphics, all graphics will remain selected. Once again, any future operations will then apply to all selected graphics.

A further way to select a group of graphics is to draw an imaginary box around them with the pointer tool. Pretend that you are drawing a box around a group of graphics, but make sure that the pointer tool is currently active. A dotted box will be drawn as the mouse button is held down (Figure 45), and once released, any graphics that are entirely enclosed by this imaginary box will be selected.

If you ever have trouble selecting a graphic, because it may be behind a guide (ruler, margin, or column) or a block of text, try holding down the Command key as you attempt to select the graphic. This will often allow hidden or hard to get at graphics to be selected.

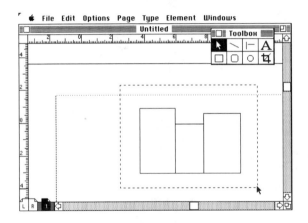

Figure 45. Drawing an imaginary box around a set of graphics will also select multiple graphics. Make sure the pointer tool is selected, and draw a border around the graphics you would like to select. Upon releasing the mouse, all the graphics within the border will be selected.

Setting the graphic default

Every graphic you create has a line thickness setting and a fill setting. It would be a nuisance to have to change every graphic you create, to use the line thickness you want, rather than the one that is set.

Setting the default line and fill values for graphics is achieved by selecting the pointer tool from the Toolbox, making sure that no graphic is currently selected, and choosing the required values from the *Line* and *Fill* sub-menus. Although you will see no immediate change on screen, every graphic that is created from now on will use the *Line* and *Fill* values you have just set by default.

240

Maintaining aspect ratio

When you create a rectangle, an ellipse, or a line, you will find it extremely difficult to create a square, a circle, or in some cases a straight line. Combine the use of the mouse with the aspect ratio of the screen, and this is almost impossible. PageMaker, however, allows you to use a technique that automatically maintains the correct aspect ratio.

When you create a graphic, or even if you are resizing a graphic, hold down the Shift key as you do so. The graphic will snap to its correct shape (square or circle) immediately. Make sure that you release the mouse button before you release the Shift key, otherwise the aspect ratio may be lost.

You can create fairly complex graphics quite easily by using these features of PageMaker. However, don't get too wrapped up in making complex graphics in PageMaker. Many graphics can be drawn easier and better in third-party packages.

Bar charts are a good example of this. Although possible to draw in PageMaker, a number of graphing programs produce such charts automatically by simply entering the actual data.

Wraparounds

All internally created PageMaker graphics can be set up as regular or irregular wraparounds. The method by which this is done is identical to the way it is done with imported graphics — and for this reason is explained in detail in modules 7 and 14 (regular wraparounds in module 7, and irregular wraparounds in module 14). All facets of wraparounds described in these modules can be applied identically to internally created graphics.

Module 6 Exercise

Creating Graphics

Module 6 Exercise
Creating Graphics

In this exercise we will create simple graphics from within PageMaker.

This training material is structured so that people of all levels of expertise with PageMaker can use it to gain maximum benefit. To do this, we have structured this material so that the bare exercise is listed below this paragraph on just one page, with no hints. The following pages contain the steps needed to complete this exercise for those that need additional prompting. The **Creating Graphics** module should be referenced if you need further help or explanations.

Module 6 exercise steps

1.   *Create a new one page publication using a Letter page, and 0.75 inch or 20 mm margins.*

2.   *Assign three columns to the first page.*

3.   *Load in the text file Lead Story using the Autoflow method.*

4.   *Insert a border of 2 points thickness around the outside of the page, with a spacing of approximately 5 mm or (.2 inches), horizontally and vertically, between the margins and the border.*

5.   *Insert intercolumn rules of 2 points thickness.*

6.   *Change the first paragraph heading to 24 points bold Palatino.*

7.   *Create a box behind the heading using a 2 point outline and a 10% fill background.*

8.   *Draw a box in the bottom right-hand corner of the third column 2 inches high, with a 2 point thickness border.*

9.   *Load in the Practice graphic file from the Basic Lesson folder, and place it into the Pasteboard area to the right of the page. Proportionally reduce its size to fit into the box of step 8 with white space all around, and then move it into this box.*

10.   *Select the box and the graphic from steps 8 and 9, delete from page 1, and place them into the top left-hand corner of page 2.*

The steps to completing this exercise are on the following pages.

The steps in detail

1. Create a new one page publication using a Letter page, and 0.75 inch or 20 mm margins.

The new publication is created using the *New* command (Figure 1). Set up the associated dialog box as shown in Figure 2.

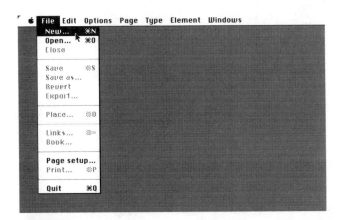

Figure 1. Use the New command to start a new PageMaker document.

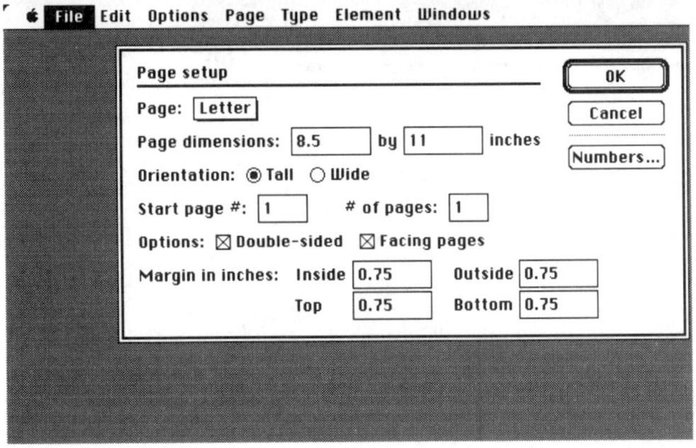

Figure 2. Set the page size to Letter in the New dialog box, one page long and 0.75 inch margins all around.

2. Assign three columns to the first page.

The page is assigned columns using the *Column guides* command from the **Options** menu (Figure 3). Insert 3 in the *Column guides* command dialog box (Figure 4).

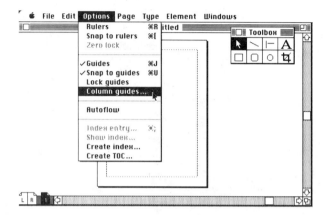

Figure 3. The Column guides *command from the* **Options** *menu allows you to set columns on the page.*

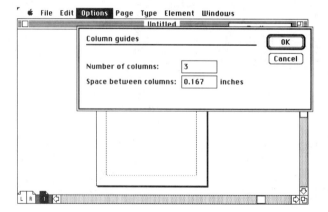

Figure 4. Set 3 columns for the page from the Column guides *dialog box.*

3. Load in the text file Lead Story using the Autoflow method.

Use the *Place* command to load in the Lead Story file from the Lesson 2 folder (within the Tutorial folder) inside the PageMaker 4 folder. Locate the Lesson 2 folder and the Lead Story file within it, and double-click on it (Figures 5 through 8).

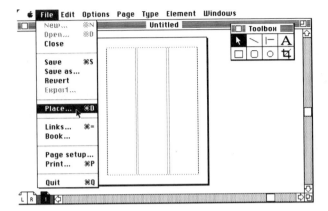

Figure 5. *The* Place *command is used to insert text
into PageMaker.*

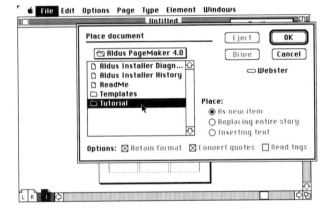

Figure 6. *Lesson 2 is located
in the Tutorial folder.*

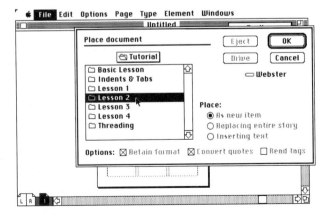

Figure 7. *Double-click on
the folder Lesson 2.*

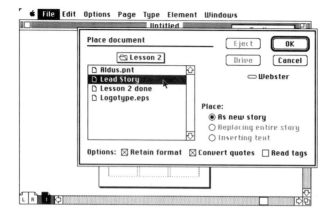

Figure 8. *Now double-click on the file Lead Story.*

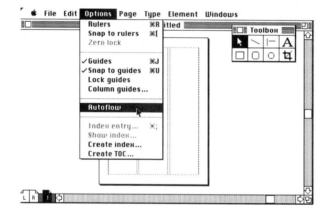

Figure 9. *Make sure the Autoflow command in the **Options** menu has a check next to it.*

To use the *Autoflow* method to flow the text, make sure this option is selected within the **Options** menu (Figure 9). It is selected when a check appears next to the command. If it has a check, leave it, and if it doesn't, select it. The mouse cursor will then appear as shown in Figure 10.

Position this mouse cursor at the top of the first column (Figure 10), and click once. After a few seconds text will have flowed into all three columns (Figure 11).

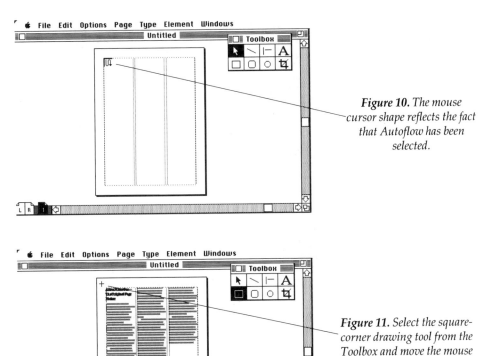

Figure 10. *The mouse cursor shape reflects the fact that Autoflow has been selected.*

Figure 11. *Select the square-corner drawing tool from the Toolbox and move the mouse cursor just above and to the left of the first column.*

4. *Insert a border of 2 points thickness around the outside of the page, with a spacing of approximately 5 mm (or .2 inches), horizontally and vertically, between the margins and the border.*

A border around a page is best created using either the square-corner or rounded-corner drawing tool. Select either of these two tools from the Toolbox. We have chosen the square-corner tool in Figure 11.

Position the mouse cursor (which will now look like a crosshair) just above the top left-hand margin (Figure 11). Hold down the mouse cursor and move it to below the bottom right-hand margin. Release the mouse button (Figure 12).

In this example we have aligned this border by eye, approximately 5 mm (or .2 inches) outside of all margins. To be more exact, you could display the rulers and adjust the settings more precisely.

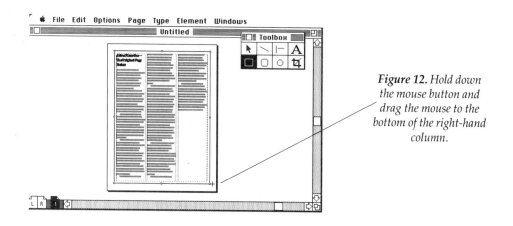

Figure 12. Hold down the mouse button and drag the mouse to the bottom of the right-hand column.

What the rectangle looks like now depends on how the default was set. However, there are two commands that should be chosen to ensure that the graphic is correctly set. The first command is to make sure that the graphic has no fill whatsoever (Figure 13).

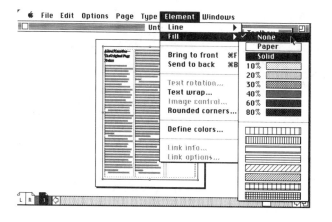

Figure 13. To make sure the setting for the shading is correct, use the Fill sub-menu under the **Element** menu to set the fill to None.

The second command makes sure that the border of the graphic is set at 2 points thickness (Figure 14). After using these two commands, the border of the page will be set correctly.

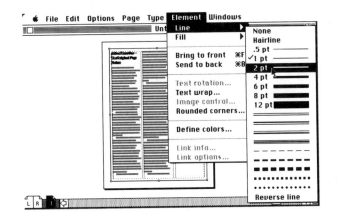

Figure 14. *Again, under the* **Element** *menu, use the Line sub-menu to set the thickness of the outline to 2 points.*

5. Insert intercolumn rules of 2 points thickness.

Intercolumn rules are inserted using the perpendicular-line drawing tool. Select this tool now from the Toolbox (Figure 15).

Before we create the intercolumn guides, try this helper. Turn the *Snap to guides* command from the **Options** menu off. It is off when there is no tick alongside it. This ensures that the line drawn does not snap to either side of the column guide, but is drawn down the middle. Move the mouse cursor to the top and between the first set of column guides (Figure 15), hold the mouse button down, drag the mouse to the bottom of this column, and release the button (Figure 16). Repeat this operation for the second set of column guides.

Set the line thickness for the intercolumn rules to 2 points as shown in Figure 17. Make sure the lines are selected to do this.

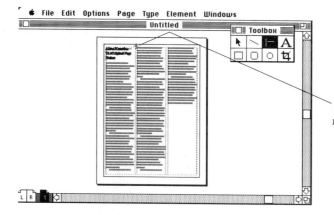

Figure 15. *To create intercolumn rules, select the perpendicular-line drawing tool, and move it to the middle and top of the first set of column guides.*

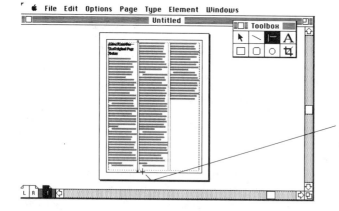

Figure 16. *Hold down the mouse button and drag it down to the bottom of the column. Repeat for the second intercolumn rule.*

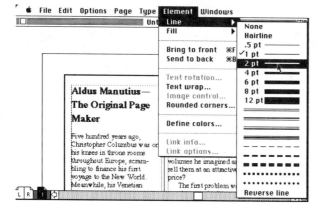

Figure 17. *Set the line thickness for the intercolumn rules to 2 points.*

6. Change the first paragraph heading to 24 points bold Palatino.

This step has to be achieved with the text cursor selected. Select this tool from the Toolbox (Figure 18).

To select the first paragraph heading, use the triple-click method. Move the mouse cursor anywhere over the heading and click the mouse button three times in succession. The paragraph will be highlighted in reverse video (Figure 18).

Figure 18. Select the heading to change its specifications.

Select the *Type specs* command from the **Type** menu to set the specifications for this paragraph (Figure 19). Set up the dialog box that appears on selecting this command as shown in Figure 20. The new heading is shown in Figure 21.

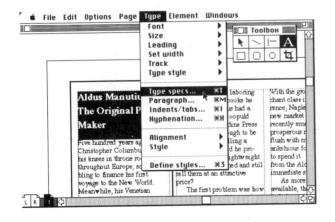

Figure 19. The Type specs *command can change the specs for the text.*

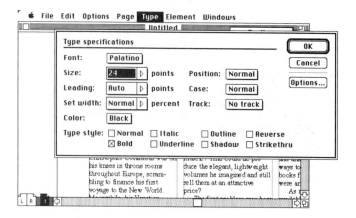

Figure 20. *Set up the* Type specs *dialog box as illustrated (Palatino Font and 24 points size).*

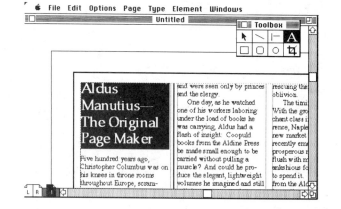

Figure 21. *The new heading resulting from the settings of Figure 20.*

7. Create a box behind the heading using a 2 point outline and a 10% fill background.

Select the square-corner drawing tool from the Toolbox, and draw a rectangle to completely cover the first paragraph as shown in Figure 22. Use the *Line* sub-menu from the **Element** menu to set the outline at 2 points (Figure 23), and the *Fill* sub-menu to set the background for this graphic to 10% (Figure 24).

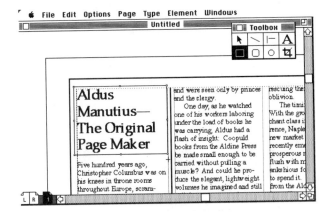

Figure 22. Select the square-corner drawing tool, hold the mouse button down, above and to the left of the heading, and drag it to the bottom right of the heading.

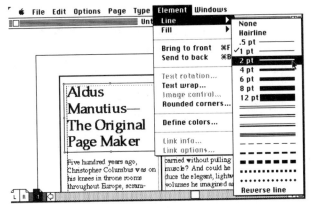

Figure 23. Set the thickness of the box outline to 2 points.

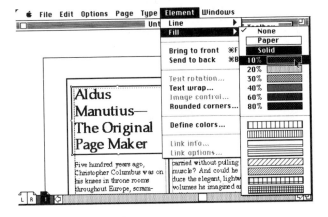

Figure 24. Also make sure that the shade for the rectangle is set to 10%.

At this stage the rectangle will be sitting on top of the text, with the text unreadable (Figure 25). Make sure the rectangle is selected, and choose the *Send to back* command from the **Element** menu (Figure 26). The text will immediately appear over the graphic (Figure 27).

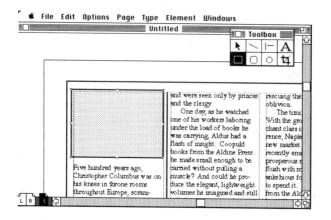

Figure 25. *Don't panic if your heading disappears.*

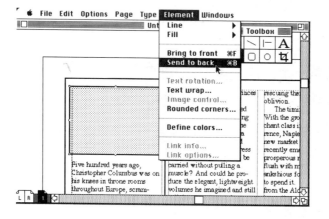

Figure 26. *Make sure the rectangle is still selected, and choose the* Send to back *command from the* **Element** *menu.*

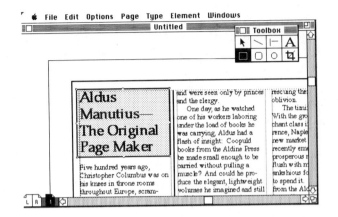

Figure 27. The heading re-appears once the shaded rectangle is sent behind the text.

8. *Draw a box in the bottom right-hand corner of the third column 2 inches high, with a 2 point thickness border.*

To ensure that we get the vertical dimension of 2 inches correctly placed, we have chosen to first show rulers through the *Rulers* command in the **Options** menu. We have then moved in *Actual size* view to the bottom right-hand column, and set up two ruler guides, as shown in Figure 28. A horizontal guide is set at the bottom margin of 10 inches. Another guide is set at 8 inches for our 2 inch box height.

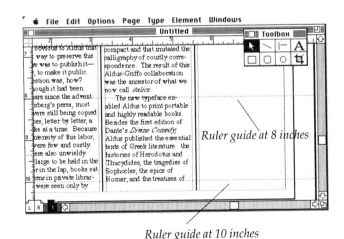

Figure 28. We are now positioned in Actual size view at the bottom right-hand corner of the page. Two ruler guides are set up at 10 and 8 inches, to help draw the 2 inches high box at the bottom of this last column.

Ruler guide at 10 inches

257

By using the square-corner drawing tool, draw the box as shown in Figure 29. The *Line* sub-menu was then used to adjust the border thickness to 2 points. You may wish to turn *Snap to guides* back on in the **Options** menu to simplify the drawing of this box.

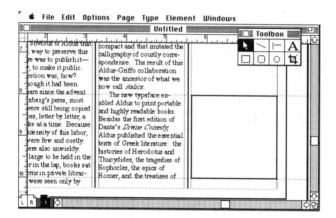

Figure 29. The box has now been drawn using the ruler and column guide as alignment tools. If the Snap to guides command was on, the box outlines would have automatically snapped to the correct positions. The border was also set to 2 points thickness using the Line sub-menu.

9. *Load in the Practice graphic file from the Basic Lesson folder, and place it initially into the Pasteboard area to the right of the page. Proportionally reduce its size to fit into the box of step 8 with white space all around, and then move it into this box.*

In Figure 30 we have reverted to the *Fit in window* view, and moved our page to the left. This is done by moving the white horizontal scroll bar, highlighted in Figure 30, to the right. The Practice graphic picture is selected,

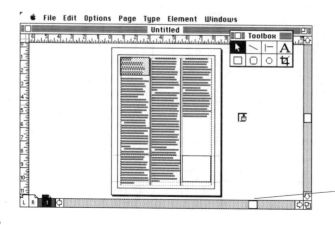

Figure 30. This is the Fit in window *view with the page moved to the left. Practice graphic has been selected from the Basic Lesson folder using the* Place *command, and the mouse cursor is positioned at a convenient location to load the picture onto the Pasteboard.*

This is pulled to the right to move the page to the left.

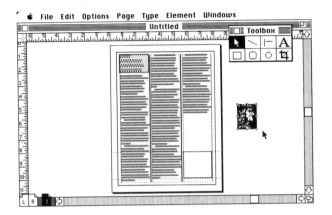

Figure 31. The mouse has been clicked and the picture is loaded onto the Pasteboard area.

through the *Place* command in the Basic Lesson folder (within the Tutorial folder), and the cursor is positioned as shown in Figure 30. At this point all you need do is click the mouse to get the result of Figure 31.

The picture now needs to be proportionately reduced to fit into the box. This is achieved by selecting the picture (it is normally selected after loading), holding down the Shift key, grabbing the bottom right handle with the mouse button down, and diagonally dragging upwards and to the left. The result of this operation is indicated in Figure 32.

Now place the mouse in the middle of the picture, hold down the button, and move it into the box as shown in Figure 33. With this figure we are back to *Actual size* view for a better look.

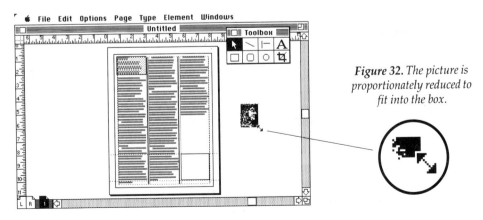

Figure 32. The picture is proportionately reduced to fit into the box.

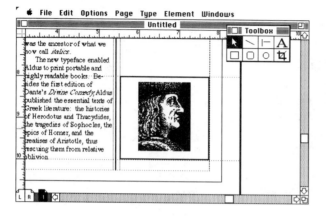

Figure 33. Actual size *view of the picture now placed inside the box.*

10. Select the box and the graphic from steps 8 and 9, delete from page 1, and place them into the top left-hand corner of page 2.

To achieve this last operation, we need to go through the following steps:

- Insert a new page, as our publication is only one page long.
- Select and cut the picture and the box from page 1.
- Move to the new page 2.
- Paste the picture into page 2. It will initially be pasted into the center of the page.
- Move the picture to the top of the first column.

Figures 34 to 39 show the steps that are required.

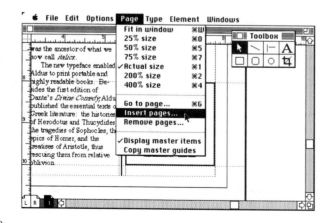

Figure 34. *The* Insert pages *command is selected from the* **Page** *menu.*

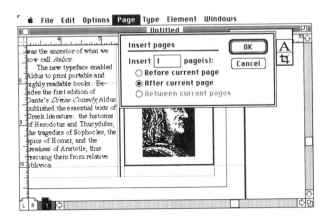

Figure 35. The Insert pages *dialog box is then completed as shown.*

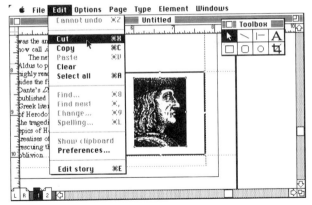

Figure 36. The picture and box were both selected and the Cut *command chosen from the* **Edit** *menu. The simplest way to select both items together is to hold down the Shift key to select the second item. If you have trouble selecting the box because it is aligned with ruler and margin guides, hold down the Command key as you select.*

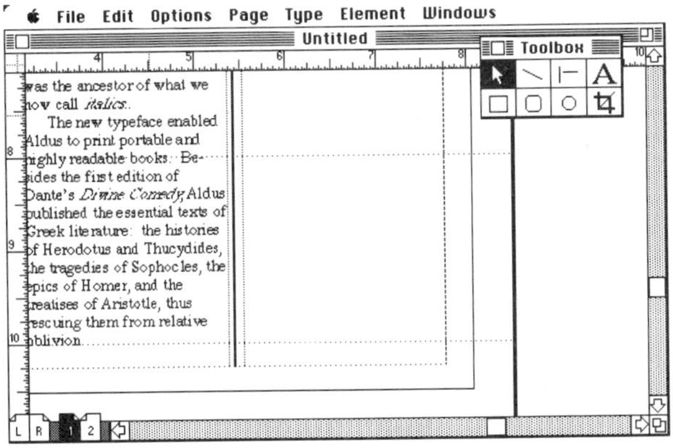

Figure 37. After the operation of Figure 36, the picture and the box are both deleted from page 1.

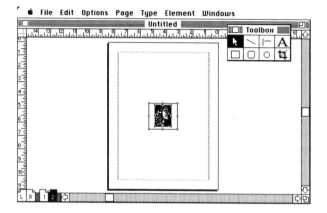

*Figure 38. We have moved to page 2 and used the **Paste** command to place the picture and box in the middle of the page..*

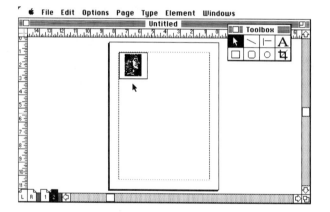

Figure 39. To finish this final step, we simply grab the picture with the mouse, hold the button down, and move it to its required position in the top left-hand corner. The mouse is then released.

Module 7

Importing Graphics

Importing Graphics

A large variety of graphics programs can be used in conjunction with PageMaker to create very professional presentations with your Macintosh. In this module we will look at the types of graphics we can import, how we import them, how we size them, crop them, move them, and alter them. In a later module we look at more complex things that can be done with imported graphics including working with irregular wraparounds and shading.

There are four different types of graphics that can be imported into PageMaker. The type of graphic that you import depends generally on the type of graphics package that creates it.

Paint-type or *bit-map* graphics are the pictures that come from MacPaint-like packages. They are generally much lower resolution than other types of drawings, usually a maximum resolution of 72 dpi (dots-per-inch).

These pictures are made up of a rectangular array of dots. PageMaker can read any documents saved in this format.

Draw-type or *object-oriented* graphics are graphics imported in the PICT format. Two PICT formats are available - PICT and PICT 2. PICT 2 has additional capabilities such as high resolution color.

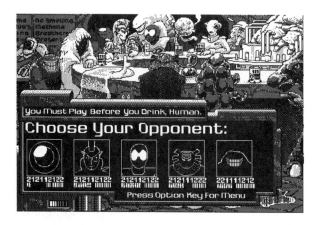

Figure 1. This graphic has been imported from FullPaint, a MacPaint-like graphics paint program. It produces images at 72 dpi — the screen resolution of the Macintosh.

Programs that produce these type of graphics include CA Draw, CA Graph, MacDraw, and others. PICT images are output device resolution dependent, meaning that the resolution they print at depends on the output device. These are generally much higher quality pictures than can be achieved with Paint-type programs.

Figure 2. This graphic, in PICT format, has been created in CA Draw. This image can be resized and still maintain crystal clear resolution.

EPS graphics are quite possibly the highest quality graphics of the lot — produced by graphics programs such as Adobe Illustrator, Aldus Freehand, and CA Draw. These types of graphics use PostScript code to create the pictures — so that unless a screen image is created when the actual graphic is created (in TIFF or PICT format), only a box will appear on screen. Most packages do, however, create a screen image to match the PostScript code. These graphics are limited in resolution only by the output device.

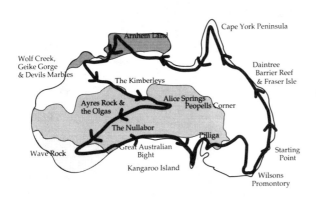

Figure 3. Both text and graphics can be manipulated and created in EPS format graphics. This image has been imported from Adobe Illustrator.

265

Scanned images are usually those in the TIFF format — although they can be imported in other formats. These images usually print at a maximum resolution of 300 dpi, and are created normally by the specialist scanning programs that come with the many scanners available in halftone, grayscale, or color formats.

Figure 4. *A TIFF image.*

Importing graphics

Before you can import any graphics into PageMaker, you must make sure that the graphics are in the correct format for importation. Using a program like CA Draw does not automatically mean that the graphic will slip directly into PageMaker. By default, the image will be saved in the CA Draw format — not the PICT or EPS format required (Figure 5). Most other programs also have a choice of what format to save the graphic under.

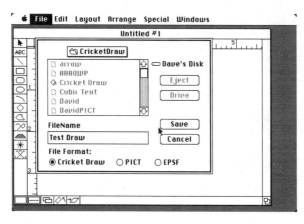

Figure 5. *Note that in this CA Draw Save dialog box, there are several formats that can be selected to save the graphic in. By default, the image will be saved in CA Draw format, which will not come into PageMaker. Either PICT or EPS file format should be chosen.*

All graphics are imported into PageMaker the same way as are text files — via the *Place* command in the **File** menu. Once imported, however, the mouse cursor takes on a different appearance—depending on the type of graphic that is imported. Figures 7 through 10 indicate the different mouse appearances, depending upon the type of graphic being imported.

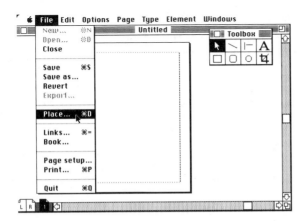

Figure 6. The Place *command is used to import all files into Page-Maker — both text and all varieties of graphics.*

Figure 7. An imported Paint-type graphic changes the mouse cursor to this.

Figure 8. A PICT graphic changes to this...

Figure 9. ...an EPS format file to this...

Figure 10. ...and a TIFF scanned image to this.

Once the mouse cursor has changed its appearance to indicate a graphics file has been loaded into memory, as shown in Figure 11, there are two ways to place it. The first way, preferable for text files, but definitely not for graphics files, is simply to click the mouse button where you want the graphic to load. The graphic will certainly load, but could be very large, and quite probably nowhere near the size that you want it to be. Extra time must then be spent to resize the picture.

In Figures 11 and 12, we are loading in the Practice graphic from the Basic Lesson folder within the Tutorial folder, using the above method. Figures 13 and 14 use a different method described on the following page.

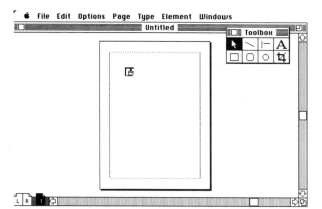

Figure 11. The easier, but not necessarily the better, way to load a graphic from this point is simply to position the mouse cursor and click the button.

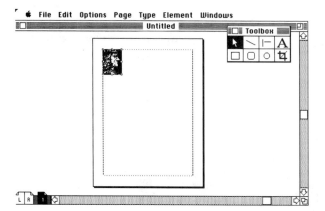

Figure 12. We were lucky here in that the graphic appeared at this size. Often the graphic appears much larger than this, causing extra work to resize it.

The better way to load a graphic file onto the page is to pretend that you are working with the square-corner drawing tool, even though the mouse cursor is loaded with one of the graphic options shown in Figures 7 through 10. You then draw a box exactly the same size as you would like the picture. Press the mouse button and drag the mouse down and across the screen (Figure 13) — release it only when the box is big enough. A temporary box will appear as the mouse button is held down. When the mouse button is released, the graphic will appear in that box (Figure 14).

With this approach, the graphic may not initially be in the correct proportion. See the section later in this module titled **Proportional resizing**, to return it to the correct aspect ratio.

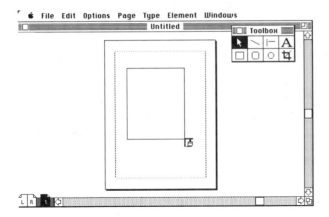

Figure 13. The best way to load the graphic is to draw an imaginary box the size you would like to see the graphic. This is done by holding down the mouse button and drawing a box.

Figure 14. Once the mouse button has been released, the graphic is loaded at exactly the same size as the box.

Moving graphics

Once the graphic is placed on the screen, chances are it may have to be moved from one area of the screen to another. To do this, hold the mouse button down inside the graphic, and move the mouse to the new position. If you move the mouse immediately after holding it down, only a box representing the graphic outline will be moved with the mouse (Figure 15). However, if you keep the mouse still for a few seconds before moving it, the entire picture will move with the mouse (Figure 16).

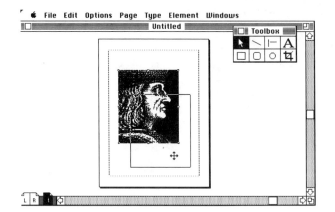

Figure 15. Here we held the mouse button down on the graphic and moved the mouse immediately. Hence only the outline of the graphic has been moved. The graphic will take up its new position as the mouse button is released.

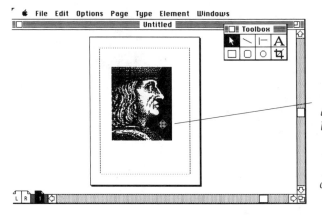

Figure 16. We are in the process here of moving this graphic across the screen. Locate the mouse cursor and see its shape. This move was achieved by holding the mouse button on the graphic, keeping it still for a few seconds, and moving the mouse. This time, the actual graphic, not a box outline, moves with the mouse.

Simple wraparounds

Before we discuss resizing and cropping the imported images, let's look at the options for setting the text wraparound for this graphic — or simply controlling how the text flows around this picture. This is achieved via the *Text wrap* command in the **Element** menu (Figure 17). This command also works the same way for graphics created within PageMaker.

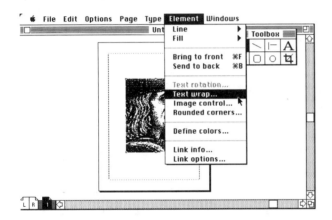

Figure 17. Simple text wraparound control is achieved via the Text *wrap command.*

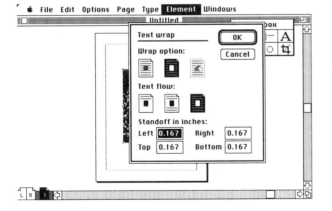

Figure 18. The Text wrap dialog box.

Under the *Wrap option* heading, you have a choice of three options. Within this dialog box, you may only choose between the first two. This choice is simple — do you want the text to flow around the graphic or not? If the answer is no, then select the first box (Figure 19). When this is done, all other commands in this dialog box become unusable and you are finished with this command. However, if your answer is yes, select the second box (Figures 20 and 21). The third box is explained in the **Advanced Picture Formatting** Module.

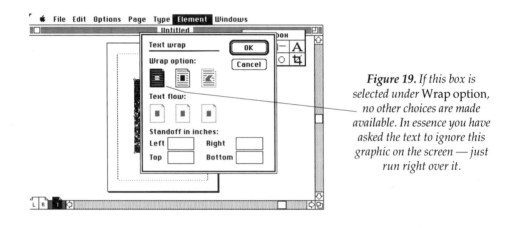

Figure 19. If this box is selected under Wrap *option, no other choices are made available. In essence you have asked the text to ignore this graphic on the screen — just run right over it.*

When the middle *Wrap option* box is selected, you must make a choice as to the *Text flow* (that is, the three page icons in the middle of the dialog box). Under this heading there are three options also, which are all very straightforward (see Figures 20 and 21). The first choice causes text to stop flowing when it reaches a graphic, but not continue unless manually. The second choice causes the text to completely jump the graphic — that is, stop when it reaches it, yet continue underneath (Figure 20). The third box will cause the text to flow around the graphic — not irregularly, but straight up and down the outsides of the graphic (Figure 21).

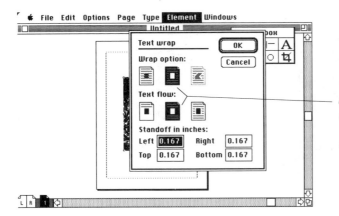

Figure 20. When the middle boxes from both the **Wrap** *option and* Text flow *have been selected, text will jump over a graphic — not down its sides, but completely jump the graphic. Alternatively, selecting the first box for* Text flow *in this instance causes the text to stop whenever it came to a graphic.*

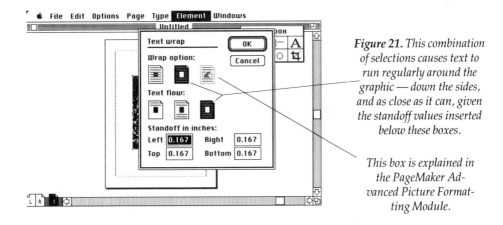

Figure 21. This combination of selections causes text to run regularly around the graphic — down the sides, and as close as it can, given the standoff values inserted below these boxes.

This box is explained in the PageMaker Advanced Picture Formatting Module.

If you chose the middle *Wrap option* (Figures 20 and 21), you must also define a *Standoff* for this graphic. This is the area around the graphic that the text cannot flow into — in effect a margin for the graphic. Insert your own figures here or keep the default values.

If you selected this command without a graphic being selected, then everything you set up in that command will become the default. If, however, a graphic was selected, the settings will only apply to that particular graphic.

273

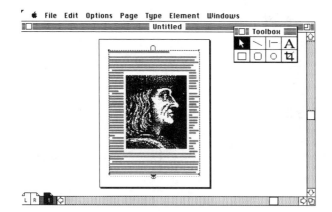

***Figure* 22.** *Here we see the practical result of a graphical wrap-around. The graphic here was set up as in the dialog box of Figure 21.*

***Figure* 23.** *Once the wrap-around has been set up, the graphic can still be moved around and the text will reflow around it.*

Graphic resizing

Any imported graphics are resized the same way as graphics created in PageMaker. Each graphic contains six handles around its edge, which are used to resize that graphic in the direction of the handle. However, you must be careful when doing this.

Depending on the *Wrap option* you set for this graphic in the *Text wrap* command, you may have two sets of handles around the graphic. The inner handles are the normal graphic selection handles, and the outer handles are associated with the middle *Text wrap* option of Figures 20 and 21. These outer handles, connected by a dotted line, indicate that the *Wrap option* is selected. In the module, **Advanced Picture Formatting**, we will be looking at the use of these outer handles, so make sure that you select the inner ones. If you would like to get rid of the outer handles altogether, move to the *Text wrap* command, and click on the first *Wrap option* as for Figure 19. The outside handles for that graphic will then disappear.

Figures 24 through 26 give examples of graphic resizing.

Figure 24. Resizing the graphic is achieved using the handles that appear around the selected graphic. The pointer tool must also be selected.

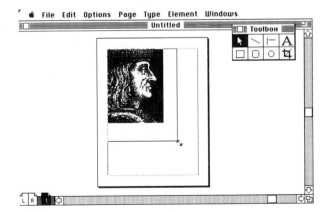

Figure 25. Hold the mouse button down on any handle until the mouse cursor changes to a two-sided arrow. Whatever direction the arrows are pointing in are the directions that the graphic can be resized. Here we are resizing it diagonally.

Figure 26. Holding the mouse button down on a side arrow allows us to resize the graphic horizontally.

Proportional resizing

If the Shift key is held down as the graphic is resized, it will snap to its correct aspect ratio from which it was created. Make sure you let go of the mouse button before the Shift key. If you hold down the Command key as well as the Shift key, the graphic will be resized according to your printer's resolution, so that it will look better when printed. Note that the graphic snaps to certain size increments when the Command key is held down.

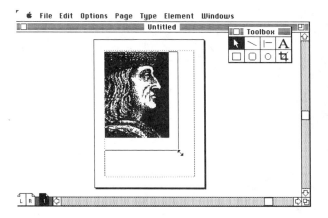

Figure 27. Hold down the Shift key and the Command key if necessary to proportionally resize a graphic. It will snap to its correct aspect ratio and size (according to your printer's resolution).

Figure 28. *After Figure 27, release the mouse button first, and then the graphic itself will snap to the correct size.*

Graphics cropping

Graphics are cropped (you may find it easier to think of it as chopped) almost the same way as they are resized, except that a different tool is used. The cropping tool is located in the bottom right-hand corner of the Toolbox (Figure 29).

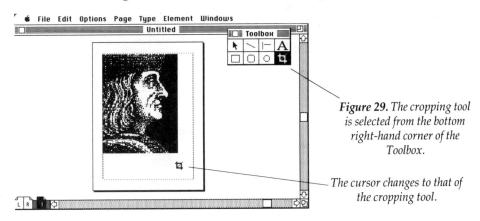

Figure 29. *The cropping tool is selected from the bottom right-hand corner of the Toolbox.*

The cursor changes to that of the cropping tool.

Once this tool is selected, locate the graphic you would like to crop. Don't worry, the removal of parts of graphics is never permanent using this method — any hidden part of the graphic can be recovered at any later stage. Click once on the graphic to be cropped, this time using the cropping tool instead of the pointer tool to make sure it is selected. Now decide which side you would like to start cropping.

Locate one handle on the side of the graphic, position the cropping tool over it with the handle showing through, and hold the mouse button down. Keep the mouse still for a few seconds until PageMaker turns the cursor into a two-headed arrow, and then move the mouse button towards the center of the graphic. This is much the same way as we used to resize the graphic — yet note that there is a dramatic difference as the mouse is moved. Depending on which handle of the graphic you select, you will be able to chop off different parts of the graphic.

We have selected the right middle handle in Figure 30 and are in the process of cropping towards the center of the graphic. Figure 31 shows the result of cropping, both from the top and the right.

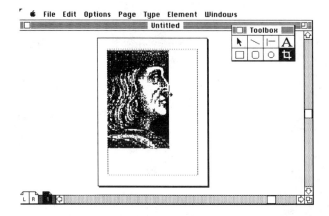

Figure 30. Pretend that you are going to resize the graphic, yet use the cropping tool. The difference will soon become apparent.

To reverse the crop at a later stage, reselect the cropping tool, select the cropped side's handle, and move the mouse away from the graphic.

Once a graphic has been cropped, another technique can be used to alter what has been cropped. This is particularly effective if the graphic has been cropped considerably. Position the cropping tool in the center of a cropped graphic, hold down the mouse button, and move it around. The cursor changes to a hand (Figure 32). Rather than the entire graphic being moved, the image itself is moved, as if behind a window — we are merely altering which part of the graphic is showing and which is hiding.

Any cropped graphic can still be moved, resized, and have the text wrap altered.

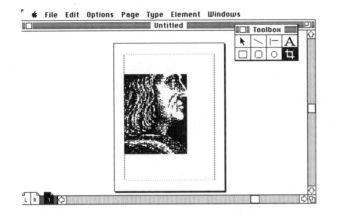

Figure 31. We have cropped this graphic from both the top and the right-hand side.

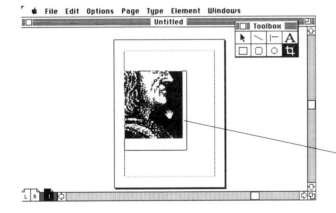

Figure 32. We can move the cropped graphic around, as if behind a window, by holding down the cropping tool positioned in the middle of a cropped graphic, and moving the mouse around.

Note the cursor changes to a hand.

Figure 33. After a graphic has been cropped, it can still be resized, moved, and have wraparounds applied to it.

Module 7 Exercise

Importing Graphics

Module 7 Exercise
Importing Graphics

In this exercise we are going to import a photograph, then manipulate it by resizing, moving, and cropping it. We will also load some text to automatically wrap around the graphic.

This training material is structured so that people of all levels of expertise with PageMaker can use it to gain maximum benefit. To do this, we have structured this material so that the bare exercise is listed below this paragraph on just one page, with no hints. The following pages contain the steps needed to complete this exercise for those that need additional prompting. The **Importing Graphics** module should be referenced if you need further help or explanations.

Module 7 exercise steps

1.   *Load the picture Practice graphic onto an A4 or Letter page (your choice).*

2.   *Resize this picture so that it measures 2.5 inches wide by 3.25 inches high exactly.*

3.   *Resize the picture proportionally so that it stays 2.5 inches wide.*

4.   *Crop the picture so that only the face is showing.*

5.   *Load the text file Lead Story into two columns on the opening page.*

6.   *Move the graphic into the middle of the screen.*

7.   *Make Lead Story wrap around all sides of the graphic.*

8.   *Make space for a border around the graphic, and then create a border.*

The steps for completing this exercise are on the following pages.

The steps in detail

1. Load the picture Practice graphic onto an A4 or Letter page (your choice).

The file Practice graphic is located in the Basic Lesson folder in the Tutorial folder. Locate and load this picture through the *Place* command in the **File** menu. Load this file onto the page by either clicking the mouse button once, or holding the mouse button down and drawing an imaginary square.

See Figures 1, 2, and 3 to perform these steps.

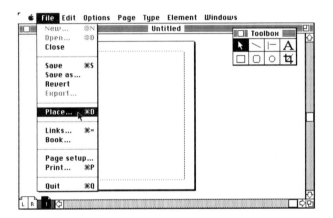

Figure 1. *Select the* Place *command from the* **File** *menu to load the file Practice graphic.*

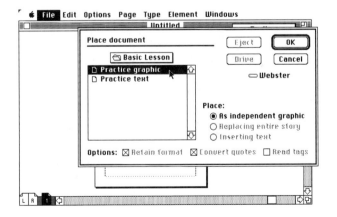

Figure 2. *Select the file Practice graphic from the Basic Lesson folder.*

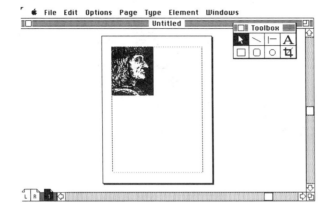

Figure 3. *The file Practice graphic is now loaded on the page — the actual size that it appears on the page depends on the method you used to load it. In this case we drew an imaginary box to the size we wanted.*

2. Resize this picture so that it measures 2.5 inches wide by 3.25 inches high.

To make sure the graphic is the correct size, you should first invoke the Page-Maker rulers. Using these rulers, and the accompanying guides, create a grid on the page of 2.5 by 3.25 inches. Figures 4 to 6 provide explanations.

Now, grab the bottom right-hand handle and resize the image (Figure 7) so that the bottom right-hand corner snaps to the bottom right-hand corner of the grid (Figure 8). The picture is now exactly 2.5 inches by 3.25 inches.

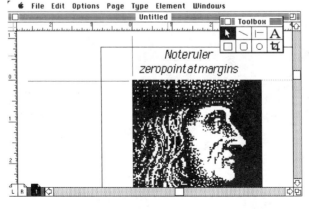

Figure 4. *To create the grid to contain the file we must first perform a few steps — use the* Rulers *command to display the rulers (the* Preferences *command can be used to ensure inches are used in the ruler), and move the zero point of the ruler to the top left margin of the page.*
The zero point of the ruler is moved by holding down the mouse button in the area where the two rulers intersect, and dragging the mouse to the spot on the screen where the new zero point will be. We have also moved to Actual size *view to see the graphic better.*

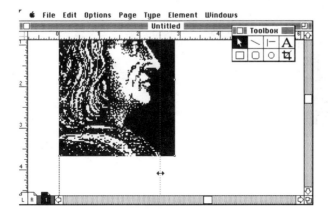

Figure 5. After the zero point of the ruler is in the correct spot, pull a ruler guide from both the vertical and horizontal rulers to align with the desired measurement. Here we have just pulled a ruler guide from the vertical ruler to align with the 2.5 inch horizontal ruler mark. Hold the mouse button down in a ruler to first obtain a guide.

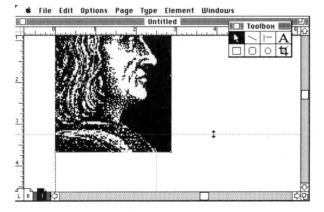

Figure 6. Here we have added a horizontal ruler guide at the 3.25 inch mark. (Make sure your zero point in the ruler is at the same place as ours.) Note your picture may be bigger or smaller than ours, depending upon how you loaded it.

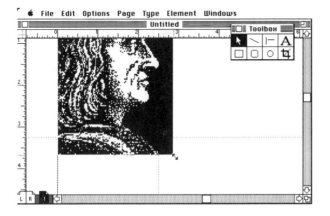

Figure 7. We can now resize the picture (make it smaller or bigger - depending on its original size) to fit it into the grid we defined. We have moved down the page slightly to see the bottom of the picture (while still seeing the grid), and began resizing by holding the mouse button down on the bottom right-hand handle and moving this corner up or down to the intersection of the two ruler guides.

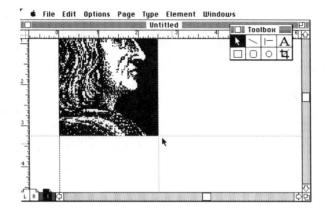

Figure 8. We have now reached the intersection of the two ruler guides. The picture has now been resized to exactly 2.5 by 3.25 inches.

3. Resize the picture proportionally so that it stays 2.5 inches wide.

Although we have resized the picture so that it is exactly 2.5 inches by 3.25 inches, it is not necessarily in its correct proportion. To make sure that it is, we must resize the picture with the Shift key held down. Once the picture is in the grid, hold the mouse button on the bottom right-hand corner of the picture, as though you were about to resize it. Now, with the mouse button held down, also hold down the Shift key.

The picture moves to its true proportion as shown in Figure 9. Note the slight gap now showing above our 3.25 inch horizontal ruler.

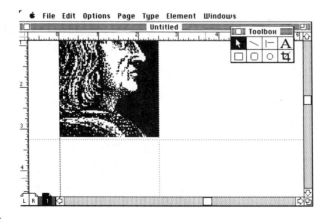

Figure 9. The true proportion of the picture at 2.5 inches wide. Although similar to what it was before, this is the result of holding down the mouse button on the bottom right-hand corner handle of Figure 8, and holding down the Shift key. The mouse was not moved at all, and was released before the Shift key was.

4. Crop the picture so that only the face is showing.

Before we can crop the picture, select the cropping tool from the Toolbox.

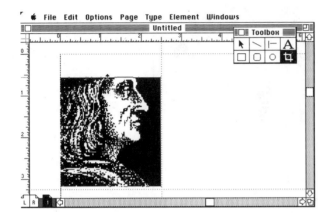

Figure 10. *Select the cropping tool from the bottom right-hand corner of the Toolbox, and start cropping from the top.*

Select the picture simply by clicking on it once with the cropping tool. From here, act as if you are going to resize the picture. Hold down the cropping tool so that the middle of this tool is over the top middle handle (Figure 10). From here, you may have to wait a second or two before you can do anything as PageMaker readies itself for the crop. After the double-arrowed vertical mouse cursor appears (Figure 10), keep the mouse button held down and move towards the center of the picture. The picture will not resize, but will be cropped.

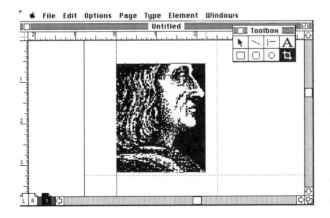

Figure 11. *We have now cropped from the top and the right.*

After cropping from one side, move to the other handles and cut additional sides off the picture. Continue cropping the picture from all four sides until only the man's face is visible (Figure 12).

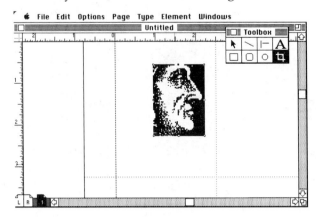

Figure 12. Here we have cropped the picture from all sides — leaving only the man's face.

5. *Load the text file Lead Story into two columns on the opening page.*

Make sure that you have two columns on the page (by using the *Column guides* command in the **Options** menu). Change to *Fit in window* view as shown in Figure 13.

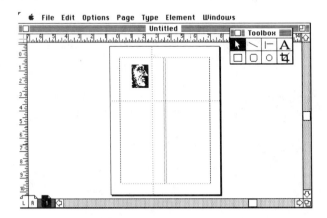

Figure 13. Move back to Fit in window *view to load the text file. Add two columns to the page via the* Column guides *command in the* **Options** *menu.*

Use the *Place* command from the **File** menu to look into the Tutorial folder and find the Lead Story file in the Lesson 2 folder (Figure 14). Select this file and flow it into the two columns on the page (Figure 15). Choose either manual or *Autoflow* methods.

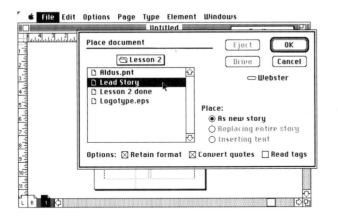

Figure 14. We are loading the
file Lead Story from the
Lesson 2 folder.

How the text reacts when it comes to the picture will depend on the setting
for the picture wraparound before starting this exercise. So far, however, it
doesn't really matter. In Figure 15, the text has run through the graphic.

6. Move the graphic into the middle of the screen.

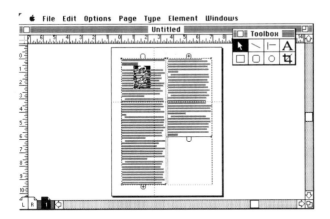

Figure 15. In our case, after
loading the file, the text has
run over the graphic.
Whether or not yours does
this does not really matter at
this stage — although it
does mean that the Com-
mand key should be held
down on the keyboard to
select the graphic for step 6.

Select the picture with the pointer tool and move it into the middle of the
screen (Figure 16). The text may reflow around the picture. If the text flows
over the picture as it has in our example, you will have to hold down the
Command key as you attempt to select the graphic.

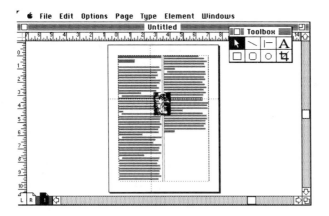

Figure 16. Here we have moved the graphic down to the middle of the page. Remember, if the text is over the graphic, you will have to hold down the Command key as you select the graphic.

7. Make Lead Story wrap around all sides of the graphic.

To do this, make sure that the picture remains selected (if it is not, simply click on it while pressing the Command key). Now, move to the *Text wrap* command in the **Element** menu (Figure 17).

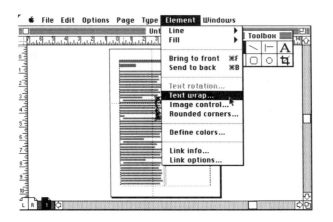

Figure 17. Making sure the graphic is still selected, choose the Text wrap *command from the* **Element** *menu.*

Within the dialog box that appears (Figure 18), set up the wraparound so that the text will wrap around all sides of the picture. See the settings of Figure 18 if you are unsure how this works.

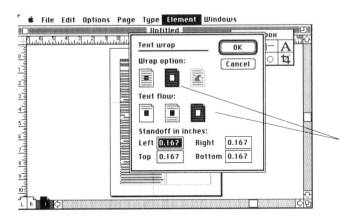

Figure 18. *Within this dialog box, make sure these options are selected. The top option ensures that the text wraps around the graphic, and the bottom option determines how the text wraps around the graphic.*

After setting up the dialog box as in Figure 18, your page should look similar to Figure 19 (in *Actual size* view).

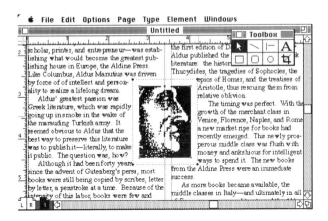

Figure 19. *Here the graphic is set at Actual view, and the text has indeed wrapped around the graphic.*

8. Make space for a border around the graphic, and then create a border.

To make space for a border around the picture we must once again move to the *Text wrap* command in the **Element** menu. It may be likely that the space for the border has already been created, but we will look at how to alter the space around the picture. Figure 20 shows the *Text wrap* dialog box again.

Notice the space above, below, and around the picture in Figure 19. This will be the forced white area around the graphic. Increase this slightly to provide a larger area around the picture for our border. Change the settings for *Standoff in inches* from the Figure 18 dialog box to those shown in Figure 20.

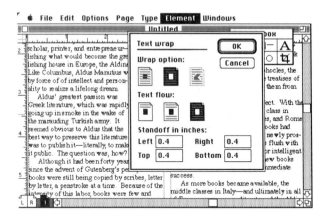

Figure 20. *Note the figures at the bottom of this dialog box that determine how close the text can flow to all sides of the graphic. We have increased these figures slightly from Figure 18 to push the text further away from the graphic. Figure 21 shows the result.*

Once you OK these changes, you will be returned back to the page. Move to *Actual size* view so that you can see the picture and the text (Figure 21). You will now see an increased amount of white space around the picture.

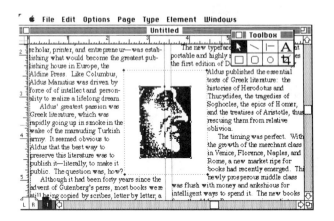

Figure 21. *The result: quite a distinct amount of white space between the photo and the text — equivalent to the numbers we inserted in Figure 20.*

Now grab the rectangle drawing tool from the toolbox, and draw a rectangle around the picture (Figure 22). If the rectangle has a shade or a color, it will overlay the picture. If it does, and you cannot see the picture, choose the *Send to back* command from the **Element** menu. You may, after choosing this command, like to apply a shade, color, and/or line thickness to the outline. The result is shown in Figure 23.

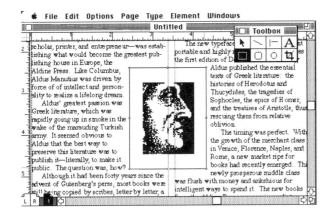

Figure 22. Select one of the graphics tools from the Toolbox (in this case the rectangle), and draw a box around the picture. If the box you create sits on top of the graphic and you cannot see it, immediately choose the Send to back *command from the* **Element** *menu.*

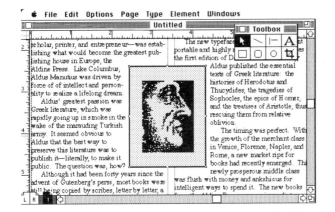

Figure 23. We increased the thickness of the line using the Line *sub-menu, and gave the box a background shade using the* Fill *sub-menu (and sent it to the back), to make it look a little different.*

Module 8

Master Pages

Master Pages

Theory

Master Pages are used when text, graphics, page numbers, headers, footers, and whatever, must be repeated on many pages throughout the document. They save having to repaste or re-create the same item on multiple pages.

Master page icons

Along the bottom left-hand corner of the screen are the page number icons. We have looked at these icons before as we changed, created, and deleted pages. However, there are two extra icons that read L and R. There will only be an R icon if your document is not set up as a Double-sided publication in the *Page setup* command from the **File** menu. These icons stand for the left and right master pages. Once you click on either of these icons, you will see either one or two blank pages; for two pages to show, the Facing pages option must be selected from the *Page setup* command. These pages are called the master pages and on the screen they look like any other (Figure 1).

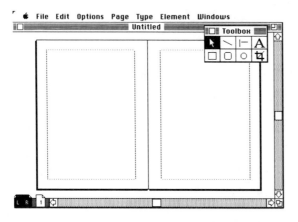

Figure 1. Note the L and R icons selected in the bottom left-hand corner of the screen: the master pages.

These master pages are exactly like any others in the way graphics, text, columns, etc., are applied to them. Anything you place on these pages, however, will repeat on all pages throughout the publication. These pages do not print. To print the contents of a master page, you first display them on a standard page and print from there.

Document changes and guides

Master pages are much like any others — they can have columns applied, have ruler guides inserted, and have their margins altered, either as individual left or right pages, or together. If we apply three columns to the right master page, all right-hand pages in the publication, already created or not, will use these three columns. The same applies to the left-hand page. Consequently, if every page in your 100-page book needs three columns, you only need define these columns on the master pages. You can change these column guides individually on each page after the master page(s) have been set. This flexibility allows you to change any specific page to look a little different from the others.

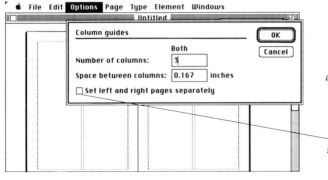

Figure 2. Here we are defining the number of column guides for both left and right master pages. This dialog box allows both left and right to be defined in one operation.

If we click the bottom left-hand square, we get the slightly different dialog box of Figure 3.

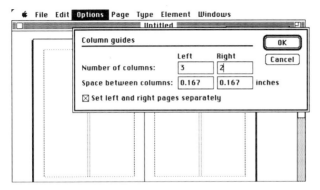

Figure 3. In this instance, it is now possible to set different columns for left and right pages. For example, we have selected 3 columns for left pages and 2 columns for the right pages.

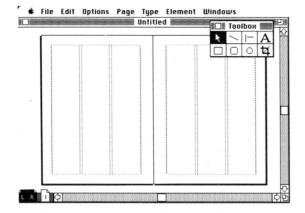

Figure 4. These column guides are a result of the Figure 2 operation. Three columns were defined for both left and right pages.

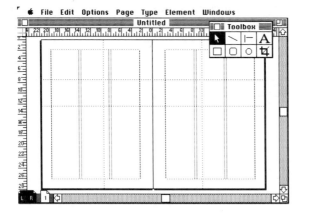

Figure 5. Two horizontal and one vertical ruler guide have been included on the master pages. These will now, like the column guides, appear on each page.

Any non-printing margin guides and/or ruler guides added to these pages will also be seen on all corresponding pages in the publication (Figure 5).

Text and graphics additions

As you might have guessed, any text or graphic placed on the master page(s) will repeat on every page. For example, a company logo, motto, and/or address and phone number can be placed on one or both of the master pages. These will then repeat exactly as they appear on the master pages on every page in the document.

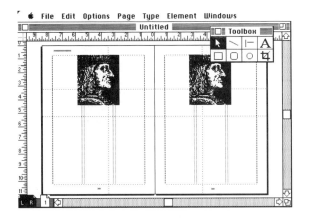

Figure 6. We have just placed a graphic onto both master pages and sized it as shown.

Headers, footers, and page numbers

Headers and footers are the repeating bits of information that appear at the top and bottom of every page in a book or magazine. This often includes such items as the book name, chapter name, chapter number, date, and/or the page number. To define these for a document, simply create them any way you like on the master page(s).

In Figure 7, we are positioned in *Actual size* view at the top left corner of the left master page. A heading that we want repeated on each page has been keyed in.

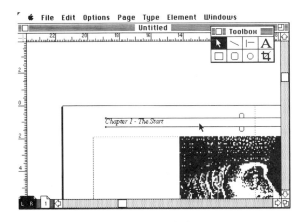

Figure 7. A header — "Chapter 1 — The Start" — has been keyed in and placed just above the border on the top left-hand corner of the left master page. We have also keyed in the same header on the top right-hand corner of the right master page.

Page numbers, however, require a slightly different technique. Simply typing a number on the master page will result in that number being printed on every page. Therefore, instead of typing the actual number, hold down the Command and Option keys and type a P (you must first select the text tool from the Toolbox and place it on the page where you want the page number to appear). On the master page, this will appear as LM on the left master and RM on the right master (Figure 8), but will appear as the correct number on all other pages (Figure 9). The correct number is taken as the number that appears on that page's icon box. To alter the number that this uses, select the *Page setup* command in the **File** menu, and see the instructions given in Figure 10.

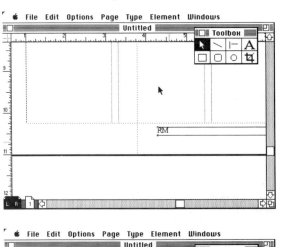

Figure 8. An automatic page number has been added to the bottom of a master page. It always shows as LM on the left page and RM on the right page.

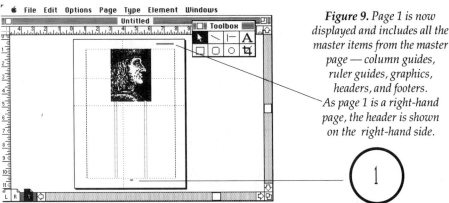

Figure 9. Page 1 is now displayed and includes all the master items from the master page — column guides, ruler guides, graphics, headers, and footers. As page 1 is a right-hand page, the header is shown on the right-hand side.

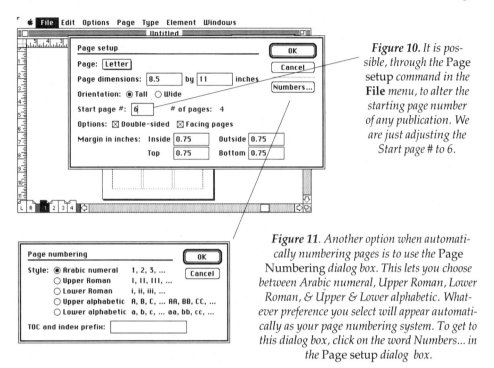

Figure 10. It is possible, through the Page setup *command in the* **File** *menu, to alter the starting page number of any publication. We are just adjusting the* Start page # *to 6.*

Figure 11. Another option when automatically numbering pages is to use the Page Numbering *dialog box. This lets you choose between Arabic numeral, Upper Roman, Lower Roman, & Upper & Lower alphabetic. Whatever preference you select will appear automatically as your page numbering system. To get to this dialog box, click on the word Numbers... in the* Page setup *dialog box.*

Composite page numbers are possible, whereby additional information is included with the basic page number. This can include such items as the word page, or chapter numbering, such as 4-1, 8-7, etc. In Figure 12 a composite page number is added to a master page.

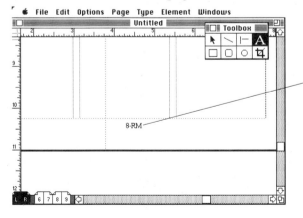

Figure 12. In this example, we would like to preface all page numbers with the chapter number 8. This is done by typing 8- in front of the Command-Option-P (auto page number) combination on the master pages.
If we moved to the first page, which is now 6, due to the Figure 10 operation, this page would reflect the number 8-6.

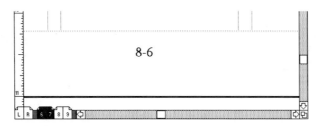

Figure 13. *A close-up view of the front page of our publication showing that our operations of Figures 10 through 12 worked correctly.*

Removing master items

There will, of course, always be pages where master items, such as logos, headers, and footers, will not be needed. The first page in a book, for example, rarely uses a header or footer.

When you come to a page that you do not want master items to appear on, you will discover that text or graphic items cannot be deleted simply by selecting and deleting them. As a matter of fact, they cannot be selected at all.

There are three ways to remove master items from a particular page. Any guides, whether column, ruler, or margin guides, can be moved out of the way as if they were created on the page. Unlike text or graphics, these can be changed or moved.

One or more master elements can be hidden from view by drawing a white box over them (this is particularly useful when you wish to remove some master elements from a page but not all). This is illustrated in Figure 14.

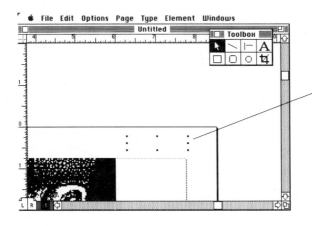

Figure 14. *This is a white graphics box (only the selection handles are shown) which has been drawn over the master page header. This item is thus removed from the page without upsetting any other master items. The white box is achieved by choosing None from the Line sub-menu and Paper from the Fill sub-menu.*

Finally, if you wish to remove all master items from a particular page, you must deselect the *Display master items* command in the **Page** menu (Figure 15). The result is shown in Figure 16.

Any pages that do not use the master items will still be included in the page number count.

As we said above, it is possible to readjust non-printing master guides (column, ruler guides) on any actual page. If you wish to revert back to the guides from the master page, select the *Copy master guides* command from the **Page** menu. All relevant non-printing guides will then reappear on your page.

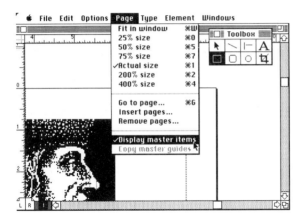

Figure 15. The Display master items *command removes all master items from your page. The result is shown in Figure 16.*

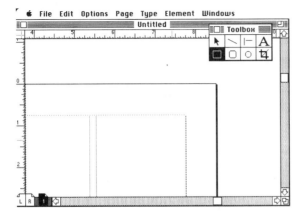

Figure 16. The result of using the command of Figure 15. All master items are deleted. They can be brought back by simply reselecting the same command.

Module 8 Exercise

Master Pages

Module 8 Exercise
Master Pages

In this exercise we will utilize master pages to set up headers, footers, and column guides. We will then remove master items from selected pages and also change column guides. This is an involved exercise that combines techniques from many of the modules we have already looked at.

This training material is structured so that people of all levels of expertise with PageMaker can use it to gain maximum benefit. To to do this, we have structured this material so that the bare exercise is listed below this paragraph on just one page, with no hints. The following pages contain the steps needed to complete this exercise for those that need additional prompting. The **Master Pages** module should be referenced if you need further help or explanations.

Module 8 exercise steps

1. *Set up a four-page publication with the following specifications: Letter size, Tall, four pages, Double-sided, Facing pages, and .75 inch margins all around.*

2. *Go to master pages to setup left page headers and footers as follows: (a) April 1990, flush left header; (b) DTP Newsletter, flush right header; (c) page number, centered footer. Set all text in Times, 10 point, italic.*

3. *Set right master pages in mirror image format to that of step 2.*

4. *Set left and right master pages in two column format with 1 point intercolumn rules.*

5. *Go to page 1 and load Practice graphic (Basic Lesson folder) into bottom half of page.*

6. *Load Lead Story (Lesson 2 folder) using Autoflow method onto pages 1 and 2. Make sure it jumps over the graphic.*

7. *Load Lead Story again using Autoflow method starting from top of column 2 on page 2.*

8. *Remove master item headers from page 1 (but not footer).*

9. *Change column guides on page 3 from 2 to 3 columns, and adjust text to fit.*

10. *Remove master items from pages 2 and 3.*

11. *Change column guides on page 3 back to 2 columns without using the Column guides command.*

The steps for completing this exercise are on the following pages.

The steps in detail.

1. Set up a four-page publication with the following specifications: Letter size, Tall, four pages, Double-sided, Facing pages, and .75 inch margins all around.

After choosing *New* from the **File** menu, set up the publication details in the *Page setup* dialog box as shown in Figure 1.

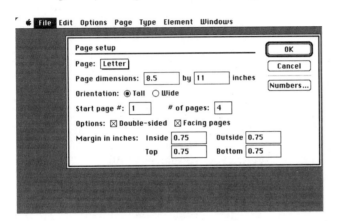

Figure 1. The initial Page setup *dialog box should be filled in to these exact specifications.*

2. Go to the master pages to set up left page headers and footers as follows: (a) April 1990, flush left header; (b) DTP Newsletter, flush right header; (c) page number, centered footer. Set all text in Times, 10 point, italic.

Figure 2 shows the left-hand master page with the flush left and flush right headers in place. They were created with the text tool and placed 0.5 inches below the top of the page.

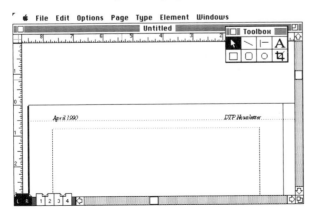

Figure 2. The top of the left-hand master page is displayed in Actual size *view showing the two headers.*

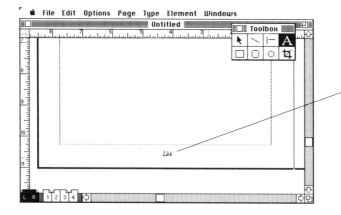

Figure 3. *The Command-Option-P automatic page number combination always shows up on the master pages as either LM or RM, which stands for Left Master or Right Master.*

The page number was then inserted in the middle of the left master page as a footer using the Command-Option-P special combination. Figure 3 shows the result in *Actual size* view. This special page number key combination always appears as either LM or RM on the master pages.

Select each block of header and footer text, and use the *Type specs* command in the **Type** menu to set these headers and footers in Times, 10 point, italic.

3. Set right master pages in mirror image format to that of step 2.

On the right master page, April 1990 should be flush right and DTP Newsletter flush left. Figure 4 shows the result. The page number footer will still be in the middle of the page as for Figure 3.

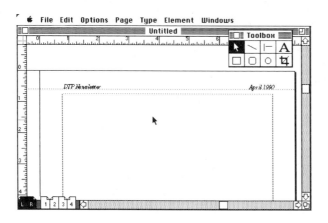

Figure 4. *The right master page is now set up with mirror image headers. Compare this with Figure 2.*

4. Set left and right master pages in two column format with 1 point intercolumn rules.

To set two columns, we go to the *Column guides* command in the **Options** menu and select 2 columns. The intercolumn guides are drawn using the perpendicular line drawing tool selected from the Toolbox. It is wise to turn off the *Snap to guides* option in the **Options** menu when drawing the intercolumn rules (Figure 5). This allows the vertical line to be drawn between the columns without its snapping to either of the column guides. The line thickness of 1 point is chosen from the *Line* sub-menu. Figure 6 shows the final results for both master pages in *Fit in window* view.

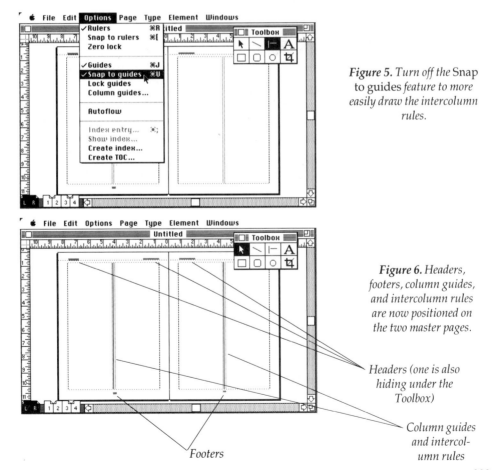

Figure 5. Turn off *the* Snap to guides *feature to more easily draw the intercolumn rules.*

Figure 6. Headers, footers, column guides, and intercolumn rules are now positioned on the two master pages.

Headers (one is also hiding under the Toolbox)

Column guides and intercolumn rules

Footers

5. Go to page 1 and load Practice graphic (Basic Lesson folder) into bottom half of page.

Click on 1 on the page icons in the bottom left-hand corner of the screen. Choose the *Place* command from the **File** menu and select Practice graphic from within the Basic lesson folder (Figure 7). Paste this picture into page 1 by drawing an imaginary box with your cursor before clicking the mouse button. Position it at approximately the same position and the same size as we have done in Figure 8.

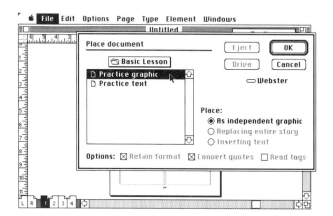

Figure 7. By selecting the Place *command from the* **File** *menu, we are provided with this dialog box. Choose* Practice graphic *from the Basic lesson folder.*

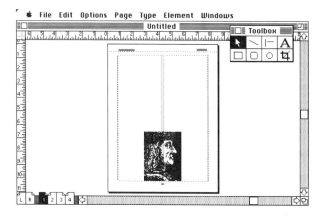

Figure 8. Put Practice graphic *on page 1 at approximately this size and in this position.*

6. *Load Lead Story (Lesson 2 folder) using Autoflow method onto pages 1 and 2. Make sure it jumps over the graphic.*

Before we select Lead story, select the picture on page 1 and adjust the picture wrap to that required. As we want the text to jump over the graphic, choose the options as shown in Figure 9. This dialog box is accessed through the *Text wrap* command in the **Element** menu.

Now choose the *Place* command from the **File** menu, and from the associated dialog box (Figure 10), select Lead Story from the Lesson 2 folder. Flow this text onto pages 1 and 2 using the *Autoflow* command (make sure the *Autoflow* command has a tick next to it in the **Options** menu). The results of this autoflow are shown in Figures 11 and 12.

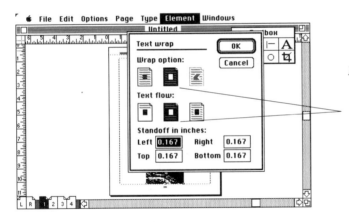

Figure 9. To make the text jump over the picture in page 1, choose these two options in the Text wrap dialog box from the **Options** *menu.*

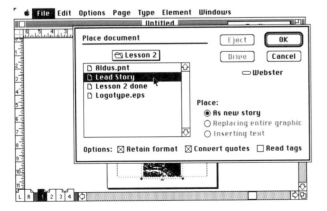

Figure 10. This is the Place *dialog box again. Choose Lead Story from the Lesson 2 folder.*

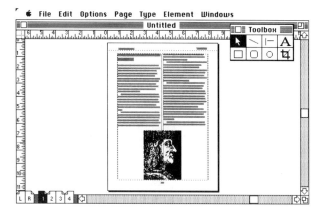

Figure 11. *Lead Story has flowed onto page 1 and has completely jumped over our picture. This is because of the Figure 9 settings.*

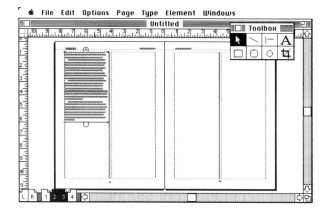

Figure 12. *As we used the Autoflow method to flow the text, Lead story has flowed automatically onto page 2.*

7. Load Lead Story again using Autoflow method starting from top of column 2 on page 2.

Figure 13 shows the reselection of Lead Story for placement onto page 2. Figure 14 indicates the position at the top of column 2 of page 2 to start flowing this new text file. Note the *Autoflow* cursor at the top of the column. Figure 15 shows the results of flowing the text.

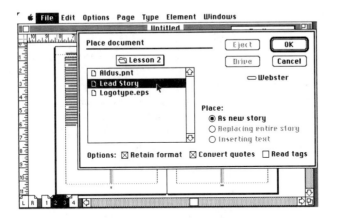

Figure 13. Lead Story is being loaded again because it is a suitable size for our exercise.

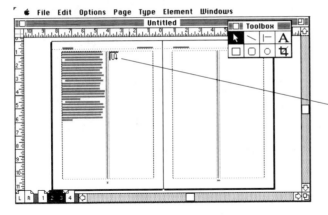

Figure 14. Note that the Autoflow cursor is positioned at the top of the second column of page 2. This is where we want to commence flowing the text.

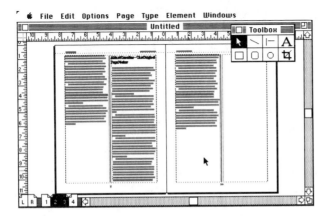

Figure 15. This is how your pages 2 and 3 should look after flowing the text.

8. Remove master item headers from page 1 (but not footer).

Under the **Page** menu, we have a command called *Display master items*. When this is selected (has a check alongside it), all master items are displayed on the page currently being viewed. When it is not selected, no master items are displayed. In this step, we have been asked to remove only some of the master items. This command cannot therefore be used as it hides or shows all master items. The simple way to perform this step is to draw boxes around the flush left and right headers and make their shade as *Paper* (through the *Fill* sub-menu) and their lines *None* (through the *Line* sub-menu).

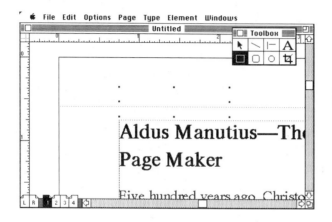

Figure 16. We are on page 1 and looking at the top left-hand corner where our flush left header should be. It cannot be seen because we have drawn a box over it, and shaded the box Paper from the Fill sub-menu and made its lines None from the Line sub-menu. The selection handles, however, can still be seen.

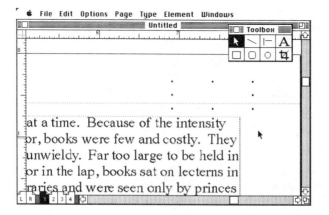

Figure 17. Similar to Figure 16, we have drawn the same sort of box around the right header on page 1. The selection handles can be plainly seen.

This is shown in Figures 16 and 17, where we can see box selection handles, but no box. This *Paper* (color white) box completely covers the two headers. As these boxes are white and have no lines, they will not appear on the printout, but will still cover the two headers.

9. Change column guides on page 3 from 2 to 3 columns, and adjust text to fit.

This step is best explained by pictures. Please read the captions associated with Figures 18 to 24.

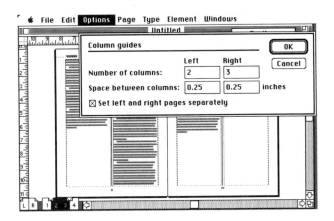

Figure 18. This is the Column gudes *dialog box. Change the right page figure from 2 to 3 columns.*

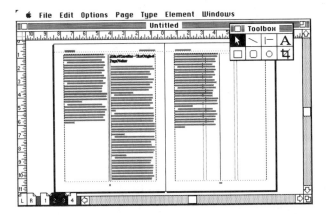

Figure 19. Note that page 3 is now showing column guides for three columns in the background of the text. Text already placed stays in its old format, however. We need to manually change it as shown in the following figures.

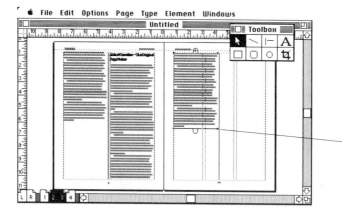

Figure 20*. First select the text in column 1 of page 3 with the pointer tool. Next grab the bottom right-hand corner handle and drag the text to the left to align with the new column guides.*

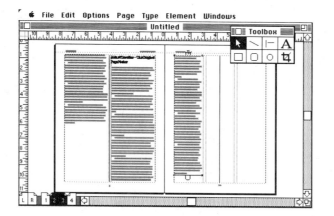

Figure 21. *The left column of the right-hand page is now aligned. Note the problem, however: the intercolumn rule drawn for two columns per page on the master page is still showing down the middle of the second column. This is fixed in the next step.*

10. Remove master items from pages 2 and 3.

As we mentioned in step 8 above, the *Display master items* command from the **Page** menu can be used to show or hide (as a group) all master items on any page. We will now select that command (Figure 22). It shows as a check in this figure indicating that it was already selected. We are currently deselecting it.

The result is indicated in Figure 23. Note that not only have we removed the intercolumn rule showing in Figure 21, but we also have removed the headers and footers on both pages.

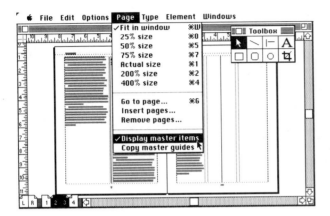

Figure 22. This is the Display master items command which allows us to show or hide items from master pages.

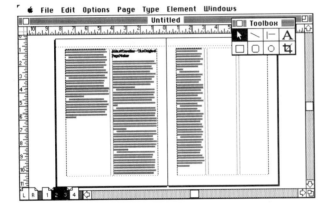

Figure 23. Here are pages 2 and 3 without master items showing. Note the headers and footers are missing, as well as the intercolumn rules. This figure is a result of choosing the command in Figure 22.

11. Change column guides on page 3 back to 2 columns without using the Column guides command.

This step reverses what we were doing in step 9. Again it is better described in pictures. Please refer to Figures 24 to 28 for details.

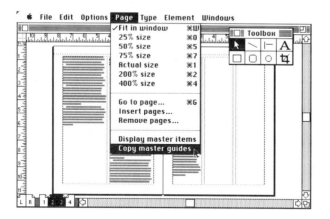

Figure 24. As our master pages were set up with two columns, it is possible to display those column guides back onto our page 3 without going through the Column guides command. Choose, as shown here, the Copy master guides command from the **Page** menu.

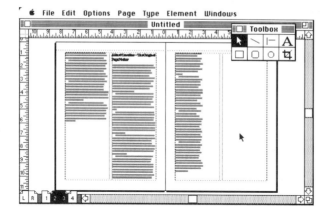

Figure 25. Column guides have now changed back to 2 after the results of Figure 24.

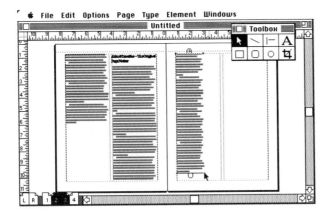

Figure 26. *Now select the first column of page 3 with the pointer tool. Grab the bottom right-hand handle and pull the text column to the right to widen it to the full width of the first column.*

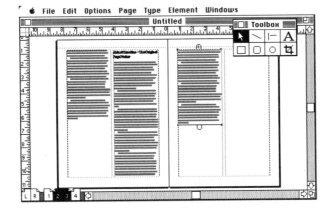

Figure 27. The first column on page 3 is now fixed.

Module 9

Printing

Printing

Print command

Your PageMaker *job* is ready to print at any time. There is no need to save before printing, and certainly no need to have completed your publication. In fact, the more often you get a chance to print your job, the better it will probably turn out. The printer always gives a clearer indication of what the document is going to look like than does the screen, thanks to the printer's higher resolution.

Several printers are available for use with PageMaker, most using the printer language PostScript. LaserWriters, QMS, Varityper, AST, Dataproducts, and others can be used with the Macintosh.

Before printing your document, you must select a printer. If you have only one printer to choose from, this step is obviously not necessary since that printer will always be used. However, if you are hooked up to several printers, use the *Chooser* command in the **Apple** ( ) menu to select the printer you want (Figure 1). After choosing this command, you will see the dialog box in Figure 2.

First, simply select the type of printer you would like to use (LaserWriter, ImageWriter, AppleTalk, etc.) After choosing the type,

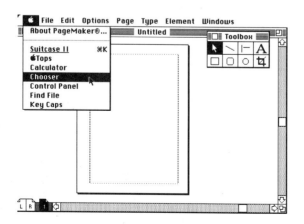

Figure 1. Use the Chooser *command to select a printer. This* **Apple** *menu is available in all Macintosh programs.*

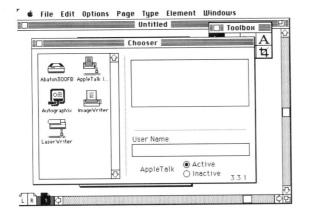

Figure 2. *The* Chooser *command dialog box looks like this, and you are prompted to select a printer. Of course, your choices may be different than those shown here depending on which printers you are hooked up to.*

all available printers will be listed in the dialog box. Now select the printer you wish to use, and this is the printer the Mac will talk to. If a printer is not listed when it should be, make sure it is turned on, is connected correctly, and has the correct settings.

In Figure 3, we selected the LaserWriter icon and one QMS PS 810 printer titled Webster & Associates (our only currently-attached printer) appeared under the *Select a LaserWriter* list at the top right-hand corner of the dialog box.

To print your document, select the *Print* command from the **File** menu (Figure 4). After selecting this command, you will see the dialog box in Figure 5.

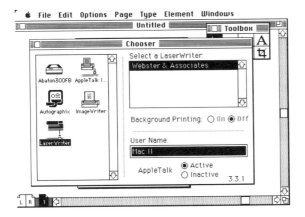

Figure 3. *After selecting the type of printer you would like to use (highlighted), all available printers of this type will be listed under the heading* Select a LaserWriter. *In this case, only one laser printer is available.*

As you can see from Figure 5, printing is not quite as easy as just saying "print." There are a variety of options available to control the print of your publication.

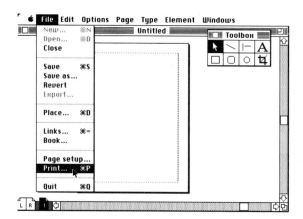

Figure 4. The Print *command from the* **File** *menu can be selected at any time — even when nothing appears on the page.*

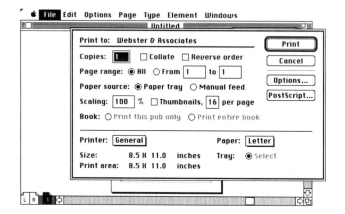

Figure 5. The Print *command dialog box.*

At the top of the Figure 5 dialog box is listed the name of the currently selected printer. If this is not the printer you wish to use, select *Cancel* from this dialog box, and look at the *Chooser* command from the **Apple** menu and review the printer choice (Figure 3 again).

Your first selection in Figure 5 is how many copies to print of your publication. You can choose from 1 to 100. (If you have a fairly low throughput printer, don't try to use it as a printing press — a photocopier or instant printer may work out far faster and more economical.)

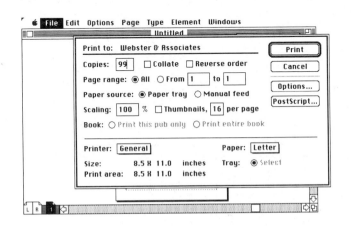

Figure 6. Here we have entered 99 as the number of copies we would like of our publication.

Next to the number of copies is the *Collate* square. If this square is selected, all copies printed will be collated as they are printed. (This will obviously only work if multiple copies of multiple pages are going to be printed.) Although this sounds like an attractive proposition, it will take much longer to print when this option is selected, as each page has to be processed individually, rather than just once for multiple copies of the same page.

Alongside the *Collate* option is the *Reverse order* option. Depending on the output tray of your printer (some flip the pages as they are coming out), you may prefer to print first page to last, or the other way around, so that when the pages are picked up they do not have to be resorted into the correct order. PageMaker will try to determine which way your printer sorts its output, and print so that the pages are in order, not necessarily first to last.

The *Page range* line is used to select the actual pages that are to be printed. Choose *All* to print the entire publication, or insert figures after *From* into the page range boxes to print specified pages (Figure 7). If you wish to print just one page, put that same page number in both the *From* and the *to* boxes.

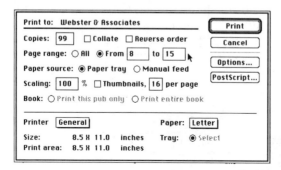

Figure 7. Here we have selected to print 99 copies of pages 8 to 15 of our document.

The *Paper source* is altered if you wish to change printing from the paper tray to printing on a manually fed page. Most printers support this feature, which allows you to insert a letterhead, an envelope, a certificate, or slightly thicker piece of paper that would not otherwise be suitable for the paper tray.

The *Scaling* option allows you to scale the print of your document, from 25 percent to 1,000 percent (Figure 8), at full PostScript resolution. In this way, higher point sizes than can be accessed through the PageMaker dialog boxes can be achieved by scaling the publication as it is printed. PageMaker centers reduced and enlarged pages on the paper.

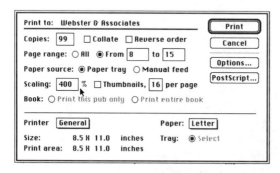

Figure 8. Here we have decided to scale the print to 400 percent.

Thumbnails is a very useful PageMaker feature that allows you to print a wide range of publication pages shrunken down to fit onto one page. This is especially useful to keep on file exactly what is in every publication rather than spending the time and money by printing them out in full. Up to 64 thumbnails can be printed per page.

The *Book* option in this dialog box is only available when the current publication contains a book list (see Module 16, **Long Document Capabilities**). The first choice you have here is to print only the current publication, by selecting the relevant circle. But if the publication does contain a book list, it is now possible to print all publications in this book list.

Printer parameters

Underneath the print options of Figure 8 are the *Printer* type, *Paper* size, and paper *Tray*. The first choice is the printer type. Click on the relevant box, and run down the menu to select your exact brand and model of printer (Figure 9).

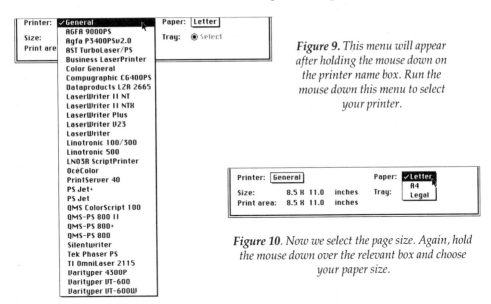

Figure 9. This menu will appear after holding the mouse down on the printer name box. Run the mouse down this menu to select your printer.

Figure 10. Now we select the page size. Again, hold the mouse down over the relevant box and choose your paper size.

Next you must select the page size that your printer is using (Figure 10). If you specify a Letter size for your laser printer, and it is using an A4 paper tray, PageMaker will prompt you, once given the command to print, to remove the A4 tray and insert the Letter tray. The page size and print area on that page is automatically indicated as you select *Paper* size in Figure 10. If the print area is larger than the page area, you need to select the *Tile* option as discussed later in this module.

If your printer has multiple paper trays, you need to select which one. Note that in Figure 9, we have chosen the General laser printer option, and the paper tray option just says *Select*. This is because the General option is assumed to have only one paper tray.

If we had, however, chosen a printer with multiple trays, then options of *Upper* and *Lower* would replace Selected. See Figure 11, for example, which shows the TI OmniLaser 2115 model selected with *Upper* and *Lower* tray options.

After finally adjusting all the hardware specifications for your printer, you are now ready to print. This is achieved, as you might have guessed, by clicking on the *Print* button. Before doing this, however, you may wish to review the next section on *Print options*.

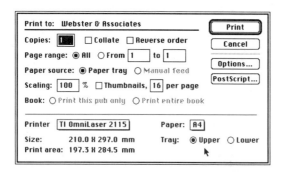

Figure 11. Unlike Figure 9, you can now see that the upper and lower tray options are available. This is because we have selected a different laser printer — one that offers two trays.

Print options dialog box

By clicking on the word *Options,* you will see the *Aldus print options* dialog box (Figure 12). The commands in this dialog box are described below.

The *Proof print* box should be checked for a speedier print — minus any imported graphics. Only text and graphics created in PageMaker will print in this case, and the imported graphics will be printed with a diagonal cross through them.

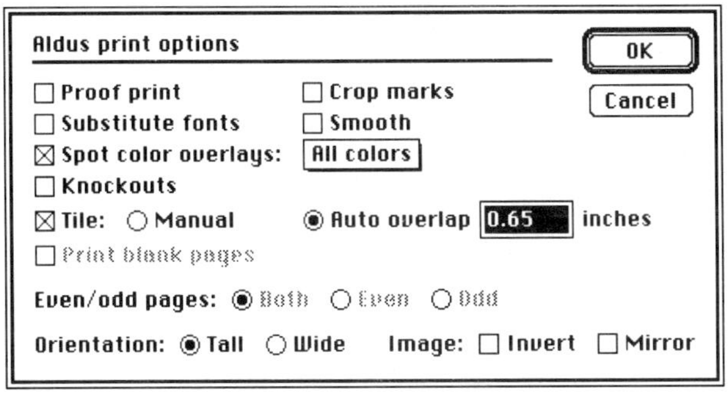

```
┌─────────────────────────────────────────────────┐
│ Aldus print options                    ┌─────────┐│
│                                        │   OK    ││
│ ☐ Proof print      ☐ Crop marks        └─────────┘│
│ ☐ Substitute fonts ☐ Smooth            ┌─────────┐│
│ ☒ Spot color overlays: │All colors│    │ Cancel  ││
│ ☐ Knockouts                            └─────────┘│
│ ☒ Tile: ○ Manual    ◉ Auto overlap │0.65│ inches │
│ ☐ Print blank pages                               │
│                                                   │
│ Even/odd pages: ◉ Both  ○ Even  ○ Odd             │
│                                                   │
│ Orientation: ◉ Tall  ○ Wide   Image: ☐ Invert ☐ Mirror │
└─────────────────────────────────────────────────┘
```

Figure 12. The Aldus print options dialog box.

Crop marks can be added to a printed page, so that a printing company can align pages together correctly and see exactly what page size they are working with. They appear as not quite joined cross hairs in every corner of the page.

Substitute fonts is usually left on. This command substitutes the existing fonts found in most PostScript printers for the screen fonts found in the Macintosh — Venice, New York, Geneva, and Monaco. If this choice is not selected, anything in your publication that uses these fonts will print at screen resolution.

Smooth is an option that sometimes increases the apparent resolution of Paint-type graphics from the Macintosh paint programs, by adding dots to the ragged edges. However, it should never be used with scanned images, and will slow printing time. Experiment with this command, as it can be pot luck as to whether it will actually make the graphic appear better than before.

Spot color overlays is a choice that is used when preparing color work to be taken to a printer for finishing. By selecting this option, every new color will be printed on a page by itself, as this is what the printer requires. The box to the right of *Spot color overlays* provides a pop-up sub-menu where you can choose to print color overlays for one color only or all colors.

Knockouts is only available when *Spot color overlays* is selected. This option is used so that different color graphics are printed separately on each overlay, in the order they were created. A blank spot will appear where the colors overlap.

When the *Print blank pages* box is checked, PageMaker will print all blank pages in your publication until you deselect it.

The *Tile* option lets you print oversize pages so that you are not limited to the page size supported by your printer (Figures 13 and 14). To print a Tabloid page size from a Letter size printer, tiling can be selected, and it will print out as several Letter pages, all overlapped (to whatever degree you like in manual tiling, or whatever overlap you specify for automatic tiling), and can be pasted together after printing. This can also be used when scaling A4 or Letter pages larger than normal.

Automatic tiling will cause PageMaker to determine the starting point of each tile, based on the specified overlap (see Figure 15). PageMaker will start at the upper left-hand corner of a page, and print all of one page's tiles before moving on to another. Automatic tiling should be used when there is no need to control what is printed (that is, preventing a complex image from printing twice, too many tiles per page, etc.).

Tiling manually is achieved by repositioning the zero point on the ruler to specify where the tile is to start. After the starting point for a tile has been specified, PageMaker prints that tile for every page in the range of pages you are printing. You then set the zero point for the second tile, and PageMaker prints that tile for all pages being printed again. In this way, if your publication consists of ten pages, manual tiling will first cause ten tiles to print (one per page), then another ten (one per page again, and so on).

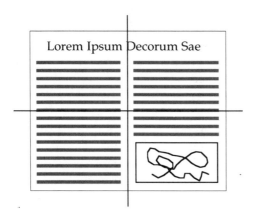

Figure 13. A page divided into four tiling segments.

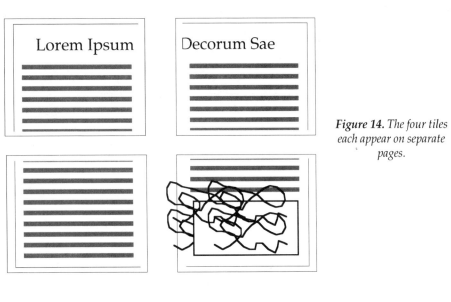

Figure 14. The four tiles each appear on separate pages.

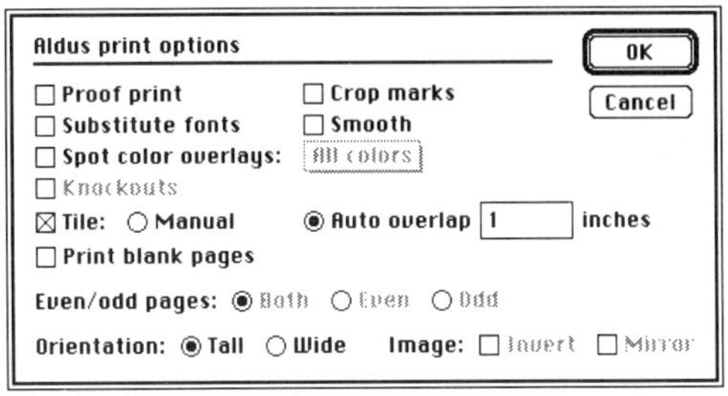

Figure 15. If we scale the output 400 percent (Figure 8), we must use the Tile option for printing (in this case with Auto overlap). This causes the large page to be printed out as several Letter pages, with a 1 inch overlap on every page, to aid in the alignment.

At the bottom of the *Aldus print options* dialog box (Figures 12 or 15) you can choose from a number of options. The *Even/odd pages* selection is used for double-sided printing. You can either print even or odd at a time, and then reverse the pages in the printer, so it will print on the other side. A mandatory option is deciding whether you want to print a landscape (*Wide*) or a portrait (*Tall*) page. Lastly, you may choose from two special effects — *Mirror* and *Invert*. These options are useful for printing to film.

Once all options in the *Aldus print options* dialog box have been selected, click on OK to return to the *Print* dialog box of Figure 5.

Errors

Several errors may occur during the print process (Figure 16). Nearly all of these are related to the connection between the Macintosh and the printer. Make sure they are connected securely with cables, as well as through the *Chooser* command in the **Apple** menu, and that the printer is switched on and selected for the Macintosh.

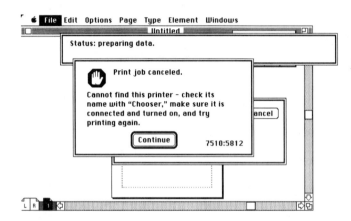

Figure 16. This is one of the several error commands that might occur when printing from PageMaker. The cause can be one of many things — in this case a missing cable.

Creating Postscript print files

We usually print directly to a printer. However, there is an option that allows us to create a PostScript print file — one that can be used in a variety of ways. This print file can be used to transmit to a service bureau, but also can serve as an EPS file that can be placed in other PageMaker documents, or other applications.

To use this approach, go about the print process in the normal way, selecting the page numbers, the quantity, tiling, and crop mark options as explained earlier in this module.

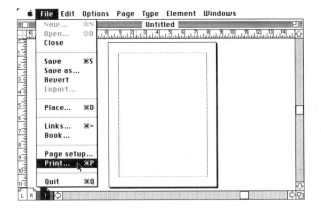

Figure 17. To create a PostScript print file you must first select the Print command as normal.

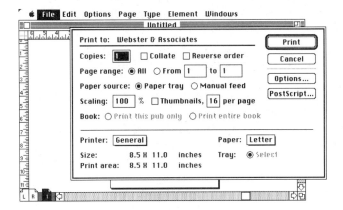

Figure 18. Set up your print options as normal, keeping in mind exactly what you would like to do with the print file.

After selecting your print preferences, click the mouse over the PostScript button underneath the Options choice. Instead of searching for a printer, PageMaker will display the dialog box of Figure 19.

We must now make another selection of the options we wish to use to create a PostScript file.

Your first option is whether or not to *Download bit-map fonts*. If you have intentionally used fonts such as New York, Geneva, or Monaco in your document, you will need to have this option

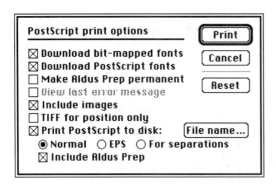

Figure 19. *The PostScript print options dialog box - achieved by clicking on the word PostScript in the Print dialog box.*

checked to make sure the screen version of this font is down-loaded to the printer, as most PostScript printers do not include PostScript versions of these fonts. This should be unchecked otherwise, to make sure the printer never prints the screen version of an accidentally included screen font.

Next, you must select whether or not to *Download PostScript fonts*. If you are printing to disk, and the printer that is finally going to print this document does not contain the fonts used, check this option to make sure that the fonts, if available, are downloaded with the print file. In most cases you will only be using PostScript fonts, which are already resident in the printer, so uncheck this command. If you attempt to download fonts to a printer in which the fonts already exist, the print job may fail. Also uncheck this option if your copy-protected PostScript fonts are initialized for a printer other than the destination printer.

Make Aldus Prep permanent downloads this printer file to the printer in question (if printing directly to a printer), until the printer is turned off. This generally should be checked, unless you fall into one of the following categories.

• You are printing with other programs as well, and would like to have as much memory free in the printer as possible.

• You are using several different versions of PageMaker.

• You are printing to disk.

Check the *View last error message* if you want PageMaker to keep displaying status messages from the printer until the publication is printed. It is a wise idea to check this option. It may alert you to problems you could be having while printing.

The next option is *Include images*. This should be selected if you are printing color comprehensives to a color PostScript printer, or printing a grayscale version of TIFF images. If you are printing color separations do not select this option.

Tiff for position only, when selected, means PageMaker will print a lower resolution version of any TIFF images in the document you wish to print.

Towards the bottom of the Figure 19 dialog box is a selection *Print PostScript to disk*. Check this if you are printing to disk rather than directly to a printer.

Next to this command are the choices *Normal*, *EPS*, or *For separations*. Check *Normal* if the file is going to a remote printer or service bureau, or if it has multiple pages. Check *EPS* if the file is a single page that is going to be used as an EPS file, either in PageMaker or another application. *For separations* prepares the publication to be sent to a color separation program.

If the printer you intend printing to contains the file Aldus Prep, there is no need to check the *Include Aldus Prep* option. This will only make the print file larger if printing to disk. However, if the printer does not contain the file Aldus Prep, make sure that this box has been checked.

Finally, you must set the file name if printing to disk. This is so both you and PageMaker know exactly what the print file is going to be called. Choose *File name* from Figure 19 to get the extra dialog box of Figure 20.

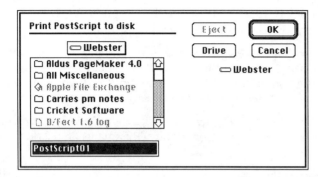

Figure 20. After clicking on the filename, you must name the file you are about to create. The default name will be PostScript01 if Normal was chosen from Figure 19.

If *Normal* was chosen in Figure 19, you will get the default Postscript01 name in the Figure 20 dialog box. If *EPS* was chosen, the default name will be Untitled.eps. If *For separations* was chosen, the default name will be Untitled.sep.

Module 9 Exercise

Printing

Module 9 Exercise
Printing

In this exercise we will look at some of the printing options available with PageMaker, although a printer is not needed.

This training material is structured so that people of all levels of expertise with PageMaker can use it to gain maximum benefit. To do this, we have structured this material so that the bare exercise is listed below this paragraph on just one page, with no hints. The following pages contain the steps needed to complete this exercise for those that need additional prompting. The **Printing** module should be referenced if you need further help or explanations.

> *Because printing is a fairly straightforward exercise (it will either work or it won't, and if it doesn't, it is probably a connection problem anyway), we will not print directly to a printer in this exercise. We will, however, look at the print procedures as well as printing to disk.*

Module 9 exercise steps

1. *Set up the print dialog box to print the first page of the template Newsletter 2 (located in the Template folder) three times. Enlarge the print by 200%, and tile the print with a 1 inch overlap. Check your dialog boxes with Figures 4 and 5 of this exercise.*

2. *Print the same file to disk as an EPS file, and name the print file EXER10PS. After printing the file to disk, start a new PageMaker publication and load in the EPS file EXER10PS. It should look exactly the same as the Newsletter 2 template of Figure 1.*

The details for completing this exercise are on the following pages.

The steps in detail

1. Set up the print dialog box to print the first page of the template Newsletter 2 (located in the Template folder) three times. Enlarge the print by 200%, and tile the print with a 1 inch overlap. Check your dialog boxes with Figures 4 and 5 of this exercise.

The first step in this exercise is to open a copy of the PageMaker template Newsletter 2, located in the Template folder (Figure 1). If you are already in PageMaker, close your current document and select *Open* to get this chapter.

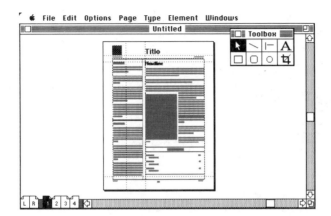

Figure 1. Make sure this Newsletter 2 file is open as a copy of the original template. Your title bar should read Untitled.

After opening this template, select the *Print* command from the **File** menu (Figure 2).

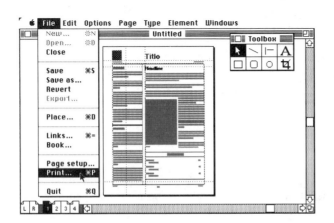

Figure 2. After opening the file, select the Print *command from the* **File** *menu.*

To print the publication three times, make sure you alter the number in the *Copies* box to 3. Adjust *Page range* from 1 to 1. See Figure 3 for both these adjustments.

To scale the print to 200 percent, alter the *Scaling* figure to 200 (Figure 4).

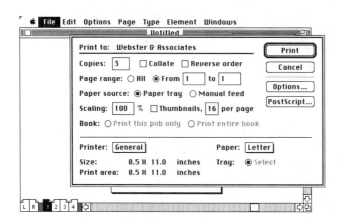

Figure 3. *Change the figure in the top left-hand corner of the dialog box (Copies) to 3. This ensures three copies of the publication are printed. The* Page range *should be set from 1 to 1, because we only want to print the first page.*

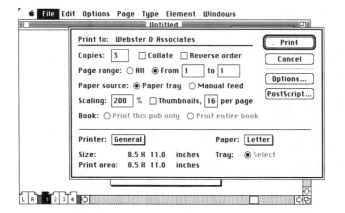

Figure 4. *Change the figure for* Scaling *to 200 to double the print size.*

Now check *Options* in the Figure 4 dialog box to get the *Aldus print options* dialog box of Figure 5. In this box, make sure the *Tile* command has been checked to ensure tiling is used. Select *Auto overlap*, and change the figure in the overlap box to 1 inch (Figure 5).

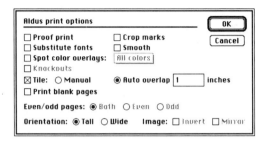

Figure 5. Select the Tile *box from the* Aldus print options *dialog box, and set the* Auto overlap *to 1 inch. Choose* Cancel *from here unless you have a printer connected and would like to see the output.*

Choose Cancel at this time, unless you wish to try out these print options.

2. Print the same file to disk as an EPS file, and name the print file EXER10PS. After printing the file to disk, start a new PageMaker publication and load in the EPS file EXER10PS. It should look exactly the same as the Newsletter 2 template of Figure 1.

With the same publication open, select again the *Print* command. However, make sure that you are only printing one copy, and that the print is not scaled or tiled at all (Figure 6).

Select the *PostScript* option at the right of the print dialog box to get the *PostScript print options* dialog box in Figure 7.

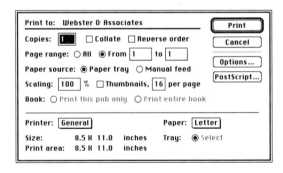

Figure 6. To create an EPS file, print a one page document only once, with no scaling or tiling.

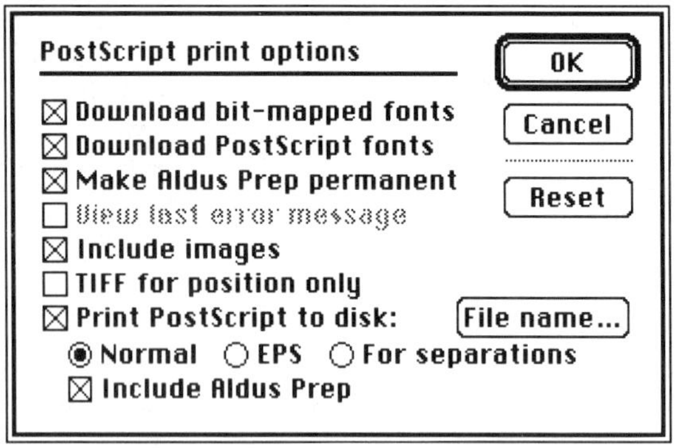

Figure 7. By selecting the word
PostScript *in the* Print *dialog box
of Figure 6, this* PostScript print
options *dialog box will be displayed.*

From the *PostScript print options* dialog box, there are a few things we must
select to print an EPS file to disk. First, click in the box that says *Print PostScript
to disk*, and select *EPS* rather than *Normal* (Figure 8). This ensures that we can
reload the file after printing. Uncheck the two top options as well.

Before we can say *Print* from the Figure 8 dialog box, we must set a name for
the resulting print file. To do this, click on the *File name* rectangle in the bottom
right of the box. You will be presented with yet another dialog box (Figure 9)
asking you to give the file a name. Simply insert the name EXER10PS in the
name rectangle as shown in Figure 9. Also adjust your folders, to print it on
your disk where you can find it.

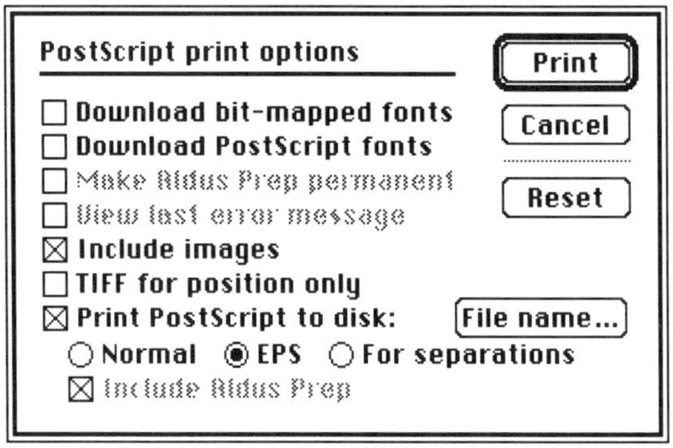

Figure 8. To print an EPS file to
disk, make sure that your dialog
box is set up as illustrated — with
Print PostScript to disk *and* EPS
checked. Also uncheck Download
bit-mapped fonts *and* Download
PostScript fonts.

After setting up these options, click on OK in Figure 9. Then click on OK in the *PostScript print options* dialog box, and then *Print* in the *Print* dialog box. After a few seconds the file will be printed to disk (Figure 10).

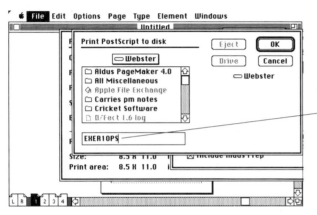

Figure 9. After clicking on File name *from Figure 8, insert the name for the print file (EXER10PS) in the rectangle provided and select* OK.

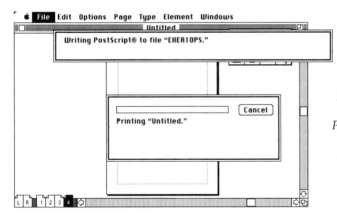

Figure 10. This is a message that will be displayed as the PostScript print file is created.

343

To reload this file, make sure that the current file has been closed and a new one opened (Figure 11).

After creating a new publication, use the *Place* command from the **File** menu (Figure 12) to insert the EPS file we have just created. From the list of files displayed (Figure 13), choose EXER10PS and flow it onto the page (Figure 14). It will be identical to the template, Newsletter 2, which was originally loaded.

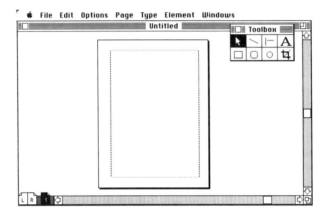

Figure 11. *Close the file that was open, and select* New *from the* **File** *menu to create a new one.*

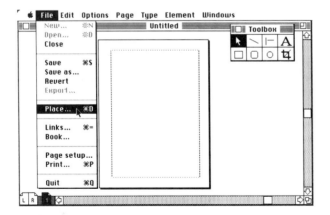

Figure 12. *Choose the* Place *command to gain access to EXER10PS — the PostScript file we just created.*

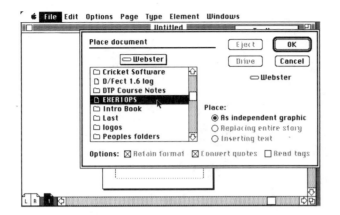

Figure 13. Select EXER10PS from the list of files presented from the Place *command.*

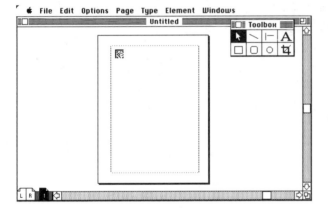

Figure 14. The mouse cursor will change to a PostScript cursor to indicate an EPS file is ready to be loaded.

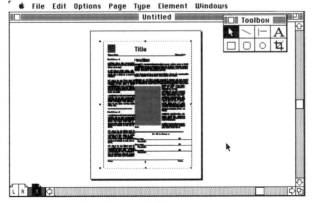

Figure 15. The file, once loaded onto the page, looks exactly like the original template — Newsletter 2 — although we can resize it, move it, and change it anyway we wish.

Module 10

Templates

Templates

PageMaker templates save you time and effort when creating new publications. You do not have to re-create the format of a document if that format exists elsewhere. The way this works is quite simple.

Templates are like partially created publications — publications that can be used over and over again without destroying the original. Let's say, for example, that every month you create a company newsletter. The specifications for this newsletter may be: eight pages, Letter page, two columns on pages 1-6, three columns on pages 7 and 8, a border around all pages, vertical rules between all columns, headers, footers, numbered pages, etc.

Initially, this would be set up from scratch in the normal way, and would take a little time. Once done, however, with all these attributes saved as a template, this template could be used as the starting point for the next month's newsletter. By using this approach, you can now spend more time concentrating on the content of the newsletter rather than the format, because the format is already created.

PageMaker 4.0 contains a library of templates covering a wide range of publication types that can be used as starting points for documents. You can either use these templates as they are, modify them slightly to meet your needs, or simply create your own. Two types of templates are included — grid templates and placeholder templates. The former are general purpose, and basically consist of a variety of document sizes with different column and grid (ruler guide) settings. The placeholder templates are specially designed for a paticular type of publication, and include text and graphics within them.

Creating templates

Creating templates is done the same way as creating a typical publication. The *New* command is selected, as many pages as you need are added, the margins and columns are defined, and text and graphics are added where necessary. This is briefly summarized in Figures 1 through 5. The difference comes when the document is saved.

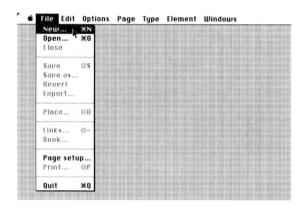

Figure 1. We are going to look at the steps in creating a simple template. Start off as you normally would — by selecting the New *command from the* **File** *menu.*

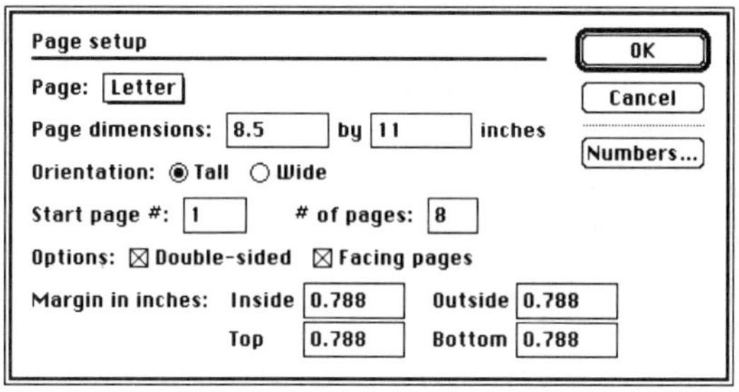

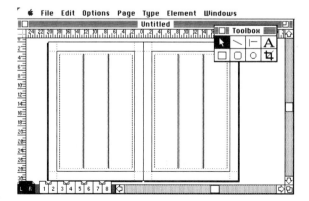

Figure 2. Define the page in the Page setup *command. In this case we have set the number of pages, new margins, etc.*

Figure 3. Once the document opens, set up all the document formatting — number of columns, borders, intercolumn rules, etc., in the master pages.

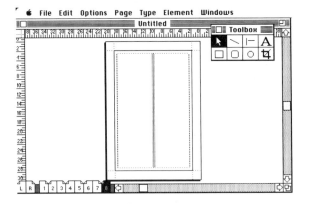

Figure 4. *Any page in the document can be set up independently of the others. Here page 8 is two columns, while all others are three.*

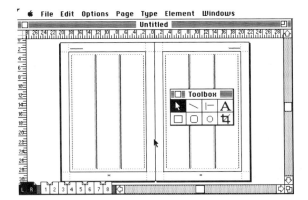

Figure 5. *Text information such as headers, footers, and page numbers can also be set up in the master pages of a template.*

Whenever you choose the *Save* command for the first time (Figure 6), or the *Save as* command from the **File** menu, you are presented with the dialog box of Figure 7. The name is entered as usual (in our case Newsletter Template), but the difference is in the option in the right-hand side of the dialog box. Here you have a choice as to how to save the document — either as a traditional *Publication* (this will be selected by default) or as a *Template*. If you choose Template, this PageMaker file then takes on special qualities.

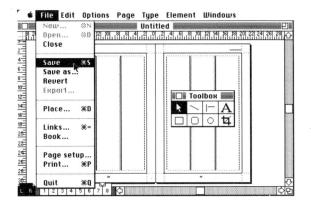

Figure 6. *Up until now, the creation of the template has been exactly the same as the creation of a publication — the difference comes during the* Save *command.*

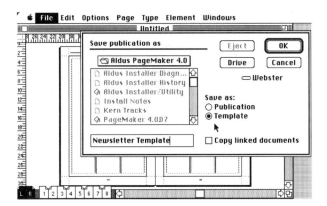

Figure 7. *Give the document a name as you normally would, but click on* Template *in the bottom right-hand corner. By default,* Publication *will be selected. Then click on OK.*

PageMaker publications and PageMaker templates can be distinguished from the desktop quite easily — see the icons below to see the difference between the two files.

Newsletter 2

Template

Lesson 2 done

Publication

351

The main difference between publications and templates are apparent when the PageMaker file is opened. If a publication is opened, the original file is opened, and any changes saved then affect that file permanently. However, if a template is selected, then by default an unnamed original (a copy) is opened. The named original remains untouched on disk to be used another time. The template copy that was opened can be added to, modified, etc., and saved this time as a new publication. Because this template opens up without a name, there is no chance of saving over the original template and destroying its contents by mistake.

In Figure 8, the *Open* dialog box shows, in the bottom right corner, the options of *Original* or *Copy*. A template always defaults to the *Copy* option, whereas a publication defaults to *Original*. Figure 9 gives further examples.

Opening copies or originals of either publications or templates can be manually overridden through the *Open* command in Figure 8. Whenever you select a PageMaker file to be opened from within this dialog box, the default conditions will occur of *Original* or *Copy* as indicated above. Once you select a template, however, you can override this and select *Original*. This is necessary, of course, if you wish to modify the original template. In the same way, you can override the *Original* default for a publication and open up a copy.

An example of opening up a copy of the Newsletter Template, which we saved in Figure 7 as a template, is shown in Figure 10.

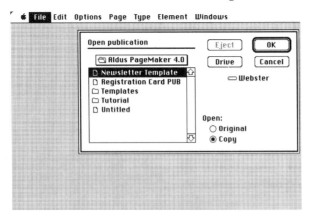

Figure 8. *Here we have used the* Open *command to gain access to this list of PageMaker files. Once we select a template to open (this was the template we just created), note how the option in the bottom right-hand switches to* Copy *rather than* Original.

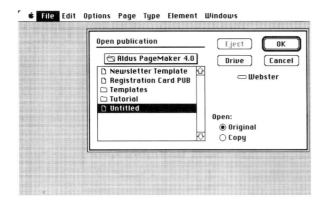

Figure 9. When we select a normal publication to open, the option now switches back to Original. This can be manually overridden if need be.

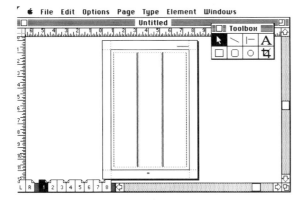

Figure 10. Here we have opened up a copy of the template we just created (Newsletter Template). Note how it looks exactly the same as the right master page of Figure 5, yet is untitled.

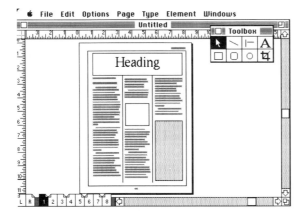

Figure 11. Once the copy of the template has been opened, we are free to add this month's text and graphics, without having to redefine page parameters.

Text and graphic placeholders

We have mentioned that a template can contain any amount of graphics or text you like. If we consider a monthly newsletter, the actual content of this newsletter will change from month to month. One would think, therefore, we cannot include much text in the template, as it will have to be updated anyway. However, by using text and graphics as "placeholders," we can include as much text and graphics in our template as we need without having to worry about this text being removed or updated. Using text and graphics placeholders in templates makes creating a publication a much easier task.

Let's say that we loaded in one major text file, several graphics files, and several headings throughout our Newsletter Template example. When we open up the template next month, the graphics, text, and headings are all there, but we now have new text, graphics, and headings that are going to replace those of last month. Replacing the old text with the new becomes very easy, and the process of replacing the old text and graphics helps us to precisely format and position the new elements.

Graphic placeholders

In a simple copy of a newsletter template of Figure 12, let's first replace one of the graphics on the first page with a new graphic. Select the old graphic that is going to be replaced, immediately before selecting the *Place* command (Figures 13 and 14). When you choose the *Place* command, locate the new graphic as in Figure 15 and select it, but do not yet choose OK.

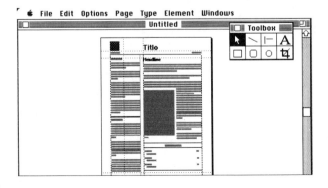

Figure 12. To work through with us in this section of the module, load the Newsletter 2 template contained in the PageMaker Templates folder. As shown in this figure, it contains various text and graphics placeholders on Page 1. We have selected the graphic in the middle of the second column to be replaced.

Figure 13. *We have changed to 75% size view so that you can see how the graphic we have selected is going to be replaced*

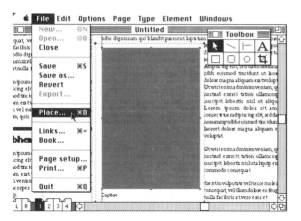

Figure 14. *With the graphic still selected, choose the* Place *command from the* **File** *menu to locate the new graphic.*

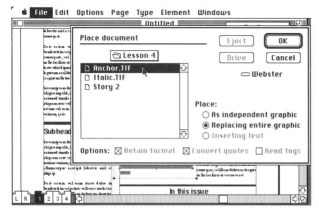

Figure 15. *The graphic we are going to use to replace the old graphic is Anchor.TIF from the Lesson 4 folder. Note that we also select the option to the right — Replacing entire graphic (see the explanation on the next page).*

There are several options within the Figure 15 dialog box that may be active depending on the steps that were taken before choosing this command. The one that should be active now is located to the right of the dialog box, and gives you the choice between two ways to load the graphic — either *As independent graphic,* which is selected by default, or *Replacing entire graphic. As independent graphic* is a picture loaded in the traditional way — the mouse cursor will change appearance, and you may choose where to load the graphic on the page.

Replacing entire graphic will insert the new graphic not only in the same area as the existing graphic, but also using the same sizing, cropping, and wraparound attributes as the previous graphic. This can, of course, be modified after the graphic has been replaced. On clicking OK, the new graphic totally replaces the old (Figure 16).

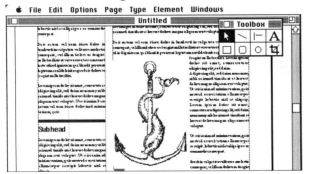

Figure 16. After choosing OK, the new graphic entirely replaces the old, taking on all its attributes.

Text placeholders

The same theory applies to text replacement as it does to graphics. Select any part of the text file that you would like to replace with a new file (use either the pointer tool or make an insertion point with the text tool), and choose the *Place* command. Locate the new text file, and note the new option to the right of the list of files. It will read *As new story* and *Replacing entire story.* As with graphics, if you select *Replacing entire story*, the new text file will completely overlay the previous file — following its exact path. If the files are of different length, this doesn't matter — as there will either be a blank space following the file if it is shorter, or more text to flow if it is longer.

See Figures 17 to 19 for examples of this approach.

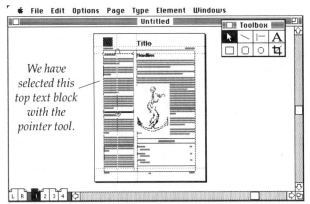

Figure 17. *The procedure for replacing existing text files with other text files works in the same way as the graphics example. First, select any text block with the pointer tool, or create an insertion point with the text tool within a story. These two options will cause the total text file to be replaced. If you wish to replace only a portion of a text file, then select part of that file using the text tool.*

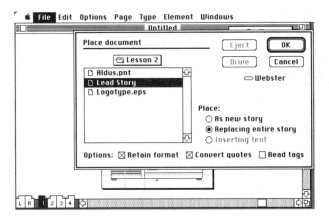

Figure 18. *After choosing the* Place *command, we select the new text file, as well as the* Replacing entire story *option. If we have selected only a portion of our text tool, then the* Inserting text *option would have been available for selection as well.*

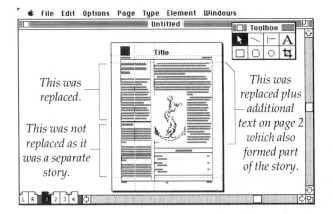

Figure 19. *By clicking OK, the new text file completely replaces the old — flowing in exactly the same pattern. The procedure replaces the entire story associated with the text block initially selected (Figure 17).*

357

Heading placeholders

Heading placeholders work in a slightly different way to other text placeholders. Because headings are generally much shorter than text files, it is much quicker to type them in PageMaker rather than in a word processor. Let's say, for example, that you have a heading in place in your template as shown in Figure 20.

Simply select the text cursor, and highlight the entire heading (Figure 20). Without pressing the *Delete* key, or using the *Cut* command, type in the new heading. The new heading will completely overwrite the old, yet use exactly the same attributes (Figure 21). The same type style, justification, and spacing will be applied to the new text.

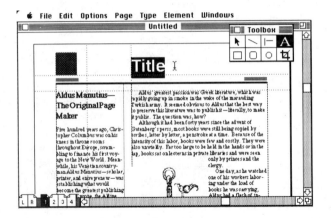

Figure 20. Replacing headings, yet keeping their formatting, is very simple. Select, using the text cursor, the old heading, but do not cut or delete the text.

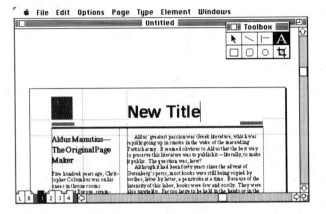

Figure 21. Simply type in the new heading. The old heading will be deleted, and the new heading will use the exact text and paragraph attributes as did the old heading.

***Figure 22.** The same principles apply to all minor text files — simply select the text. Here we are changing the first subhead.*

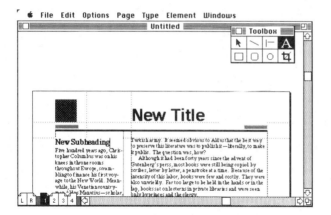

***Figure 23.** The new sub-heading is now typed over the old.*

All text and graphics placeholders can be regular or simulated. Provided with PageMaker are several "dummy" files that can be used to create a template, so that real files do not have to be created and used.

Module 10 Exercise

Templates

Module 10 Exercise
Templates

In this exercise we will illustrate the use of templates and show how to work effectively with them.

This training material is structured so that people of all levels of expertise with PageMaker can use it to gain maximum benefit. To do this, we have structured this material so that the bare exercise is listed below this paragraph on just one page, with no hints. The following pages contain the steps needed to complete this exercise for those that need additional prompting. The **Templates** module should be referenced if you need further help or explanations.

Module 10 exercise steps

1. *Load the template Tabloid from the Templates folder.*

2. *On page 1 of this template, we are going to replace four major sections — the graphic in the first column, the title, the column one, page one text, and the graphic at the top of the middle column. Make sure you understand which parts of page 1 we are talking about when we refer to these (see Figure 1 to get a better idea).*

3. *Replace the graphic in column 1 with the file Practice graphic from the Basic Lesson folder.*

4. *Replace the column one, page one text with the file Story 2 from the Lesson 4 folder.*

5. *Replace the graphic at the top of the middle column with the file Anchor.TIF from the Lesson 4 folder.*

6. *Replace the title with a title of your own choosing.*

7. *Save the template as a publication called Template Exercise.*

The steps to completing this exercise are on the following pages.

The steps in detail.

1. Load the template Tabloid from the Templates folder.

This step can be achieved using either of two methods — depending on whether or not PageMaker is open at the current time. If it is, then the *Open* command from the **File** menu must be used to access this template from the Templates folder (Figures 2 and 3).

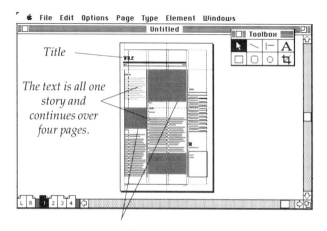

Figure 1. *The Tabloid template.*

Graphics we will replace

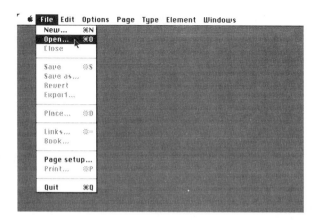

Figure 2. *The Open command from the **File** menu is the way to get access to both publications and templates.*

If you are at the Macintosh desktop, you can open the file from there by locating it and double-clicking on it (Figure 4). In both cases, because the file is a template, a copy will be opened by default. Notice that *Copy* is automatically selected in Figure 3.

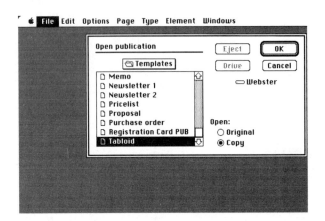

Figure 3. The Tabloid *template is located in the Templates folder inside the PageMaker 4 folder. Note we are opening a copy of this template.*

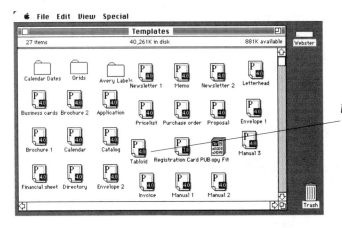

Figure 4. Alternatively, a template or publication can be opened by locating the file on the Macintosh desktop and double-clicking on it.

2. *On page 1 of this template, we are going to replace four major sections—the graphic in the first column, the title, the column one, page one text, and the graphic at the top of the middle column. Make sure you understand which parts of page 1 we are talking about when we refer to these (see Figure 1 to get a better idea).*

See Figure 1 to make sure you understand what we refer to as the title, the page one text, and the graphics.

3. *Replace the graphic in column one with the file Practice graphic from the Basic Lesson folder.*

If you are not in *75% size* view, move to this view now through the **Page** menu. Select the existing graphic, or in our case a gray shaded square, in the first column by clicking on it (Figure 5). Now move to the *Place* command in the **File** menu (Figure 6).

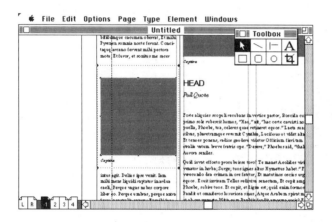

Figure 5. *The first step in replacing a graphic is to select the graphic being replaced.*

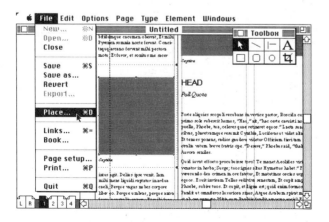

Figure 6. *After Figure 5, move to the Place command in the **File** menu to choose the graphic to replace the selected one.*

Locate the file Practice graphic in the Basic Lesson folder (Figure 7). After selecting it in this dialog box (by clicking on it once, not twice) check the option *Replacing entire graphic* to the right of the list of files. This will make sure that the current graphic is deleted and replaced by the new one at the same place and size. Click on OK. The new graphic then replaces the old (Figure 8).

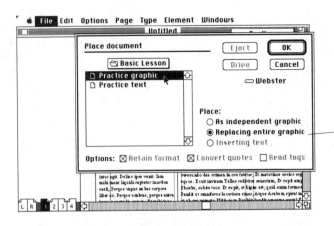

Figure 7. Select the file Practice graphic to replace the graphic we had originally selected on the page in Figure 5. Make sure you also choose Replacing entire graphic.

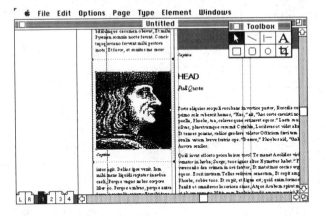

Figure 8. After clicking on OK in Figure 7, the new graphic will, after a few seconds, replace the old.

4. Replace the column one, page one text with the file Story 2 from the Lesson 4 folder.

The same steps are used to replace one story with another, as are used to replace graphics. In this case we are only replacing column one, page one text, not the entire story. In this template, the text is basically one whole story. We therefore need to select just the first column of the page one text with the text tool (Figure 9).

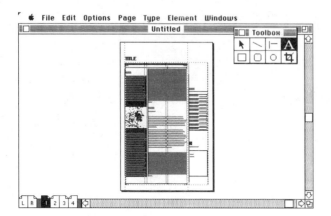

Figure 9. *To replace a portion of a text file, select tthe portion (in our case column one of page one) with the text tool.*

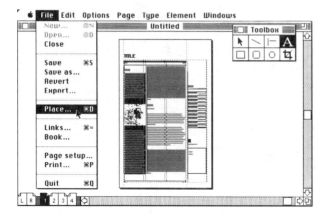

Figure 10. *Once again, after selecting the section to be replaced using the text tool, move directly to the Place command in the* **File** *menu.*

Locate the file Story 2 from the Lesson 4 folder (Figure 11). Notice that the *Replacing entire story* as well as the *Replacing selected text* commands can be selected, while the file Story 2 is selected in the list of files. Check the *Replacing selected text* option (Figure 11) and click on OK. By selecting *Replacing selected text*, Story 2 will replace all text in column one, and continue through the publication until it runs out. Story 2 is only a small file and it finishes halfway down the middle column. The rest of the original text in Tabloid will remain. If you selected *Replacing entire story*, Story 2 will fill the same amount of space, and the rest of the text belonging to this same story in Tabloid will disappear.

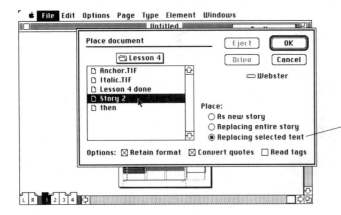

Figure 11. *Select the file Story 2 to replace the text in column one, page one. Make sure you also choose* Replacing selected text *and then click on OK.*

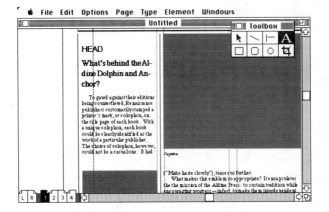

Figure 12. *The new file will replace the old column one text and will continue until it runs out. Sometimes, however, this replacement may require a little tidying up.*

5. *Replace the graphic at the top of the middle column with the file Anchor.TIF from the Lesson 4 folder.*

The graphic we refer to here is actually the gray square at the top of the middle column. See Figure 1 again if in doubt. Move across the page so that you can see this graphic (Figure 13).

After spotting this space set aside for a graphic and selecting it, move to the *Place* command (Figure 14), select the file Anchor.TIF, and check the *Replacing entire graphic* option (Figure 15).

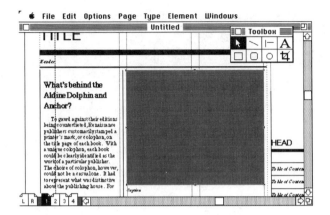

Figure 13. Locate the graphic placeholder at the top of the middle column and select it.

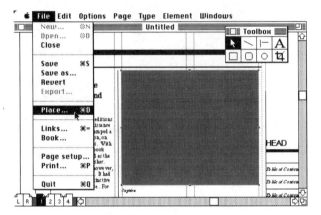

Figure 14. After selecting the space set aside for the graphic, move directly to the Place *command in the* **File** *menu.*

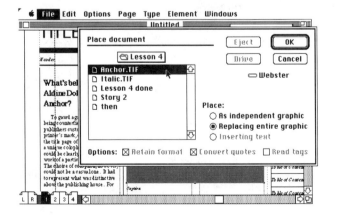

Figure 15. Choose the file Anchor.TIF, and check the Replacing entire graphic *option. Click on OK.*

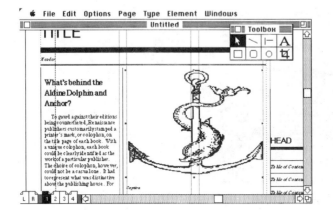

Figure 16. The file Anchor.TIF will entirely replace the graphic place-holder and take up no extra room.

6. Replace the title with a title of your own choosing.

Move up to the top of the page and locate the title. This is the title placeholder — it has defined the position as well as the type specifications of the title. In fact, we could replace this in either of two ways — by selecting it using the pointer or text tool, and loading a new text file to replace this one; or by selecting the title with the text tool, and simply typing in the new option. Because the title is small, the latter method is probably the easier of the two.

Select the title in text mode, and simply type in your new one (Figures 17 and 18).

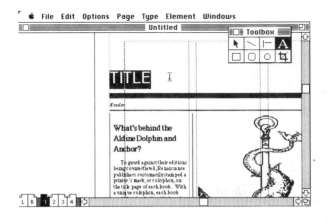

Figure 17. For this step we have selected the title using the text editing mode.

Figure 18. Type in
immediately what
you want the new
title to say.

7. Save the template as a publication called Template Exercise.

You should note that the template you are working with is actually called *Untitled* — indicating that we are working on a copy of the original. We must now save it as a new publication. Use the *Save* command in the **File** menu (Figure 19) and insert the name Template Exercise in the name rectangle (Figures 20 and 21).

Figure 19. It is a good idea
to save before you finish. At
any stage you can save
your work by choosing the
Save command from the
File menu.

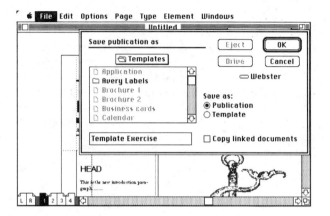

Figure 20. Insert the name in the name rectangle as shown. Here we have called the publication Template Exercise.

Figure 21. The name of the publication replaces Untitled in the menu bar at the top of the screen.

Module 11

Style Sheets

Style Sheets

A PageMaker style sheet comes with every template or publication that you open. A style sheet contains several different groups of text characteristics, identified by style names, that can be applied to text. For example, a style sheet may contain four different style types — Heading, Body text, Subheading, and Footnote. (These style names can be anything you want them to be.) Heading may be defined as Bookman, 24 point, Bold, Centered, 1 inch of space below, indented 0.5 inches from the left and right, etc. All other style names are defined differently again. You decide what attributes are saved under what name.

After you load in text and are ready to format, previously you would have had to move through a lot of menus and commands to format such things as headings, as described above. However, with style sheets, you can apply the style name Heading to a paragraph on the page, and all attributes defined for this style are applied immediately. This is a far quicker way to format text than just using the **Type** menu.

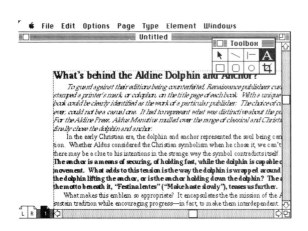

Figure 1. All these paragraphs on this page were formatted in a matter of seconds using style sheets, as opposed to minutes using the **Type** *menu.*

The benefits of style sheets do not end there. Let's say, for example, that you have applied the style Heading to a hundred or so paragraphs throughout a very large publication. This Heading style may be defined as Palatino 24 point bold, yet you decide that it would look better if it were Bookman 24 point bold. Instead of having to find every single paragraph and alter its appearance, all you have to do is alter the attributes of the style name Heading. Every time this style occurs in the text it will be automatically altered.

Style sheets can be copied from publications and templates to other publications or templates. Style sheets can also link up to word processors, like Microsoft Word, that use style sheets.

Don't get style sheets confused with type styles—which include bold, italic, underline, etc. When we talk about applying a style, we mean applying one of the style names in a style sheet to text.

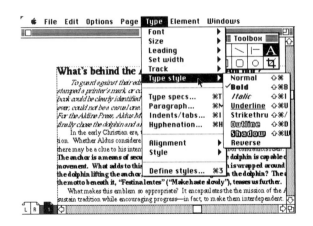

Figure 2. Don't get the type styles shown here confused with styles from the style sheet — they are separate.

Adding new styles to a style sheet

You can add new styles to a publication's style sheet by (1) defining styles from scratch, (2) basing a new style's definition on one of the current publication's existing documents, (3) copying an existing style sheet from another publication, (4) importing styles with imported word-processed documents, or (5) importing style names from a word processing program.

We will look at each of these methods soon, but first we will look at the default styles in every style sheet.

As already mentioned, every template or publication contains a style sheet, even if you are not really aware of it. To see the styles that are used in your current document, choose the *Style palette* command from the **Windows** menu (Figure 3). Just below the Toolbox will appear a small window as shown in Figure 4.

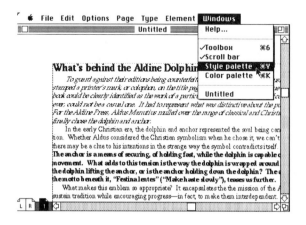

Figure 3. When using style sheets, make sure that the Style palette is shown by choosing the Style palette command in the **Windows** menu.

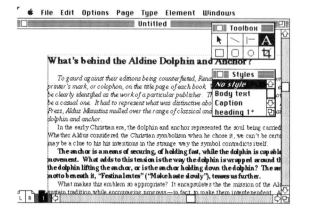

Figure 4. The Style palette will appear somewhere below the Toolbox, and can be moved around similar to the Toolbox.

Inside this Style palette there may be listed several different names. However, if this is a new publication (that is, it contains no imported text) it will contain several style names by default— *No style* and *Body text,* as well as *Caption, Headline, Subhead 1,* and *Subhead 2.*

Body text, by default, includes such attributes as Times 12 point, auto leading, flush left paragraphs, first indent and hyphenation on. We will show you in this module how to modify all default styles, and how to create your own, among other things.

Defining styles from scratch

Once you become familiar with PageMaker's style sheets, you will continue to add new styles — maybe some to represent headings, others for footnotes, formulas, headers, and footers, etc. The alternative PageMaker method that you can also use to format text, involves selecting text, moving through the commands in the **Type** menu, and applying characteristics one at a time. We covered this in detail in Module 4. This latter method can still be used in conjunction with style sheets, so that you can phase in the use of style sheets if they are a little confusing at first.

Before we start looking at creating new styles, load some text onto the page to see the effect of creating these new styles. We have used the Story 2 file from the Lesson 4 folder in the Tutorial folder, and loaded it into a single column. If, upon loading the text, new styles appear in the style sheet, ignore them for now. Don't worry if the formatting of your Story 2 file looks different to our Figure 5; we'll adjust this later on in Figure 16.

New styles are created using the *Define styles* command in the **Type** menu (Figure 5). Select this command now. The dialog box of Figure 6 appears.

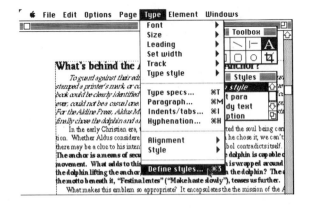

Figure 5. The Define styles *command is used to create new styles to add to the style sheet.*

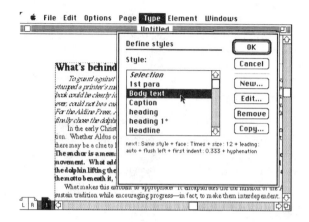

Figure 6. The Define styles *dialog box. Don't worry if your dialog box has some different styles to ours — it does not matter.*

At the left of this dialog box is the list of all the styles in this publication's style sheet. It should include *Selection* and *Body text*. Listed below these names may well be other styles that are different to our Figure 6. This does not matter. Next to these styles are several commands we will use to create and edit new styles.

Click the mouse on the word Selection at the top (Figure 7). Below the list of names will appear a list of type specifications. This reflects exactly the attributes of the selected text (if any is selected). If you click on the word Body text (Figure 6), the text specifications now reflect exactly how the style Body text is set up. It is possible that Body text and Selection are set up exactly the same or they may differ.

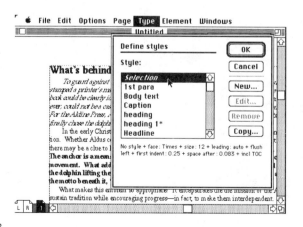

Figure 7. Compare Figures 6 and 7 to see the type specifications defined below the list of styles.

To create a new style, you must click on the command *New* within the Figures 6 or 7 dialog box. A New dialog box of Figure 8 will appear. This relates to having the word Selection actually highlighted, as we have done in Figure 7. If Body text or other styles had been selected, then this selected style would appear in the *Based on*: rectangle in Figure 8. The words No style should appear in the *Based on*: rectangle.

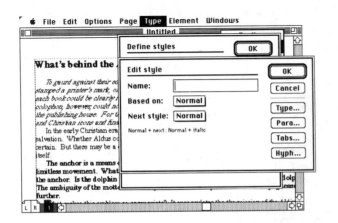

Figure 8. Upon selecting the New command from the dialog box in Figure 7, you will see this dialog box.

Insert a name for the style in the Figure 9 dialog box. You can call it anything you like, but make it applicable to its use so it can be recognized later on. We called ours 'title' in Figure 9.

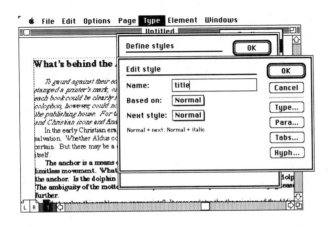

Figure 9. Your first step in this dialog box is to name the style you are about to create. Try to name it something applicable — it makes things a lot easier later on.

To the right of the Figures 8 and 9 dialog box are four commands — *Type*, *Para*, *Tabs*, and *Hyphenation*. As you click on any one of these, the appropriate dialog box relating to these commands is shown (Figures 10 through 13). In these dialog boxes, adjust this style we have just created so that it is fairly big — or at least a little different from Body text. Every time you use one of these commands in Figures 10 through 13 and click on OK, you are returned back to the dialog box of Figure 9 to use another command. When you have finished defining the style exactly as you want it, click OK to return to the previous *Define styles* dialog box, shown in Figure 14.

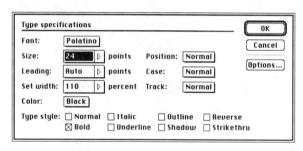

Figure 10. This dialog box is invoked after clicking once on the Type command in the dialog box of Figure 9. Change your box to reflect these selections.

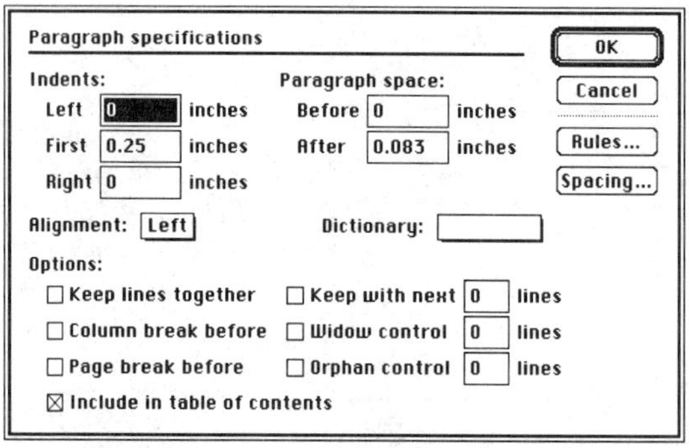

Figure 11. This dialog box is accessed by clicking on the Para *command from the Figure 9 dialog box. Adjust your box to the same as this.*

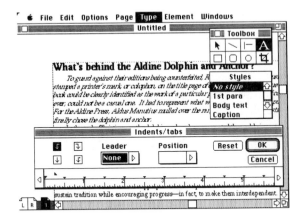

Figure 12. *This box comes from selecting the* Tabs *command. Keep it as is.*

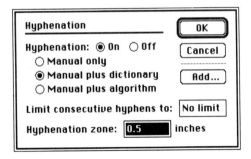

Figure 13. *This box is from selecting the* Hyphenation *command. Keep it as is.*

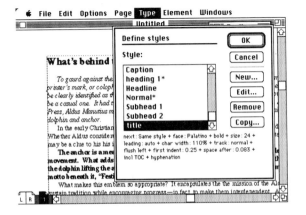

Figure 14. *Using these commands, we selected the attributes of the style we created. Note the list of new attributes we have assigned to the new title style at the bottom of the dialog box.*

Click on OK in the Figure 9 dialog box to return to the Figure 14 *Define styles* dialog box. In Figure 14, the new style name (title) joins the list of styles. Underneath the list, the type specifications for this new style are listed. Click OK again to return back to the page. Joining the *Style palette* is the new title style we created (Figure 15). The *Define styles* command can be used as many times as is necessary to create all the styles you need.

For example, in Figure 14 after defining the title style, we could have chosen *New* to create more styles if we wished.

Figure 15. The style we created, title, has been added to the list of styles in the Style *palette.*

Applying styles

Styles are very simple to apply to paragraphs on the page. If you want one paragraph alone to use the new style you created, move to the text cursor. Insert this text cursor inside the paragraph, or simply select the entire paragraph if that makes it easier. Now move back to the *Style palette* and click on the style you would like to apply to the paragraph. Instantly, any attributes you created with that style are applied to the paragraph on screen. Whatever attributes it had previously have been overwritten.

Several paragraphs in sequence can be applied a style at once, simply by selecting more than one paragraph before you select the style.

Styles can also be applied via the *Style* command in the **Type** menu (Figure 18).

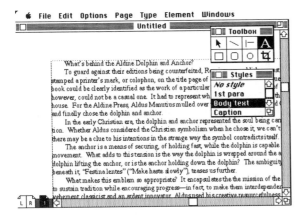

Figure 16. To illustrate how we can apply styles to unformatted text, we have changed all the paragraphs of our Story 2 text file to look the same. We applied the Body text style to everything by simply selecting all text and clicking on Body text in the Style palette.

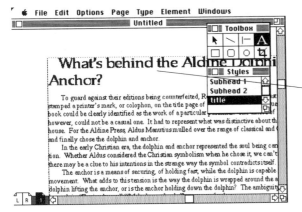

Figure 17. To apply styles to single or multiple paragraphs of text, we insert the text cursor in the first paragraph (or whatever paragraph(s) we like), and click on title in the Style palette. The attributes we defined in creating the title style (Figure 14) are instantly applied to that paragraph.

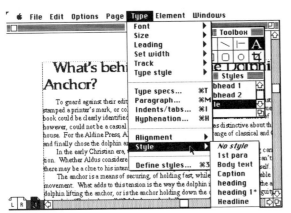

Figure 18. Apart from clicking on the style name in the Style palette, styles can also be applied via the Style command in the **Type** menu. Simply insert the text cursor in the paragraph(s) concerned, and choose the Style command and then the style name of your choice.

Editing styles

Let's say you have applied the style Body text to most of your publication, and now decide that it must be changed. As we mentioned, when looking at the benefits of style sheets, there is no need to find all the paragraphs that use the Body text style. Simply edit the Body text style itself, and all paragraphs using this style will change. To perform this example, we first of all change all text back to Body text, as shown in Figure 19, except for the first paragraph heading.

Select once again the *Define styles* command from the **Type** menu. From the list of styles presented (Figure 20), select the style you would like to edit, and choose the *Edit* command to the right of this box. You will then get the Figure 21 Edit style dialog box. Alternatively, you can click on the name of the style you would like to edit in the *Style palette*, with the Command key depressed, to go immediately to Figure 21. We have chosen to edit Body text.

In either case, you will see the dialog box in Figure 21 that was also used to create a new style. You can edit the style the same way you created a new one. When editing styles, the name comes up automatically in the *Name* rectangle at the top of the dialog box.

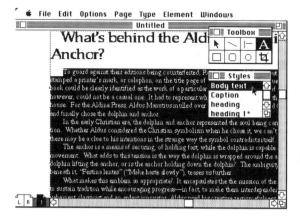

Figure 19. Every paragraph in this document has been applied the Body text *style (apart from the first paragraph). We now want to change the look of* Body text, *without having to select every paragraph before we do it. To work through this, first change back to* Body text *style, as we have done here, if you have been experimenting with other styles in the* Style *palette. Simply select the whole page (except for the first paragraph) with the text tool, and click on* Body text *in the* Style *palette.*

Select the four commands one at a time — *Type, Para, Tabs*, and *Hyphenation* — and edit the style as you see fit. Choose OK twice when you are happy with the newly edited style.

Figures 20 through 23 provide examples of using the *Edit* function with the *Body text* style.

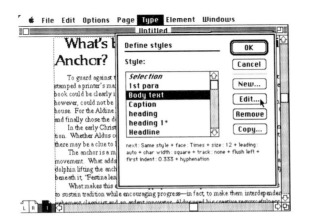

Figure 20. Our first step in editing Body text *is to select the* Define styles *command again. From the dialog box that then appears, select* Body text *(or whatever style you would like to edit), and choose the* Edit *command.*

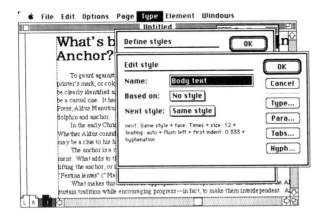

Figure 21. After selecting Edit *from Figure 20, this dialog box will appear. Note how the name* Body text *already appears next to* Name.

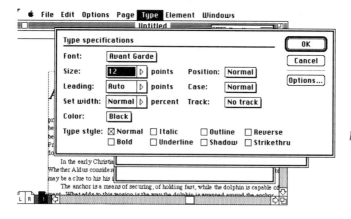

Figure 22. We chose the Type command from Figure 21, and were presented with this dialog box. We changed the font from Palatino to Avant Garde.

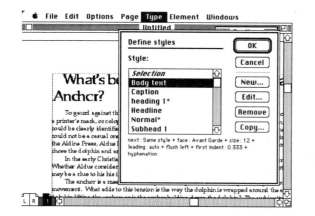

Figure 23. Note how the definition of Body text has changed to reflect the new attributes. Compare with Figure 20 —Avant Garde has now replaced Times as the font.

In Figures 20 through 23, we have only changed the type specifications to Avant Garde. *Para, Tabs,* and *Hyphenation* commands were not changed. The result is shown in Figure 24. All the paragraphs throughout the document that use the Body text style will be updated with its new characteristics.

One other option in the *Edit style* dialog box of Figure 21 is *Next style.* This allows you to set the style of the following paragraph. For example: a paragraph defined as heading and a *Next style* as Body text: every time you start a new paragraph after a heading, it will always be Body text (Figure 25).

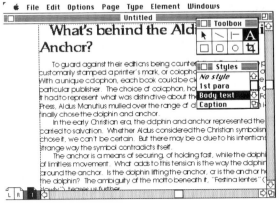

Figure 24. All paragraphs that use the Body text *style have changed, while all paragraphs that use other styles remain as they were. Compare this* Body text *style with that of Figure 19.*

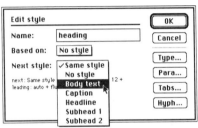

Figure 25. The Next style *option lets you establish what attributes a following paragraph will have. This is helpful when you want a certain style of paragraph to always follow a specific style.*

Removing styles

Removing a style is even easier than creating or editing a style. Choose *Define styles*, select the style from the list you would like to remove, and choose the *Remove* command (Figures 26 through 28).

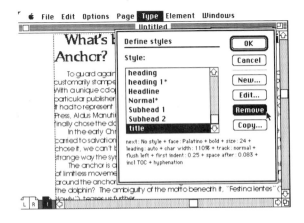

Figure 26. Removing a style is as simple as selecting it from within the Define styles *dialog box and clicking on* Remove.

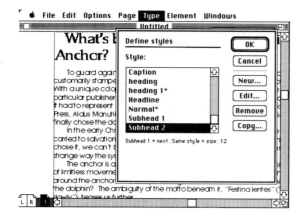

Figure 27. The style name is immediately dropped from the style sheet.

Figure 28. All paragraphs that use the style we just deleted remain as they were, but they now use the style name No Style.

Basing a new style's definition on an existing style

Let's say that you have now created several styles in this style sheet, one of which may be a heading style. Now you want to create another heading style that is similar to the existing heading style but with only minor changes. Instead of creating the new style from scratch, it would be nice to be able to start with the old heading attributes, and modify them to create the new style. This is quite possible.

We have a Style name in our style sheet called 'heading' (see Figure 29). We are now going to use it to produce a new style. You can follow on with us, if you wish, using any style name of your choice. The principle is the same.

When you choose the *Define styles* command from the **Type** menu, you would normally go straight to the *New* command to create the new heading style. However, before you do this, click in the list of styles on the original heading style before you choose *New* (Figure 29). Upon choosing this style first, in the *Based on* box in the *New* dialog box of Figure 30 will be the name of that style. Insert the name of the new style (in our case, heading 2) and change what you have to. In this way, new styles can be created with a minimum of fuss (Figures 30 through 33).

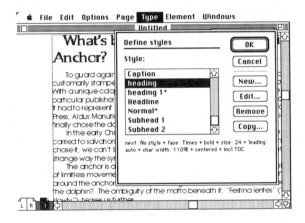

Figure 29. To create a style similar to another style, select that style in the **Define** styles dialog box before selecting the New command.

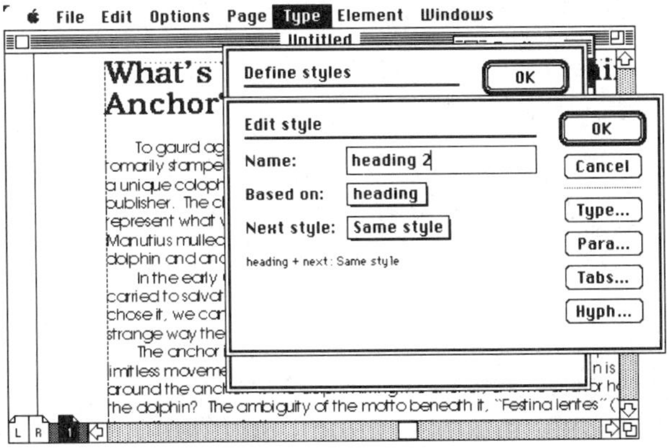

Figure 30. In the New dialog box that then appears, a name will appear in the **Based** on box. This will be the name of the style selected before selecting New (heading). Enter the name of the new style above this name (heading 2).

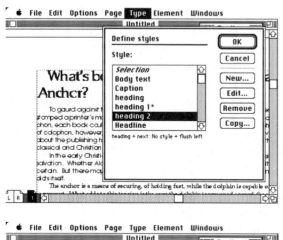

Figure 31. We used the Para command from the dialog box in Figure 30 to slightly alter the appearance of the new style. Note, however, the description of the new style below the list tells us that heading 2 is exactly the same as heading except that it is flush left. Note that in Figure 29, one of the attributes of a heading paragraph was that it was centered.

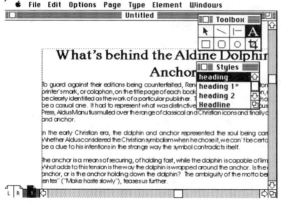

Figure 32. To see the difference between the styles of heading and heading 2 (note how heading 2 has been added to the Style palette), we have selected the first paragraph and tagged it with our original heading style (which included centering). Note how this paragraph is centered. Now ensure the text cursor is still in this first paragraph....

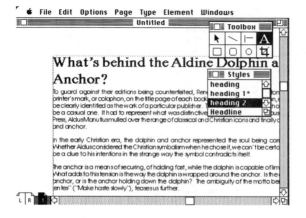

Figure 33. ... and click on the style heading 2 in the Styles palette. The paragraph now looks basically the same as the heading style, yet is flush left.

Renaming styles

The easiest way to rename a style is to create one exactly the same with the new name (using the method described above), and then remove the one with the old name. Effectively, you have renamed the style.

Copying an existing style sheet from another publication

Copying a style sheet from a separate publication or template into another document will combine the two style sheets together. Once again, to use this function, you must choose the *Define styles* command. This time, however, select the *Copy* command (Figure 34).

You must know which document you want to copy a style sheet from. When the *Copy* command is chosen, you are presented with a list of publications (you can move to other folders), from which you must select a publication or template (Figure 35). Once you select the new document (Figure 36), PageMaker spends a few seconds combining the two style sheets together, and you are returned to the new *Define styles* dialog box. It now contains a list of styles from both style sheets (Figure 37).

The *Style palette* will then also reflect the new list of styles that have been added (Figure 38).

Figure 34. *To copy the style from an existing style sheet (resident in another publication or template), get to the* Define styles *dialog box, and then click on the* Copy *command.*

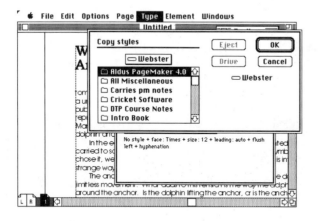

Figure 35. You will then see the list of publications and templates in the currently open folder. Locate the publication or template you know has the other style in it, and click OK.

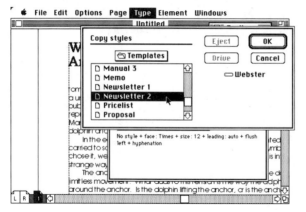

Figure 36. We are going to copy the styles from a file called Newsletter 2 from the Templates folder.

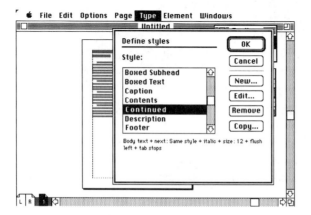

Figure 37. After a few seconds, the styles from Newsletter 2 are combined with the styles that already exist in this publication. Note the new styles listed in this dialog box, as compared to Figure 31.

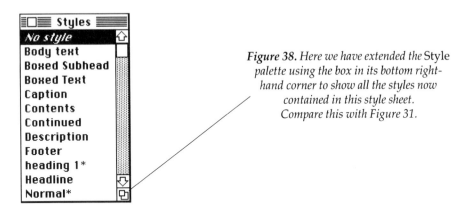

Figure 38. Here we have extended the Style palette using the box in its bottom right-hand corner to show all the styles now contained in this style sheet. Compare this with Figure 31.

When copying styles, you may get a message asking you if you want to copy over existing files. Click OK for yes or Cancel for no.

Importing styles and style names with word-processed documents

This can be achieved in two different ways. First, if your word processor uses style sheets, they can be applied and created with all style names being carried through into PageMaker. If the style names already exist in PageMaker, then the imported paragraphs that use that style are applied the attributes of PageMaker's style. Don't forget to ensure that *Retain format* is checked in the *Place* dialog box (Figure 39).

If your word processing document does not support style sheets, it is still possible to have the imported text formatted to a pre-defined PageMaker style. All you need to do is type style name tags in angle brackets (<>) at the beginning of each paragraph, making sure that these tags match the correct style names in your publication's style sheet.

Figure 39, which shows the *Place* command dialog box, indicates the different options to choose from in deciding how to import text with styles intact. The *Retain format* option brings in all the style information intact from word processors that support style sheets. The *Read tags* option reads the tag names you have typed into your word-processed document using angle brackets.

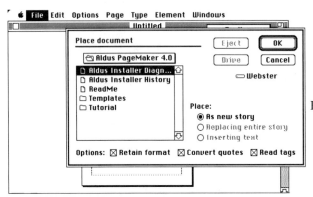

Figure 39. The Place *command dialog box. Note the* Retain format *and* Read tags *options at the bottom of the dialog box.*

Figure 40. Styles are recognized from word processing programs. Here we are looking at the dialog box for the Define Styles *command within Microsoft Word.*

Overriding styles

Any style can be overridden by selecting the text and applying any type specifications from the **Type** menu. If you apply a new style altogether to a paragraph that currently uses an overridden style, only type style changes (such as italic or bold) will survive the style change.

Changing styles from story editor view

To change a style from story editor view, you must first activate the *Style palette* from the **Windows** menu so it appears on screen. Let's say we wanted to change the highlighted paragraph style of Figure 41 from Normal to Caption. We can either highlight a paragraph by dragging the text tool over the text, or by simply clicking on the paragraph style name in the left column. Then go to the *Style palette* and select Caption. This paragraph will assume the new style and the new name will appear at the left (Figure 42).

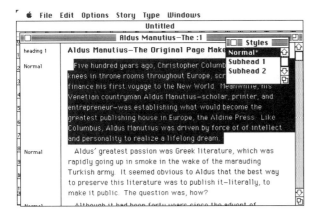

Figure 41. *In story editor view the paragraph styles appear in the left margin. The style of a selected paragraph will also be highlighted in the* Style *palette. To change the style of a paragraph in story editor view, highlight the paragraph and select the new style from the* Style *palette.*

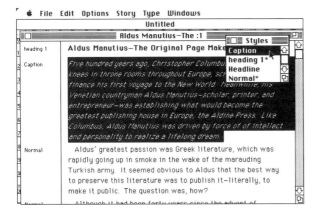

Figure 42. *We have changed the style of the selected paragraph to* Caption. *The new style name also appears in the left margin at the beginning of the paragraph.*

Module 11 Exercise

Style Sheets

Module 11 Exercise
Style Sheets

In this exercise we will work with style sheets and see how quickly we can format text using this method.

This training material is structured so that people of all levels of expertise with PageMaker can use it to gain maximum benefit. To do this, we have structured this material so that the bare exercise is listed below this paragraph on just one page, with no hints. The following pages contain the steps needed to complete this exercise for those that need additional prompting. The **Style Sheets** module should be referenced if you need further help or explanations.

Module 11 exercise steps

1. *Create a new document, using one Letter vertical page with margins of your choice.*

2. *Create and/or modify three style sheets using these names and parameters:*

    (a) Body text
    10 point Helvetica
    Left justified
    Automatic leading
    .1 inch paragraph spacing
    .1 inch first line indent
    2 inch left indent

    (b) Heading
    24 point Times Bold
    Centered
    Automatic leading
    .2 inch above and below para spacing

    (c) Introduction
    14 point Times Italic
    Centered
    15 point line spacing
    .12 inch above and below para spacing

3. *Load the file Lead Story from the Lesson 2 folder.*

4. *Apply the **Heading** style to the first paragraph of the text file, the style **Introduction** to the second paragraph, and the style **Body text** to the rest of the paragraphs.*

5. *Change the **Body text** style so that it uses the font Times Roman and is 12 point.*

The steps to completing this exercise are found on the following pages.

The steps in detail

1. Create a new document, using one Letter vertical page with margins of your choice.

Start PageMaker using the *New* command from the **File** menu. If a publication is already open, remember that you will have to close this publication using the *Close* command before another can be opened. In the *New* dialog box, make sure that a Letter page is selected, and that only one page is in the publication.

See Figures 1 and 2 for this first step.

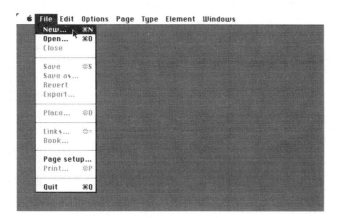

Figure 1. Select the New command from the **File** menu to create a new publication.

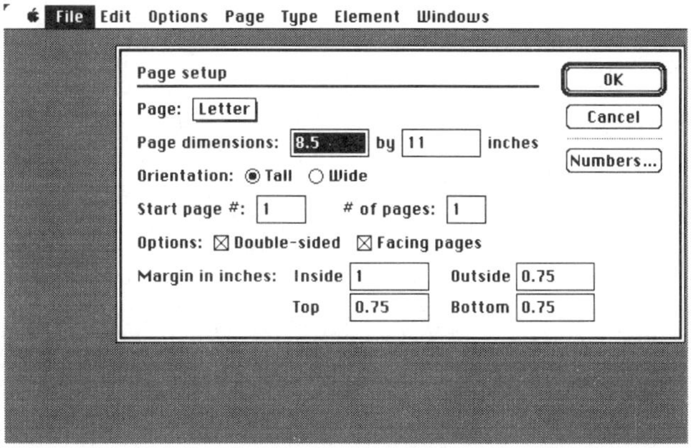

Figure 2. Set up a single vertical Letter page (the other settings do not matter for this exercise).

2. Create and/or modify three styles using these names and parameters:

(a) Body text
10 point Helvetica
Left justified
Automatic leading
.1 inch paragraph spacing
.1 inch first line indent
2 inch left indent

Body text is a style that will have to be modified rather than created, as it always exists by default in every publication. In order to modify how it is set, first choose the *Define styles* command in the **Type** menu (Figure 3).

Figure 3. The Define *styles command from the* **Type** *menu is used to alter and create styles.*

In the dialog box that then appears (Figure 4), click on the line that reads Body text. When you do this, the bottom of this dialog box will list all the attributes currently assigned to Body text — these are the ones we will change. Some may be set up already — it depends on how Body text is currently set for your publication.

To alter the settings for Body text, we must click on the *Edit* command within the Figure 4 dialog box. By doing this, you will see the additional dialog box of Figure 5.

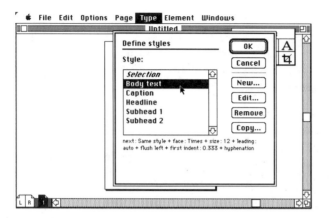

Figure 4. The Define styles *dialog box — note how we have clicked on Body text to select it. The current attributes for Body text are then shown in the bottom of this dialog box. Your settings may differ — it really doesn't matter at this moment.*

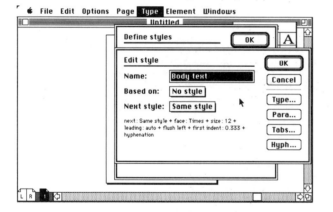

Figure 5. After clicking on the Edit *command in Figure 4, you will see the* Edit style *dialog box.*

   This *Edit style* dialog box will have the name of the style we are editing at the top of its dialog box against Name (in our case Body text), as well as the current attributes of this style at the bottom. To the right of this box are four commands — *Type, Para, Tabs,* and *Hyphenation.* Each one of these commands allows us to alter a different part of the style. The two commands we will look at to change the style according to our step 2 (a) specifications for Body text, are the *Type* and *Para* commands. Click first on the *Type* command.

Yet another dialog box will appear (Figure 6) — the type specifications of the style Body text. Part of our specifications for step 2 tells us that we must change Body text to 10 point Helvetica. Just change the *Font* and *Size* commands to that shown in Figure 7.

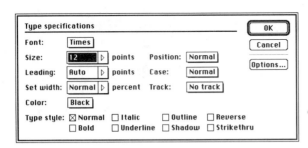

Figure 6. After selecting the Type *command from Figure 5, you will see this dialog box. Don't worry if it contains different values than this — it depends on the defaults currently set for your copy of Page-Maker.*

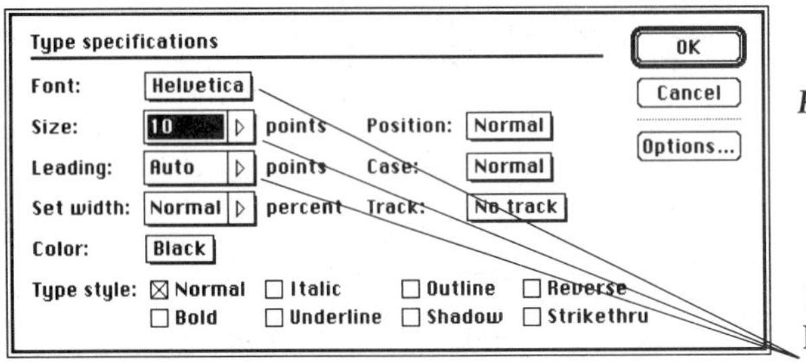

Figure 7. Change your settings to match these, as defined in the specifications for this step.

We have changed to Helvetica for Font *and 10 points for* Size. *Also make sure that* Leading *is set to Auto.*

The *Leading* must also be set to Auto. Click on OK once you have set the text attributes correctly, and you will be returned to the *Edit style* dialog box (Figure 8).

Notice in the Figure 8 dialog box that the current settings for Body text have been altered. Compare Figure 8 with the settings of Figure 5.

Figure 8. Read the attributes for Body text now in this dialog box — they have changed to reflect the changes we just made. Compare with Figure 5.

Now click on the *Para* command in the Figure 8 dialog box to alter the other settings for Body text. Once again you will see a new dialog box, shown in Figure 9.

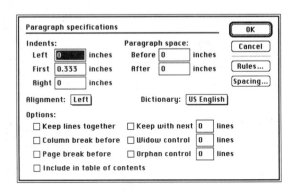

*Figure 9. The Para dialog box is identical to the Paragraph command in the **Type** menu — although this time it applies to a style rather than /.;selected text.*

Here we must set a .1 inch paragraph spacing, a .1 inch first line indent, and a 2 inch global left indent. If you find that you are working in millimeters, don't worry or try to change to inches using the *Preferences* command from the **Edit** menu. Remember, we can still set measures in inches even if millimeters is selected (just put an 'i' after your value).

To set the paragraph spacing, choose .1 inch in the *After* rectangle (Figure 10), or in the *Before* rectangle, if you so desire.

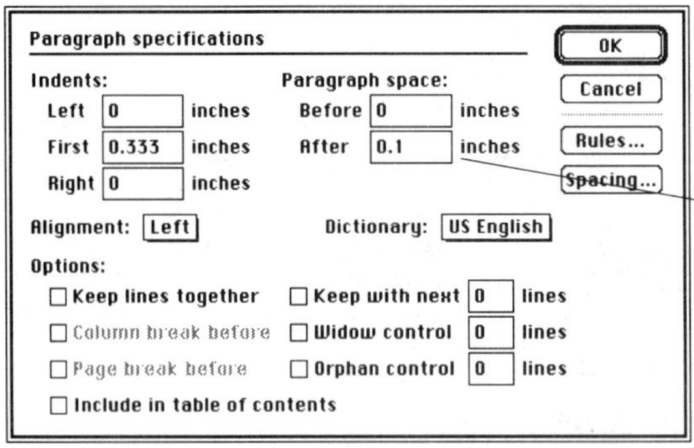

Figure 10. Here we have inserted 0.1 inches of paragraph space in the After *rectangle.*

The first line indent is set using the *First* rectangle — put a .1 inch in it also (Figure 11). To set a global left indent of 2 inches, you must insert 2 in the *Left* rectangle (Figure 11).

Finally, make sure that the setting for *Alignment* is Left as per our specifications of Left justified (Figure 11).

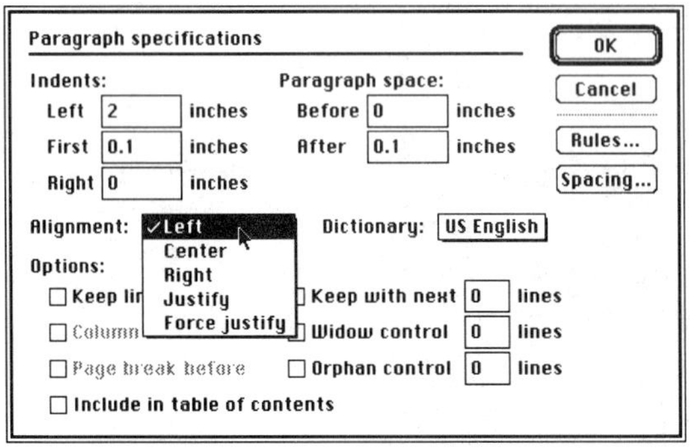

Figure 11. Here we have set a global left indent of 2 inches and a first line indent of .1 inches.

Note we have also checked Left as our preferred alignment.

After making these settings, click OK in Figure 11. Click on OK again to return you to the *Define styles* dialog box of Figure 12. In it, you can see all the settings we have altered for Body text.

From here we can go about creating the other styles we were asked to create.

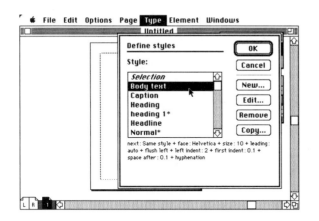

Figure 12. *After clicking OK from the dialog box in Figure 11, and then OK from the* Edit style *dialog box, we are returned to the original* Define styles *dialog box. Note all the new settings for Body text.*

(b) Heading
24 point Times Bold
Centered
Automatic leading
.2 inch above and below para spacing

To create any new style, click on the *New* command from the *Define styles* dialog box of Figure 12. The *Edit style* dialog box is shown again (Figure 13), although this time it is slightly different. It has no name in the Name box. Notice that the *Based on:* box includes the name Body text. This is because we had Body text selected in the *Define styles* box before clicking on *New*. This doesn't matter, as we can still define the new Heading style as we like.

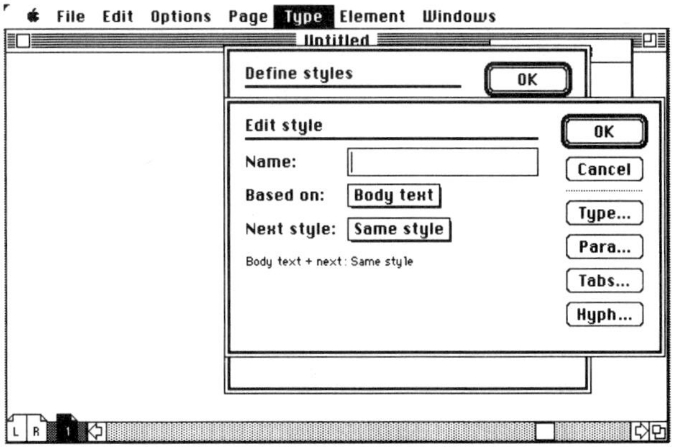

Figure 13. *The* New *dialog box is very similar to the* Edit style *dialog box — but this time we must insert a name for the new style (Figure 14).*

405

We must name the style before we create it. Simply type the name of this style — the mouse cursor is correctly positioned to receive the name, which in this case is *Heading* (Figure 14).

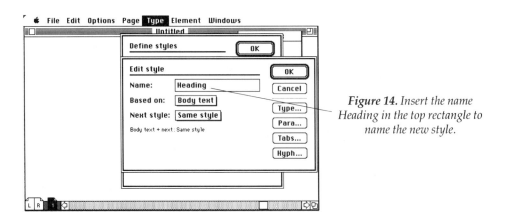

Figure 14. *Insert the name Heading in the top rectangle to name the new style.*

After naming the new style, use the four commands in this dialog box to alter the settings for the Heading style, although the *Type* and *Para* commands are still the main ones. Select *Type* to get to Figure 15.

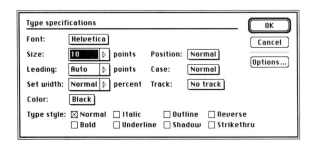

Figure 15. *This is the dialog box we get after selecting the* Type *command from Figure 14. This needs to be altered to that of Figure 16.*

Within this command we must make the size 24 point, the font Times, and the type style Bold. We must also make sure the leading is set at Automatic. Perform these steps as you would normally do as shown in Figure 16, then click OK. You will then be returned to the Figure 14 dialog box. Click on the *Para* command to get to Figure 17.

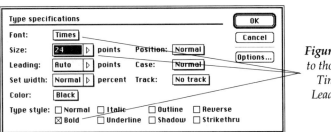

Figure 16. Change the settings to those defined in this step — Times, 24 point, and bold. Leading is Auto as required. Then click on OK.

Use the Figure 17 dialog box to center the paragraph, and also put .2 inches of space before and after it (Figure 18). Click OK twice to return to the *Define styles* dialog box of Figure 19.

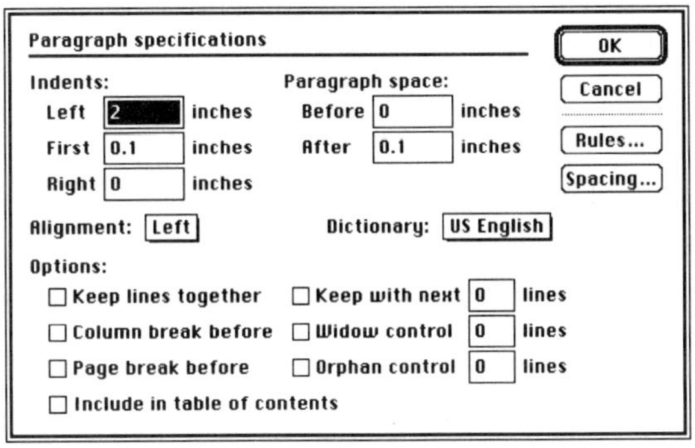

Figure 17. The dialog box for the Para command may initially look like this. However, all we want for Heading is space before and after — not left, first, or right. See modifications performed in Figure 18.

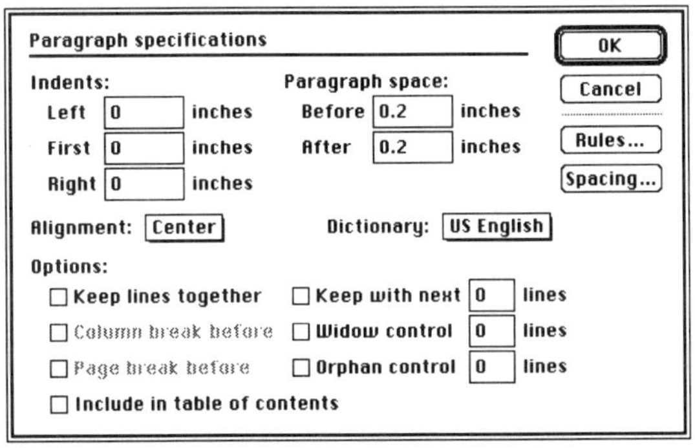

Figure 18. We must change to zero all the Indents rectangles on the left, and insert .2 inches of space in the Before and After Spacing rectangles. We have also changed the Alignment to Center.

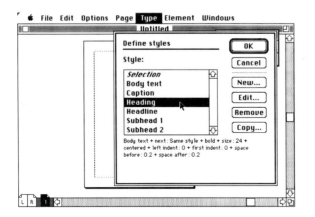

Figure 19. *After returning once again to the* Define styles *dialog box, you will find* Heading *has been added to the list of styles. If selected, its attributes will then be listed at the bottom of the dialog box as shown here.*

The Heading style just created is now in the Figure 19 dialog box, as well as its attributes at the bottom of the screen. Click on the name Body text in the list and the attributes will change again as indicated in Figure 20.

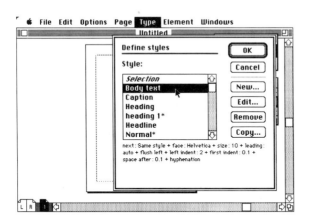

Figure 20. *If Body text is selected within this dialog box, then its settings are immediately reflected beneath the list of styles.*

We must create one more tag from within this dialog box.

(c) Introduction
14 point Times Italic
Centered
15 point line spacing
.12 inch above and below para spacing

3. Load the file Lead Story from the Lesson 2 folder.

This file is loaded via the *Place* command in the **File** Menu, and exists in the Lesson 2 folder.

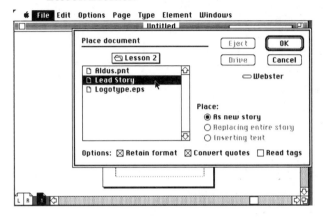

Figure 21. Here we are loading in the file Lead Story.

Once loaded, flow the file onto the first page as indicated in Figure 22 (this should only have one column in it).

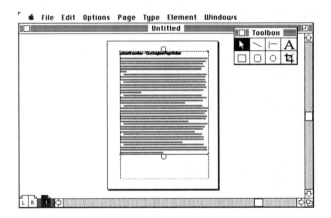

Figure 22. Lead Story loaded onto the page.

*4. Apply the **Heading** style to the first paragraph of the text file, the style **Introduction** to the second paragraph, and make sure that the rest of the paragraphs in the text file use the style **Body text**.*

After the text has been loaded onto the page, applying tags is simple. You must, however, first make sure that the *Style palette* is visible through the *Style palette* command in the **Windows** menu (Figures 23 and 24).

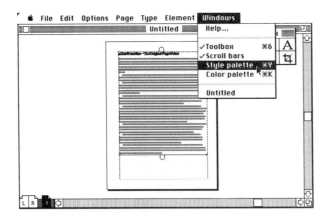

Figure 23. The Style *palette is accessed via the command of the same name in the* **Windows** *menu.*

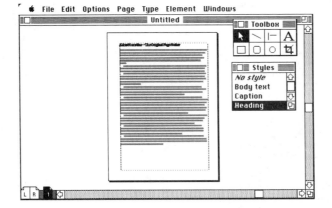

Figure 24. The Style *palette is now visible complete with default styles, the styles we created, and any styles that may have been carried through from the word processor that created the text.*

We have been asked to apply the tag Heading to the first paragraph in the text file. This is achieved by simply inserting the text cursor (make sure this is selected in the Toolbox) somewhere in this first paragraph. The whole paragraph need not be selected. From here, move to the *Style palette* and click on the style Heading (Figures 25 and 26). All the attributes we gave to Heading will be instantly applied to this paragraph.

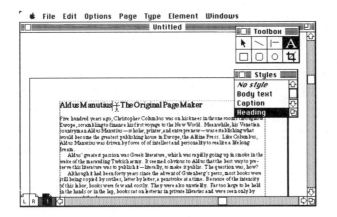

***Figure** 25. Select the paragraph that you would like to apply a new style ...*

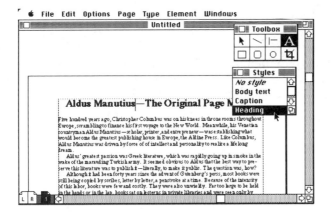

***Figure** 26... and click on the name of the style in the* Style *pallete.*

To apply the tag Introduction to the second paragraph, the steps are the same: insert the text cursor in this paragraph, and click on the style Introduction in the *Style* palette. Once again, everything that was set up for Introduction is applied to the paragraph with the text cursor in it.

Figure 27 illustrates the result.

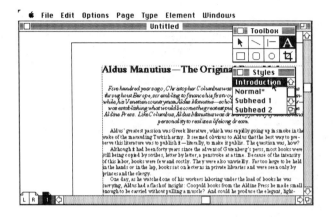

Figure 27. Here we have inserted the text cursor in the second paragraph on the page, and clicked on the style Introduction. Immediately the text has been altered to reflect this (italic, centered, etc).

Finally, to make sure that all other paragraphs are using the style Body text, select the rest of the page using the text editing tool and click on the style Body text in the *Style* palette (Figure 28). All the text will change to Body text if it was not already using it. For example, note the 2 inch left indent in Figure 28, which was part of our Body text definition. Don't worry about the extra tags that may have entered the *Style palette* — these are merely carried through from the word processor — we will not use them.

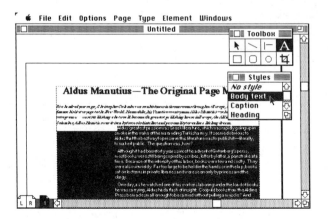

Figure 28. All other paragraphs were selected and applied the style Body text in one operation. Remember, when applying a style to more than one paragraph, select these paragraphs before clicking on the style in the Style palette.

5. *Change the* **Body text** *style so that it uses the font Times Roman and is 12 point.*

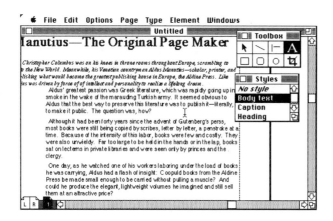

Figure 29. Here we see in Actual size view the look of Body text at 10 point Helvetica. We wil now change all Body text to 12 point Times by making one simple change.

The style Body text can be altered without having to select any text. Merely move to the *Define styles* command in the **Type** menu, and select the style Body text from the list (Figures 30 and 31).

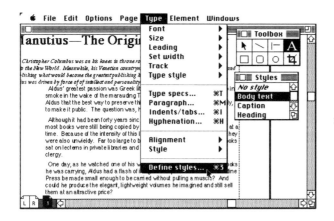

Figure 30. Move to the Define styles *command in the* **Type** *menu to change the attributes of Body text style.*

From here, choose the *Edit* command (Figure 31), and from within the *Edit* style dialog box choose the *Type* command (Figure 32).

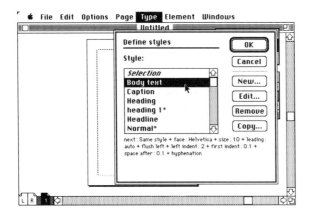

Figure 31. From the Define *styles dialog box select the style Body text and choose the* Edit *command.*

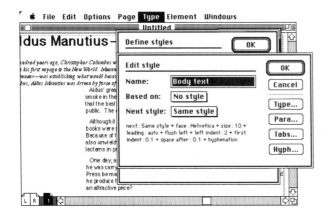

Figure 32. Once in the Edit *style dialog box, choose the* Type *command. Note that the Body text name is already included, as we had selected it in Figure 31. Now move to Figure 33.*

From within the *Type* dialog box in Figure 33, change the Body text to Times 12 point. When you then return to the page, all paragraphs with the Body text tag will change to this new style (Figures 34 and 35).

Compare Figure 35 to that of Figure 29.

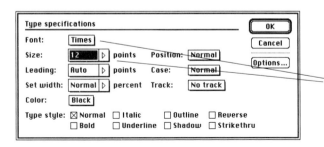

Figure 33. *Change the settings for the Type specifications of Body text to reflect this dialog box — that is, Times at 12 points.*

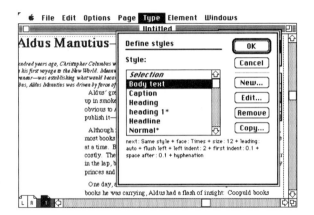

Figure 34. *When you return back to the Define styles dialog box, the attributes for Body text listed along the bottom of this box have changed to reflect the new settings.*

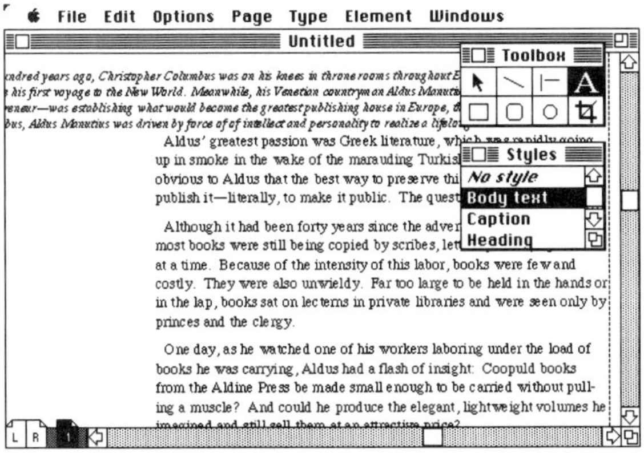

Figure 35. *Back on the page, all Body text paragraphs have been altered to reflect the new settings for Body text. Compare to Figure 29.*

Module 12

Setting Defaults

Setting Defaults

Introduction

At times it is useful to be able to utilize certain preset options within PageMaker without having to readjust them each time PageMaker is opened. Of course, you could set up a template to do this (one that used all the settings you want to), but there are times when we just don't need to use a template.

So far we have looked at many options that can be invoked within PageMaker. *Rulers, Column guides,* and *Style palette* are but a few of the things that can be invoked when entering PageMaker. Suppose, however, that you always wanted the *Style* and *Color palette*, you always wanted *Rulers*, and you always wanted to use an A3 page with pre-defined margins all around (Figure 1). Setting this up each time you opened PageMaker would not be very productive.

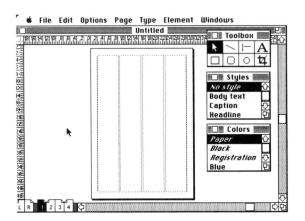

Figure 1. *If all of your documents start off like this (Rulers, Style palette, Color palette, four columns, A3 page size), it would take a fair amount of setting up each time.*

PageMaker is normally shipped with pre-defined options for many of its settings. These are referred to as the default settings and may differ for the U.S. and non-U.S. versions. The settings for all standard defaults are listed in the Appendix of the PageMaker Reference Manual.

What we would like to do, for ease of operation, is to sometimes change these defaults to those of our own choosing. This can be done in two ways through the Application defaults or Publication defaults.

Application defaults

To customize the use of PageMaker with Application defaults, you must have no publication currently open. This will involve either using the *Close* command to get rid of the current document, or simply restarting PageMaker (it always opens at the Page-Maker desktop without a publication).

You may have noticed that even with no publication open, all the menus appear at the top of the screen, and all can be invoked (Figures 2 and 3). Further, many of the commands within these menus can be selected.

Any command that can be selected while no publication is open, can be set up as a default. For example, we could select the *Rulers* command, and although no rulers would show now, we could see that it has a tick alongside. This indicates that its default status is On (Figure 3). If we wish the rulers not to come up automatically in any of our publications, we would select this command now to uncheck it. Whenever a new publication is now opened, the rulers would not appear. In this way, you can set up defaults in the following areas:

Type Size, Face, Leading, and Style;

Page Size and Margins;

Rulers command;

Text flow;

All guide commands;

Line and Fill;

Preferences;

Palettes;

Colors; and so on.

Remember that any of these commands, if altered while no publication is opened, will become the new default. Any time a new publication is opened, it will use these settings. These defaults can be changed, if wished, for a single publication.

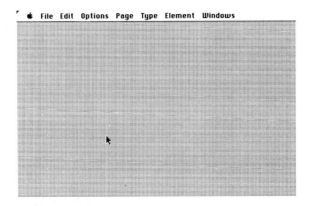

Figure 2. *PageMaker opened without a publication will look like this.*

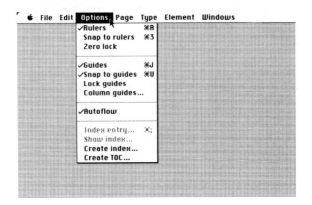

Figure 3. *All menus and many commands can be used even though no publication has been opened.*

Publication defaults

Publication defaults differ from Application defaults in that Publication defaults are set up inside a publication, and are only defaults for that particular document. For instance, you may decide that in one publication you wish to draw lines of 8 point thickness. Before you draw any lines, you would move to the *Line* command in the **Element** menu, and select an 8 point thickness line (Figure 4). Any line now drawn within this publication will automatically be of 8 point thickness (Figure 5).

To create these Publication defaults, it is important that the pointer tool is chosen and no text or graphics is selected.

As another example, if you want the *Style palette* to always appear on screen for a particular publication, turn it on in the **Windows** menu, and it will appear on screen every time this publication is opened and used.

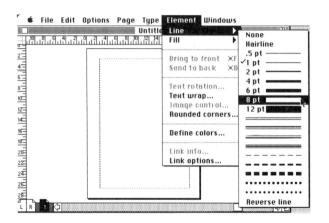

Figure 4. Publication defaults are set up within a publication. In this case, because a line is not selected as we set a line thickness, all future lines will be of 8 point thickness.

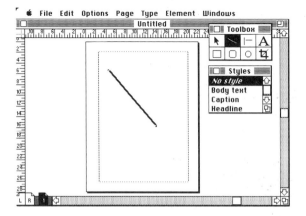

Figure 5. Any line drawn now is 8 points thick.

More default settings

You will most likely not set up defaults for every single Page-Maker option or command, but only the most commonly used functions. We will go through some of the more common ones and show you how to set up or change the default to suit your needs.

Open PageMaker 4, or if you are already in it close your current document. For the rest of this module we will be setting Publication defaults, which will only apply to the current document.

First, select *New* from the **File** menu.

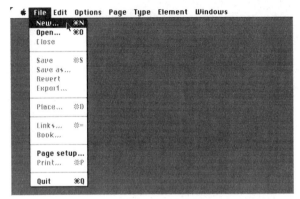

Figure 6. Choose New *to start up a new PageMaker document.*

We have now been confronted with the *Page Setup* dialog box (Figure 7). Here we have stayed with the Letter option for the page size. We want this document to be in portrait format so we select *Tall* for *Page orientation.* Next we have given ourselves five pages. Both *Double-sided* and *Facing pages* should be set already by default, so we'll leave them as they are. Lastly, we will give our page a one inch margin around the whole page.

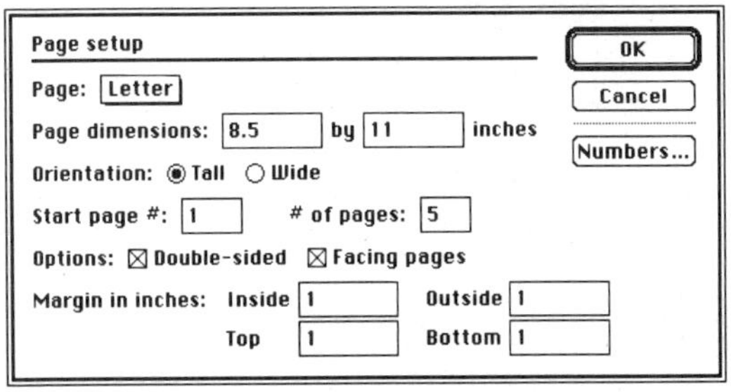

Figure 7. These are the defaults we set in the Page setup *dialog box as discussed above.*

After clicking on OK, the document will open to our specified defaults. We can then set up some more defaults before doing anything. First, select the *Column guides* command under the **Options** menu.

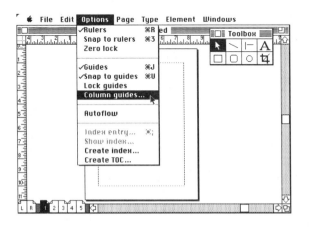

Figure 8. To set up your columns for this publication, go to the Column *guides command under the* Options *menu.*

Here we will give ourselves four columns and leave the 0.167 inch spacing (Figure 9). Click on OK, and now the page will have four columns.

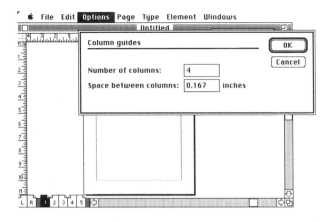

Figure 9. The Column *guides dialog box where we give our document four columns.*

Now select the *Paragraph* command in the **Type** menu.

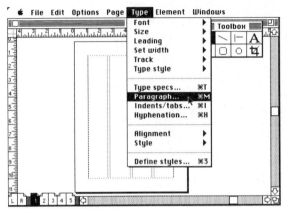

Figure 10. Our next step is to set the defaults in the Paragraph *specifications dialog box.*

In the *Paragraph* specifications dialog box (Figure 11), set a first line indent of 0.25 inches, and the same amount of space before and after each paragraph. Also set the alignment to *Justify* and put *Widow* and *Orphan* control on three lines.

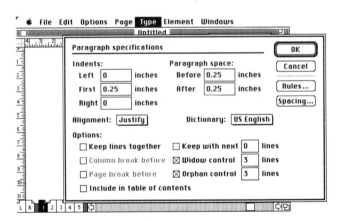

Figure 11. Our default settings for the Paragraph specifications dialog box.

Under the **Edit** menu is the *Preferences* command. In this dialog box (Figure 12), we are going to change the measurement system to millimeters and the Vertical ruler to millimeters. There are other options here to change, but we are going to keep them at their original default values. After clicking on OK, notice the measurement system of the ruler change from inches to millimeters.

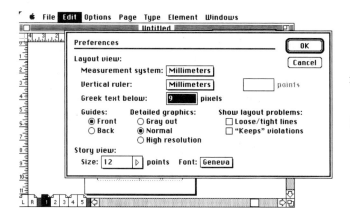

Figure 12. The Measurement system *in this dialog box controls all measurements in PageMaker. We have chosen millimeters for our general measurements and the vertical ruler.*

Looking under the **Options** menu (Figure 13), we can see we have a few more choices here that can be altered for this publication. There's the *Rulers* command, which gives you the choice of having *Rulers* on or off, or the *Snap to rulers, Guides, Snap to guides* and *Lock guides* commands, that you can also have on or off for your current document.

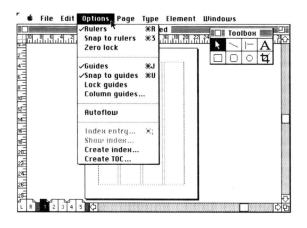

Figure 13. The **Options** *menu has a number of choices that you can set at the beginning of your document so they can stay in use the whole time. Another choice here is the* Autoflow *command that can be set so text automatically flows onto your page.*

Under the **Type** menu (Figure 14) we can go into the *Type specifications* dialog box and set up defaults for our text.

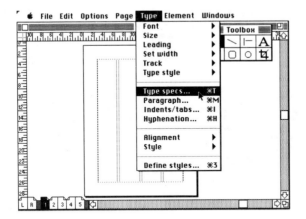

Figure 14. The Type
specs *dialog box is
accessed through the*
Type *menu.*

Here we are going to change the font to Palatino, with 11 as the
new point size. Then we will change the Leading to 13, which
works well with 11 point text. The only other change we will make
here is the type style to italic.

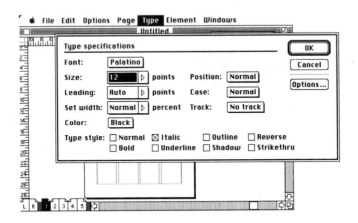

Figure 15. The Type
specs *dialog box after
we made our changes.*

The finished result of all these default changes can't really be
observed until you start putting text onto the page.

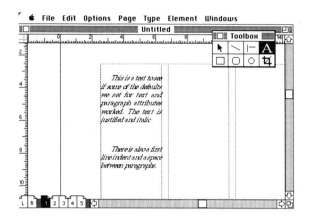

Figure 16. *This figure shows some of the defaults we have set. For example, Palatino 12 point italic text, justified, on a four column page, with a 0.25 inch first indent.*

Some of the defaults we set for *Type* and *Paragraph*, as shown in Figure 16, all worked correctly. If we now saved this as a new publication and re-opened it, all the new defaults set in this module would still apply. Try it if you wish. If all our future documents were the same, or very similar to this document, we could have set all these defaults as Application defaults before the document had been opened.

Many more defaults can be set in PageMaker. For a comprehensive list of all U.S. and English defaults, see the Appendix of your PageMaker Reference Manual. The procedure for setting all other Application and Publication defaults is as simple as selecting them and changing them to your own requirements.

Module 12 Exercise

Setting Defaults

Module 12 Exercise

Setting Defaults

In this exercise we are going to set different defaults, both Application and Publication, to illustrate how easy this is to do within PageMaker.

This training material is structured so that people of all levels of expertise with PageMaker can use it to gain maximum benefit. To do this, we have structured this material so that the bare exercise is listed below this paragraph on just one page, with no hints. The following pages contain the steps needed to complete this exercise for those that need additional prompting. The **Setting Defaults** module should be referenced if you need further help or explanations.

Module 12 exercise steps

1. *Set the Application default for PageMaker as follows:*
   Letter size page
   2 columns
   20 mm margins top, bottom, left, and right
   Style and Color palettes showing.

2. *Start a new publication to check if the new defaults have worked.*

3. *Once you have started the new publication, new Publication defaults as follows:*
   Lines at 2 point thickness
   Shades at 10 percent black
   Text must be 14 point Helvetica Bold, justified

4. *Test both graphics and text to determine if you were successful.*

The steps to completing this exercise are found on the following pages.

The steps in detail

1. Set the Application default for PageMaker as follows:
   Letter size page
   2 columns
   20 mm margins top, bottom, left, and right
   Style and Color palettes showing.

Application defaults are the defaults that are set when no publication is open, yet will apply to all publications that are created subsequently. So, to set these defaults, make sure that only PageMaker (and not a publication or template) is open. By double-clicking on the PageMaker 4 option at the Macintosh desktop, you will get the screen as shown in Figure 1.

Alternatively, if you are in an existing PageMaker publication, even with a blank page you must choose *Close* from the **File** menu (not *Quit*). Your screen will then look like Figure 1.

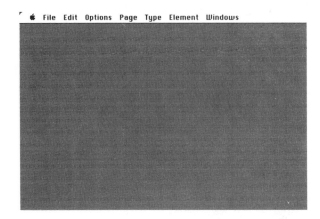

Figure 1. PageMaker without a publication open will look like this.

To set the page size and margin defaults, choose the *Page setup* command in the **File** menu as shown in Figure 2 (remember do not open or create a new publication). In the dialog box that appears (Figure 3), set up Letter page size, and change all four margins to 20 mm.

The columns default figure must be set using the *Column guides* command in the **Options** menu (Figure 4). Set the number to 2 in the ensuing dialog box (Figure 5).

Module 12 Exercise - Setting Defaults

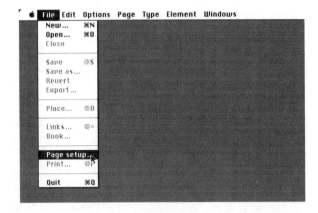

*Figure 2. Select the Page setup command in the **File** menu.*

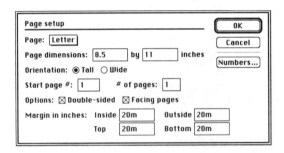

Figure 3. Change the page size to Letter (it may already be there), and change all margins to 20 mm. Click on OK.

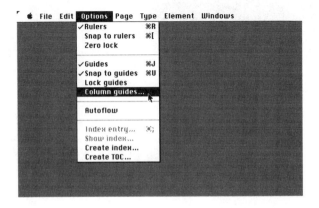

*Figure 4. Select the Column guides command from the **Options** menu.*

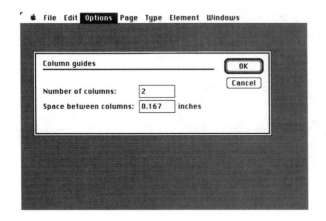

Figure 5. In the dialog box that ensues, insert 2 for the number of columns. Once again, this number of columns will become the default.

Finally, to make sure that the *Style* and *Color palettes* are showing, select these options from the **Windows** menu (Figures 6 and 7). Although once again you will not see anything happen, you will know these palettes will show, if the options are checked in this menu.

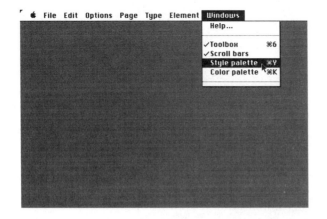

Figure 6. Select the Style palette *command from the* **Windows** *menu.*

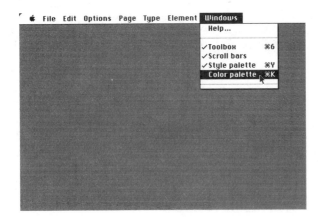

Figure 7. Also select the Color palette *command from the same menu.*

2. Start a new publication to check if the new defaults have worked.

Select *New* from the **File** menu — all the options we set in step 1 should be visible on the page. See Figure 8 for what to expect. The *Page setup* dialog box will also have appeared before the Figure 8 screen, allowing you to check that margins were 20mm (or 0.788 inches), and the page was of Letter size.

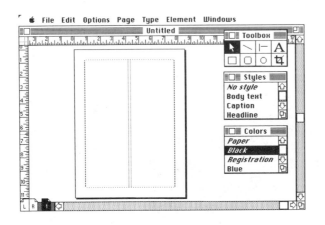

Figure 8. Your PageMaker *publication, opened using the* New *command from the* **File** *menu, now shows the options displayed in this figure — including both palettes and two columns.*

3. Once you have started the new publication, set new Publication defaults as follows:
Lines at 2 point thickness
Shades at 10 percent black
Text must be 14 point Helvetica Bold, justified

Publication defaults are set when a publication is opened. These defaults will not affect any other publications, but will affect the future operation of this publication.

To set the line thickness default, make sure that there are no selected lines on the page and the pointer tool is highlighted. To make sure, do not draw any lines or even select the line drawing tool. Move to the *Line* sub-menu in the **Element** menu, and select the 2 points thickness line (Figure 9). As with Application defaults, you will not see anything happen as yet.

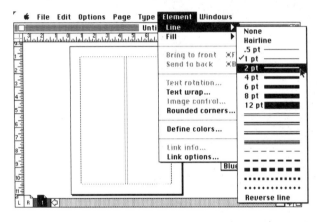

Figure 9. Select the 2 pt option in the Line *sub-menu to ensure the default for all lines drawn in this publication is 2 points. Make sure before you do this that NO lines are selected on the page, because if they are, only those lines are affected by this command.*

The same procedure is followed to set the graphic fill pattern — make sure there are no selected graphics on the page, your pointer tool is selected, and move to the *Fill* sub-menu under the **Element** menu. Within this menu, select 10% as the fill pattern (Figure 10).

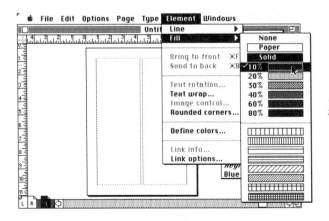

Figure 10. Select the 10% command from the Fill *sub-menu to set this graphic default.*

435

The text default setting also works in a similar way. Make sure the pointer tool is selected, move to the **Type** menu, and select the *Font* command. Run the mouse down the typefaces and select Helvetica (Figure 11).

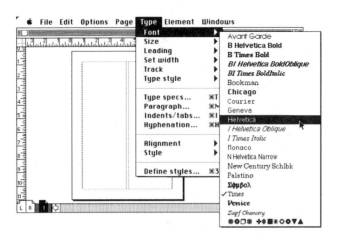

Figure 11. Here we set the Font default to Helvetica.

Select next the *Size* command from the **Type** menu, and run the mouse down to 14 point (Figure 12).

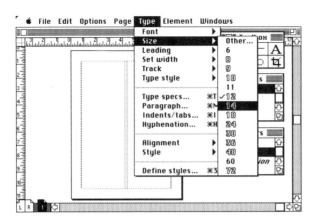

Figure 12. The size default is set to 14 point.

The next step is to select the *Type style* command and choose Bold from the sub-menu (Figure 13).

Finally, select Justify from the *Alignment* command towards the bottom of the **Type** menu. All of these settings could have been selected at one time through the *Type specs* command and its associated dialog box.

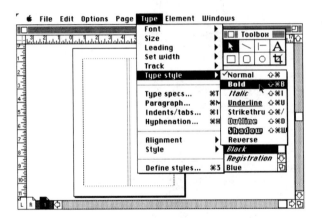

Figure 13. *The type style default is set to Bold.*

4. *Test both graphics and text to determine if you were successful.*

To test whether the Publication defaults we set were successful, draw a rectangle on the page. It should have a 2 point outline and a 10% shade. Go to *Actual size* view and compare your graphic to Figure 14. Test both line thickness and fill shade settings through the *Line* and *Fill* sub-menus.

To test the type specification defaults, we must type some text onto the screen. Make sure you are in a view that allows you to read the text, select the text tool, click on the page, and tap on the keyboard. Although you may not immediately be able to tell how the text is set up (Figure 15), select the text and move through the **Type** menu to see exactly what its attributes are.

Module 12 Exercise - Setting Defaults

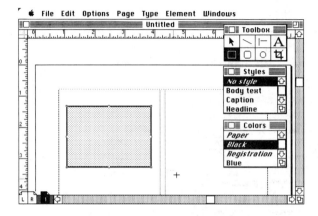

Figure 14. *Here we have selected the rectangle tool and drawn a rectangle on the page to test the default settings. Go to the Line and Fill sub-menus to check that 2 point thickness and 10% fill actually apply to this box. Unless you have made an error in step 3 (Figures 9 and 10), this should be the case.*

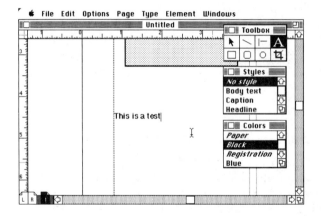

Figure 15. *Now we select the text tool and type some text on the page. Once again, it appears as though the default settings we created have worked. However, to make sure, select the text and check its attributes through the* **Type** *menu.*

Module 13

Color

Color

PageMaker 4 supports color operation on both the screen and output devices. Although no low-cost laser printers are available for use with color as yet, there are continuous new developments in this area. At the moment, the ImageWriter range of printers using color ribbons are providing quite good results.

To see PageMaker in color you need a Macintosh with the appropriate color monitor. Monitors with the Macintosh can display up to 16 million colors, with 256 showing at any one time. All the features of PageMaker involving color can also be run on monochrome monitors, although it becomes a little more difficult to follow, define, and apply colors.

Color can be set using the Macintosh control panel, where menus, commands, and background shades can be set for all applications, regardless of whether or not the individual publications themselves support color.

On a monochrome monitor, the PageMaker page appears as a black outline, with a dotted line representing the margin inside that page. On a color monitor, all guides appear as solid colors, making them easy to see, and to quickly see which are printing

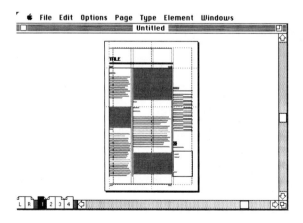

Figure 1. PageMaker still works with color on monochrome monitors. This page, with the appropriate printer, will print in full color.

Using color

Two commands, the *Define colors* from the **Element** menu and the *Color palette* from the **Windows** menu, both need to be invoked to see how color works within PageMaker. Select first the *Color palette* command as shown in Figure 2.

The *Color palette*, which then appears (Figure 3), looks very similar to the *Style palette*, and in fact works in a very similar way. Colors can be defined much as styles are, and can be applied to any selected portion of the page simply by clicking on the color you want from the palette. This is a virtually identical process to that of applying styles as discussed in Module 11.

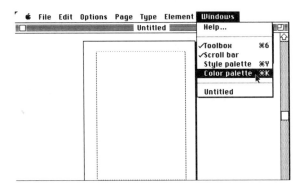

Figure 2. Choosing the Color palette *command in the* **Windows** *menu will make visible the* Color palette *as shown in Figure 3 (assuming that it is not already visible).*

Three colors are defined within the *Color palette* (Figure 3) by default. These are *Paper, Black,* and *Registration.* We will look quickly at what each of these mean before we start creating and applying other colors.

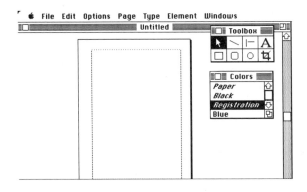

Figure 3. The Color palette *looks very similar to the* Style palette *used by PageMaker. Your* Color palette *may also include Red, Blue, and Green colors by default.*

441

Paper, Black and Registration

Paper is set to white by default — you can change it, however, to any color you wish.

Black is the tone black and cannot be altered. It is more or less the normal color — the color you apply to an element on the page in the absence of any other color. Black initially applies to all text.

Registration is not really a color, but it can be applied to any element of the page. It is used when color separations are to be created directly from PageMaker. Normally, for separations, every new color is printed on a page by itself. Any page element that uses the color Registration, however, will be printed on every page in the document.

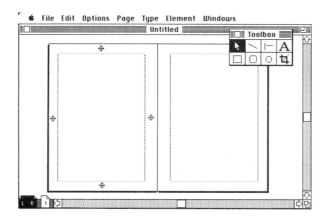

Figure 4. The color Registration is applied to Registration marks placed on the master pages of your document. These Registration-colored markers help a printer align color separations much more accurately. These Registration markers print on every page when using color separations.

that publication occupies an entire page. You produce them on any blank area on the master pages (Figure 4) and they will then be replicated throughout the document. The color Registration is then assigned to these marks, allowing them to print on every page irrespective of the overlay's color. Registration marks are created so that the page can be aligned perfectly when color printing is being done.

If your publication's page is smaller than the printed page, PageMaker can then automatically add the Registration marks. This is done by checking *Spot color overlays* and *Crop marks* in the *Print options* dialog box.

Other default colors

Red, Blue, and Green are the other default colors that may be defined and may appear in your *Color palette*.

Registration marks are added manually to a publication when

Creating new colors

To create a new color, you must select the *Define colors* command in the **Element** menu (Figure 5). The dialog box of Figure 6 then appears.

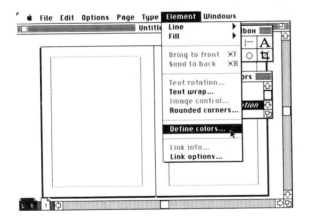

Figure 5. The Define colors *command is used to create your own colors. It causes the dialog box of Figure 6 to occur.*

As you can see, the process of creating new colors is almost identical to creating new styles, up to this point at least. Select *New* in the dialog box of Figure 6 to define a new color.

After selecting *New*, you will be presented with the additional dialog box of Figure 7.

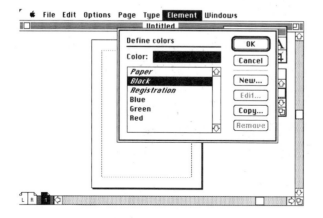

Figure 6. *The* Define colors *dialog box looks like this — much like the* Define styles *dialog box.*

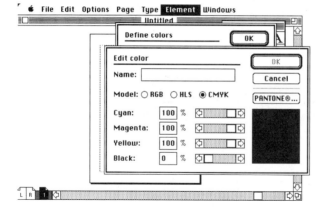

Figure 7. *After selecting* New *from the dialog box in Figure 6, this additional dialog box appears.*

Figure 8. *Enter a name for your color in the rectangle to the top of the dialog box — the same way as you would name a new style.*

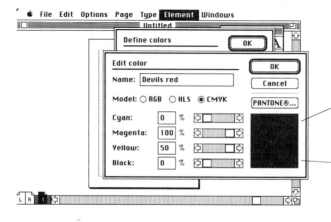

This box is actually in two parts. The top half reflects the color as it is edited. On a color monitor, it constantly changes to reflect any changes made to the percentages to the left. The bottom half of the box will reflect the current color as it is defined.

There are several ways to create the new color. First give the color a name, in much the same way in which we gave the style its name. In Figure 8, we have chosen Devils red.

Your next choice is the Model to be used to create the color. The reason that you can select between four models — *RGB, HLS, CMYK* — and *Pantone* is because traditionally these are the four ways in which colors can be defined. Depending on your background, your available information, and the output device you are using, you can opt for any one of the four.

Process and spot colors

PageMaker gives you the choice of using either process or spot color for your publication. Process coloring is the blending of four separate colors to create the colors for your publication. For process colors to work, four color separations are needed. The CMYK color model is used when defining process colors and they are generally used for photographs, where colors are required to blend. Spot colors are defined in the Pantone section. Only one spot color can be applied to an object at a time and this concept is generally used for logos and such, when one solid color is needed.

RGB

The *Red, Green,* and *Blue* method is perhaps the easiest and most common of the three methods for defining colors. It relies on the defining of a percentage of each of the three colors (Figures 8 and 9) — which gives a wide range of possibilities as to actual colors, although not quite as many as the other methods. Use the horizontal scroll bars (Figure 9) to adjust the percentage of each color.

This is much like mixing red, green, and blue paint in different proportions to create a new color.

Model: ◉ RGB ○ HLS ○ CMYK

Red: [90] % ◁▦▦□▦▷   *Figure 9. Here we have defined a color using*
Green: [5] % ◁□▦▦▦▷   *different values for Red, Green, and Blue using the*
Blue: [10] % ◁□▦▦▦▷   *RGB method.*

At the extreme right of the Figure 8 dialog box, a small rectangle showing the current color will constantly update, giving you some idea of what color you have created (this is assuming that you have a color screen — you are working blind with a monochrome monitor). With a monochrome monitor, you must have some idea beforehand as to what percentage makeup you require for your color(s).

HLS

The *Hue, Lightness,* and *Saturation* method (Figure 10) works in a very similar way to the RGB method, only Hue is defined from 0 to 360 degrees, while Lightness and Saturation are defined as percentages. Once again, the color being created will constantly update next to the percentage bars on color monitors.

Note: The HLS model cannot be used to create new colors — only to edit or change existing ones.

Model: ○ RGB ◉ HLS ○ CMYK

Hue: [356] ° ◁▦▦▦□▷   *Figure 10. This color, defined using the HLS model,*
Lightness: [47] % ◁▦□▦▦▷   *is exactly the same as the color defined in Figure 9*
Saturation: [89] % ◁▦▦□▦▷   *using the RGB method.*

CMYK

The *Cyan, Magenta, Yellow,* and *Black* method is the most precise of all — each of these four colors and tones can be defined in percentages. Otherwise, it works in exactly the same way as the two methods described above. The CMYK model is commonly used in four-color printing. It is the method to use for defining process colors.

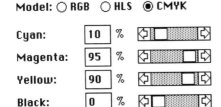

Figure 11. Once again we have the same color defined as in the last two figures, yet this time using the CMYK model.

Note that with any of the above three methods you use to describe a color, selecting a new method will cause the percentage bars to display that color in the new method (see examples in Figures 9 to 11).

After defining the required color, selecting a name (Devils red in our case in Figure 12), and selecting OK from Figure 12, the new color has been created. It will appear in the *Define colors* dialog box of Figure 13, and the *Color palette* of Figure 14. It is then available for selection when required.

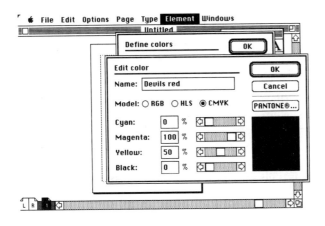

Figure 12. After having gone this far — naming the color, and defining the color using any of the three models so far discussed, you are ready to click on OK. We have called our new color Devils red.

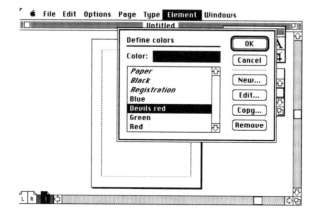

Figure 13. *After clicking OK in the previous dialog box of Figure 12, you will be returned to this dialog box. The new color is now listed with the default colors, and on a color monitor, will be displayed in the rectangle next to the word Color.*

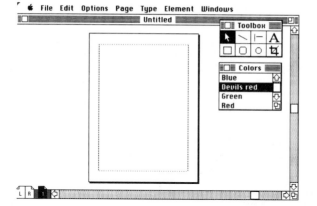

Figure 14. *After exiting the Figure 13 dialog box, the new color will also be listed in the Color palette.*

Pantone

The fourth color option is based on the Pantone colors. Pantone Color system is a library of standard industry colors used by printers and graphic designers. PageMaker now contains this library of colors in the *Pantone Color* dialog box, accessible through the *Edit color* dialog box (Figure 15). The Pantone color library is well suited for defining spot colors.

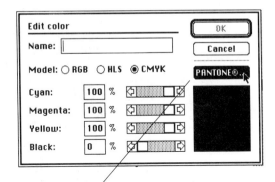

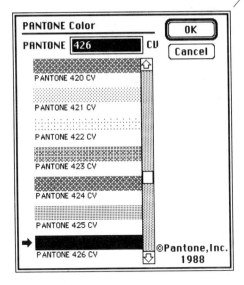

Figure 15. The Pantone Color *dialog box is accessed through the* Edit color *dialog box. It is a library of standard industry colors where each color is represented by a number.*

The vertical scroll bar to the right of the colors in the *Pantone Color* dialog box is used like any other scroll bar in PageMaker. By holding the mouse down on either the up or down arrow, all color possibilities can be viewed. When you've found the color you want, you click on it once, and then click on OK.

449

Because Pantone colors are recognized by number, if you know the number of the color you want, you can key it directly in the box above the colors. On returning to the *Define colors* dialog box, you will see the Pantone color you selected in the list of colors. After leaving this dialog box, you will also see the new Pantone color in the *Color palette*. This new color is applied to text and graphics the same way all other colors are. See Figures 16 through 18 for more details.

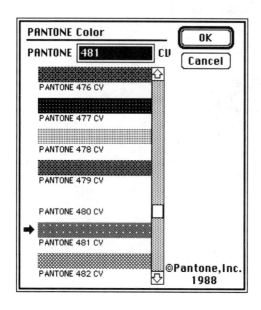

Figure 16. *We selected Pantone 481 by simply clicking over it. It now has the large arrow to the left of it, and the number is reflected in the rectangle above the colors. Now see Figures 17 and 18.*

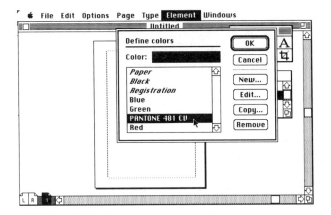

Figure 17. On returning to the Define colors *dialog box, we see the Pantone color we selected in our list of colors.*

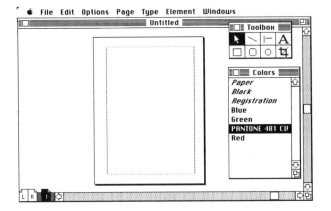

Figure 18. The color is also displayed in the Color palette.

Editing colors

Any color besides Black and Registration can be edited using the *Edit* command in the Figures 6 or 17 *Define colors* dialog box. Select the color you would like to edit — note that the defined color is displayed above the list of colors for color monitors. Now select the *Edit* command from this same dialog box. What will be displayed is the same dialog box as for creating a new color (Figure 7), but with a name already included in the Name rectangle. From here you can simply change the percentages for the color, using any of the four models, and then click on OK.

The only difference in editing versus creating a new color, is that with editing we do not have to type in a new name as we did in Figure 8 for color creation. The name of the color to edit will already appear in the Name section of the dialog box.

Removing colors

Colors are also removed using the *Define colors* dialog box shown again in Figure 19. Select the color you would like to remove from this list, and choose the *Remove* command. The color is then permanently removed from the *Color palette*. See further notes in this regard in the Figure 19 caption.

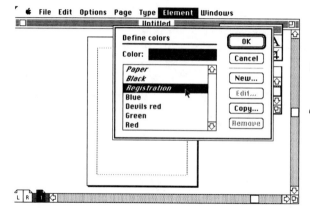

Figure 19. The colors Paper, Black, and Registration cannot be removed. Black and Registration cannot be edited either. Note in this figure that the Edit and Remove commands are grayed and not available when Registration is selected.

Copying colors

Copying colors into your publication is also a simple process. After choosing *Define colors* from the **Element** menu to get the Figure 19 dialog box, you choose the *Copy* command at the bottom of the box. The *Copy colors* dialog box (Figure 20) then appears. This provides a list of publications from which it is possible to copy color descriptions.

Select the publication (or even template) whose colors you wish to copy into your current publication, and click on OK in Figure 20. Any new colors will now be added to your *Define colors* box and *Color palette*, as shown in Figures 21 and 22.

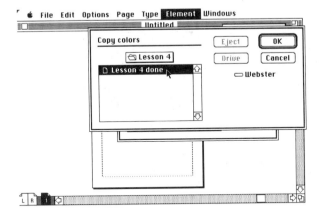

Figure 20. *The* Copy colors *dialog box lists publications and templates that can be used to copy color descriptions into your currently opened document.*

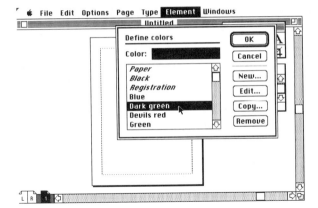

Figure 21. *Using the* Copy *procedure of Figure 20, we have added Dark green to our list of colors. This now appears in the* Define colors *dialog box. See also Figure 22.*

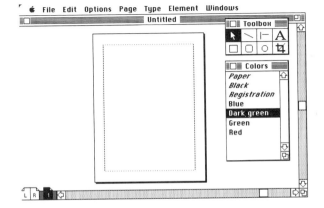

Figure 22. *The new color Dark green, added through the* Copy *process, also appears in the* Color *palette as well as the* Define colors *dialog box of Figure 21.*

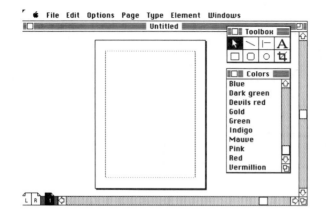

Figure 23. Here we have created a wider range of colors for use — the number that can actually be created is virtually unlimited.

Applying colors

Colors are applied exactly as are styles. If a dialog box is still showing, click OK to remove it from the screen. Any printing element on the screen can be applied a color; whether it be text, created graphics, or imported graphics. Simply select the element you would like to color; text using the text cursor (Figure 24), other elements using the pointer tool.

As the object is selected, one option is to move to the *Color palette* (if this is not showing, choose the command *Color palette* from the **Windows** menu) and click on the color you want to use. On color monitors this becomes apparent immediately, and on color output devices the color will be matched as closely as the output device can make it.

The other option of applying color is to use the *Define colors* command from the **Element** menu. Again select the object, move to this command, and then, in the resulting dialog box (same as Figure 21), select the required color from the list shown.

Color PICT, EPS, and TIFF graphics which have been imported into PageMaker can also have colors applied to them, but these colors will not appear until the publication has printed. A selected object's color will be highlighted in both the *Color palette* and the *Define colors* dialog box. Any text or graphic not assigned a color, by default will be black. Color can be applied to individual text characters, lines and all graphics created in PageMaker. However, only one color can be applied to an element at a time.

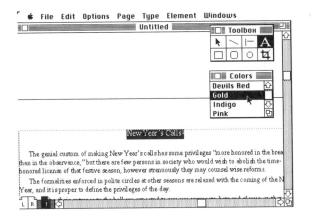

Figure 24. *To apply a color to any element on the page, select the element, and select a color from the* Color pallete. *Although not visible on a monochrome monitor, the Color has been applied to that graphic or text element.*

Macintosh II Color Wheel

The Mac II allows another method to define colors — using the Mac II color wheel.

You can only access the Mac II color wheel if you have a Mac II. Then, as you choose the *Edit* command within the *Define colors* box (of Figure 17), hold down the Shift key and you will see the color wheel.

You may either alter the figures on the left of the wheel, or run the mouse over the color wheel itself. A small box reflects the constantly updated color. Figure 25 shows the Mac II color wheel.

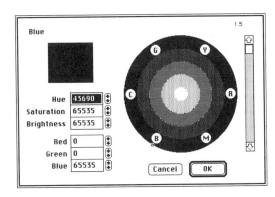

Figure 25. *The Mac II color wheel. When it is in black and white it will have letters showing which color represents what area of the wheel. By clicking the mouse on an area or running it around the wheel the color will change. In color, the box to the left will reflect the color you have chosen, but always the numbers below this box will change as you change the color. Moving the scroll bar down, to the right of the dialog box, will result in a darkening of the whole color wheel.*

Module 13 Exercise

Color

Module 13 Exercise

Color

In this exercise we will work with color within PageMaker. A color screen or printer is not necessary to complete this exercise, although it would make it a little easier.

This training material is structured so that people of all levels of expertise with PageMaker can use it to gain maximum benefit. To do this, we have structured this material so that the bare exercise is listed below this paragraph on just one page, with no hints. The following pages contain the steps needed to complete this exercise for those that need additional prompting. The **Color** module should be referenced if you need further help or explanations.

Module 13 exercise steps

1   *Open up the publication Lesson 2 done from the Lesson 2 folder.*

2.   *Define three new colors — **orange, purple,** and **aqua**. Use the RGB method to do this. Set orange to 100% red and 40% green; purple to 100% blue, 75% red; and aqua to 100% green and 100% blue.*

3.   *Show the Color palette.*

4.   *Make the heading purple, and the graphic orange. The Portrait graphic at the top of the page must be aqua.*

5.   *The frame around the page must also be aqua (you will have to move to the master page to do this).*

6.   *Create registration marks on the master pages, at the top and bottom of the page, and make sure they are correctly colored for registration.*

The steps to completing this exercise are on the following pages.

The steps in detail

1. Open up the publication Lesson 2 done from the Lesson 2 folder.

This file is located in the Lesson 2 folder — it can be accessed either from the Macintosh desktop, or from the *Open* command in the **File** menu, if you are already in PageMaker.

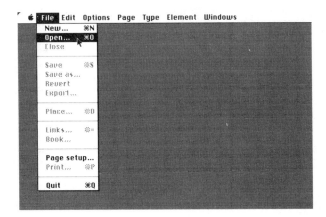

Figure 1. Use either the Open *command (as shown here) or open directly from the Macintosh desktop.*

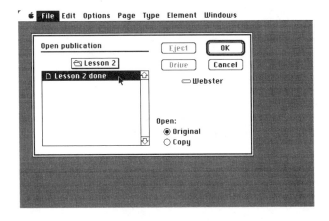

Figure 2. Open the Lesson 2 done file from the Lesson 2 folder.*

459

Figure 3. The publication
Lesson 2 done will look like
this on your screen in Fit in
window *view.*

2. *Define three new colors —* **orange**, **purple**, *and* **aqua**. *Use the RGB method to do this. Set orange to 100% red, 40% green; purple to 100% blue, 75% red; and aqua to 100% green and 100% blue.*

Defining any colors is done through the *Define colors* command in the **Element** menu (Figure 4). You will then see the dialog box of Figure 5.

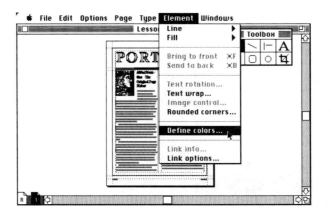

Figure 4. Choose the Define
colors *command from the*
Element *menu to create and
use new colors.*

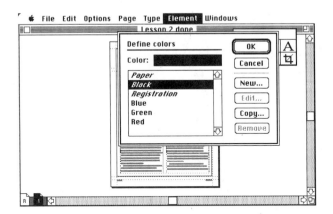

Figure 5. The Define colors *dialog box. Red, Blue, and Green can be included in this box as default colors.*

The Figure 5 dialog box will have three colors defined by default — Paper, Black, and Registration. It may also include Red, Blue, and Green.To create new colors, click on the *New* option. You will then see with the Figure 6 dialog box.

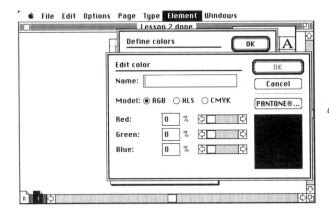

Figure 6. The Define colors New *dialog box is actually the same as the* Define colors Edit *dialog box. The only difference is that with clicking on New in Figure 5, you need to type in a new name in the* Name *rectangle.*

Before we create this new color we must name it. Type in the name of the new color in the rectangle at the top of the dialog box — first of all, orange (Figure 7).

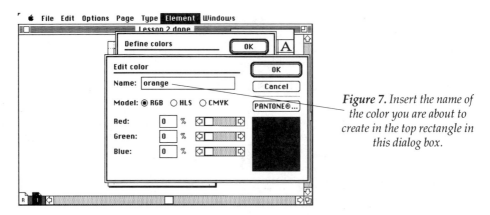

Figure 7. Insert the name of the color you are about to create in the top rectangle in this dialog box.

We have been asked to create three colors using the RGB method — the method selected by default. Using this method, you will see sliding scale bars — one representing Red, one Green, and one Blue. To create orange, move the red sliding scale to 100%, the green to 40%, and the blue to 0% (Figure 8). Although it is not noticeable on monochrome screens, the color orange has been created and is represented in the bar to the right of these sliding scales. Now click on OK.

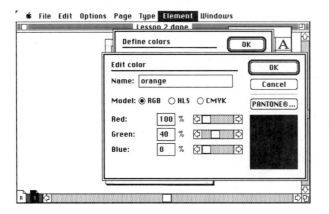

Figure 8. To create the color orange, use the scroll bars on the sliding scales to set the Red bar at 100%, the green at 40%, and the blue at 0%.

You will then be returned to the previous dialog box (shown again in Figure 9), to which the color orange will have been added. From here, click on *New* again to create the next two colors. Creating purple is shown in Figures 10 through 12; aqua is shown in Figure 13.

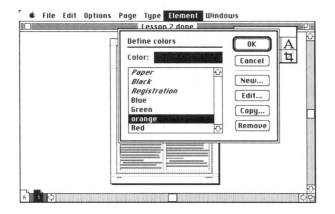

Figure 9. After clicking OK from the box in Figure 8, you will be returned to this dialog box, and the orange color you just created will be included in the list of colors.

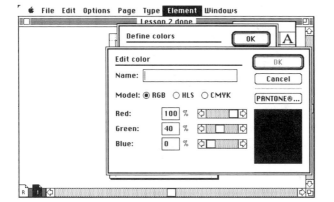

Figure 10. You must click on New again from the dialog box in Figure 9, and once again you will be presented with this dialog box.

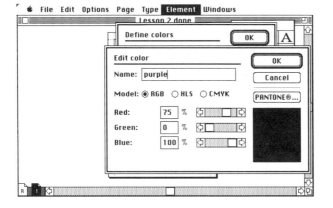

Figure 11. For the color purple, insert its name at the top, and set the blue scale at 100%, the red at 75%, and the green at 0%.

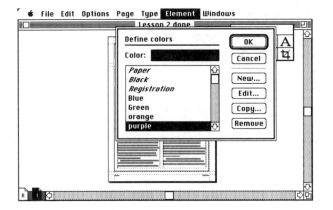

Figure 12. *After clicking OK from Figure 11, you will once again be returned to this dialog box with the color purple added to it.*

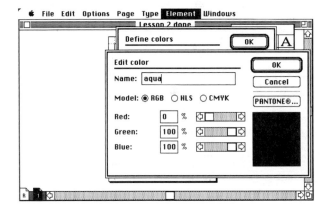

Figure 13. *Match your dialog box with this one (after choosing New again from Figure 12) to create the color aqua.*

After getting this far, click on OK twice to get back past the two dialog boxes and onto the PageMaker page.

3. Show the Color palette.

The *Color palette* can be accessed via the *Color palette* option in the **Windows** menu (Figure 14). In this *Color palette* will be listed all the colors we have just created. You may want to resize the *Color palette* so that you can see all the colors (Figure 15).

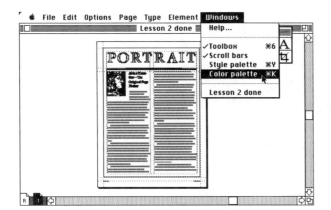

Figure 14. *Choose the* Color palette *command from the* **Windows** *menu to display the Color palette on screen.*

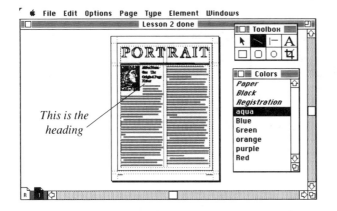

Figure 15. *Here the* Color palette *has not only been displayed, but we have increased it in size, so we can see all the colors listed.*

4. *Make the heading purple, and the graphic orange. The Portrait graphic at the top of the page must be aqua.*

To make any text a certain color is a simple procedure. Select that text using the text editing tool, and click on the required color in the *Color palette.* That selected text will then be registered as that color. Although these colors can be applied with style sheets, none has been defined for this publication, so we will apply colors manually. See Figures 16 through 21 for these operations.

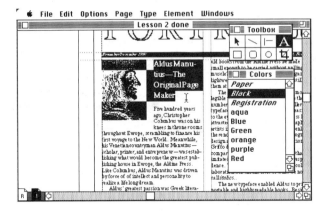

Figure 16. 75% view has been used here to allow us to read the text, and see most of the page. To turn the heading purple, select it, as shown here using the text editing tool.

Figure 17. Click on the color purple in the Color *palette.*

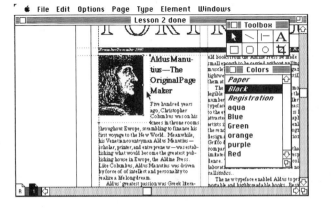

Figure 18. Select the graphic next to it with the pointer tool.

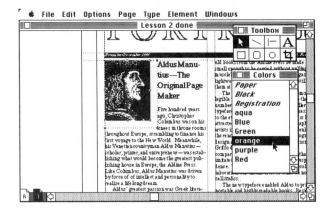

Figure 19. ...and click on orange from the Color *palette.*

Graphics must be selected using the pointer tool, but are applied colors the same way as text. Once the graphic is selected, click on the correct color in the *Color palette* and the graphic will then assume that color (Figure 19).

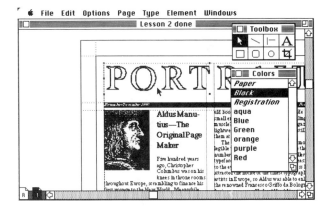

Figure 20. Move to the top of the page and select the graphic at the top of the page with the pointer tool.

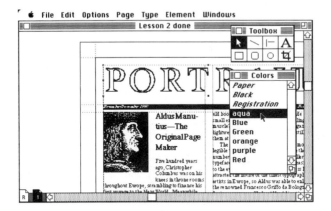

Figure 21. Click on the color aqua in the Color palette to turn the graphic this color. Note that PICT, EPS and color TIFF graphics are not displayed on screen in their assigned colors.

5. *The frame around the page must also be aqua (you will have to move to the master page to do this).*

Because the frame is on the master page, you will not be able to select it from page 1. Click on the R icon in the bottom left-hand corner of the page to move to the master page (Figure 22).

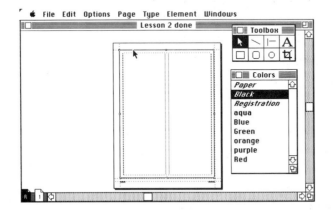

Figure 22. Note that the R icon in the bottom left-hand corner of the page has been selected — the right master page. Note the frame around the page that has been selected.

Select the frame using the pointer tool and click on aqua from the *Color palette* (Figure 23). This frame is now treated as aqua.

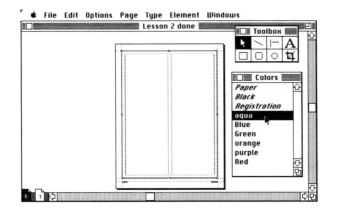

Figure 23. Here we have selected aqua from the Color palette to turn the frame this color.

6. *Create registration marks on the master pages, at the top and bottom of the page, and make sure they are correctly colored for registration.*

These registration marks are only created as a guide to the printer — they help align color separations. They are also very simple to do, and are created on the master page.

Create, at the top of the master page, a fairly small symbol (Figure 24) and repeat it at the bottom of the page (Figure 25). The symbol we've created is shown in Figure 24.

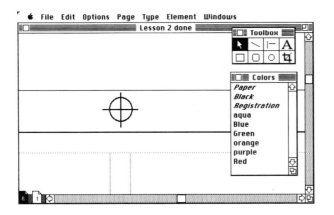

Figure 24. This symbol has been created using the graphic drawing tools within Page-Maker. Copy this graphic and paste it at the bottom of the page as well.

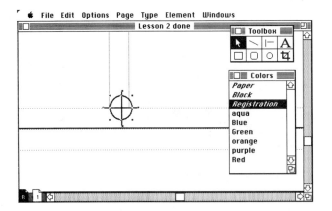

Figure 25. *The graphic has been copied and pasted at the bottom of the page.*

After creating a symbol and placing it at the top and bottom of the page, make sure that all parts of both symbols are colored Registration by using the Registration color from the *Color palette* (Figure 26). This ensures that these registration marks will print on every page, if color separations are created at print time.

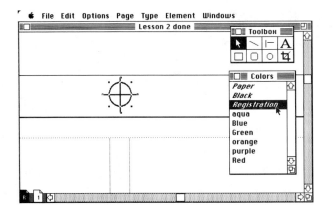

Figure 26. *Assign the color Registration to the special symbol marks. This ensures that these registration marks will print on every page of color separations.*

Module 14

Advanced Picture Formatting

Advanced Picture Formatting

Introduction

We have already described in Module 7 how we can import pictures and how we can resize and move these pictures in various ways. In this module we will look at more complex wraparounds, and how we can alter the composition of the picture itself.

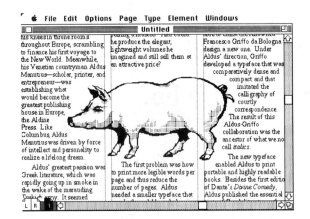

Figure 1. An example of an irregular wraparound achieved using PageMaker 4's advanced techniques.

Irregular wraparounds

In module 7, we looked at creating simple wraparounds with graphics using the *Text wrap* command in the **Element** menu. Depending on your choice, text can be made to skip over a graphic, stop at a graphic, run through a graphic, or wrap regularly around the border of the graphic. What we will look at now is how to make text wrap *irregularly* around the edge of the graphic.

To follow this example, load the text file Lead Story into a three-column page, and load the picture file Anchor.TIF (in Lesson 4 folder within the Tutorial folder) somewhere on top of this text. Make the graphic about 4 inches (10 cm) square (see Figures 2, 3, and 4 for details).

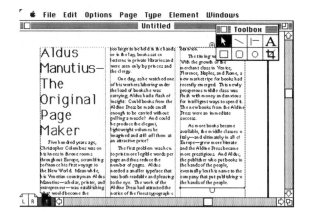

Figure 2. The file Lead Story will not quite fill three columns, but should look something like this. This is the actual view at the top of the page.

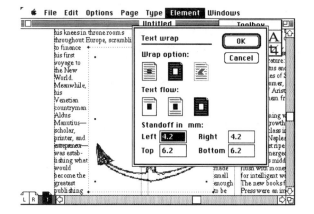

Figure 3. To make sure that the text wraps correctly around the image loaded in, alter the Text wrap command so that it reads the same as shown here. Your image should be selected before moving to this command.

Every picture, when selected, will have two sets of handles around it. The inside handles are the ones used to resize the picture. We have already looked at the use of these handles in previous modules. The outside handles, connected by dotted lines, are used to create a wraparound for the graphic. Each outside handle is called a "vertex" by PageMaker. Before these handles can be used, however, the *Text wrap* command must be set up similar to Figure 3. Make sure your graphic is selected.

Now size the graphic so that it fits across two columns as shown in the *Actual size* view of Figure 4.

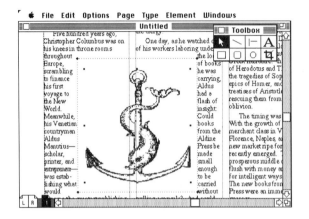

Figure 4. *Size the graphic so that it fits nicely across two columns. Text will flow down both sides of the graphic, as long as you followed the instructions in Figure 3.*

Initially, the outside set of handles around a selected graphic consists of a dot or vertex in every corner. You can hold the mouse button down on any of these corners, as if you were going to resize the graphic, and change the shape of the wraparound. Move the top right-hand dot a little to the right (Figure 5), and watch how the text will change its flow to compensate for this movement (Figures 6 and 7). Any of the four corner dots can be moved in this way, and the text will change its flow each time.

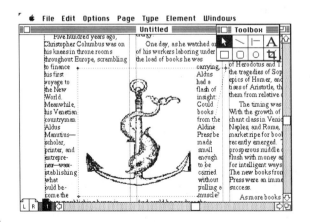

Figure 5. *Here we are altering the position of the right-hand outside text flow margin of the graphic. See the next figure to see the result.*

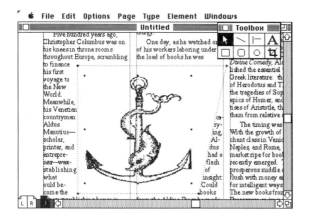

Figure 6. *After moving one of the outside dots slightly, the text reformats to compensate for this movement.*

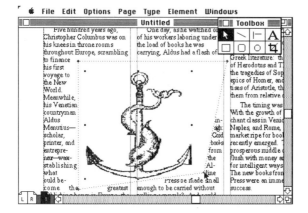

Figure 7. *Here we have also moved the bottom right-hand corner dot up slightly. Notice how much text has reformatted to compensate for this.*

Moving the four dots in this way will alter text flow, but will hardly create an irregular wraparound. We need to have more than four dots to achieve a correct irregular wraparound. We can actually create more to suit our purpose.

Move the mouse cursor to a point on the dotted outline where another vertex would come in handy. Think of it as moving to a point where a bend in the outline would be necessary. Click once, and a new vertex will be created (Figure 8). After clicking once, hold the mouse button down on this vertex and move it around. You will notice that there is now a new bend in the outline of the graphic (Figure 9).

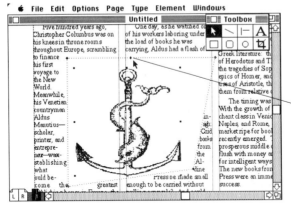

Figure 8. *We have decided that the dotted outline, in order to best "hug" the graphic, needs a bend in it. Simply click where you want the bend, and a new vertex appears with all the properties of the corner dots.*

This vertex can be moved in any direction, including along the line itself. As many dots as needed can be created to make an irregular wraparound. Simply click on the dotted outline of the graphic wherever you need to bend the line.

Figures 10 through 12 show additional manipulations to make the text wrap exactly as we would like. With this irregular wraparound created, the graphic can still be resized and moved, using the inside handles, without losing the actual shape of the wraparound (Figure 13).

Every time a vertex is moved or created, the text reflows to compensate. If this slows you down, annoys you, or you simply don't want it to happen, hold down the space bar as you move or create vertexes. The text will reformat when the space bar is released. You can move several vertexes before the space bar is released.

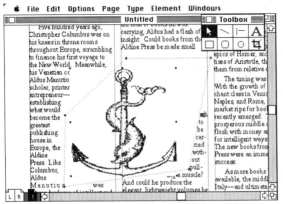

Figure 9. *After we created this new vertex, notice how, after we move the top left-hand vertex, the line now bends at the new position.*

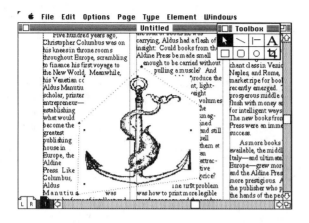

Figure 10. *We can also move down the right-hand corner vertex thanks to that new vertex we created.*

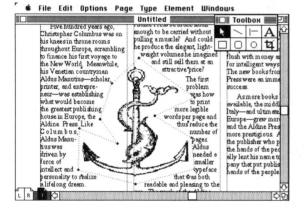

Figure 11. *Almost finished... we have created several new dots, simply by clicking on the dotted line where we felt it necessary, and moving these new dots around.*

Figure 12. *After we finished the wraparound, we deselected the graphic and hid the column guides. This now gives a good indication of how the printed graphic will appear.*

477

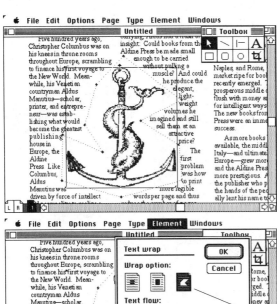

Figure 13. We can still enlarge the graphic without any worries about losing the wraparound. The handles to resize the graphic may be a little hard to see.

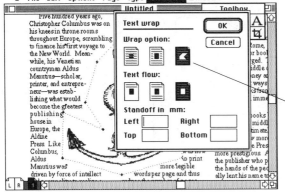

Figure 14. Once the text wraparound has been manually altered, the dialog box for the Text wrap *command from the* **Element** *menu will reflect that change. This option will then be automatically selected.*

Altering the appearance of graphics

Several controls exist to alter the appearance of certain imported graphics, such as scanned images or Paint-type graphics created in any of the packages compatible with PageMaker. Graphics imported in EPS format, Draw-type package images, or internally created graphics cannot be altered in this way.

The controls for altering these graphics are contained within the *Image control* command in the **Element** menu. Before this command can be activated, a graphic must be on the screen and be selected.

Several things can be altered about an imported graphic. These include the lightness, contrast, gray levels, and screen pattern of the graphic.

Adjusting the lightness of a graphic will affect the entire image. Blacks, for example, can be lightened until they appear a light shade of gray. Light images can be darkened so that they appear totally black.

Adjusting the contrast of an image involves lightening dark areas and darkening light areas. A high-contrast picture has very dark areas and very light areas — without much in between. A low-contrast picture is one where there is little difference between the dark areas and the light areas of a picture — for instance a photo that is taken in very poor light. Contrast can be increased or decreased using PageMaker's *Image control*.

For the examples in this module we have loaded Practice graphic from the Basic lesson folder and a scanned image, Photo. TIF from PageMaker 3's Getting Started folder. This image is not available with PageMaker 4.

Figure 15. Here we are going to alter two different types of imported graphics — a black and white image and a scanned image with sixteen levels of gray.

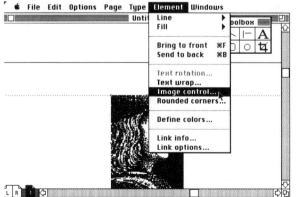

Figure 16. Select the image you would like to alter, and choose the Image control *command from the* **Element** *menu. We have selected the black and white image to look at first.*

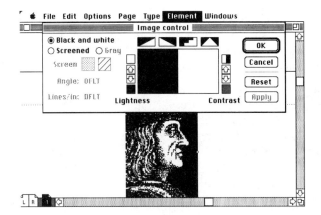

Figure 17. This is the Image control *dialog box for a two tone image. Gray shade images create a slightly different dialog box. See Figure 27 as an example.*

With a two-tone black and white image (as from Paint-type packages), the dialog box will appear as in Figure 17. In the top left-hand corner *Black and white* is selected by default, and although this limits a little what we can do with the selected image, we still can change it. In the middle of the dialog box we have two bars — one for each shade of gray (black and white).

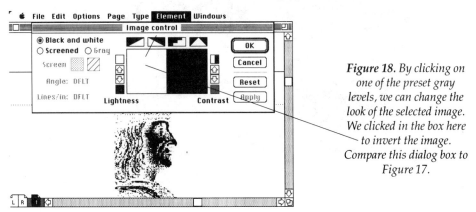

Figure 18. By clicking on one of the preset gray levels, we can change the look of the selected image. We clicked in the box here to invert the image. Compare this dialog box to Figure 17.

Above these two bars are some preset gray levels (contained in four small rectangular boxes) that can be applied to a graphic. Only the second choice will have any effect — it will invert the image (Figure 18). The first choice will return it to normal. The other choices will only work with screened images. The *Lightness* and *Contrast* cannot be changed for images that are not screened and therefore the scroll bars above these commands will not work.

We can, however, turn this black and white image into a screened image simply by clicking on *Screened* in the top left-hand corner of the dialog box (Figure 19). It is then possible to play around with the lightness, contrast, and other commands.

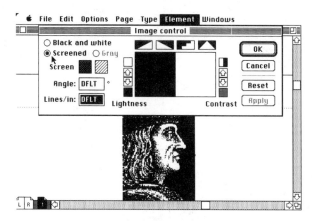

Figure 19. We can turn the black and white image into a screened image simply by selecting the Screened *selection below the* Black and white *selection.*

After we have "screened" this image, we can do much more to it. All four boxes above the two gray level bars have an effect on the graphic, as do the Lightness and Contrast controls. However, although clicking on any one of the four gray level boxes causes an immediate change in the appearance of the selected graphic, you must click on the *Apply* command to see a change in the graphic when using the Lightness and Contrast controls.

Figures 20 to 22 provide further examples of these operations.

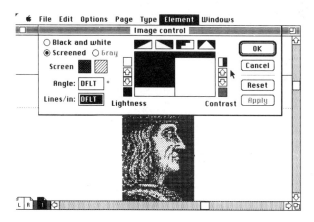

Figure 20. By clicking on the scroll bars to adjust lightness and contrast of the image, two things will happen. The length of the two bars in the middle of the dialog box will alter to reflect the changes, and after you click on Apply, *the image will also change to reflect the changes you have made.*

481

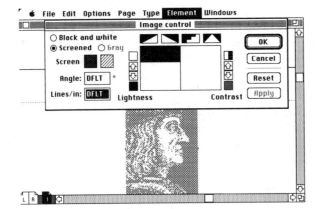

Figure 21. The higher these bars appear in their squares (the smaller the black area in these bars) the lighter the image is. In other words, if both bars were nearly all black, the image would appear very dark; and if they were nearly all white, the image would appear very light. The lightness is increased by clicking on the top arrow of the Lightness control.

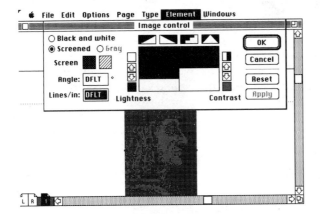

Figure 22. The closer the two bars appear, the less contrast there is in the image. In this figure, both bars are nearly the same in areas of black. Hence, the contrast of the image is poor. Contrast is changed by clicking on the top or bottom Contrast arrows. If both bars contain the same amount of black, the image becomes all one shade of gray.

The Lightness and Contrast settings can also be changed by clicking the mouse button in the gray scale bars.

Remember that when dealing with screened images, results are often far better on a printer than they appear on screen. It would be a good idea to experiment with a few settings, when altering a picture, to see exactly which give the best results. On the following page (Figures 23 through 26), we have created some examples on a printer to show exactly how two-tone, paint-type graphics can be manipulated using the PageMaker *Image control* command.

Figure 23. *This image has been printed exactly as it was created — no changes have been made. Its black and white dialog box is the same as Figure 19.*

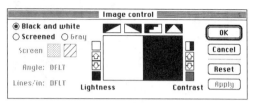

Figure 24. *This image was reversed before it was printed.*

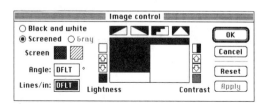

Figure 25. *This image was screened and the contrast lowered.*

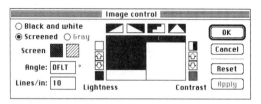

Figure 26. *Here we have screened the image again, changed the screen pattern to lines, and the lines per inch to ten. The screen pattern options are described later in this module.*

Scanned graphics are a slightly different story. They contain more shades of gray, and more precise manipulation of these graphics is possible.

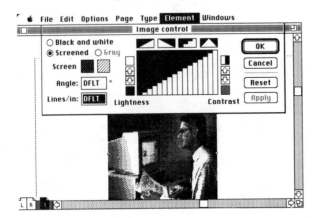

Figure 27. The dialog box for a graphic, usually scanned, that contains sixteen gray levels.

For example, with the photograph of Figure 27 selected, note how this time the dialog box creates more bars to represent the number of gray scales the selected image uses, in this case sixteen. The Screened selection at the top left-hand corner of the dialog box is selected by default as well. Perhaps the first thing to notice is that the preselected gray level boxes have more effect on the selected graphic this time. This is shown in Figures 28 and 29.

Figures 30 and 31 show other methods of modifying the gray scale settings.

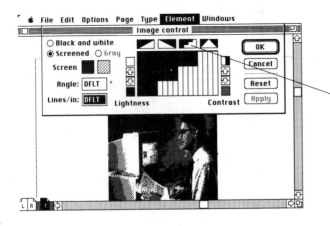

Figure 28. Here we have chosen one of the preselected gray level settings to slightly change the appearance of the graphic. Note the gray level bars have also changed to reflect this new setting.

Figure 29. Another prese-lected gray level setting which creates other effects with the graphic.

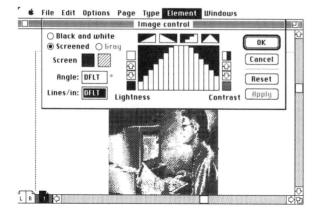

Figure 30. As with all two-tone graphics, the lightness and contrast can be adjusted by clicking on the various up and down scroll arrows. Remember to click on Apply to see the result.

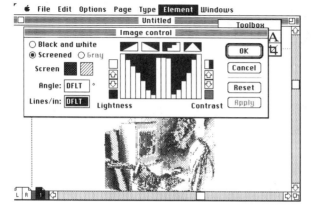

Figure 31. Random setting of the gray levels can be achieved by clicking the mouse in the different vertical bar areas.

Any screened image can also be adjusted in a unique way — by altering the screen pattern itself. Intially the screen pattern consists of dots, but it can be changed to lines to create special effects. This is achieved using the controls next to the Screened option.

Apart from changing the screen pattern to lines or dots, you may also adjust the frequency of these lines or dots, and the angle at which they lie. The controls for these commands are at the left of the dialog box (Figure 32).

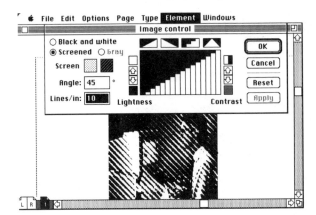

Figure 32. Here we have changed the screen pattern to lines rather then dots, and changed the frequency of the lines from the default 53 per inch to 10 per inch.

You may also create a two gray level image from a sixteen gray level image by clicking on Black and white instead of Screened in the top left-hand corner of the dialog box (Figure 33). Some other examples of gray level settings are shown in Figures 34 to 36.

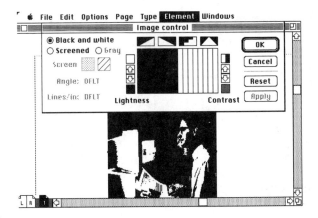

Figure 33. A scanned image turned black and white.

Figure 34. *This is the scanned image as it would normally appear using the gray level box as shown in Figure 27.*

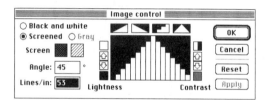

Figure 35. *Here we have altered the image in the above manner.*

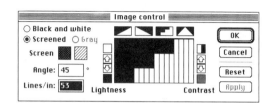

Figure 36. *Here once again we have selected a preset gray level setting to achieve this result.*

Inline graphics

Inline graphics are graphics that are added to your text so that they actually become part of the text. This enables your graphic to move with the text, if you happen to change your page layout. This feature is best suited for small graphics when used with body text. Text that a graphic is linked to will not wrap around the graphic. If your graphic is large, and you insert it in the middle of your text block, it will act as a large text character and widely separate your lines of text. You can, however, insert the graphic at the end of a text block, without affecting the actual layout.

Inserting an inline graphic

To insert a graphic into the text so it becomes part of that text block, follow these steps. First, load the text file Story 2 onto a one column page. Move the page to 75% size view and, with the text tool, place the flashing cursor somewhere in the middle of your text. (Figure 37).

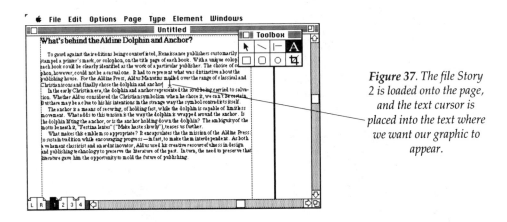

Figure 37. The file Story 2 is loaded onto the page, and the text cursor is placed into the text where we want our graphic to appear.

We are going to load the graphic Anchor.TIF onto the page as an inline graphic. Keeping the text tool selected, choose the Place command and find the file Anchor.TIF from the Lesson 4 folder. You will notice that, once this file is selected in the dialog box (Figure 38), you will be given two choices as how to load this graphic.

As independent graphic is your first choice (Figure 38). If you select this, the graphic you place will not be part of the text but a separate object on the page. Because we placed the text cursor in the middle of our text, the *As inline graphic* choice is selected. If we hadn't placed the text cursor in our text, the *As inline graphic* choice would not be available.

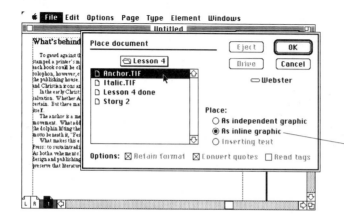

Figure 38. The Place *dialog box is giving us two choices on how to load our graphic. Because we inserted the flashing cursor into the text, the* As inline graphic *choice is selected automatically.*

After clicking on OK, the graphic appears where you placed the cursor. You will notice that it is probably a little large (Figure 39). Before we shrink the graphic though, we can see the flashing cursor next to the image is as large, as though the graphic is a piece of text. Double-click over the graphic, and you'll see that it can in fact be selected as a piece of text. Now move to the *Alignment* command in the **Type** menu, and change the alignment to center and you'll see that it can be aligned just like text.

Inline graphics can be resized just like normal graphics. We suggest you do this. Select it with the pointer tool, and shrink it using the bottom right handle. Decrease it so it is just slightly larger than your text. The graphics may now be indistinguishable but not to worry, we can still see what has happened. See Figures 39 through 41 for more details.

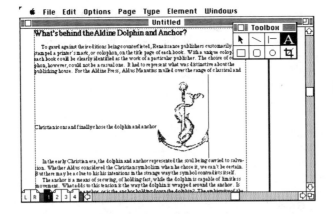

Figure 39. *The graphic is placed as an inline graphic, but also has certain characteristics of text. Notice the flashing cursor next to the graphic.*

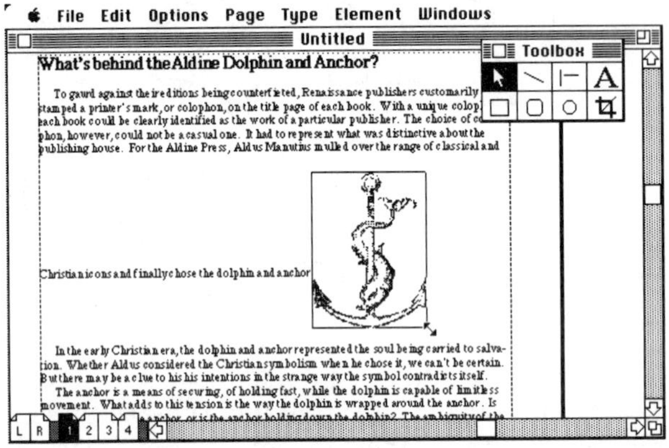

Figure 40. *Generally, the graphic should be shrunk so it will not affect the layout of text. This, of course, depends on what effects you are trying to achieve. Select it with the pointer tool and change its size as though it is a normal graphic.*

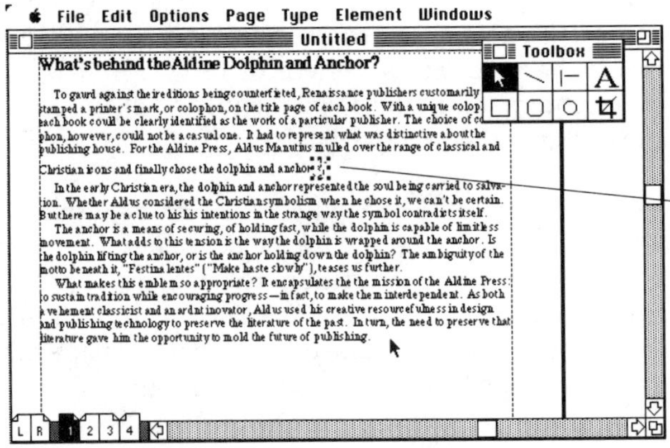

Figure 41. *The graphic is reduced in size so it fits into the text much-better.*

To prove that the inline graphic moves with the text, take your pointer tool, place it anywhere in the text, and keep your finger on the mouse. Now, move the mouse around, and see how the graphic follows with the text (Figure 42). If you try and move the graphic now it can't be done. It can be moved slightly up and down on the baseline, but because it's part of the text, it can't be moved to the left or right.

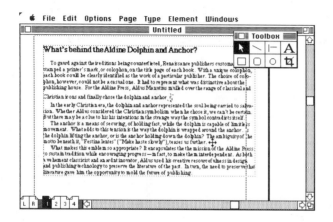

Figure 42. *You will see that if you move the text anywhere on the page now, the graphic will follow.*

Separating inline graphics and text

If you later decide you want an inline graphic to be an independent graphic, this is easily achieved. First, select the graphic with your pointer tool. Now, move to the **Edit** menu and activate the *Cut* command. Straight after this, use the *Paste* command. Your graphic reappears in the same position. Using the pointer tool, move in and pull the graphic away from the text, with your finger on the mouse the whole time. You'll see that it is now an independent graphic, and can be moved as such. Figures 43 through 46 illustrate this process.

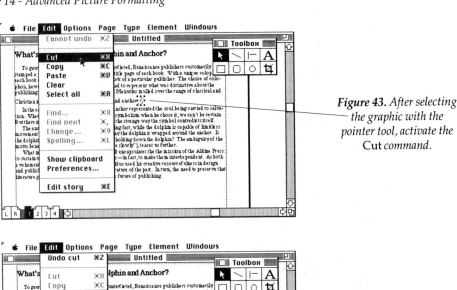

Figure 43. After selecting the graphic with the pointer tool, activate the Cut command.

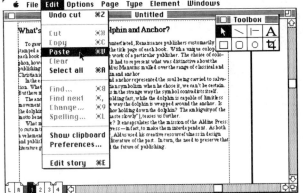

Figure 44. Next choose the Paste command so that the graphic will reappear onto your page.

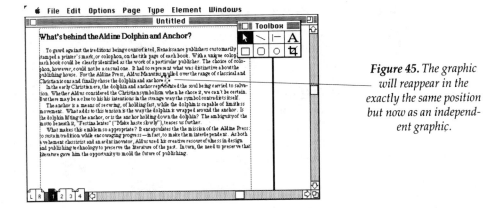

Figure 45. The graphic will reappear in the exactly the same position but now as an independent graphic.

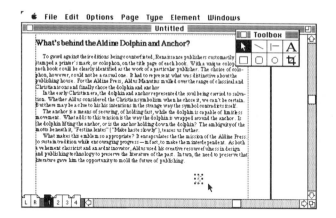

Figure 46. The graphic can now be moved away from the text

Joining graphics and text already on the page

If your graphic and text are already on the page, and you want to join them, similar steps are followed. First, select your graphic with the pointer tool and choose *Cut*. Next, select the text tool and insert it where you would like your graphic to be placed. Then simply choose *Paste* and it is now an inline graphic. Figures 47 through 50 illustrate this approach.

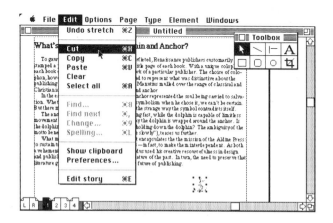

Figure 47. When making a graphic, that is already on the page, an inline graphic, first select it with the pointer tool. Then activate the Cut command.

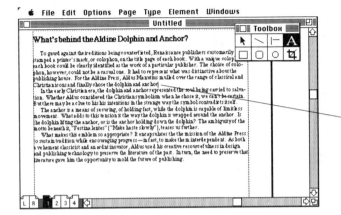

Figure 48. *After cutting the graphic from your screen, select the text tool, and place the flashing cursor where you want the graphic to be placed.*

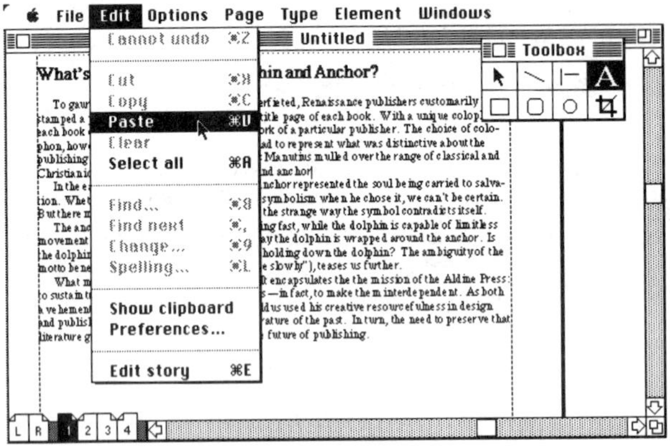

Fifure 49. *To bring the graphic back onto the page as an inline graphic, choose* Paste.

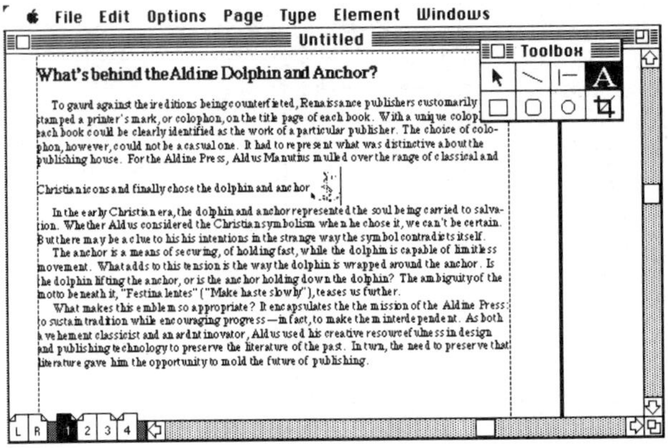

Figure 50. *It is now an inline graphic, at the location of the text cursor, and will move with the text.*

Inline graphics can be loaded in story view as well. Story view is part of the story editor discussed in Module 5. The procedure is almost the same. Place the flashing cursor in the text where you would like the graphic to appear. Then, instead of choosing the *Place* command, choose the *Import* command from the **Story** menu. The graphic will show up as a little marker, and can only be manipulated once out of story mode. See Figures 51 through 54 for details.

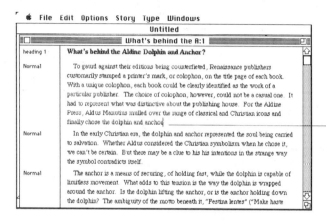

Figure 51. *To place an inline graphic in story view first place the flashing cursor somewhere in the text.*

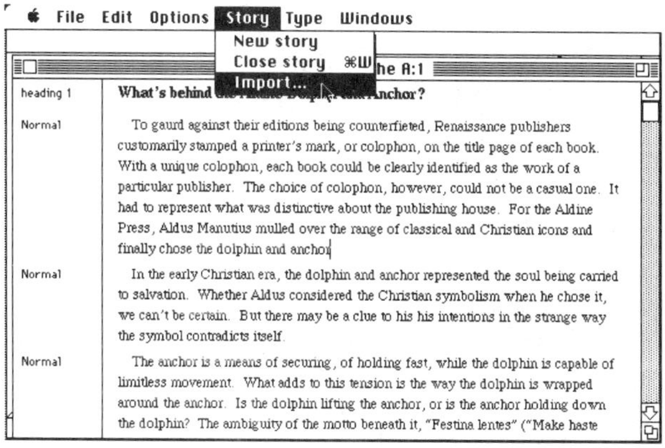

Figure 52. *The Import command is selected from the* **Story** *menu*

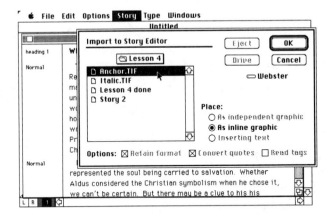

Figure 53. The Import to Story Editor *dialog box will appear. This is the same as the* Place *dialog box, so the same steps are followed. Again, because we placed the flashing cursor in the text, the As inline graphic choice is selected.*

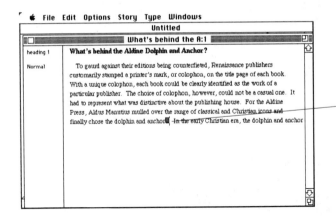

Figure 54. The placed graphic in story view will show up as a marker, and can only be manipulated once out of story view.

Inline graphics are also affected by the *Leading* command. Your best option here is to have Auto leading selected. In some cases, the graphic may be to large, as we mentioned earlier, and your lines of text will be altered. Sometimes moving the graphic slightly up or down, or shrinking it more, can alleviate the problem of breaking up text.

Module 14 Exercise

Advanced Picture Formatting

Module 14 Exercise
Advanced Picture Formatting

In this exercise we will import different types of pictures into PageMaker, and look at the advanced options that are available to alter the look and properties of these pictures. We will also work with irregular wraparounds of graphics.

This training material is structured so that people of all levels of expertise with PageMaker can use it to gain maximum benefit. To do this, we have structured this material so that the bare exercise is listed below this paragraph on just one page, with no hints. The following pages contain the steps needed to complete this exercise for those that need additional prompting. The **Advanced Picture Formatting** module should be referenced if you need further help or explanations.

Module 14 exercise steps

1. *In this exercise we are going to load three files — Anchor.TIF, Practice graphic, and Lead Story. Load these files now so that Lead Story is in two columns on the page, and the two graphics are positioned on the page. Text must also wrap regularly around these graphics. If you are unsure about what we mean here, look at Figure 1 over the page.*

2. *Select the file Practice graphic. Change it from a black and white image to a screened image, and make it slightly darker. Now reverse the image — turn white black and black white.*

3. *For the second graphics file, Anchor.TIF, create a wraparound with this image that will cause the text to run irregularly around the image — to hug the image. (See Figure 2 on the next page if you are unsure about what we mean here.)*

4. *The second part of this exercise is to create an inline graphic. Add another page to this document, and load the file Story 2 onto a one column page. Place the file Logotype.eps as an inline graphic anywhere in your text (preferably beginning at the left-hand margin, as the graphic will most likely spread right across the page). Shrink it slightly so it fits nicely across the page.*

5. *Now make it an independent graphic, and move it so it sits under the text on the page.*

The steps for completing this exercise are on the following pages.

The steps in detail

1. *In this exercise we are going to load three files — Anchor.TIF, Practice graphic, and Lead Story. Load these files now so that Lead Story is in two columns on the page, and the two graphics are positioned on the page. Text must also wrap regularly around these graphics. If you are unsure about what we mean here, look at Figure 1.*

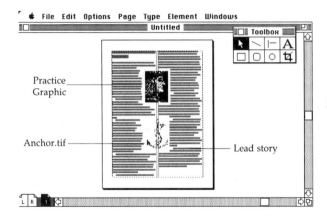

Figure 1. This is the result we want after step 1.

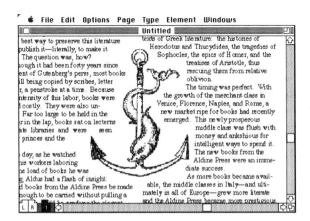

Figure 2. This is the result we want after step 3.

To achieve the page shown in Figure 1, follow these steps:

Select *New* to create the publication, and choose an A4 or Letter size page.

Use the *Column guides* command in the **Options** menu to create two columns (Figure 3).

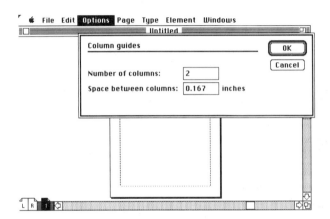

Figure 3. In the Column guides *dialog box, insert the figure 2.*

Load the file Lead Story from the Lesson 2 folder into these two columns (Figures 4 and 5).

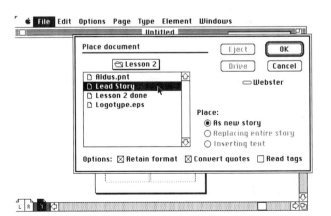

Figure 4. Load the file Lead Story from the Lesson 2 folder. This is the dialog box obtained from the Place *command in the* **File** *menu.*

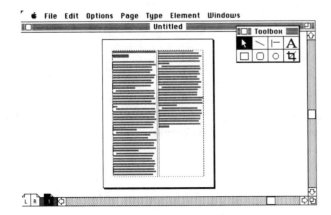

Figure 5. The Lead Story file is loaded into two columns on an A4 or Letter size page.

Before loading any pictures, move to the *Text wrap* command in the **Element** menu, and set up the dialog box for a regular wrap as illustrated in Figure 6. Make sure the pointer tool is selected, and make sure also that no text block is selected — as the text wrap setting will then only apply to that text block.

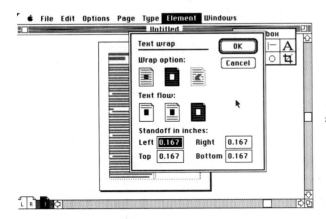

Figure 6. It is a good idea to set the Text wrap *dialog box up as such, before actually loading any pictures. This ensures all pictures, when loaded, automatically take on this setting.*

Load both Anchor.TIF (Lesson 4 folder) and Practice graphic (Basic Lesson folder) onto the page using the *Place* command from the **File** menu. Position them approximately as shown in Figure 1. Resize these pictures, if necessary, so that they are around the size of those in this figure.

If the text did not run around the pictures as in Figure 1, the step you took in Figure 6 did not work. Simply select each picture, choose the *Text Wrap* command, and set it up as Figure 6 for each picture.

2. Select the file Practice graphic. Change it from a black and white image to a screened image, and make it slightly darker. Now reverse the image.

Select the file Practice graphic on the page simply by clicking on it, and choose the *Image control* command from the **Element** menu (Figure 8). If this command cannot be chosen, make sure that the correct graphic is selected on the page. The Image control dialog box of Figure 9 then appears. Also change to *Actual size* view as shown in Figures 7 and 8.

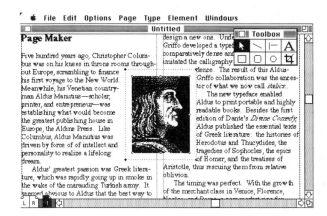

Figure 7. Select the file Practice graphic. Also make sure that you are in Actual size *view so that you can see the changes we make to this picture.*

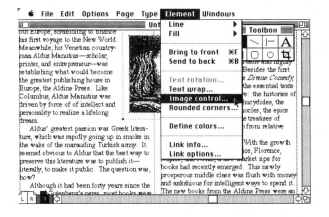

Figure 8. After selecting the graphic, choose the Image control *command from the* **Element** *menu.*

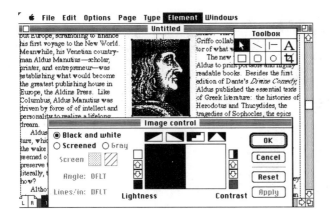

Figure 9. The Image control
dialog box.

We now have to do several things — change the image to a screened image, darken it slightly, and reverse the image.

To do this, first click on the option in the top left-hand corner of the dialog box — Screened. This changes the image from two shades to an image made up of either lines or dots. You will notice no apparent change in the picture until you darken it slightly (Figure 10). The picture could not have been darkened when it was a black and white image. Now we need to reverse the image.

To change the image to a reverse video image, click on the second preset gray scale level. Immediately the image will become reverse video (Figure 11).

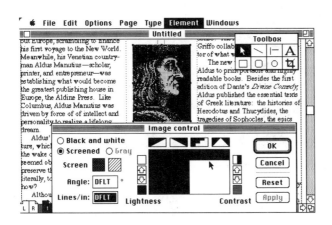

*Figure 10. We now have
selected the Screened option
and darkened the image by
adjusting the contrast arrow.
Don't forget to click the
Apply button to see the
results.*

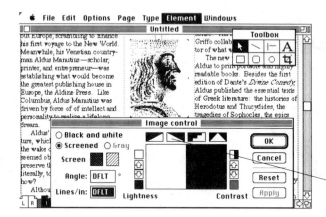

Figure 11. *In order to reverse the video of the image, we have clicked on the second preset gray scale box. Note the change in the actual graphic.*

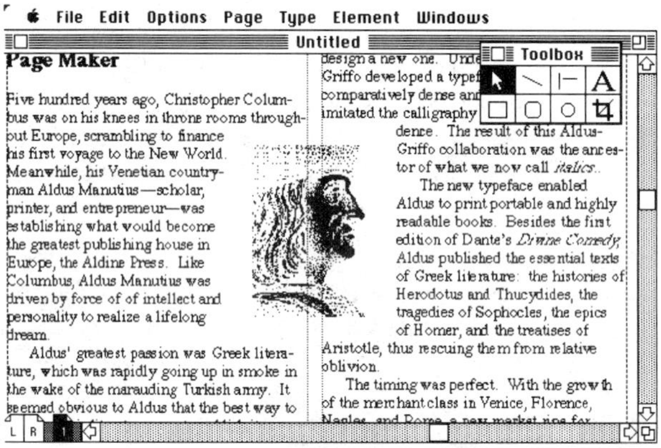

Figure 12. *The final result of our changes to the graphic.*

3. *For the second graphics file, Anchor.TIF, create a wraparound with this image that will cause the text to run irregularly around the image — to hug the image. (See Figure 2 at the start of this exercise, if you are unsure about what we mean here.)*

Stay in *Actual size* view and move down the page to view the graphic Anchor.TIF. Also, select the image so that you can see the handles around the image (Figure 13). In fact, there should be two sets of handles showing.

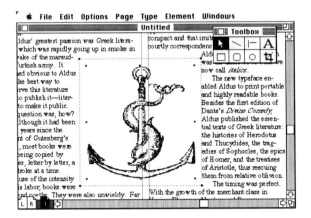

Figure 13. Move down to the second graphics file, Anchor.TIF, and select it. Note the two sets of handles showing.

The outside diamond handles that are joined by the dotted lines are called vertexes. These are the ones that control the irregular wraparound. We will use these to create our wraparound.

Every time you click the mouse button on the dotted line, a new vertex is created. Several of these vertexes will have to be created at strategic points on the dotted line, in order to create the wraparound. From here, however, we will guide you with pictures — which can explain the procedure far more easily than can be done with words.

See Figures 14 to 25 for details.

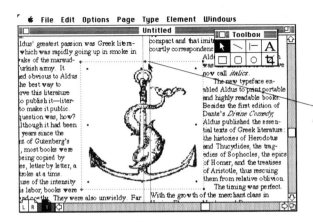

Figure 14. To add a corner, or vertex, to the dotted line, we simply click on it. In this figure we have added another corner (it looks at the moment like another handle on the dotted line), in the middle of the top horizontal line.

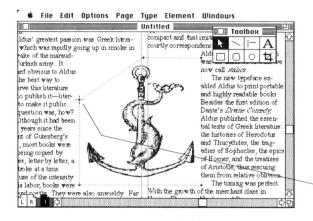

Figure 15. *To change the shape of the dotted square (and hence the wraparound), hold the mouse button down on one of its vertexes and move it towards the graphic. Here we are holding the mouse button down on the top left-hand corner vertex and moving it towards the graphic. Be careful to hold the mouse button down only on vertexes on the dotted line — not the other selection handles within the lines.*

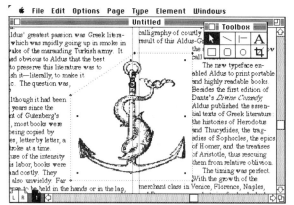

Figure 16. *Upon releasing the mouse button after performing the step in figure 15, the text reflows around the new border of the dotted polygon. If some of your text is still hidden, select* Send to back *from the* **Element** *menu.*

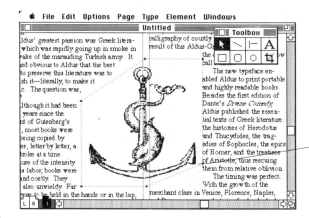

Figure 17. *Once again we are in the process of changing the wraparound — this time by holding down the mouse button on the bottom right-hand handle and moving it towards the graphic.*

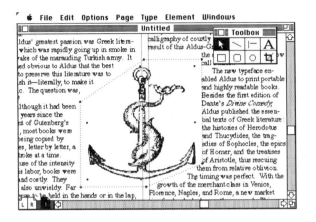

Figure 18. *After releasing the mouse button, the text reflows around the graphic.*

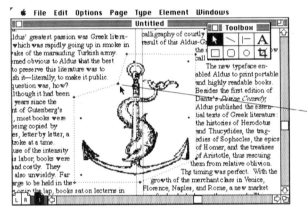

Figure 19. *We must again add another vertex to the dotted line — this time in the middle of the left-hand line. After creating the vertex, move the line closer to the graphic so the text hugs the image.*

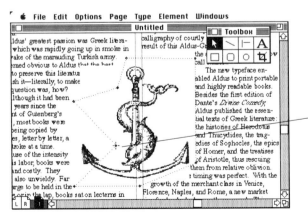

Figure 20. *Keep adding as many vertexes as you need, to complete the irregular text wraparound of the image. Because the shape of this image is so irregular, you may have to create quite a few additional vertexes. Here we are in the process of moving another vertex we have created. Figure 21 shows you the final result of this move.*

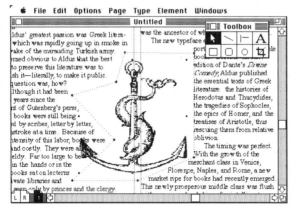

Figure 21. Notice the text has reflowed to fit in with the direction we just moved our line to.

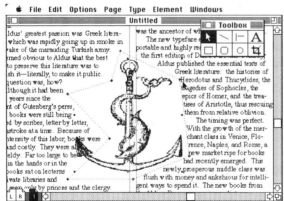

Figure 22. This figure is the result of moving yet another vertex towards the graphic — this time the top right handle.

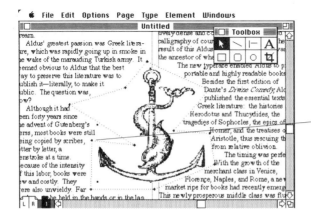

Figure 23. Once again another vertex has been added near the bottom left of the graphic...

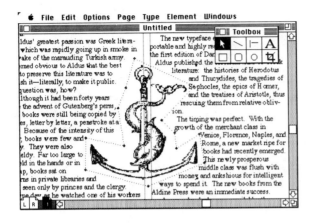

Figure 24... More vertexes have been added and moved to complete the wraparound.

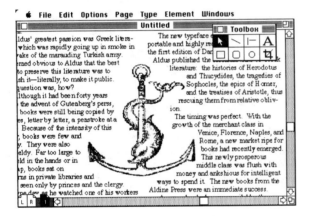

Figure 25. And here is how the wraparound will finally look on the screen, once guides are hidden and the graphic is deselected. (This simply gives us a better view of the graphic — it is certainly not necessary.)

4. The second part of this exercise is to create an inline graphic. Add another page to this document, and load the file Story 2 onto a one column page. Place the file Logotype.eps as an inline graphic anywhere in your text (preferably beginning at the left-hand margin, as the graphic will most likely spread right across the page). Shrink it slightly so it fits nicely across the page.

On the second page, load in the file Story 2 from the Lesson 4 folder (Figure 26), and move to 75% view for a better perspective. Place the flashing text cursor somewhere in your text, as in Figure 27. Because the graphic will be placed from where you inserted the cursor, it is a good idea to position the text cursor against the left-hand margin. This will allow enough room for the placed graphic to load.

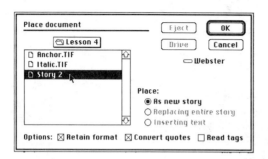

Figure 26. The Story 2 file is located in the Lesson 4 folder. Double-click on it for placement onto page 2.

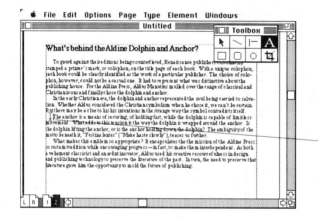

Figure 27. Story 2 is loaded onto page 2. Move to 75% view and place the flashing cursor into your text. We placed ours at the beginning of the third paragraph.

The next step is to load in your inline graphic. Move again to the *Place* command and locate the file Logotype.eps (Figure 28). Because we placed our cursor in the text, the *As inline graphic* choice will be available and automatically selected.

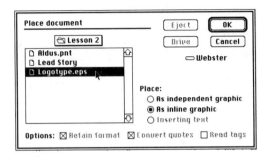

Figure 28. The Logotype.eps file can be found in the Lesson 2 folder. Note that the As inline graphic choice is automatically selected.

Figure 29. The graphic is loaded into the text and is now an inline graphic. Whenever the text block is moved around the page, the graphic will follow.

After the graphic has been loaded on to the page, you will probably notice that it is a little wide and slightly hangs over the right margin. If it doesn't, good, you won't have to resize it. If it does, simply select it with the pointer tool, and reduce it in size as you would any graphic. Use the bottom right handle and push it back over the margin so it fits on your page (Figure 30).

Figure 30. The reduced graphic now fits into the margins of the page. If you reduce it too far, the text below will start to come up on the right-hand side. If this happens, just enlarge the graphic slightly to push the text down to the next line.

5. Now make it an independent graphic, and move it so it sits under the text on the page.

Now to make it an independent graphic. First, with the pointer tool, select the graphic. Then activate the *Cut* command from the **Edit** menu. The graphic will disappear from the screen. From the **Edit** menu once more, choose the *Paste* command. The graphic will appear in exactly the same position as it was before. Now that it is no longer part of the text, move the graphic down and place it underneath the text. Follow Figures 31 to 34 to see how this is done.

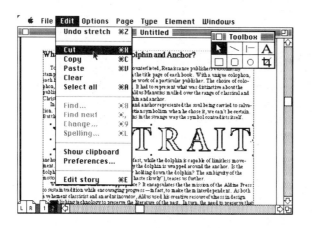

Figure 31. Cut the graphic from the screen, but only after you have selected it with the pointer tool.

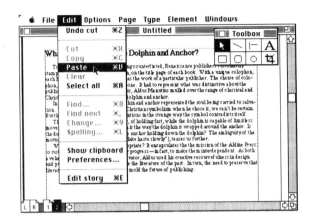

Figure 32. *The next step is to* Paste *the graphic back on to the page.*

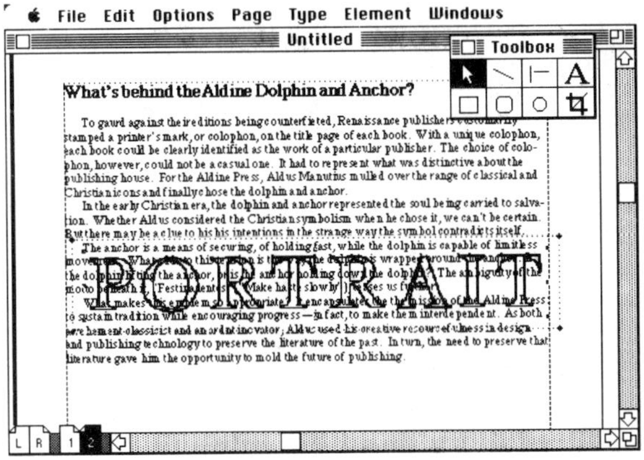

Figure 33. *The graphic is pasted back on to the page, but it is now completely separate from the text.*

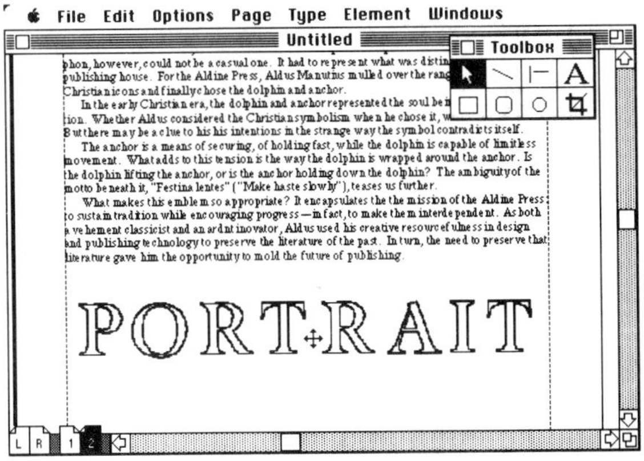

Figure 34. *The graphic is now moved away from the text and placed below it.*

Module 15

Linking Files

Linking Files

PageMaker automatically links text and graphics that you place in a publication with the original, external files. This feature allows you to automatically update the linked text or graphic files, replacing it with changes from the most current version of the external file. It also gives you access to information on when the file was created, when it was last modified, and whether or not the linked element is up to date. This version control is especially valuable in a work situation, where several people may be working on a publication that is continually being revised.

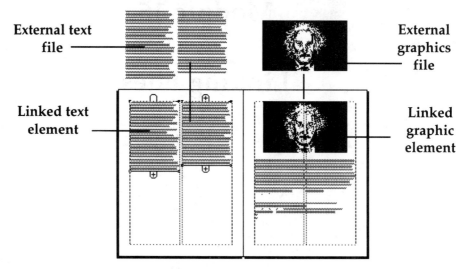

Figure 1. *Publications can be updated when changes are made to external text or graphics files.*

It is possible to change a graphic in the originating graphics program, and PageMaker will notify you that the linked graphic is different from the revised external file. You can then update the linked graphic without having to place the file manually again.

Generally, all text or graphic files that you import into Page-Maker, using the *Place* or *Import* command, are automatically linked to their original, external files.

To find out status information on any linked file, you select the *Links* command in the **File** menu (Figure 2).

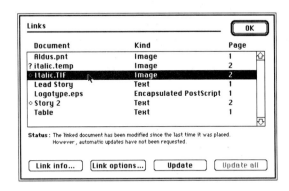

Figure 2. **File** *menu and* Links *dialog box displayed.*

When you select a file on the list, its status is displayed underneath (Figure 2). Below is a list of each symbol that can appear to the left of each file name and what they indicate.

Link status indicator

No indicator	Link is up to date or not linked
◆	Linked file has been modified and will be automatically updated
◊	Linked file has been modified and will not be automatically updated
Δ	Both the linked file and the internal Page-Maker file have been modified.
(x)	Publication does not contain complete copy
?	Cannot find the external file

The 'Page'column in Figure 2 may display the following symbols (as well as the actual page number):

Page #	The linked inline graphic element is in a story that has not yet been composed; the page number is therefore unknown.
LM	The left master page
RM	The right master page
PB	The pasteboard
OV	The linked text element - an inline graphic, for example, is not displayed because it is part of a text block that is overset, or not fully flowed.
X	The linked text element is an open story that has not yet been placed.

In the Figure 2 *Links* dialog box, there are four buttons available at the bottom. The first two, *Link info* and *Link options* display dialog boxes, and are described in the next sections.

The *Update* option is for updating single linked elements. This option will be dim if there is no existing linked file, or if the highlighted file name is currently up to date.

The *Update all* option allows you to update all internal publication files that are linked to external ones, but only those that have *Update automatically* selected in the *Link options* dialog box (Figure 4 in the following sections). This option will be dim if the selected linked element is up to date or if you have not selected *Update automatically* for that element.

Link info dialog box

When you select *Link info* from Figure 2, the dialog box in Figure 3 appears. This box can also be selected from the *Link info* command in the **Element** menu. It cannot be selected through the **Element** menu, however, unless you have a graphic or text block selected.

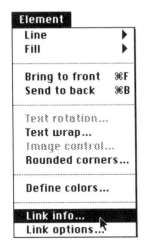

Figure 3. Link info *dialog box and the Link info command in the* **Element** *menu. This dialog box can also be selected from clicking on* Link info *in the Figure 2* Links *dialog box.*

In the Figure 3 dialog box, you can update or re-establish a link between a text or graphic element and its external file, and you can display file information. Relinking may be necessary if the external file is moved to a different folder, or if its name has been changed. To update a link, select the required external file, and then click on *Link*.

To the right of the *Link info* dialog box of Figure 3 is displayed important information about the linked element.

Link options dialog box

There are two ways you can activate the *Link options* dialog box (Figure 4). First, you can select a file from the list in the *Links* dialog box of Figure 2 and then click on *Link options*, or you can select a linked element in the publication and choose *Link options* from the **Element** menu. Either way will get you to Figure 4(b). To select the *Link options: Defaults* dialog box of Figure 4(c), choose *Link options* from the **Element** menu when no publication is open, or no element is selected.

In this dialog box, you determine how PageMaker will store and update linked elements with external files. You can either set up, or change, the default options for all publications you open during a session, or modify the options for a single linked element. Any settings you change for a single element override the default settings.

519

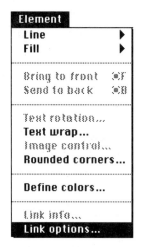

Figure 4(a). *The two* Link options *dialog boxes and the* Link options *command from the* **Element** *menu.*

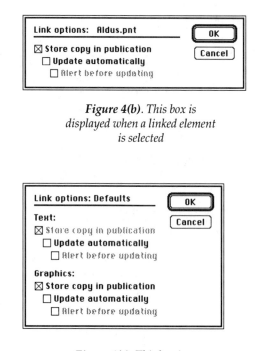

Figure 4(b). *This box is displayed when a linked element is selected*

Figure 4(c). *This box is displayed when nothing is selected and can be used to set default values.*

The options in these dialog boxes are interdependent: each lower option becomes available only when the one above is selected. Each option provides a different layer of control over how linked files are updated.

Store copy in publication: This option is always selected for text and EPS files. For graphics files, if this is deselected, it is necessary for PageMaker to use the external files when printing. It is also useful when the graphic file is larger than 64K, as this would increase the size of the publication considerably, slowing down processing time.

Update automatically: If you select this option, any changes you make to the external file will automatically update the linked version within the publication. Updating occurs whenever you open the publication, or when you select *Update all* in the *Links* dialog box.

Alert before updating: With this option selected, you can prevent a linked element from being updated (Figure 5).

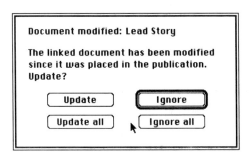

Document modified: Lead Story

The linked document has been modified since it was placed in the publication. Update?

Update   Ignore
Update all   Ignore all

Figure 5. This alert appears if you have selected Alert *before updating in Figures 4(b) or 4(c).*

If you are placing a graphic in your publication larger than 256K, or if the updated version of the graphic file has increased beyond 256K, PageMaker will display an alert asking you if you want to continue storing a copy of that file in the publication. If you choose not to, the publication will become smaller and easier to work with, but only a low resolution screen version of the graphic will be updated.

Which files can be linked?

PageMaker can only establish a link to files stored on a disk, where a file has a definable location. For this reason, a text block or a graphic copied from one program (for example Microsoft Word) to the Clipboard, and pasted into a PageMaker publication from the Clipboard, has no link to an external file. However, if you cut a linked graphic or text file, and paste into another publication, the link is also transferred.

It is also possible to create a text file from within PageMaker and export it into a word processing program. This feature allows you to edit the text in your word processor, as well as giving you the option of being able to use the same linked document in more than one publication if necessary.

When you open a publication that has links to external files, PageMaker must find all these files before it can open the publication. If the file has been deleted, or moved into a different folder, PageMaker will search the folder containing your publication. If it cannot find the file, it displays the dialog box of Figure 6.

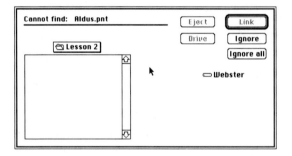

Figure 6. This dialog box is displayed when PageMaker cannot locate a file while you are opening a publication.

From this dialog box, you can search through different folders to find the missing file. Once you have located it, highlight it with your mouse, and click on *Link* to re-establish the link and automatically update the file.

If you select *Ignore* in the *Cannot find* dialog box, you are accepting a broken link. This file will not be updated with the current external file version, until you re-establish the link again. If a graphics link is broken, only a low resolution screen version of the graphic will be displayed until the link is re-established.

Printing a publication that contains links

When printing a publication that contains any linked elements, PageMaker searches for the linked external files, as it does when opening a publication. If there are any files not found, the dialog box of Figure 7 will be displayed.

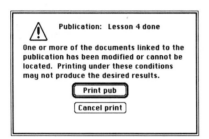

Figure 7. This alert will be displayed when PageMaker cannot find a link during printing.

If you are copying a publication to disk to take to a commercial printing house, make sure you select the *Copy linked documents* option in the *Save publication as* dialog box (Figure 8).

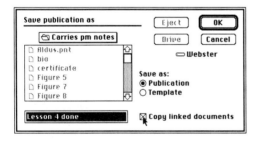

Figure 8. You must select the Copy linked documents *option if you are taking your publication to a commercial printing house.*

Note: To keep link management tasks to a minimum, be careful when moving files into different folders, or when changing the names of files, folders or disk drives. All these changes break links between external files and their linked elements in a publication, which means you must re-establish the links with each individual file.

Module 15 Exercise

Linking Files

Module 15 Exercise
Linking Files

In this exercise we will illustrate the advantages of linking publications with external files, and how to use some of these features.

This training material is structured so that people of all levels of expertise with PageMaker can use it to gain maximum benefit. To do this, we have structured this material so that the bare exercise is listed below this paragraph on just one page, with no hints. The following pages contain the steps needed to complete this exercise for those that need additional prompting. The **Linking Files** module should be referenced if you need further help or explanation.

Module 15 exercise steps

1. *In a new PageMaker publication, place on the first page the files:*

   Story 2 (located in the Tutorial folder in Lesson 4) and Anchor.TIF (in the same folder).

2. *In the Links dialog box, make the following changes:*

   For Story 2, in the Link options dialog box, check the Update automatically option.

   For Anchor.TIF, in the Link options dialog box, uncheck the Store copy in publication option.

3. *Save the publication with the name Linked publication, and check the option Copy linked documents.*

The steps for completing this exercise are on the following pages.

The steps in detail

1. *In a new PageMaker publication, place on the first page the following files:*

Story 2 (located in the Tutorial folder in Lesson 4) and Anchor.TIF (in the same folder).

Go to the **File** menu, select the *Place* command, and locate the file Story 2 in the Lesson 4 folder (Figure 1). Place Story 2 on the page in two column format.

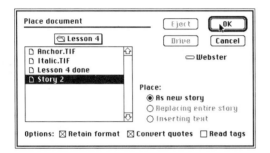

Figure 1. Locate Story 2 in the Lesson 4 folder.

Go to the **File** menu again, select the *Place* command and locate Anchor.TIF, also in the same folder. Place it at the top of the second column. Figure 3 indicates how your page should now look.

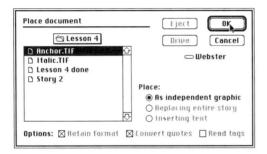

Figure 2. Anchor.TIF is also located in the Lesson 4 folder.

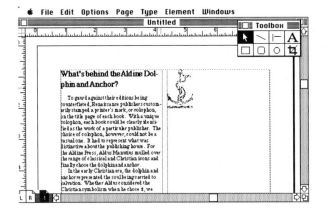

Figure 3. *Your page with the two files placed.*

2. *In the Links dialog box, make the following changes:*

For Story 2, in the Link options dialog box, check the Update automatically option.

For Anchor.TIF, in the Link options dialog box, uncheck the Store copy in publication option.

Now go to the **File** menu and select the *Links* command. The Figure 5 dialog box will now appear.

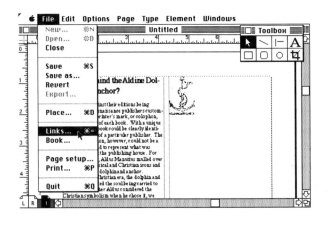

Figure 4. *Select the* Links *command from the* **File** *menu.*

Highlight Story 2 with your mouse and then select the *Link options* button (Figure 5).

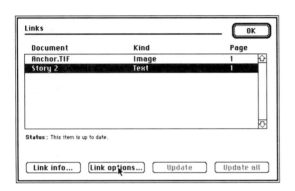

Figure 5. Select the Link options *button with your mouse.*

When the *Link options* dialog box is activated, Figure 6, click your mouse on the *Update automatically* option and then select OK. This will ensure that any changes made to the text, outside of PageMaker, will automatically be included the next time this PageMaker document is opened.

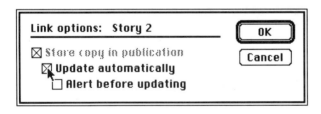

Figure 6. Click on the Update automatically *option with your mouse.*

To modify the *Link options* for the Anchor.TIF file, highlight the file name, and then select the *Link options* button again (Figure 7).

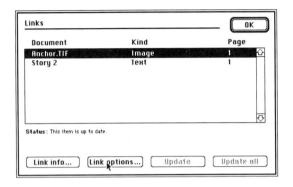

Figure 7. Make sure you highlight the Anchor.TIF file before you select the Link options button for this next step.

When the *Link options* dialog box of Figure 8 appears, deselect the *Store copy in publication* option. This option is useful to cut down the memory size of the publication so it is easier to work with.

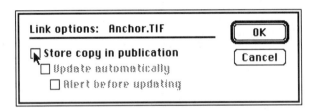

Figure 8. Deselect the Store copy in publication option.

3. *Save the publication with the name Linked publication, and check the option Copy linked documents.*

Use the *Save as* command in the **File** menu to save the publication with the name Linked publication (Figure 9). Click on the *Copy linked documents* option in this dialog box. This option is essential if you are making a copy of your publication onto a floppy disk. It copies all externally located files to the folder where you are saving your publication.

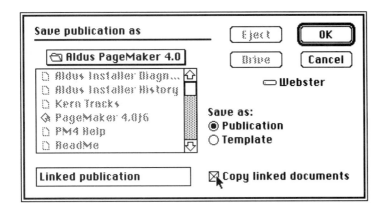

Figure 9. Make sure you check the Copy linked documents *option when you save this publication. Select OK.*

Module 16

Long Document Capabilities

Long Document Capabilities

PageMaker allows you to create large documents by linking many PageMaker publications together. Linking publications to form a long document allows you to generate a table of contents and an index that cross references between publications.

It can also be used as a multiple printing device — you may set up many publications to print without operator intervention. The multiple publication features can be accessed via the *Book* command in the **File** menu (Figure 1).

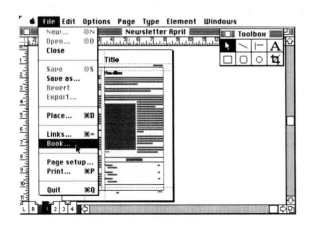

Figure 1. Select the Book *command in the* **File** *menu to access the multiple publication capabilities.*

After selecting the *Book* command from the **File** menu, the *Book publication list* dialog box of Figure 2 appears. Publications are linked together through this dialog box. The list of publications is normally included in the first publication in your book (or other type of large document). As an example of this process, we have opened, in Figure 1, a copy of the template, Newsletter 2, from the Templates folder, and called it Newsletter April.

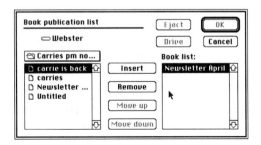

Figure 2. The Book *dialog box should look something like this. It does not matter if your list is empty.*

Note that in the Book list rectangle at the right of the dialog box, Newsletter April is already included.To add further PageMaker publications to your Book list, you must locate the specific documents on your hard disk (in the rectangle to the left in Figure 2), highlight the document name, and click on the *Insert* button (Figure 3).

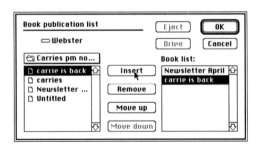

Figure 3. Once you have clicked on the Insert *button, the document name at the left will appear in the* Book list *on the right, as illustrated here.*

By using this procedure, you can keep adding documents to your Book list until it is complete. Double-clicking on a document name on the left, causes it to be automatically added to the Book list. To delete a document is just as simple. Highlight in the Book list to the right, and click on the *Remove* button (Figure 4).

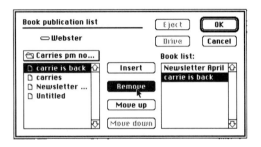

Figure 4. Highlight the document name on the right that you wish to delete, and then select the Remove *button. It will disappear from the book list.*

535

The *Move up/Move down* options move the selected document up or down one position in the Book list.

Note: *A document's position in the list represents its position in the book, which is significant when creating a table of contents, an index, or printing out the whole Book list.*

Once you have created your Book list, you will be able to use this list in conjunction with the *Create TOC, Create index* commands from the **Options** menu, and the *Print* command from the **File** menu.

If you wish to print your entire Book list, simply select the *Print entire book* option in the *Print* command, as illustrated in Figure 5.

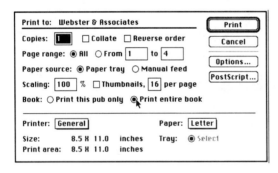

Figure 5. This is the selection that will allow you to print the entire Book list *(in the print command under the* **File** *menu). Multiple publications will then be automatically selected and printed.*

Module 16 Exercise

Long Document Capabilities

Module 16 Exercise
Long Document Capabilities

This short, but important exercise will help you more fully understand the process of creating a Book list.

This training material is structured so that people of all levels of expertise with PageMaker can use it to gain maximum benefit. To do this, we have structured this material so that the bare exercise is listed below this paragraph on just one page, with no hints. The following pages contain the steps needed to complete this exercise for those that need additional prompting. The **Long Document Capabilities** module should be referenced if you need any further help or explanations.

Module 16 Exercise steps

1. *Open up a copy of the Newsletter 2 template from the Templates folder, and call it Newsletter April.*

2. *Create a Book list containing the following example templates:*

   Brochure 1
   Brochure 2
   Directory
   Financial sheet
   Manual 2
   Pricelist

   in addition to Newsletter April at the top of the list.

3. *Remove the documents Directory and Manual 2.*

4. *Rearrange the order of the chapters so that they appear like this:*

   Pricelist
   Brochure 1
   Financial sheet
   Brochure 2
   Newsletter April

Read the following pages for the steps to complete this exercise.

The steps in detail

1. Open up a copy of the Newsletter 2 template from the Templates folder, and call it Newsletter April.

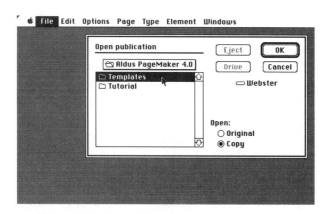

Figure 1. The Newsletter 2 template is located in the Templates folder, from the PageMaker 4 folder.

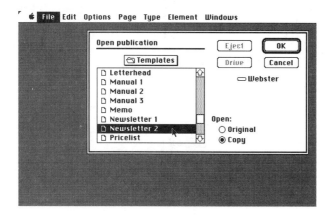

Figure 2. Before double-clicking on Newsletter 2 make sure that you don't open the original template. Selecting Copy *ensures you don't.*

2. Create a Book list containing the following example templates:

Brochure 1
Brochure 2
Directory
Financial sheet
Manual 2
Pricelist

in addition to Newsletter April at the top of the list.

Figures 3 through 6 explain these steps.

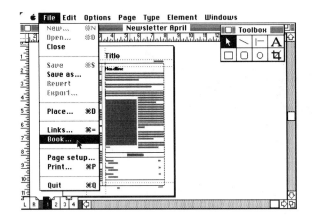

Figure 3. Select the Book command in the **File** menu. By selecting this command with Newsletter April open, you are telling PageMaker that Newsletter April is effectively your first publication in the list. This command leads to the dialog box of Figure 4.

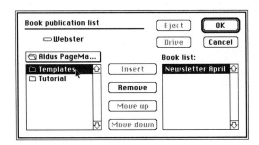

Figure 4. By double-clicking on the Templates folder within the PageMaker 4 folder, locate the list of files needed to compile this Book list.

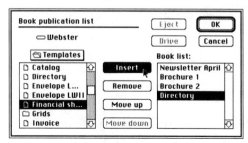

Figure 5. *Select each document individually, and then select the* Insert *button, so the document appears in the* Book list *on the right. Remember, the order you select the documents in, is the order they will appear in the* Book list. *This order can be changed with the* Move up/down *commands, however.*

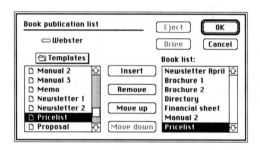

Figure 6. *Once you have selected all six documents (plus the Newsletter April document), your list should look like the one in this example.*

3. Remove the documents Directory and Manual 2.

Highlight Directory in the Book list rectangle to the right, and click on the *Remove* button. Repeat for Manual 2 (Figure 7).

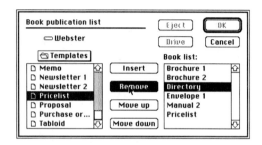

Figure 7. *To remove a document from the publication, highlight the document and select* Remove.

4. Rearrange the order of the chapters so that they appear like this:

Pricelist
Brochure 1
Financial sheet
Brochure 2
Newsletter April

Changing the order in which the documents appear involves highlighting the name, and selecting either the *Move up* or *Move down* button. This will have to be done a few times to get the documents in the correct order (Figure 8).

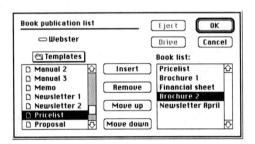

Figure 8. Here we have arranged the documents in the required positions by selecting each document individually, and choosing either the Move up *or* Move down *buttons.*

Module 17

Table of Contents

Table of Contents

Generation

PageMaker can automatically generate a table of contents at the completion of your publication or publications. You can create a table of contents for single or multiple publications that make up the one long document.

A table of contents is the list at the start of a chapter, publication, report, book, or whatever, that lists both the major contents and the page number on which they start. To create a table of contents automatically, find the important contents of your publication, and note the page numbers on which they begin.

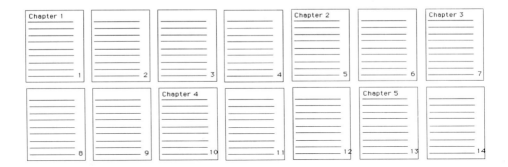

Figure 1. *This diagram shows every page of a book that would generate the table of contents as shown on the next page.*

Let's assume we have a 14-page book. This book has 5 chapters in it. Chapter 1 starts on page 1, chapter 2 on page 5, chapter 3 on page 7, chapter 4 on page 10, and chapter 5 on page 13. If we were to manually create a table of contents for this book, it might look something like the example on the following page.

Contents for our Book

What we are going to look at here is how to get this exact result, using the automatic *Create TOC* command found in the **Options** menu.

The most effective way in which PageMaker is able to do this is through the paragraph styles found in the *Style palette*. When creating a table of contents, you are asking PageMaker to search through the document for the occurrence of a particular paragraph style, and then to compile them in order of sequence with the page number that they occur on.

If we look at Figure 1 again, you can see that we have used two paragraph styles in the creation of our book. One style is Body text, and the other we might have called Chapter Head. The paragraph style, Chapter Head, would be applied to the paragraphs that read Chapter 1, Chapter 2, Chapter 3, Chapter 4, and Chapter 5 (Figure 2). This paragraph would have *Include in table of contents* selected as one of its attributes (found in the *Paragraph* command). The Body text style does not. Apart from this selection, it does not matter how this paragraph style was set up, and it does not matter what the style was called. Chapter Head is only an example.

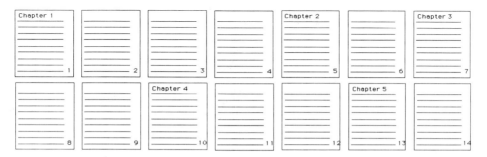

Figure 2. *In our simplified example, we have used only two paragraph styles - Body text and Chapter Head. To create a table of contents, we simply select* Create TOC, *and PageMaker searches for the paragraph style that has* Include in table of contents *selected.*

Creating your table of contents

In order for PageMaker to generate a table of contents, you must first apply a chosen paragraph style from the *Style palette* to every heading, subheading or paragraph in your document that is to become part of the table of contents. PageMaker creates the table of contents by searching through the document for every paragraph style that has the option *Include in table of contents* as one of its attributes. (Refer back to the module on style sheets if you are unsure how paragraph styles work.)

It is also possible to mark separate individual paragraphs (even without style names) to be included in the contents. This is not a recommended approach, as it may lead to inconsistent results.

For an example to work on in this module, we have opened a copy of the template, Manual 2. Go to pages 6, 7, and 8 of this copy, and replace each 'Level Head' using the text tool, as follows:

Replace 'First Level Head' (page 6) with 'Editorial'; replace 'Second Level Head' (page 7) with 'What's New?'; and the next 'Second Level Head' (page 8) with 'Tips and Tricks'.

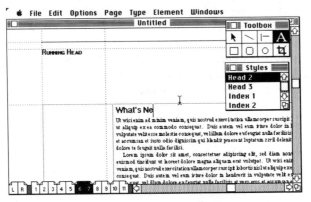

Figure 3. We have selected *'Second Level Head' on page 7 with the text tool to change to 'What's New?'*

Make sure the *Style palette* is showing on your screen. If it is not, go into the **Windows** menu and select *Style palette*.

Starting at page 6 of the document, select 'Editorial' with the text tool, and apply the *Head 1* paragraph style to it from the *Style palette*. It may already have this by default. Select 'What's new?' (page 7) and 'Tips and Tricks' (page 8), and also apply the *Head 1* style to each one separately (Figure 4).

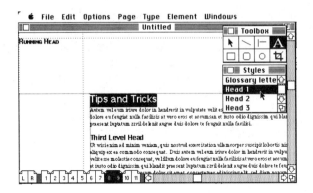

Figure 4. *Here we are applying the style 'Head 1' to the three headings we changed.*

Select *Define styles* in the **Type** Menu. Highlight Head 1, and choose to *Edit* this style. This is after we have decided that these particular headings are to be part of the table of contents. Select the *Para* command, from the *Edit style* dialog box, and click on *Include in table of contents* in the *Paragraph specifications* dialog box (Figure 5).

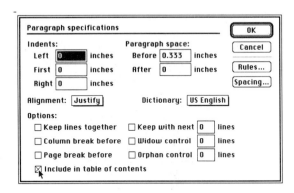

Figure 5. *We are editing the Head 1 style through the* Define styles *command, by selecting the Include in table of contents option.*

The method described above is a quick way of including paragraphs in the table of contents that have a particular paragraph style applied to them. But you may also wish to include a single paragraph that you do not wish to set up a paragraph style for.

For example, as well as all the headings we have applied the 'Head 1' style to, we may also want to include the subheading 'Third Level Head' which only occurs once in the whole document. In this case, you may select that particular item with the text tool (page 8), and select the *Include in table of contents* option, also found under the **Type** Menu, in the *Paragraph* command.

Select 'Third Level Head' with your text tool, and go to the *Paragraph* command in the **Type** menu (Figure 6).

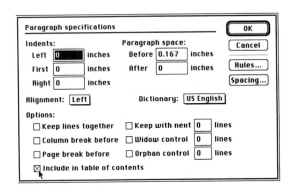

Figure 6. We have now selected the option Include in table of contents *for Third Level Head on page 8.*

It is also possible to have more than one paragraph style with the *Include in table of contents* option selected, as PageMaker will list each item in order of its appearance throughout the document, when generating the table of contents (Figure 7).

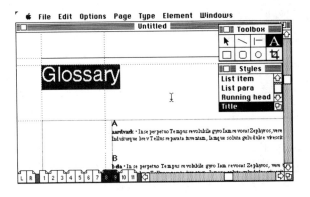

Figure 7. Both the Glossary (page 9) and the Appendix Contents (page 10) have the style 'Title' already applied (as do earlier headings in the document). We selected the Define styles *command and then selected* Include in table of contents *option for the Title style.*

Note that from Figure 7, we will also include all paragraphs with the style name 'Title' in our table of contents option.

After selecting all chosen paragraph styles for the table of contents, insert one or two blank pages at the beginning of your document (Figure 8). This is where the table of contents can be placed after it has been generated. Alternatively, the table of contents can be placed into a new or already existing PageMaker document.

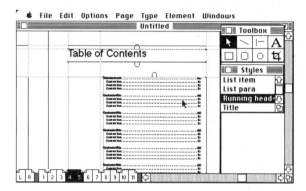

Figure 8. For our example, we deleted the two text blocks on page 5, which was the example table of contents. Our new table of contents will be placed here.

We are now ready to generate the table of contents. To do this, select *Create TOC* in the **Options** menu. The dialog box of Figure 9 will appear.

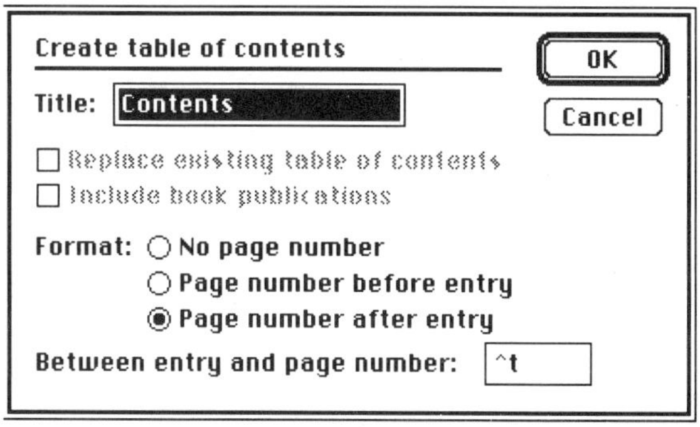

Figure 9. This dialog box will appear when you select Create TOC.

The *Title* option allows you to give your table of contents a title of up to 30 letters, or you may delete 'Contents' and leave it blank. The *Replacing existing table of contents* option will only be available if you have previously generated a table of contents, in which case you can replace it with a revised version.

If *Include book publications* is selected, PageMaker will generate a single table of contents for all the documents in the Book list, (provided one has been created). Refer to Module 16, **Long Document Capabilities** for more details on Book lists.

If you are creating a table of contents for multiple publications, you will need to follow the procedure described here for each individual document and then to create a 'Book list' including each publication name. Make sure that when you are generating your table of contents that you have the publication opened where you wish to place the contents, or alternatively have a new untitled publication opened.

The next three options refer to the formatting of the table of contents. You can select to have *No page number*, *Page number before entry*, or *Page number after entry* (default). It is not referring to the actual page number that your table of contents is placed on.

The default setting for *Between entry and page number* option is '^t', being the symbol for a leader tab (.....). This will appear between each entry and the page number (see Figure 10). This symbol can be changed. The Pagemaker Reference Manual Appendix lists other characters that can be used.

We chose to have the numbers displayed after the entry. Once you have made your choices, select OK.

After a few moments, you should have a loaded cursor on your page. You are now ready to place the new table of contents on the page 5 we chose as our contents page (Figure 10).

You will notice that PageMaker creates its own default paragraph styles, for each entry that has had a paragraph style applied to it. For example, if the style 'Head 1' is included in the table of contents, all 'Head 1' table of contents entries will now have the style 'TOC Head 1'.

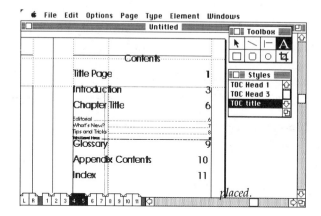

Figure 10. *We have placed our newly generated table of contents on page 5. You will probably notice that when a table of contents is first placed, the page numbers aren't vertically aligned. To fix this problem we aligned the numbers ourselves after the table of contents was*

To see the paragraph styles that have been generated, select the table of contents entries individually with the text tool, and each particular style will be displayed in the *Style palette*. By default, the generated styles are all in the Times font, but the point size and style (eg. bold, italic) will be identical to the original paragraph style (Figure 11).

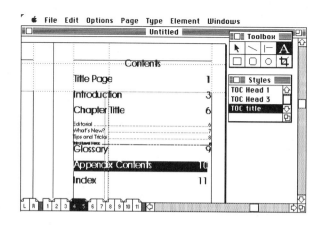

Figure 11. *We have selected this paragraph to see the 'TOC' paragraph style that has been generated by PageMaker.*

These paragraph styles can now be edited and changed in the same way as you would change them for any text file. Be careful not to change the names of the paragraph styles, only the attributes, as subsequent regenerations of the table of contents will overlook the name changes, but it will accept the attribute changes (for example, spacing, font, leading etc.). If you do apply other paragraph styles to the table of contents, or if you make any other style changes that are not made through the *Define styles* command, these changes will be lost when you generate a new table of contents.

Module 17 Exercise

Table of Contents

Module 17 Exercise
Table of Contents

This exercise will help you produce a simple table of contents.

This training material is structured so that people of all levels of expertise with Page-Maker can use it to gain maximum benefit. To do this, we have structured it so that the bare exercise is listed below this paragraph on just one page, with no hints. The following pages contain the steps needed to complete this exercise, for those that need additional prompting. The **Table of Contents** module should be kept on hand in case you need further help or explanations.

Module 17 exercise steps

1. *Open a copy of the template 'Manual 1'.*

2. *Include Subhead on pages 6, 7 and 8 as part of the table of contents. Change each one in turn to Chapter 1 through Chapter 6.*

3. *Create a blank page at the beginning of the document to place the table of contents.*

4. *Edit the paragraph style of Subhead 2 and Subhead 3, so that both have Include in table of contents selected.*

5. *Generate a table of contents.*

6. *Place the table of contents.*

7. *Change the style that has been generated for the first line of the contents page, so that there is 0.2" paragraph spacing above and below it.*

8. *Go to page 5 and select Title Placeholder, and change its attributes so that it will become part of the table of contents.*

9. *Regenerate the table of contents to replace existing contents file on page two.*

The steps in detail

1. Open a copy of the template 'Manual 1'.

Open a copy of the file 'Manual 1' from the Templates folder.

2. Include Subhead on pages 6, 7 and 8 as part of the table of contents. Change each one in turn to Chapter 1 through Chapter 6.

See Figure 1 caption for details. Once this is complete, select one of the Chapter X insertions on your page with the text tool, to check what style has been applied. You will see that pages 6 and 7 have Subhead 2, and page 8 has Subhead 3 (Figure 2).

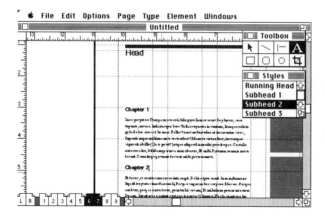

Figure 1. With your text tool, go to pages 6, 7 and 8, select every word Subhead (an actual bolded subhead) and replace each one with a chapter number (1 through 6). You should have 6 when you reach the end. (Do not change anything on page 5.)

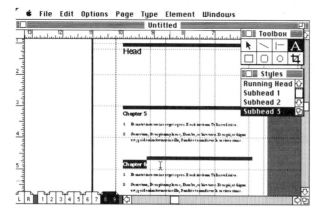

Figure 2. On selecting Chapter 6 on page 8, we can see that the Subhead 3 style becomes highlighted.

3. *Create a blank page at the beginning of the document to place the table of contents.*

Go to page one of the document, and insert one page after the current page, by selecting *Insert pages* from the **Page** menu.

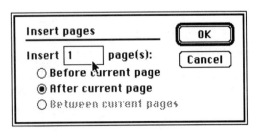

Figure 3. *On page 1, select the* Insert pages *command in the* **Page** *menu. The final result will give you a blank page on page 2 for placing the table of contents.*

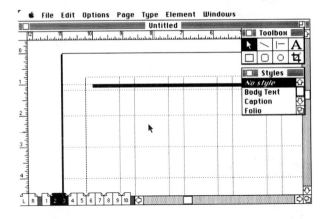

Figure 4. Page 2 is now ready to place the table of contents.

4. *Edit the paragraph style of Subhead 2 and Subhead 3, so that both have Include in table of contents selected.*

Go into the *Define styles* command in the **Type** Menu, and highlight the Subhead 2 style (Figure 5).Then select the *Edit* option.

See Figures 6 and 7 for how to ensure this style is included in the table of contents. Now, on your own, repeat this process for Subhead 3.

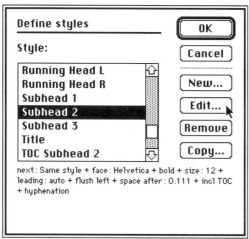

Define styles

OK

Style:

Cancel

| Running Head L |
| Running Head R |
| Subhead 1 |
| **Subhead 2** |
| Subhead 3 |
| Title |
| TOC Subhead 2 |

New...

Edit...

Remove

Copy...

next : Same style + face : Helvetica + bold + size : 12 +
leading : auto + flush left + space after : 0.111 + incl TOC
+ hyphenation

Figure 5. Highlight Subhead 2 and select the Edit option.

Edit style

OK

Name: **Subhead 2**

Cancel

Based on: **No style**

Next style: **Same style**

Type...

Para...

next : Same style + face : Helvetica + bold + size :
12 + leading : auto + flush left + space after : 0.111
+ hyphenation

Tabs...

Hyph...

Figure 6. When the Edit style dialog box appears, select the Para option.

Paragraph specifications

OK

Indents:

Paragraph space:

Cancel

Left **0** inches   Before **0** inches

First **0** inches   After **0.111** inches

Rules...

Right **0** inches

Spacing...

Alignment: **Left**   Dictionary: **US English**

Options:

☐ Keep lines together   ☐ Keep with next **0** lines

☐ Column break before   ☐ Widow control **0** lines

☐ Page break before   ☐ Orphan control **0** lines

☒ Include in table of contents

Figure 7. In the Paragraph specifications dialog box make sure the Include table of contents option is selected.

5. *Generate a table of contents.*

You are now ready to generate the table of contents. Go to page 2 of your document where the generated TOC will be placed. Select *Create TOC* from the **Options** menu (Figure 8) to get the *Create table of contents* dialog box (Figure 9). Leave the default settings of Figure 9 as shown for this example.

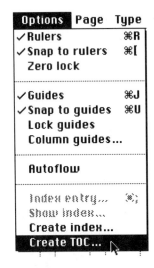

Figure 8. *Go into the* Options *menu and select* Create TOC.

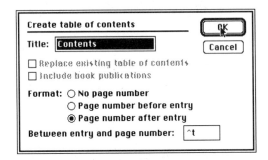

Figure 9. *In this* TOC *dialog box, we have left the default settings as our choice for creating our table of contents, but these can be modified accordingly.*

6. *Place the table of contents.*

When the loaded cursor appears on your page, place the text. On placing the cursor in the top left-hand corner of the page, and just clicking the mouse, the generated table of contents file will flow down the first narrow column to the left. To ensure the text flows right across the page, draw an imaginary box from the top-left hand corner to the bottom right, before releasing the loaded cursor. It will then look similar to Figure 10.

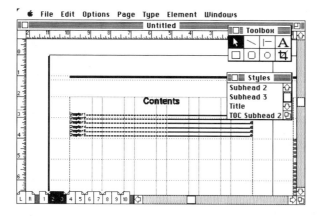

Figure 10. This is how your Contents page should look at this stage.

7. *Change the style that has been generated for the first line of the contents page, so that there is 0.2" paragraph spacing above and below it.*

Select the first line with the text tool. The style TOC Subhead 2 will be highlighted (Figure 11).

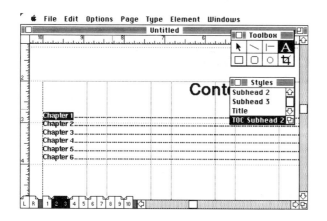

Figure 11. When we select the first line, the TOC Subhead 2 style becomes highlighted in the Style palette.

Go into *Define styles* in the **Type** menu, and highlight *TOC Subhead 2.*

You need to select the *Edit* option in the *Define styles* dialog box to change TOC Subhead 2 paragraph spacing to 0.2" above and 0.2" below. From the *Edit style* dialog box, select the *Para* command to get the Figure 12 dialog box for *Paragraph specifications.*

Paragraph specifications			OK

Indents: **Paragraph space:** Cancel
Left `0.25` inches Before `.2` inches Rules...
First `-0.25` inches After `.2` inches Spacing...
Right `0` inches

Alignment: `Left` **Dictionary:** `US English`

Options:
☐ Keep lines together ☐ Keep with next `0` lines
☐ Column break before ☐ Widow control `0` lines
☐ Page break before ☐ Orphan control `0` lines
☐ Include in table of contents

Figure 12 After selecting the Para option, we are able to insert 0.2" of spacing above and below. Select OK several times, to get back to page 2.

Notice what has now happened to our contents. The lines starting Chapter 1, Chapter 2, Chapter 3 and Chapter 4 all have 0.2" spacing, before and after. This is because they all use the same style — TOC Subhead 2, which we have just altered. The lines beginning Chapter 5 and Chapter 6, do not have the extra spacings as they use the style TOC Subhead 3 (Figure 13).

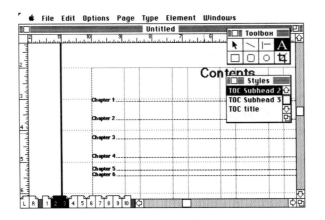

Figure 13. Your Table of Contents will now look similar to this.

8. Go to page 5 and select Title Placeholder, and change its attributes so that it will become part of the table of contents

Select Title Placeholder with the text tool (Figure 14). Choose the **Type** menu, and select the *Paragraph* command. In this dialog box, select the *Include in table of contents* option (Figure 15). Note we are changing this paragraph's specifications without altering its style definition. This is generally not good practice.

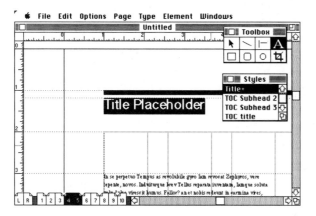

Figure 14. Highlight the text
with the text tool.

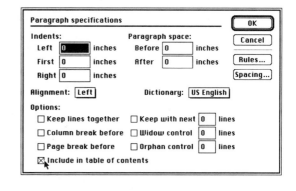

Figure 15. Select the Paragraph *option in the* **Type** *menu.*
Click on the Include in table of contents *option with your mouse.*
Select OK.

9. Regenerate the table of contents to replace existing contents file on page two.

Go back to Page 2 and select the *Create TOC* command in the **Options** menu.
Make sure that *Replace existing table of contents* is checked (Figure 16). Select
OK.

Module 17 Exercise - Table of Contents Creation

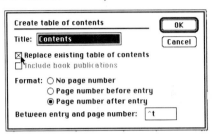

Figure 16. *Select* Replace existing table of contents *in the dialog box. It may already be checked by default. Click on OK.*

The new contents page should still have the paragraph spacing, and also the new edition (Title Placeholder) that was just selected for inclusion. Your table of contents will look like Figure 17.

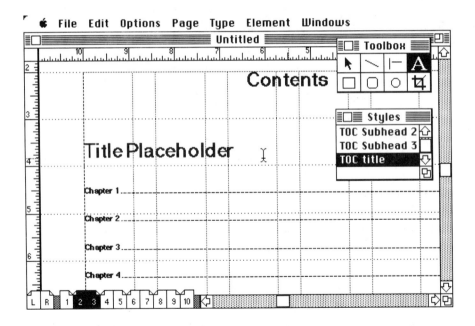

Figure 17. *This is how your table of contents will now look.*

Module 18

Generating an Index

Generating an Index

Creating an index

PageMaker can automatically generate an index from reference words that you select and identify in the text. From this selection, PageMaker then searches through the text to generate a list of words, which have been specifically chosen by you to become part of the index.

Creating an index involves:

- Identifying the important topics.

- Developing a hierarchy of related words for each topic.

- Identifying alternative wordings, and related information for cross referencing of each topic.

You'll need to spend time planning your index. Try to think of as many ways of describing each topic as you can. For example, 'delete' may be described as 'cut' or 'clear'. It is only once you have completed this stage, that you will be ready to move onto the next step involving the 'index entry'.

PageMaker allows you enter up to three levels for each index entry. The primary entry will be the topic that you have selected, for example 'Printer', the secondary level could be 'PostScript' and the tertiary entry might be 'Paper'. PageMaker also allows you to cross reference other index entries from the current document, and even from other documents that are part of a Book list (see **Module 16, Long Document Capabilities**).

Once you have a list of the words and related cross reference words, that are to become part of the index, the next step is to systematically go through the document and select each of these words for inclusion.

Each word must be selected individually (PageMaker does not, for example, search through the whole document for the occurrence of the the word 'Printer'; only the one you have selected). Each occurrence of a particular word may be in a different context.

For example, the first occurrence of the word 'Printer' may be in relation to 'laser printers', and the second occurrence may be in relation to 'outside bureau printers'. That is why every index entry must be inserted individually, although once you have built up a fair number of index entries, you are able to cross reference entries of the same word very quickly.

Once you have completed all the index entries and cross references, you then select *Create index* in the **Options** menu, choose the format you want, and PageMaker generates an index that you place onto a new page, or in a new document.

If you add any more text or graphics to your publication, which causes the page numbering to change, PageMaker allows you to generate a new updated version to replace the old index.

Let's have a look, step by step at how it's done.

Creating index entries

To illustrate index entry, we have placed the text file Lead Story from the Lesson 2 folder. On the first page, if we want, say, *Aldus Manutius* as one of our index entry topics, we must 'mark' these words for inclusion. There are two ways we can do this. The first way is illustrated in Figure 1, the second in Figure 2.

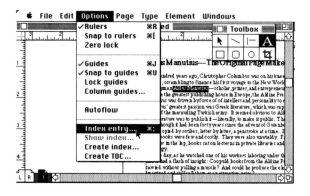

*Figure 1. With the text tool, highlight the words **Aldus Manutius**. Select* Index entry *from the* **Options** *menu. The highlighted word will appear as shown in the Figure 3* Create index entry *dialog box. It can then be edited, if required, with the text tool.*

The Figure 1 method is used when the text you want in the index is the same as the text you have selected. The Figure 2 method opens up the Figure 3 dialog box but without, in our example, any words in the Topic rectangles. We are free to enter our own entry, which may differ slightly from the actual word or phrase in the text.

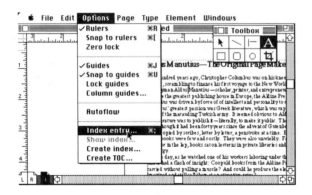

*Figure 2. With the text tool, insert the flashing cursor close to the words **Aldus Manutius**. Select* Index entry *from the* **Options** *menu, and you can then type the word into the first* Topic edit *box of the Figure 3* Create index entry *dialog box.*

Note: *All index entry topics can be up to 50 characters long.*

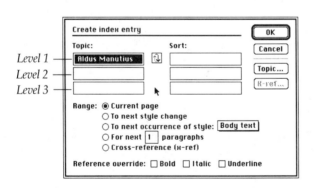

Figure 3. There are three levels of index entry in the Create index entry *dialog box, for primary, secondary, and tertiary levels.*

The *Create index entry* dialog box of Figure 3 contains three levels of index entry — primary, secondary, and tertiary. Secondary and tertiary are optional. When you insert an entry, as we have done in Figures 1 or 2, PageMaker places an index marker in text, which is visible in story view.

If we enter in the *Create index entry* dialog box 'Desktop' as the first entry, 'publishing' as the second entry, and 'PageMaker' as the third entry (as shown in Figure 4), PageMaker will display the generated index like this:

D

Desktop

   publishing

      PageMaker **1**

Or like this:

D

Desktop: publishing: PageMaker **1**

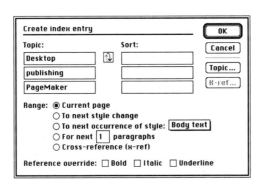

Figure 4. An example of the Create index entry *dialog box with all the levels utilized.*

You may want to create several primary entries for each topic to ensure the reader will find what they are looking for. So, if it is necessary to create such a comprehensive index, you will need to enter, for example, 'publishing' and 'PageMaker' also as first entries.

If you use the cross reference option, no page number is displayed at all. It could look like this:

D

Desktop

   See **publishing: PageMaker**

Let's look at the other sections of the *Create Index entry* dialog box of Figures 3 or 5.

Using the *Sort* edit boxes allows you to specify how each corresponding entry will be sorted in the index. (Figure 5 displays an example of its use.)

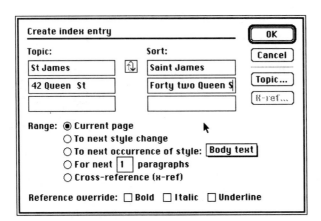

Figure 5. If the Sort *edit box is left empty, PageMaker will list the entry as it appears in the* Topic *edit box. However if you have an entry, such as a number, it is wise to spell out its sort details, otherwise it may not appear at the correct place in the index.*

The options that follow the *Range* command in the Figures 3 or 5 *Create index entry* dialog boxes, refer to the number of pages PageMaker will include for the current index entry listing. For example, if the topic 'Desktop' is referred to constantly on pages 1 through to 2, then in the index you would want the 'Desktop' listing to display, for example:

D

Desktop **1-2**

We have used 'Desktop' as an example here, but anything can be substituted.

Current page option: If 'Desktop' information is complete on this page select this.

To next style change option: If 'Desktop' information continues until the next change in paragraph style select this.

To next occurrence of style option: If 'Desktop' information continues beyond the next style change, here you can select the paragraph style that marks the end of this section.

For next   paragraphs option: Here you can enter in the specified number of paragraphs that 'Desktop' information continues for.

Reference override option: These three options allow you to modify the style for the page numbers and cross reference sections only of the index. These selections remain until changed again.

Cross-reference (x-ref) option: Click this option to select the *X-ref* option so that 'Desktop' can be cross-referenced with any other index entry that has previously been entered.

We will look at this last option in more detail in the next section. It is always advisable to leave cross-referencing until **after** all the index entries have been made, as PageMaker provides a list of all existing index topics in your publication to make selection easier.

Topic button: Clicking on this button will display the *Select topic* dialog box. This dialog box simplifies the mutiple entry of identical topics. Simply select, in alphabetical order, from the list of index topics and click on OK.

X-ref button: Clicking on this button will display the *Select cross-reference topic* dialog box. This box allows you to now cross-reference what is in your *Create index entry* dialog box as an index topic, with any other topic already entered.

One final note: If you choose *Index entry* without first selecting text or inserting the text tool, only the *Cross-reference* option becomes available at this point.

Cross referencing within single and multiple publications

As we indicated above, it is wise not to attempt any serious cross referencing of index entries until all index entries have been entered. We will now look at an example of how to use PageMaker's cross referencing capabilities within index generation.

Say, for example, we wanted to cross-reference 'Desktop' with 'Publishing', both having already been entered into the *Create index entry* dialog box of Figures 3 or 5.

First, select the *Show index* command in the **Options** Menu.

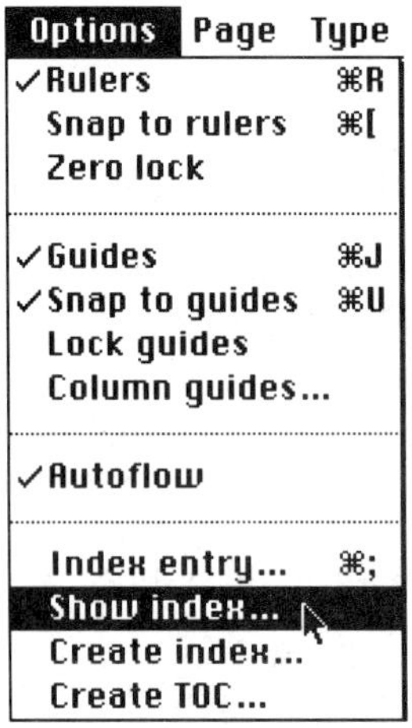

Figure 6. *Select the* Show index *command in the* Options *menu when you need to edit, remove, or cross reference current index entries.*

A dialog box like the one in Figure 7 will appear. For this example, we have already entered a number of index entries. The *Show index* dialog box alphabetically lists all index entries. You can scroll through this list, by clicking on the letter after *Index section* in the top left corner of the dialog box (Figure 7). An alphabetical sub-menu appears and you can select whichever letter you require. We have chosen 'D' for Figure 7. This gives us the Desktop entry we are looking for. Click on this entry, as we have done in Figure 7, to highlight it. Then click on the *Add* button in the bottom of the dialog box to get the Figure 8 *Create index entry* dialog box.

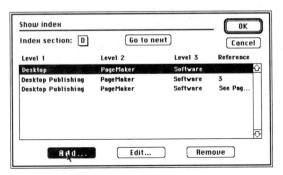

Figure 7. Locate Desktop *and highlight this entry. Click on the* Add *button to activate another dialog box, as shown in Figure 8.*

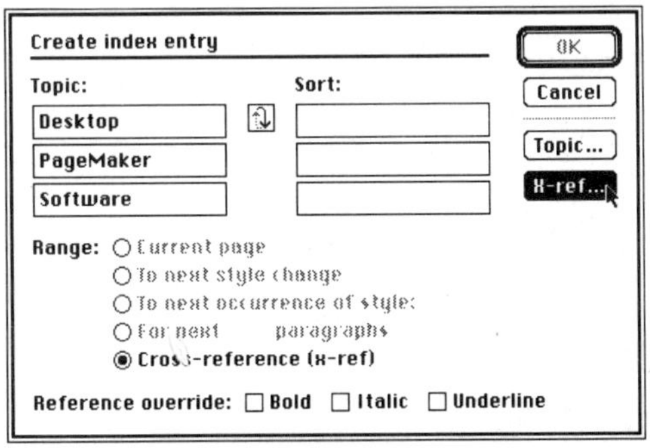

Figure 8. Select the Cross-reference *option, and then select the* X-ref *button. Figure 9 will now appear.*

Se-

lect the cross-reference option by clicking on *Cross-reference* at the bottom of Figure 8, and then the *X-ref* button at the right. A dialog box like Figure 9 will appear. This is the *Select cross-reference topic* dialog box. We are looking for the index entry 'Publishing' in this box.

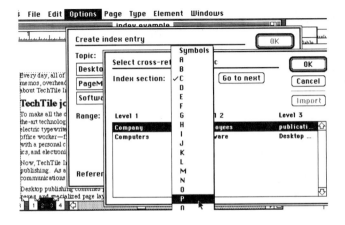

Figure 9. Each index entry is listed alphabetically. To go to 'P' (as we are looking for publishing) you can click on Go to next *until you come to it, or hold your mouse down on the box displaying the letter. When the sub-menu appears, you can select the required letter with your mouse and release.*

By clicking on the letter to the right of the *Index section* in this box, you get the single-letter sub-menu shown in Figure 9. Run your mouse down the menu, and select 'P' for Publishing. Highlight the word 'Publishing', as we have done in Figure 10, and then click on OK twice to return to Figure 11.

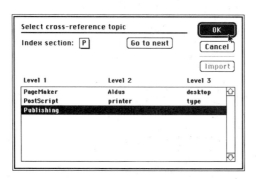

Figure 10. Once Publishing is highlighted, select OK twice to return to the Figure 11 Show index *dialog box.*

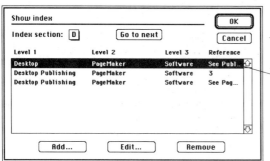

Figure 11. This is how the Show Index *dialog box will display the cross referenced topic.*

From the Figure 11 Show index dialog box, we can now see that 'Desktop' is cross-referenced in the index with 'Publishing'. Once the index has been generated, it will look similar to either one of these examples:

D

Desktop. *See* **Publishing**

or

D

Desktop

See **Publishing**

PageMaker also allows you to cross-reference topics from other publications. All selected publications must be placed in a 'Book list' (described in Module 16) so that PageMaker will know which documents to display the index entries for cross referencing.

For utilizing multiple publications, the next step is to go into *Show index* in the **Options** menu, which is the same approach as for a single publication. Highlight the entry that you would like to cross reference and then select the *Add* button.

In the *Create index entry* dialog box, you must select the *X-ref* option (again as for Figure 8 in single publications), and it is within this next dialog box, *Select cross-reference topic* (similar to Figure 10), that you are able to select *Import*.

Once you have done this, PageMaker displays every index entry from every publication in the the current publication's 'Book list'. You are now able to select the entry you wish to cross-reference with the original topic you chose.

Editing

When you have completed your index entries, as well as any cross references, you may still need to edit, add or delete an entry at a later stage, before you create your index.

This is simply done by selecting the *Show index* command in the **Options** menu (as we have already done above for creating cross references). The dialog box that appears is shown again in Figure 12. Highlight the entry you wish to edit, add to or remove as shown in Figure 12 below.

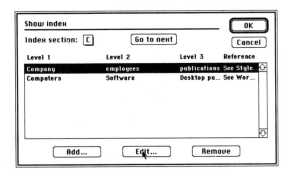

Figure 12. The Add *button allows you to add a cross reference to the selected index entry. The* Edit *button displays the* Edit index entry *dialog box, allowing you to edit any section of this, and the* Remove *button removes the highlighted index entry.*

Another example of the *Topic* button, discussed under the *Create index entry* dialog box of Figures 3 and 5 can be shown here. If we had several different entries for the same topic, for example, 'Desktop' and 'Desktop Publishing', they would appear under separate index entries, even though they are the same topic. To stop this happening, you must select either one of these entries through the *Show index* command and select the *Edit* option. Once inside the *Edit index entry* dialog box of Figure 13, you select the *Topic* button as shown. The *Select topic* box of Figure 14 then appears. From this figure, select the preferred topic name and click on OK.

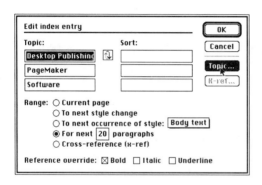

Figure 13. We selected Desktop Publishing in the Show index *dialog box, then the* Edit *button, and now we will select the* Topic *button from this* Edit index entry *dialog box.*

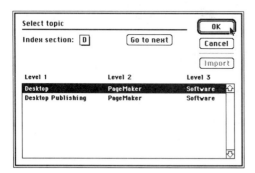

Figure 14 In the Select topic *dialog box, we simply select the index entry topic we would prefer to use, in our case we are selecting the 'Desktop' entry. Click on OK and the process is complete.*

We are now ready to create our index. Before this is done, we need to decide if it is to go onto a blank page at the end of the document, onto the paste board area, or into a new document altogether.

Once you have the appropriate page of your document opened, select *Create index* in the **Options** menu. A dialog box similar to that of Figure 15 will appear on your screen. The *Title* of the index can be edited with the text tool, and can have up to thirty letters.

By selecting the *Format* button, a second dialog box (Figure 16) will appear.

Figure 15. In the Create index *dialog box, the* Replace existing index *option will not be available if this is the first time you have asked PageMaker to generate this index. The* Include book publications *will also be unavailable if you have not set up a 'Book list' previously. If you select* Remove unreferenced *topics, index topics imported from other publications that are not used as entries or cross-references in the current publication are removed. Any index topics that have no references are also removed.*

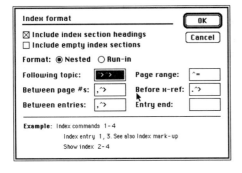

Figure 16. PageMaker offers you two default settings for the index format, Nested *and* Run-in. *By clicking on either alternative, an example of the format is displayed at the bottom of the dialog box.*

Because PageMaker automatically generates each section heading of the index (for example, A, B and C), you must deselect *Include Index section headings* in Figure 16, if you wish not to have these included. PageMaker, however, will still insert spacing in between each alphabetical section.

If you select *Include empty index sections*, PageMaker will list every section included in your index, but the empty sections will read 'no entries'.

Choose *Nested* or *Run-in* to determine the format of your index. Examples are shown at the bottom of the Figure 16 dialog box. The rest of this dialog box highlights the different characters used between index entries, page numbers, etc. The Appendix of the PageMaker Reference manual provides details of these characters.

Once you have made your selections in the *Index format* dialog box, click on OK. Now select OK again, and PageMaker will generate an index.

After a short time, you will have a loaded cursor on your page which you can place in the same way as any other text file. If you checked *Replace existing index*, then your new index will automatically replace the old.

As with the generated table of contents, PageMaker creates its own paragraph styles for the index as well. You are also able to make additions and deletions to any index entries after the index has been created. To update the index, simply select *Replace existing index* in the *Create index* dialog box, and PageMaker will regenerate and replace the old version.

Module 18 Exercise

Generating an Index

Module 18 Exercise
Generating an Index

This exercise is designed to illustrate the concepts of index generation within PageMaker. Although it only refers to a single-page publication, the major requirements to generate an index are covered.

This training material is structured so that people of all levels of expertise with PageMaker can use it to gain maximum benefit. To do this, we have structured this material so that the bare exercise is listed below this paragraph on just one page, with no hints. The following pages contain the steps needed to complete this exercise for those that need additional prompting. The **Generating an Index** module should be referenced if you need further help or explanations.

Module 18 exercise steps

1. *Open a new 2 page publication, and place Lead Story from the Lesson 2 folder, across three columns. This will be used to create an index.*

2. *The items that are to be indexed are Francesco Griffo da Bologna, italics, Greek literature, Homer and Aristotle. Some of these will be primary entries, others secondary.*

3. *Index the items so the resulting index file will look like this:*

A
Artists
    Francesco Griffo da Bologna   *1*
F
Fonts
    Italics   *1*
G
Greek Literature
    Aristotle   *1*
    Homer   *1*
I
Italics. *See Fonts: italics*

4. *Place the text on a page inserted at the end of the publication, so it looks similar to the example of Figure 16.*

The steps in detail

1. Open a new 2 page publication, and place Lead Story from the Lesson 2 folder, across three columns. This will be used to create an index.

Figure 1. *Lead Story placed on a three column page. This figure may make it easier for you to identify the parts of the text to be indexed in step 2 of this exercise.*

2. *The items that are to be indexed are Francesco Griffo da Bologna, italics, Greek literature, Homer, and Aristotle. Some of these will be primary entries, others secondary.*

The first step when creating an index is to change to the text tool. This allows us to move through the text and select the index entries that we want.

The first item to index is around the middle of the center column. If we look at how this entry occurs in our example index, we see that it is actually a secondary entry — under the primary entry of 'Artists'. See Figures 2 through 4 for the steps to achieve this.

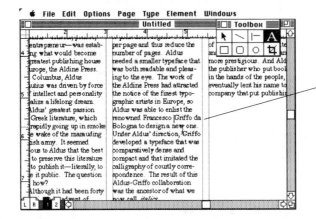

Figure 2. *Insert the text cursor near the words Francesco Griffo da Bologna. It does not matter exactly where the cursor lies as long as it is close to these words.*

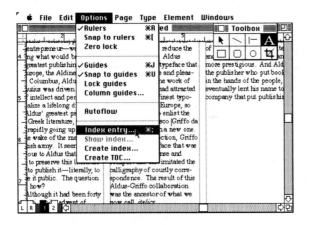

Figure 3. *After inserting the text cursor in or near the word or words you would like to index, select the Index entry command in the* **Options** *menu.*

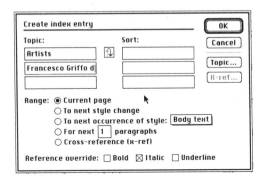

Figure 4. Because Francesco Griffo da Bologna is a secondary entry under the primary entry 'Artists', the Create index entry dialog box should be filled out as illustrated in this figure. Also choose Italic for Reference override, to give us italic page numbers. Select OK to record your entry.

We move now to the next phrase to be indexed — **italics,** just below Francesco. As we look at the index example at the front of this exercise, we see that this also is a secondary entry under the heading **Fonts.** See Figures 5 through 7 for the steps to do this.

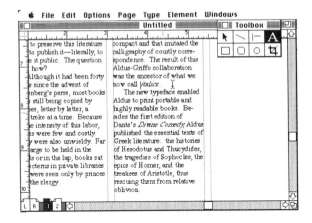

Figure 5. Insert the text tool anywhere near the words italics. It does not matter exactly where the cursor lies as long as it is close to these words.

Figure 6. After inserting the text cursor, remember to choose this command.

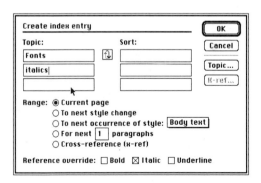

Figure 7. Because italics is a secondary entry, it must be inserted in the correct box. The word Fonts should be inserted on the first line. Select OK.

The next two entries — **Aristotle** and **Homer** — occur as secondary entries under the same primary entry. To do this, you must be very careful to spell the primary entry correctly, as it has to be entered twice, once for each secondary heading. Apart from being careful to spell everything correctly, these two phrases are notated as index entries in exactly the same way as the previous one. (Figures 8 through 11).

Optionally, for keying in the second secondary entry of **Aristotle** (Figure 11), we could have first chosen the *Topic* button and selected Greek Literature from the *Select topic* dialog box that appears. That way we would have ensured that the spelling was correct.

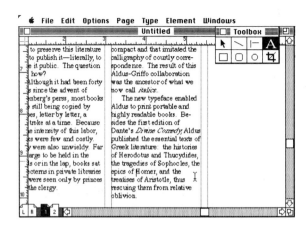

Figure 8. Insert the text cursor anywhere near the word Homer. It does not matter exactly where the cursor lies as long as it is close to these words.

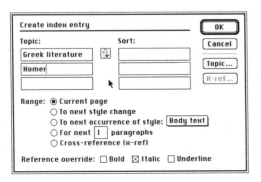

Figure 9. *Fill out the dialog box as illustrated. Make sure Greek literature is spelled correctly, as it will be referenced again. Select OK.*

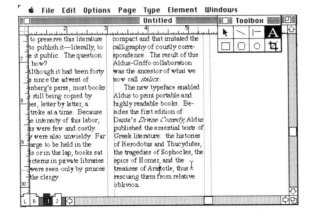

Figure 10. *Insert the text cursor in the word Aristotle.*

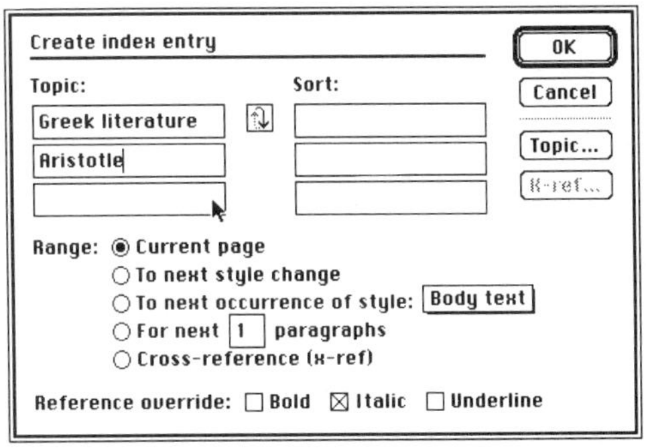

Figure 11. *Under the* **Options** *menu select* Index entry *command, and when the dialog box appears, fill it out as per this figure. Select OK.*

The final index entry involves the *X-ref* option in the *Create index entry* dialog box. On the example index at the front, note the entry under I. It reads:

I

Italics. *See Fonts: italics*

When we create this sort of index entry, we do not have to worry about inserting the text cursor anywhere near the words **italics** or **Fonts**, although the cursor may be embedded in the text. We can also choose the *Index entry* command with the pointer tool selected, which by default only allows you to select the *X-ref* command in this dialog box. This is because there are no page numbers displayed with the 'See' entries.

To complete this last entry, insert your text cursor anywhere in the document, or select the pointer tool, and then choose the *Index entry* command in the **Options** menu. This gives you the Figure 12 dialog box.

Make sure *Cross-Reference* is selected, and then click on the *X-ref* button. In the *Select cross-reference topic* dialog box of Figure 13, you must then find **Fonts** under the letter **F** and highlight it. Select OK twice, to get back to your page.

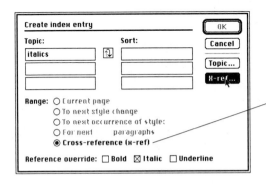

Figure 12. The entries should look like this. Select the cross reference option and click on X-ref.

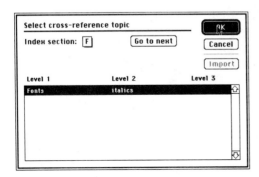

Figure 13. Once Fonts has been located and highlighted, by selecting OK, PageMaker lists Fonts as a cross reference to italics.

3. Index the items so the resulting index file will look like that shown below.

4. Place the text on a page inserted at the end of the publication so it looks similar to the example of Figure 16.

A

Artist

  Francesco Griffo da Bologna *1*

F

Font

  Italics *1*

G

Greek Literature

  Aristotle *1*

  Homer *1*

I

Italics. *See Fonts: italics*

Select *Create index* from the **Options** menu. See Figures 14 and 15 to complete this process.

Figure 14. The options in the Create index *dialog box will look like this. Now select the* Format *button.*

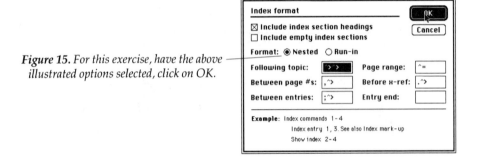

Figure 15. For this exercise, have the above illustrated options selected, click on OK.

You are now ready to select OK in the *Create index* dialog box. When the loaded cursor appears on your blank page, place the text. Your final index page will look like the example in Figure 16.

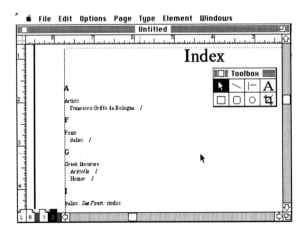

Figure 16. The completed index.

About the Authors

Tony Webster was awarded the 1986 McGraw-Hill award for Distinguished Achievement in New Product Development for his work in publishing. He is the author of several books, including *PageMaker 3 by Example* (M&T Books, 1989) and *Dynamics of Desktop Publishing Design* (M&T Books, 1989).

David Webster is a contributing editor to the *Australian Desktop Publishing Magazine* and co-author of PageMaker 3 by Example (M&T Books, 1989).

Index

A Library of Technical References from M&T Books

NetWare User's Guide
by Edward Liebing

Endorsed by Novell, this book informs NetWare users of the services and utilities available, and how to effectively put them to use. Contained is a complete task-oriented reference that introduces users to NetWare and guides them through the basics of NetWare menu-driven utilities and command line utilities. Each utility is illustrated, thus providing a visual frame of reference. You will find general information about the utilities, then specific procedures to perform the task in mind. Utilities discussed include NetWare v2.1 through v2.15. For advanced users, a workstation troubleshooting section is included, describing the errors that occur. Two appendixes, describing briefly the services available in each NetWare menu or command line utility are also included.

Book only   **Item #071-0**   **$24.95**

Blueprint of a LAN
by Craig Chaiken

Blueprint of a LAN provides a hands-on introduction to microcomputer networks. For programmers, numerous valuable programming techniques are detailed. Network administrators will learn how to build and install LAN communication cables, configure and troubleshoot network hardware and software, and provide continuing support to users. Included are a very inexpensive zero-slot, star topology network, remote printer and file sharing, remote command execution, electronic mail, parallel processing support, high-level language support, and more. Also contained is the complete Intel 8086 assembly language source code that will help you build an inexpensive to install, local area network. An optional disk containing all source code is available.

Book & Disk (MS-DOS)   **Item #066-4**   **$39.95**
Book only   **Item #052-4**   **$29.95**

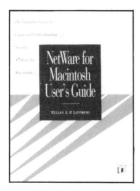

NetWare for Macintosh User's Guide
by Kelley J. P. Lindberg

NetWare for Macintosh User's Guide is the definitive reference to using Novell's NetWare on Macintosh computers. Whether a novice or advanced user, this comprehensive text provides the information readers need to get the most from their NetWare network. It includes an overview of network operations and detailed explanations of all NetWare for Macintosh menu and command line utilities. Detailed tutorials cover such tasks as logging in, working with directories and files, and printing over a network. Advanced users will benefit from the information on managing workstation environments and troubleshooting.

Book only   **Item #126-1**   **$29.95**

NetWare 386 User's Guide
by Christine Milligan

NetWare 386 User's Guide is a complete guide to using and understanding Novell's NetWare 386. It is an excellent reference for 386. Detailed tutorials cover tasks such as logging in, working with directories and files, and printing over a network. Complete explanations of the basic concepts underlying NetWare 386, along with a summary of the differences between NetWare 286 and 386, are included. Advanced users will benefit from the information on managing workstation environments and the troubleshooting index that fully examines NetWare 386 error messages.

Book only   **Item #101-6**   **$29.95**

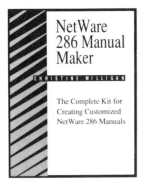

The Complete Kit for
Creating Customized
NetWare 286 Manuals

The NetWare Manual Makers
Complete Kits for Creating Customized NetWare Manuals

Developed to meet the tremendous demand for customized
manuals, The NetWare Manual Makers enables the NetWare
supervisor and administrator to create network training
manuals specific to their individual sites. Administrators
simply fill in the blanks on the template provided on disk and
print the file to create customized manuals and command
cards. Included are general "how-to" information on using a
network, as well as fill-in-the-blank sections that help administrators explain and document procedures unique to a
particular site. The disk files are provided in WordPerfect and
ASCII formats. The WordPerfect file creates a manual that
looks exactly like the one in the book. The ASCII file can be
imported into any desktop publishing or word processing
software.

The Complete Kit for
Creating Customized
NetWare 386 Manuals

The NetWare 286 Manual Maker
The Complete Kit for Creating Customized NetWare 286
Manuals
by Christine Milligan

Book/Disk   **Item #119-9**   **$49.95**

The NetWare 386 Manual Maker
The Complete Kit for Creating Customized NetWare 386
Manuals
by Christine Milligan

Book/Disk   **Item #120-2**   **$49.95**

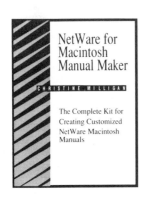

The Complete Kit for
Creating Customized
NetWare Macintosh
Manuals

The NetWare for Macintosh Manual Maker
The Complete Kit for Creating Customized NetWare for
Macintosh Manuals
by Kelley J. P. Lindberg

Book/Disk   **Item #130-X**   **$49.95**

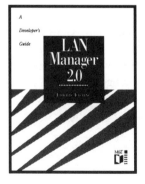

Running WordPerfect on Netware
by Greg McMurdie and Joni Taylor

Written by NetWare and WordPerfect experts, the book contains practical information for both system administrators and network WordPerfect users. Administrators will learn how to install, maintain, and troubleshoot WordPerfect on the network. Users will find answers to everyday questions such as how to print over the network, how to handle error messages, and how to use WordPerfect's tutorial on NetWare.

Book only   Item #145-8 $29.95

Graphics Programming in C
by Roger T. Stevens

All the information you need to program graphics in C, including source code, is presented. You'll find complete discussions of ROM BIOS, VGA, EGA, and CGA inherent capabilities; methods of displaying points on a screen; improved, faster algorithms for drawing and filling lines, rectangles, rounded polygons, ovals, circles, and arcs; graphic cursors; and much more! Both Turbo C and Microsoft C are supported.

Book/Disk (MS-DOS)   Item #019-4 $36.95

Book only   Item #018-4 $26.95

Object-Oriented Programming for Presentation Manager
by William G. Wong

Written for programmers and developers interested in OS/2 Presentation Manager (PM), as well as DOS programmers who are just beginning to explore Object-Oriented Programming and PM. Topics include a thorough overview of Presentation Manager and Object-Oriented Programming, Object-Oriented Programming languages and techniques, developing Presentation Manager applications using C and OOP techniques, and more.

Book/Disk (MS-DOS)   Item #079-6 $39.95

Book only   Item #074-5 $29.95

1-800-533-4372 (in CA 1-800-356-2002)

Fractal Programming in C
by Roger T. Stevens

If you are a programmer wanting to learn more about fractals, this book is for you. Learn how to create pictures that have both beauty and an underlying mathematical meaning. Included are over 50 black and white pictures and 32 full color fractals. All source code to reproduce these pictures is provided on disk in MS-DOS format and requires an IBM PC or clone with an EGA or VGA card, a color monitor, and a Turbo C, Quick C, or Microsoft C compiler.

Book/Disk (MS-DOS)	**Item #038-9**	**$36.95**
Book only	**Item #037-0**	**$26.95**

Fractal Programming in Turbo Pascal
by Roger T. Stevens

This book equips Turbo pascal programmers with the tools needed to program dynamic fractal curves. It is a reference that gives full attention to developing the reader's understanding of various fractal curves. More than 100 black and white and 32 full color fractals are illustrated throughout the book. All source code to reproduce the fractals is available on disk in MS/PC-DOS format. Requires a PC or clone with EGA or VGA, color monitor, and Turbo Pascal 4.0 or better.

Book/Disk (MS-DOS)	**Item #107-5**	**$39.95**
Book	**Item #106-7**	**$29.95**

Programming the 8514/A
by Jake Richter and Bud Smith

Written for programmers who want to develop software for the 8514/A, this complete reference includes information on both the 8514/A register and adapter Interface. Topics include an introduction to the 8514/A and its architecture, a discussion on programming to the applications interface specification, a complete section on programming the hardware, and more. A sample source code and programs are available on the optional disk in MS-DOS format.

Book/Disk (MS-DOS)	**Item #103-2**	**$39.95**
Book only	**Item #086-9**	**$29.95**

Advanced Graphics Programming in Turbo Pascal Roger T. Stevens and Christopher D. Watkins	## Advanced Graphics Programming in Turbo Pascal **by Roger T. Stevens and Christopher D. Watkins**

This new book is must reading for Turbo Pascal programmers who want to create impressive graphic designs on IBM PC's and compatibles. There's 16 pages of full color graphic displays along with the source code to create these dramatic pictures. Complete explanations are provided on how to tailor the graphics to suit the programmer's needs. Covered are algorithms for creating complex 2-D shapes including lines, circles and squares; how to create advanced 3-D shapes, wire-frame graphics, and solid images; numerous tips and techniques for varying pixel intensities to give the appearance or roundness to an object; and more.

Book/Disk (MS-DOS)	**Item #132-6**	**$39.95**
Book only	**Item #131-8**	**$29.95**

Advanced Graphics Programming in C and C++ Roger T. Stevens	## Advanced Graphics Programming in C and C++ **by Roger T. Stevens**

This book is for all C and C++ programmers who want to create impressive graphic designs on thier IBM PC or compatible. Though in-depth discussions and numerous sample programs, readers will learn how to create advanced 3-D shapes, wire-frame graphics, solid images, and more. All source code is available on disk in MS/PC-DOS format. Contains 16 pages of full color graphics.

Book/Disk (MS-DOS)	**Item #173-3**	**$39.95**
Book only	**Item #171-7**	**$29.95**

Graphics Programming with Microsoft C 6.0 Mark Mallet	## Graphics Programming with Microsoft C 6.0 **by Mark Mallet**

Written for all C programmrs, this book explores graphics programming with Microsoft C 6.0, including full coverage of Microsoft C's built-in graphics libraries. Sample programs will help readers learn the techniques needed to create spectacular graphic designs, including 3-D figures, solid images, and more. All source code in book is available on disk in MS/PC-DOS format. Includes 16 pages of full-color graphics.

Book/Disk (MS-DOS)	**Item #167-9**	**$39.95**
Book only	**Item #165-2**	**$29.95**

1-800-533-4372 (in CA 1-800-356-2002)

The Verbum Book of PostScript Illustration
by Michael Gosney, Linnea Dayton, and Janet Ashford

This is the premier instruction book for designers, illustrators and desktop publishers using Postscript. Each chapter highlights the talents of top illustrators who demonstrate the electronic artmaking process. The artist's narrative keys readers in on the conceptual vision, providing valuable insight into the creative thought processes that go into a real-world PostScript illustration project.

Book only   Item #089-3 $29.95

Object-Oriented Turbo Pascal
by Alex Lane

This comprehensive reference explains OOP techniques as they apply to Turbo Pascal 5.5, and teaches programmers how to use objects in Turbo Pascal programs. Extensive explanations familiarize readers with essential OOP concepts, including objects—the focus of OOP, inheritance and methods. Readers will also learn how to apply objects to artificial intelligence, database, and graphics applications. All source code is available on disk in MS/PC-DOS format.

Book/Disk (MS-DOS)   Item #109-1 $36.95

Book only   Item #087-7 $26.95

The Tao of Objects:
A Beginner's Guide to Object-Oriented Programming

Gary Entsminger and Bruce Eckel

The Tao of Objects:
A Beginner's Guide to Object-Oriented Programming
by Gary Entsminger and Bruce Eckel

The Tao of Objects is clearly written, user-friendly guide to object-oriented programming (OOP). Easy-to-understand discussions detail OOP techniques teaching programmers teaching programmers who are new to OOP where and how to use them. Useful programming examples in C++ and Turbo Pascal illustrate the concepts discussed in real-life applications.

Book only   Item #155-5 $26.95

1-800-533-4372 (in CA 1-800-356-2002)

FoxPro: A Developer's Guide

FoxPro: A Developer's Guide
Application Programming Techniques
by Pat Adams and Jordan Powell

Picking up where the FoxPro manual leaves off, this book shows programmers how to master the exceptional power of FoxPro. Useful tips and techniques, along with FoxPro's features, commands, and functions are all covered. Special attention is given to networking issues. Contains discussions on running FoxPro applications on both PCs and Macs that are on the same network. All source code is available on disk in MS/ PC-DOS format.

Book/Disk (MS-DOS)	Item #084-2	$39.95
Book only	Item #083-4	$29.95

SQL
and
Relational
Basics

SQL and Relational Basics
by Fabian Pascal

SQL and Relational Basics was written to help PC users apply sound and general objectives to evaluating, selecting, and using database management systems. Misconceptions about relational data management and SQL are addressed and corrected. The book concentrates on the practical objectives of the relational approach as they pertain to the micro environment. Users will be able to design and correctly implement relational databases and applications, and work around product deficiencies to minimize future maintenance.

Book only:	Item #063-X	$28.95

A Small C Compiler
2nd Edition

James E. Hendrix

A Small C Compiler, Second Edition
by James Hendrix

This is a solid resource for all programmers who want to learn to program in C. It thoroughly explains Small C's structure, syntax, and features. It succinctly covers the theory of compiler operation and design, discussing Small C's compatibility with C, explaining how to modify the compiler to generate new versions of itself, and more. A full-working Small C compiler, plus all the source code and files are provided on disk in MS/ PC-DOS format.

Book/Disk (MS-DOS)	Item #124-5	$29.95

1-800-533-4372 (in CA 1-800-356-2002)

The One Minute Memory Manager
Every PC user's Guide to Faster More Efficient Computing
by Phillip Robinson

Readers will learn why memory is important, how and when to install more, and how to wring the most out of their memory. Clear, concise instructions teach users how to manage their computer's memory to multiply its speed and ability to run programs simultaneously. Tips and techniques also show users how to conserve memory when working with popular software programs.

Book only: **Item #102-4**   **$24.95**

Windows 3.0: A Developer's Guide
Jeffrey M. Richter

This example-packed guide is for all experienced C programmers developing applications for Windows 3.0. This book describes every feature, function, and components of the Windows Application Programming Interface, teaching programmers how to take full advantage of its many capabilities. Diagrams and source code examples are used to demonstrate advanced topics, including window subclassing, dynamic memory mamagement, and software installation techniques.

Book/Disk (MS-DOS)   **Item #164-4**   **$39.95**

Book   **Item #162-8**   **$29.95**

Windows 3.0 By Example
by Michael Hearst

Here is a hands-on guide to Windows 3.0. Written for all users new to Windows, this book provides thorough, easy-to-follow explanations of every Windows 3.0 feature and function. Numerous exercises and helpful practice sessions help readers further develop their understanding of Windows 3.0

Book only   **Item #180-6**   **$26.95**

The Verbum Book of Digital Typography
by Michael Gosney, Linnea Dayton, and Jason Levine

The Verbum Book of Digital Typography combines information on good design principles with effective typography techniques, showing designers, illustrators, and desk-top publishers how to create attractive printed materials that communicate effectively. Each chapter highlights the talents of professional type designers as they step readers through interesting real-like projects. Readers will learn how to develop letterforms and typefaces, modify type outlines, and create special effects.

Book only   **Item #092-3**   **$29.95**

The Verbum Book of Electronic Design
by Michael Gosney and Linnea Dayton

This particular volume introduces designers, illustrators, and desktop publishers to the electronic page layout medium and various application programs, such as PageMaker, QuarkXPress, Design Studio, and Ventura Publishing. Each chapter highlights the talents of a top designer who guides readers through the thinking as well as the "mousing" that leads to the creation of various projects. These projects range in complexity from a trifold black and white brochure to a catalog produced with QuarkXPress. More than 100 illustrations, with 32 pages in full-color, are included.

Book only   **Item #088-5**   **$29.95**

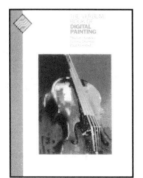

The Verbum Book of Digital Painting
by Michael Gosney, Linnea Dayton, and Paul Goethel

Contained herein are a series of entertaining projects that teach readers how to create compelling designs using the myriad of graphics tools available in commercial painting programs. Presented by professional designers, these projects range from a simple greeting card to a complex street scene. This book also includes portfolios of paintings created by the featured artists, plus an extensive gallery of works from other accomplished artists and 64 pages of full-color paintings.

Book only   **Item #090-7**   **$29.95**

ORDER FORM

To Order:

Return this form with your payment to M&T books, 501 Galveston Drive, Redwood City, CA 94063 or **call toll-free 1-800-533-4372 (in California, call 1-800-356-2002).**

ITEM #	DESCRIPTION	DISK	PRICE

Subtotal

CA residents add sales tax ____%

Add $3.50 per item for shipping and handling

TOTAL

Charge my:

☐ **Visa**

☐ **MasterCard**

☐ **AmExpress**

☐ **Check enclosed, payable to M&T Books.**

CARD NO. _____

SIGNATURE _____   EXP. DATE _____

NAME _____

ADDRESS _____

CITY _____

STATE _____   ZIP _____

M&T GUARANTEE: If your are not satisfied with your order for any reason, return it to us within 25 days of receipt for a full refund. Note: Refunds on disks apply only when returned with book within guarantee period. Disks damaged in transit or defective will be promptly replaced, but cannot be exchanged for a disk from a different title.

PageMaker 4 by Example
Macintosh Disk

PageMaker 4 by Example is a self-paced, hands-on guide to learning PageMaker 4.0, the premier desktop publishing program in the microcomputer market. Readers will learn how to load files into PageMaker, edit and manipulate text, and much more. The exercise disk supplements the book's exercises and teaches readers how to apply its concepts to practical desktop publishing projects. It includes tips on creating projects such as newsletters, advertisements, and press releases.

To Order: Return this coupon with your payment to:
M&T Books
501 Galveston Drive
Redwood City, CA 94063
Or **CALL TOLL-FREE 1-800-533-4372 (in CA 1-800-356-2002)**

☐ **YES!** Please send me the *PageMaker 4 by Example* Macintosh Disk for
$20.00 _____
CA residents add 7.25% sales tax _____
Total _____

☐ Check enclosed, payable to M&T Books.
Charge my ☐ VISA ☐ MC ☐ AmEx
Card no. _____ Exp. Date _____
Signature_____
Name _____
Address _____
City _____ State _____ Zip _____

Note: Disks may be returned for a replacement if damaged. No refunds or credits given. Prices subject to change without notice.

7093

BUSINESS REPLY MAIL

FIRST CLASS PERMIT 871 REDWOOD CITY, CA

POSTAGE WILL BE PAID BY ADDRESSEE

M&T BOOKS

501 Galveston Drive
Redwood City, CA 94063-9929

PLEASE FOLD ALONG LINE AND STAPLE OR TAPE CLOSED